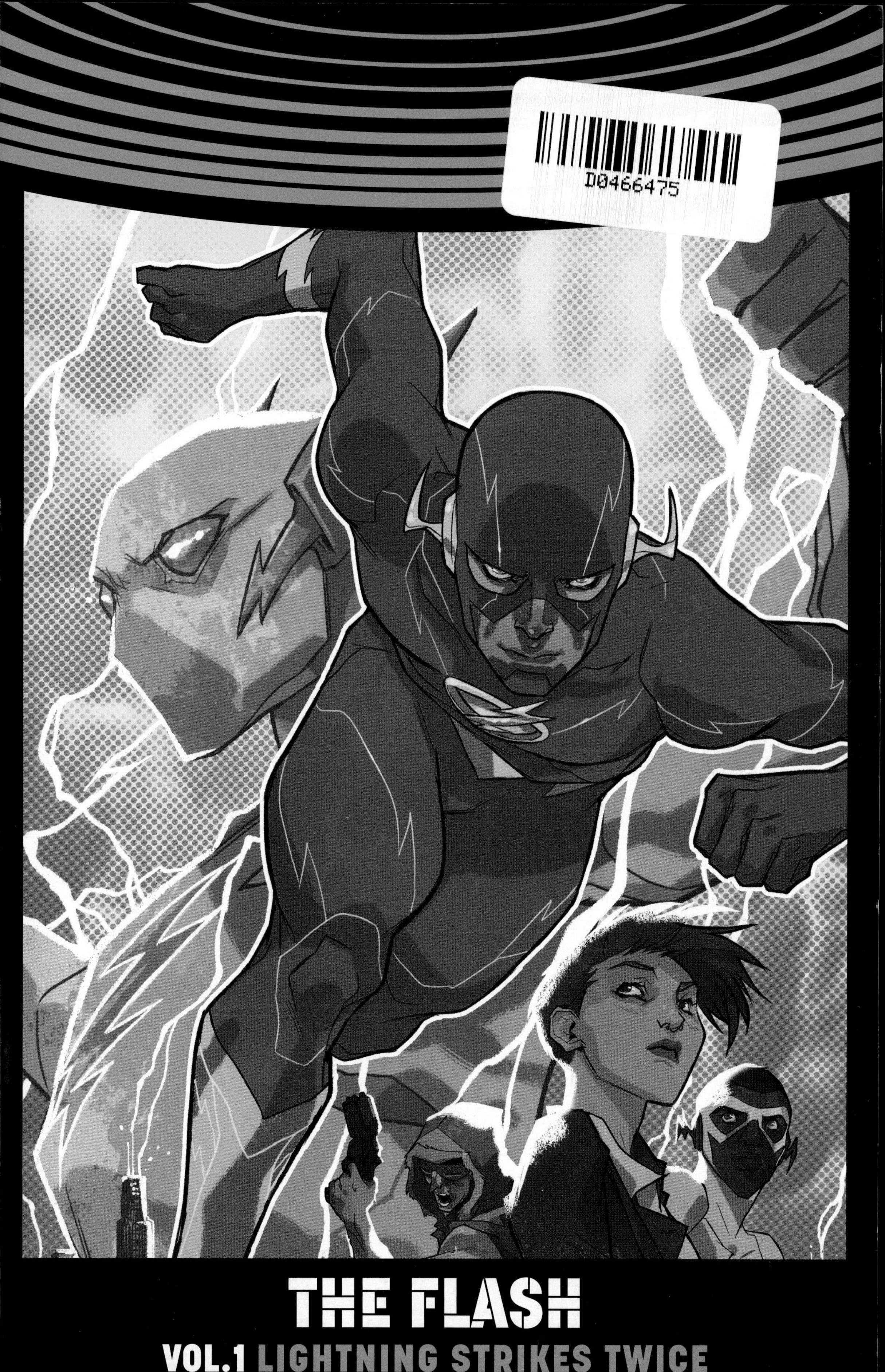

THE FLASH

VOL.1 LIGHTNING STRIKES TWICE

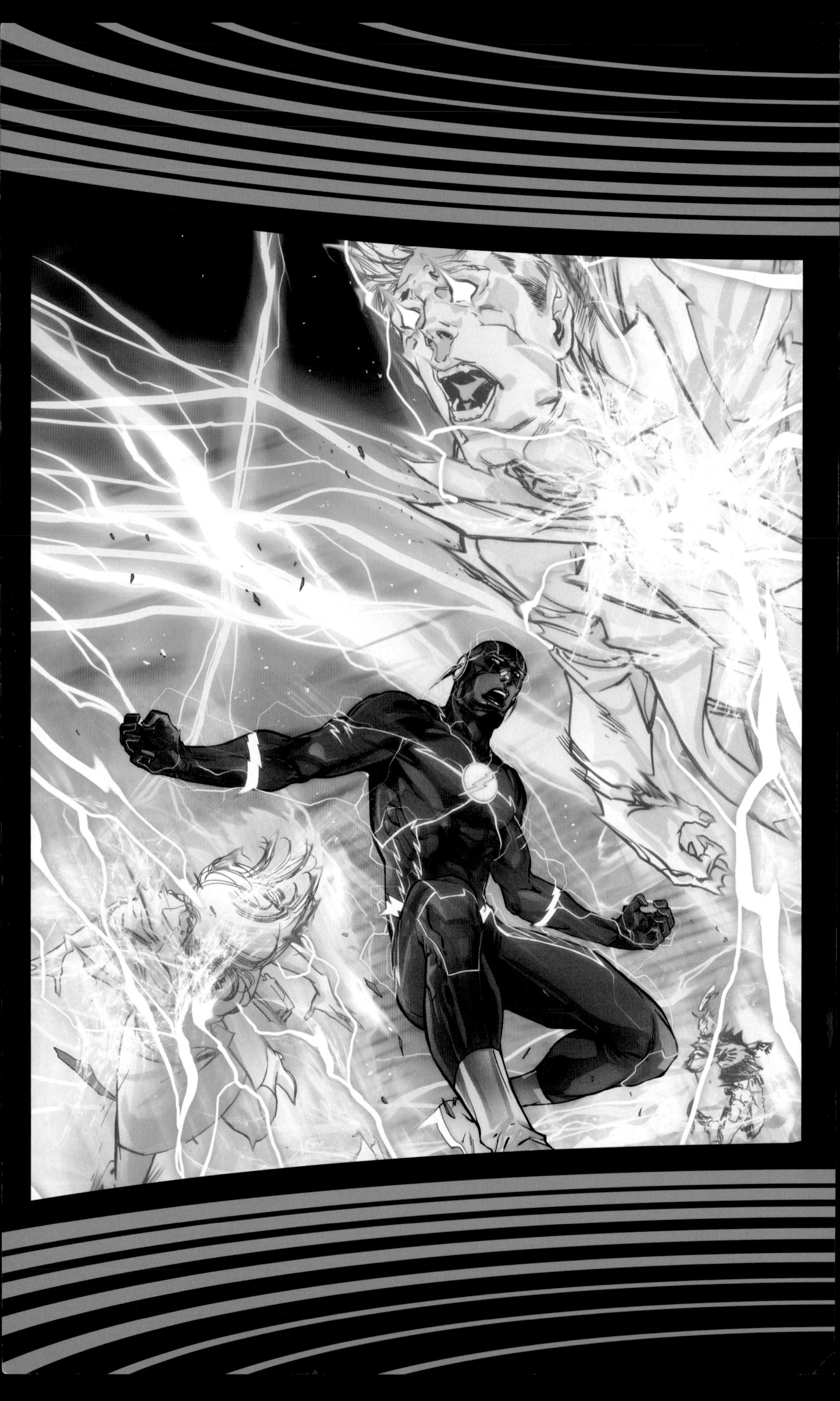

THE FLASH
VOL.1 LIGHTNING STRIKES TWICE

JOSHUA WILLIAMSON
writer

CARMINE DI GIANDOMENICO
NEIL GOOGE * **FELIPE WATANABE** * **ANDREW CURRIE** * **OCLAIR ALBERT**
artists

IVAN PLASCENCIA
colorist

STEVE WANDS
letterer

KARL KERSCHL
collection cover artist

BRIAN CUNNINGHAM Editor - Original Series ✳ **AMEDEO TURTURRO DIEGO LOPEZ** Assistant Editors - Original Series
JEB WOODARD Group Editor - Collected Editions ✳ **PAUL SANTOS** Editor - Collected Edition ✳ **STEVE COOK** Design Director - Books ✳ **DAMIAN RYLAND** Publication Design

BOB HARRAS Senior VP - Editor-in-Chief, DC Comics

DIANE NELSON President ✳ **DAN DiDIO** Publisher ✳ **JIM LEE** Publisher ✳ **GEOFF JOHNS** President & Chief Creative Officer
AMIT DESAI Executive VP - Business & Marketing Strategy, Direct to Consumer & Global Franchise Management ✳ **SAM ADES** Senior VP - Direct to Consumer
BOBBIE CHASE VP - Talent Development ✳ **MARK CHIARELLO** Senior VP - Art, Design & Collected Editions
JOHN CUNNINGHAM Senior VP - Sales & Trade Marketing ✳ **ANNE DePIES** Senior VP - Business Strategy, Finance & Administration
DON FALLETTI VP - Manufacturing Operations ✳ **LAWRENCE GANEM** VP - Editorial Administration & Talent Relations
ALISON GILL Senior VP - Manufacturing & Operations ✳ **HANK KANALZ** Senior VP - Editorial Strategy & Administration
JAY KOGAN VP - Legal Affairs ✳ **THOMAS LOFTUS** VP - Business Affairs
JACK MAHAN VP - Business Affairs ✳ **NICK J. NAPOLITANO** VP - Manufacturing Administration
EDDIE SCANNELL VP - Consumer Marketing ✳ **COURTNEY SIMMONS** Senior VP - Publicity & Communications
JIM (SKI) SOKOLOWSKI VP - Comic Book Specialty Sales & Trade Marketing ✳ **NANCY SPEARS** VP - Mass, Book, Digital Sales & Trade Marketing

THE FLASH VOL. 1 LIGHTNING STRIKES TWICE

Published by DC Comics. Compilation and all new material Copyright © 2017 DC Comics. All Rights Reserved. Originally published in single magazine form in
THE FLASH REBIRTH 1 and THE FLASH 1-8. Copyright © 2016 DC Comics. All Rights Reserved. All characters, their distinctive likenesses and related elements featured
in this publication are trademarks of DC Comics. The stories, characters and incidents featured in this publication are entirely fictional.
DC Comics does not read or accept unsolicited submissions of ideas, stories or artwork.

DC Comics, 2900 West Alameda Ave., Burbank, CA 91505. Printed by LSC Communications, Kendallville, IN, USA. 7/21/17.
Second Printing. ISBN: 978-1-4012-6784-1

Library of Congress Cataloging-in-Publication Data is available.

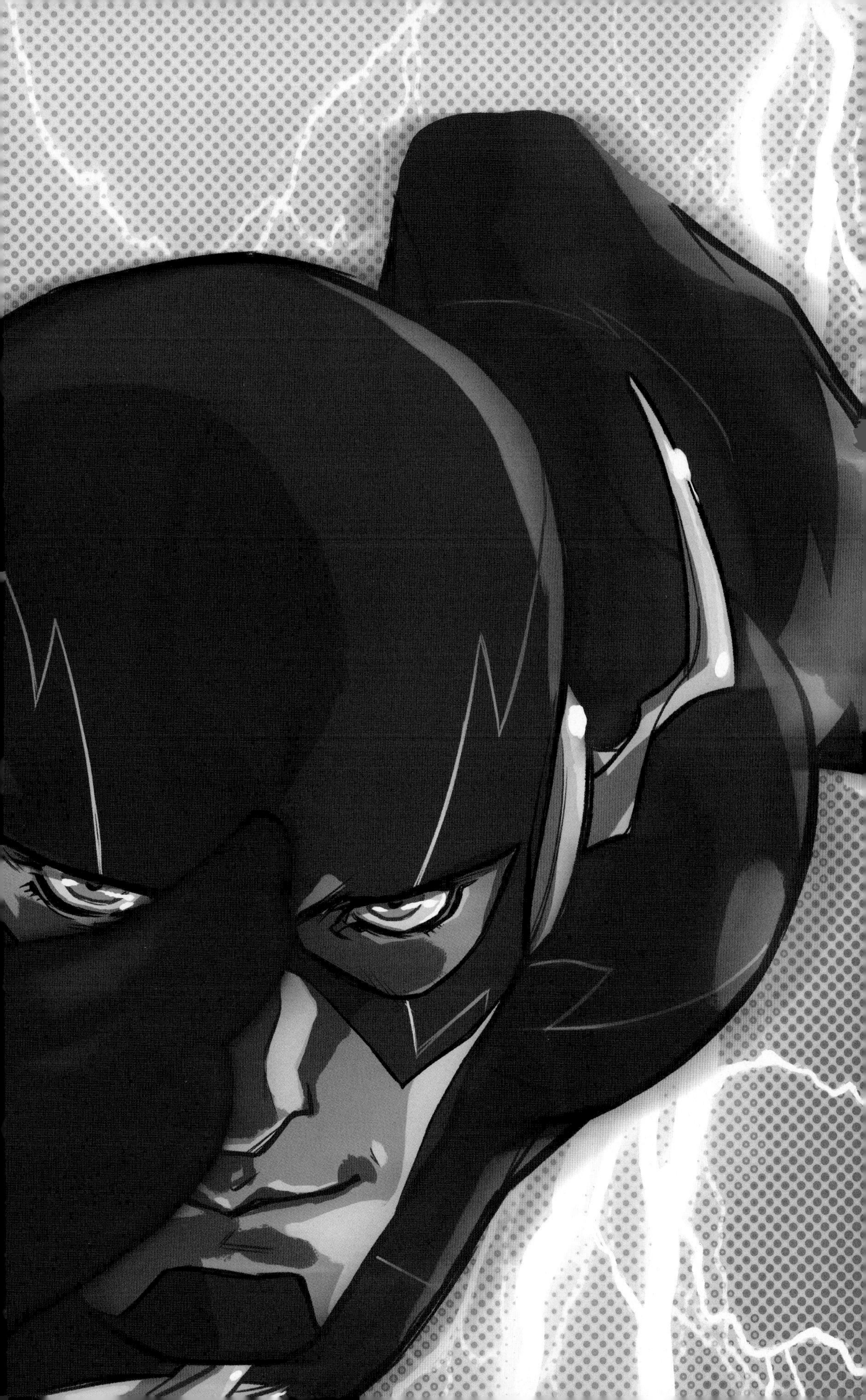

...DOOMED TO REPEAT IT...

CARMINE DI GIANDOMENICO artist * KARL KERSCHL cover artist

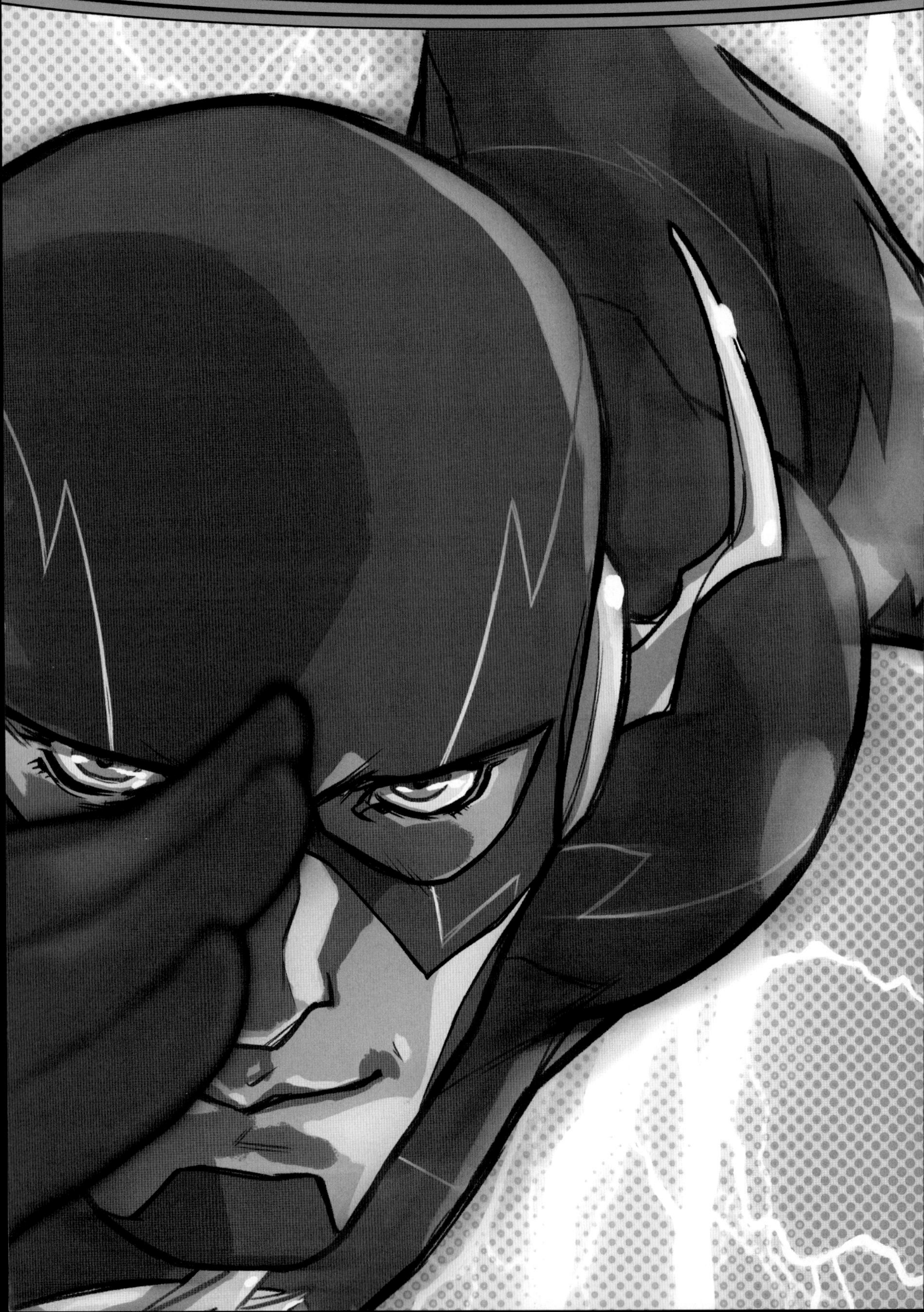

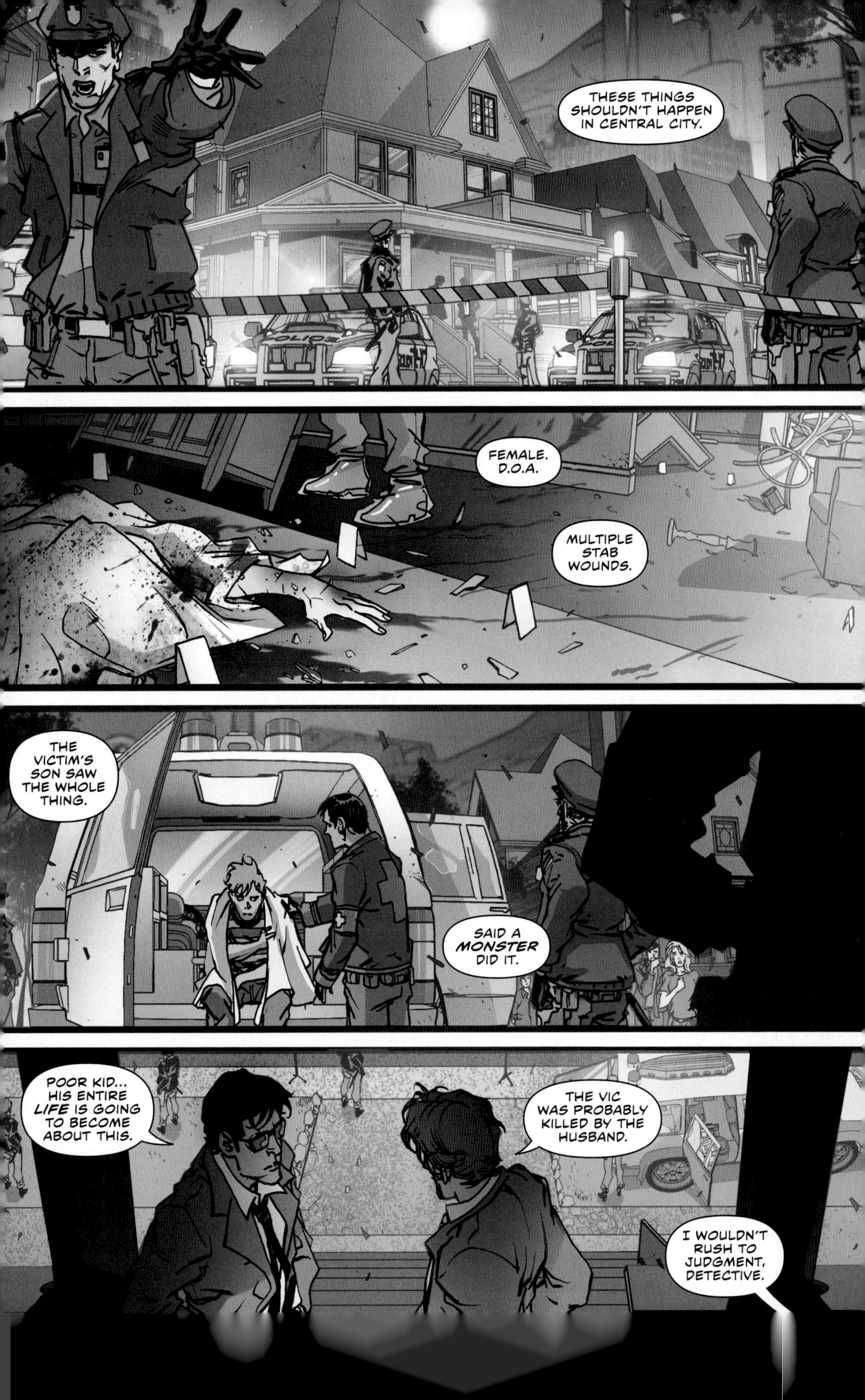
THESE THINGS SHOULDN'T HAPPEN IN CENTRAL CITY.
FEMALE. D.O.A.
MULTIPLE STAB WOUNDS.
THE VICTIM'S SON SAW THE WHOLE THING.
SAID A MONSTER DID IT.
POOR KID... HIS ENTIRE LIFE IS GOING TO BECOME ABOUT THIS.
THE VIC WAS PROBABLY KILLED BY THE HUSBAND.
I WOULDN'T RUSH TO JUDGMENT, DETECTIVE.

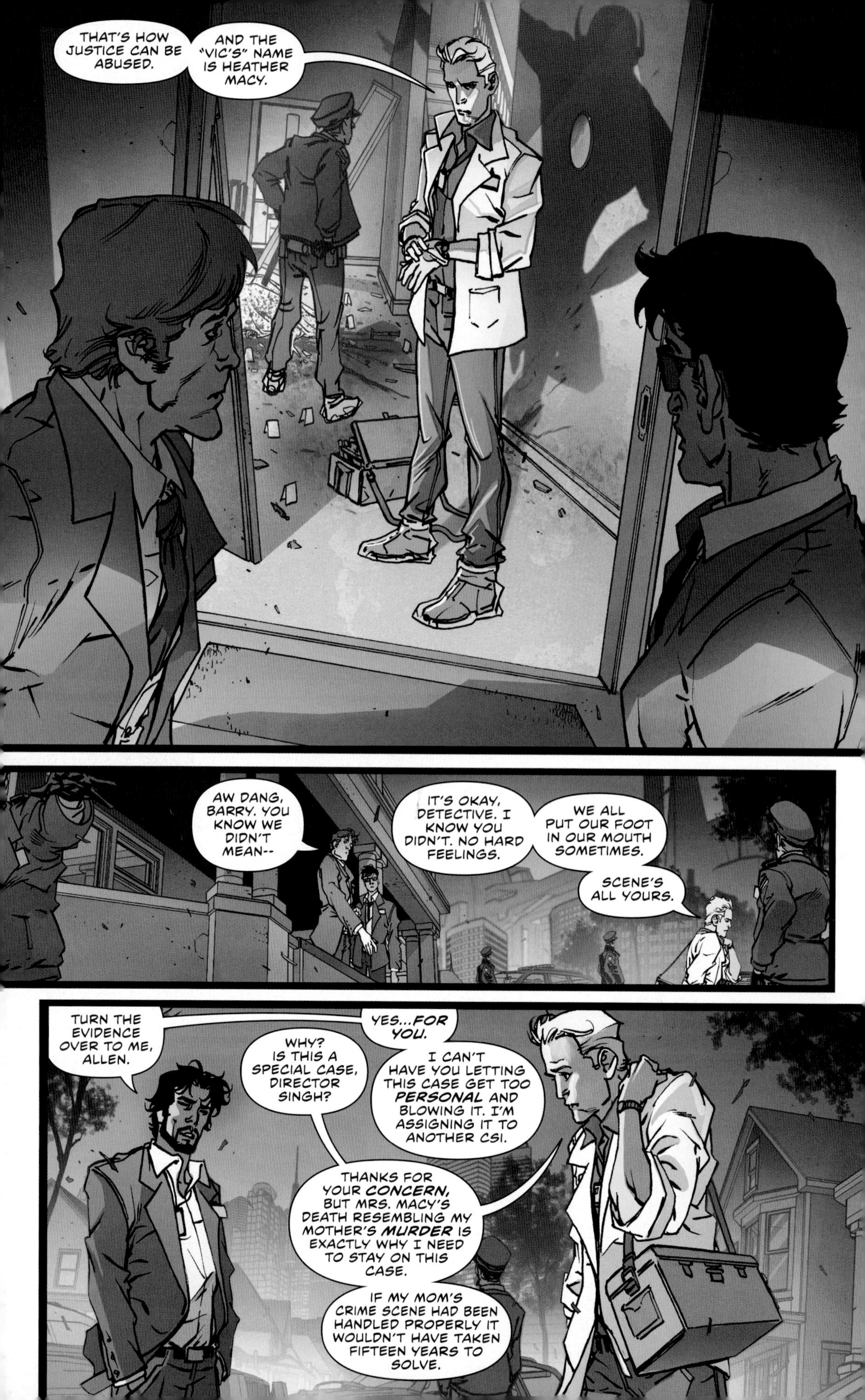
THAT'S HOW JUSTICE CAN BE ABUSED.
AND THE "VIC'S" NAME IS HEATHER MACY.
AW DANG, BARRY. YOU KNOW WE DIDN'T MEAN--
IT'S OKAY, DETECTIVE. I KNOW YOU DIDN'T. NO HARD FEELINGS.
WE ALL PUT OUR FOOT IN OUR MOUTH SOMETIMES.
SCENE'S ALL YOURS.
TURN THE EVIDENCE OVER TO ME, ALLEN.
WHY? IS THIS A SPECIAL CASE, DIRECTOR SINGH?
YES...*FOR YOU.*
I CAN'T HAVE YOU LETTING THIS CASE GET TOO *PERSONAL* AND BLOWING IT. I'M ASSIGNING IT TO ANOTHER CSI.
THANKS FOR YOUR *CONCERN,* BUT MRS. MACY'S DEATH RESEMBLING MY MOTHER'S *MURDER* IS EXACTLY WHY I NEED TO STAY ON THIS CASE.
IF MY MOM'S CRIME SCENE HAD BEEN HANDLED PROPERLY IT WOULDN'T HAVE TAKEN FIFTEEN YEARS TO SOLVE.

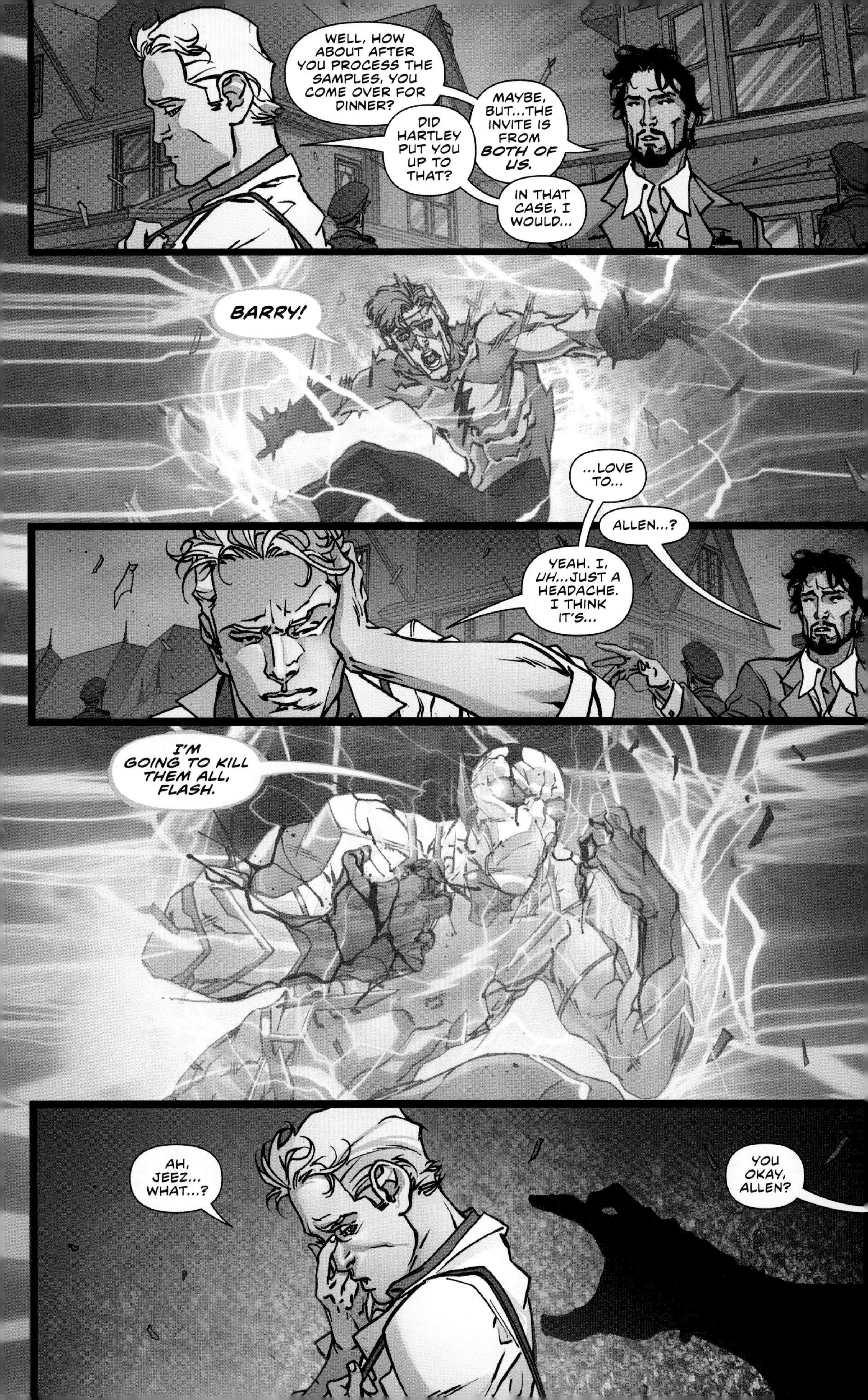
WELL, HOW ABOUT AFTER YOU PROCESS THE SAMPLES, YOU COME OVER FOR DINNER?
DID HARTLEY PUT YOU UP TO THAT?
MAYBE, BUT...THE INVITE IS FROM *BOTH OF US.*
IN THAT CASE, I WOULD...
BARRY!
...LOVE TO...
ALLEN...?
YEAH. I, *UH*...JUST A HEADACHE. I THINK IT'S...
I'M GOING TO KILL THEM ALL, FLASH.
AH, JEEZ... WHAT...?
YOU OKAY, ALLEN?

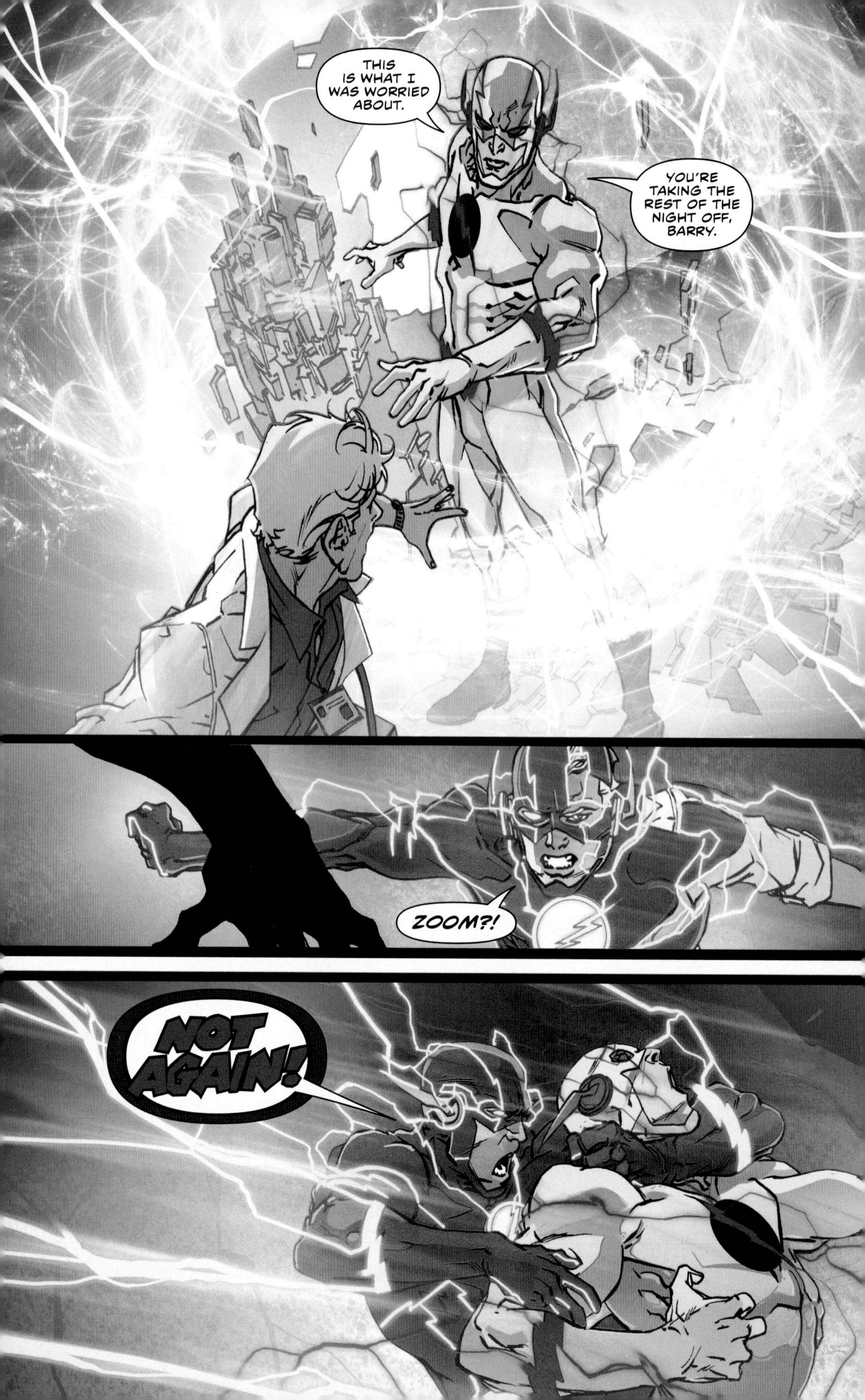
THIS IS WHAT I WAS WORRIED ABOUT.
YOU'RE TAKING THE REST OF THE NIGHT OFF, BARRY.
ZOOM?!
NOT AGAIN!

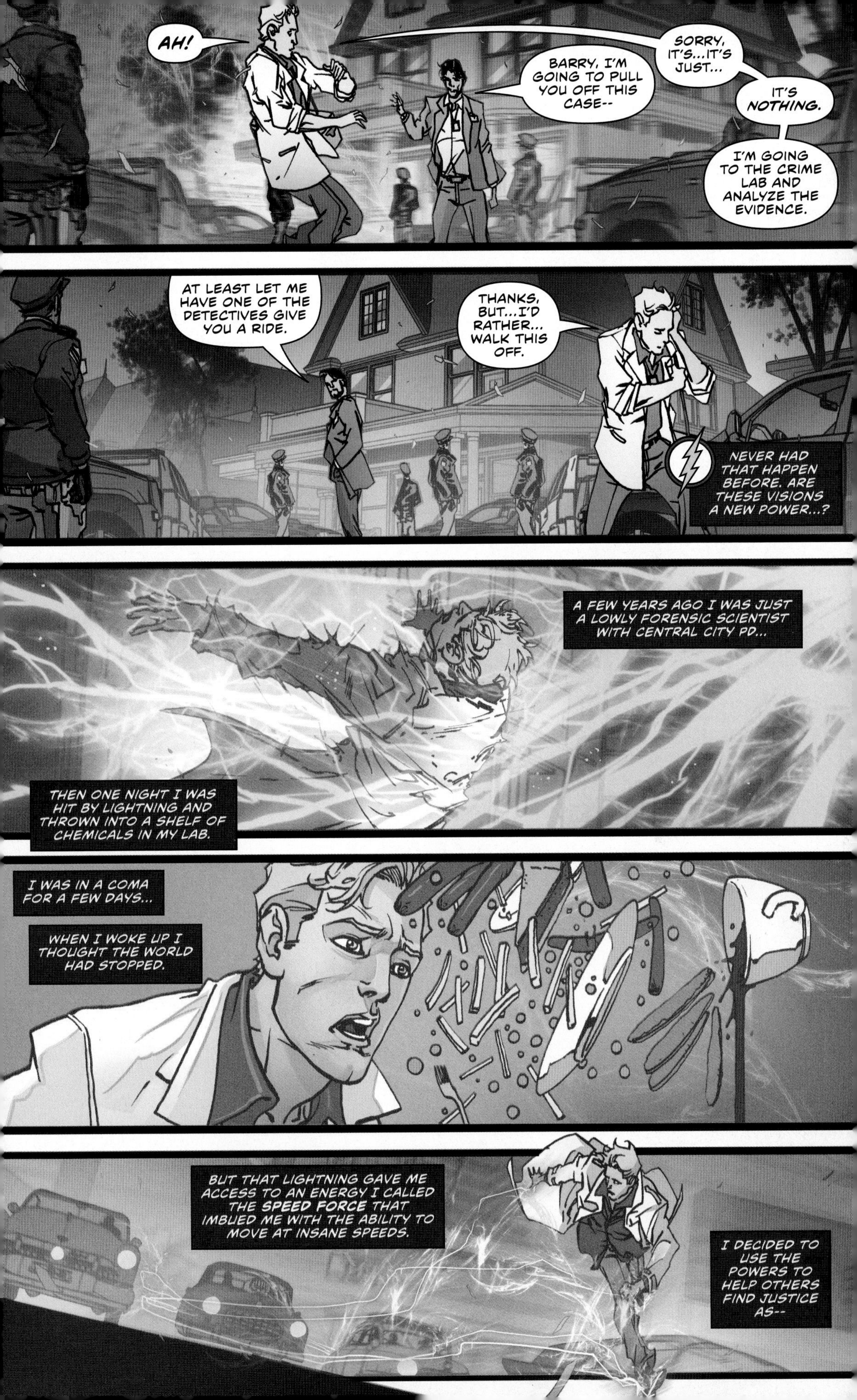
AH!
BARRY, I'M GOING TO PULL YOU OFF THIS CASE--
SORRY, IT'S...IT'S JUST...
IT'S NOTHING.
I'M GOING TO THE CRIME LAB AND ANALYZE THE EVIDENCE.
AT LEAST LET ME HAVE ONE OF THE DETECTIVES GIVE YOU A RIDE.
THANKS, BUT...I'D RATHER... WALK THIS OFF.
NEVER HAD THAT HAPPEN BEFORE. ARE THESE VISIONS A NEW POWER...?
A FEW YEARS AGO I WAS JUST A LOWLY FORENSIC SCIENTIST WITH CENTRAL CITY PD...
THEN ONE NIGHT I WAS HIT BY LIGHTNING AND THROWN INTO A SHELF OF CHEMICALS IN MY LAB.
I WAS IN A COMA FOR A FEW DAYS...
WHEN I WOKE UP I THOUGHT THE WORLD HAD STOPPED.
BUT THAT LIGHTNING GAVE ME ACCESS TO AN ENERGY I CALLED THE SPEED FORCE THAT IMBUED ME WITH THE ABILITY TO MOVE AT INSANE SPEEDS.
I DECIDED TO USE THE POWERS TO HELP OTHERS FIND JUSTICE AS--

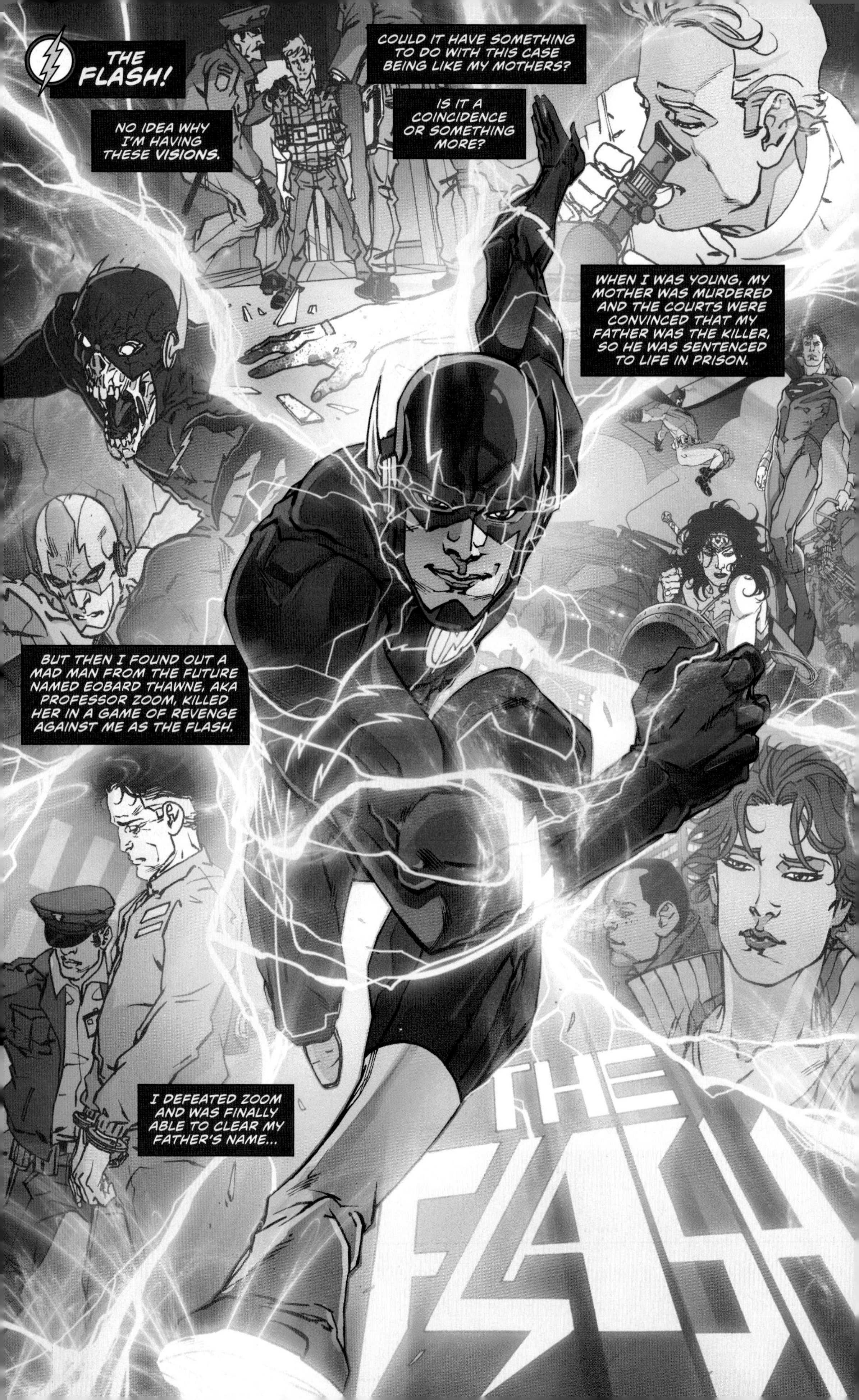
THE FLASH!
NO IDEA WHY I'M HAVING THESE VISIONS.
COULD IT HAVE SOMETHING TO DO WITH THIS CASE BEING LIKE MY MOTHERS?
IS IT A COINCIDENCE OR SOMETHING MORE?
WHEN I WAS YOUNG, MY MOTHER WAS MURDERED AND THE COURTS WERE CONVINCED THAT MY FATHER WAS THE KILLER, SO HE WAS SENTENCED TO LIFE IN PRISON.
BUT THEN I FOUND OUT A MAD MAN FROM THE FUTURE NAMED EOBARD THAWNE, AKA PROFESSOR ZOOM, KILLED HER IN A GAME OF REVENGE AGAINST ME AS THE FLASH.
I DEFEATED ZOOM AND WAS FINALLY ABLE TO CLEAR MY FATHER'S NAME...
THE FLASH

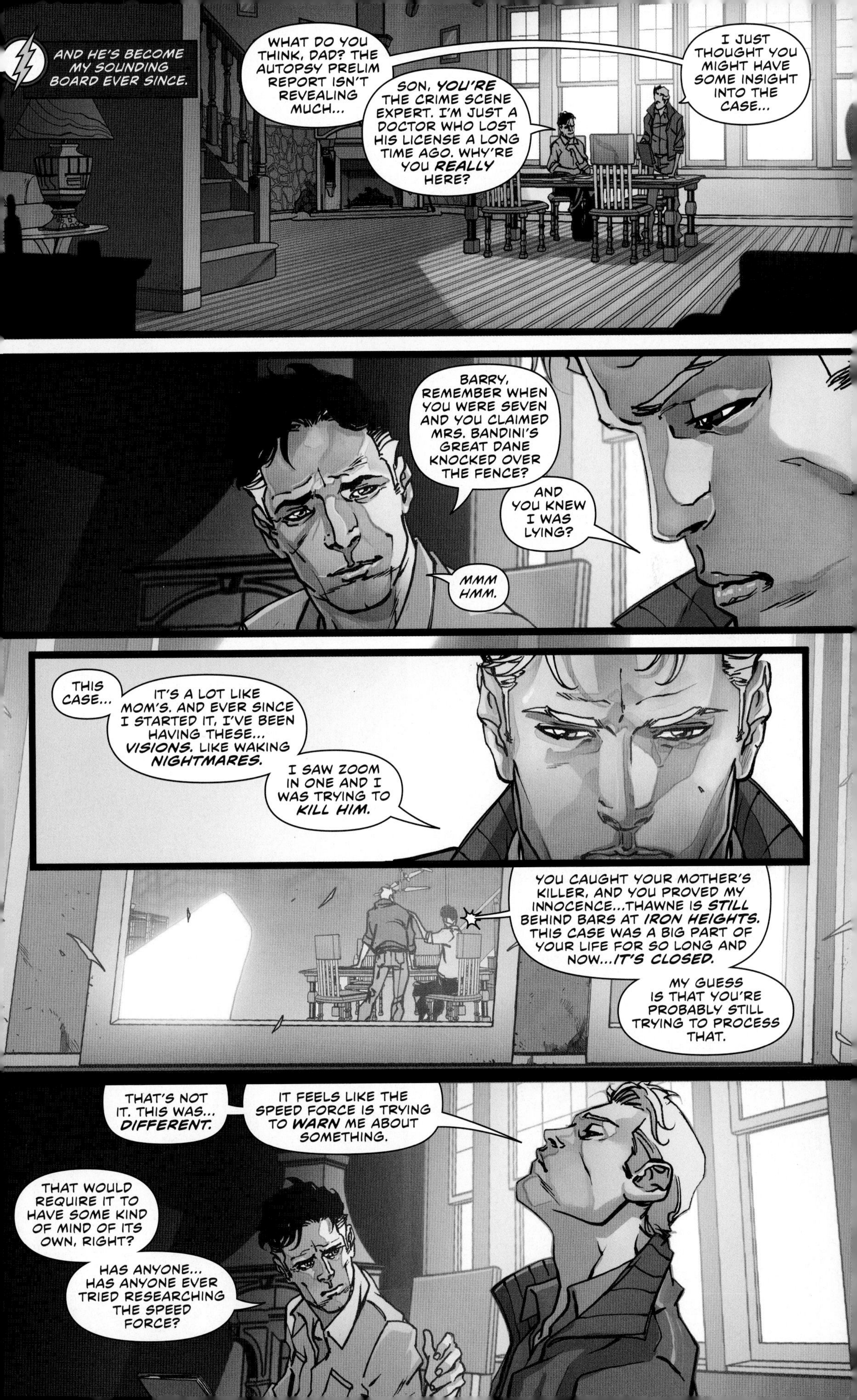
AND HE'S BECOME MY SOUNDING BOARD EVER SINCE.
WHAT DO YOU THINK, DAD? THE AUTOPSY PRELIM REPORT ISN'T REVEALING MUCH...
I JUST THOUGHT YOU MIGHT HAVE SOME INSIGHT INTO THE CASE...
SON, YOU'RE THE CRIME SCENE EXPERT. I'M JUST A DOCTOR WHO LOST HIS LICENSE A LONG TIME AGO. WHY'RE YOU REALLY HERE?
BARRY, REMEMBER WHEN YOU WERE SEVEN AND YOU CLAIMED MRS. BANDINI'S GREAT DANE KNOCKED OVER THE FENCE?
AND YOU KNEW I WAS LYING?
MMM HMM.
THIS CASE...
IT'S A LOT LIKE MOM'S. AND EVER SINCE I STARTED IT, I'VE BEEN HAVING THESE... VISIONS. LIKE WAKING NIGHTMARES.
I SAW ZOOM IN ONE AND I WAS TRYING TO KILL HIM.
YOU CAUGHT YOUR MOTHER'S KILLER, AND YOU PROVED MY INNOCENCE...THAWNE IS STILL BEHIND BARS AT IRON HEIGHTS. THIS CASE WAS A BIG PART OF YOUR LIFE FOR SO LONG AND NOW...IT'S CLOSED.
MY GUESS IS THAT YOU'RE PROBABLY STILL TRYING TO PROCESS THAT.
THAT'S NOT IT. THIS WAS... DIFFERENT.
IT FEELS LIKE THE SPEED FORCE IS TRYING TO WARN ME ABOUT SOMETHING.
THAT WOULD REQUIRE IT TO HAVE SOME KIND OF MIND OF ITS OWN, RIGHT?
HAS ANYONE... HAS ANYONE EVER TRIED RESEARCHING THE SPEED FORCE?

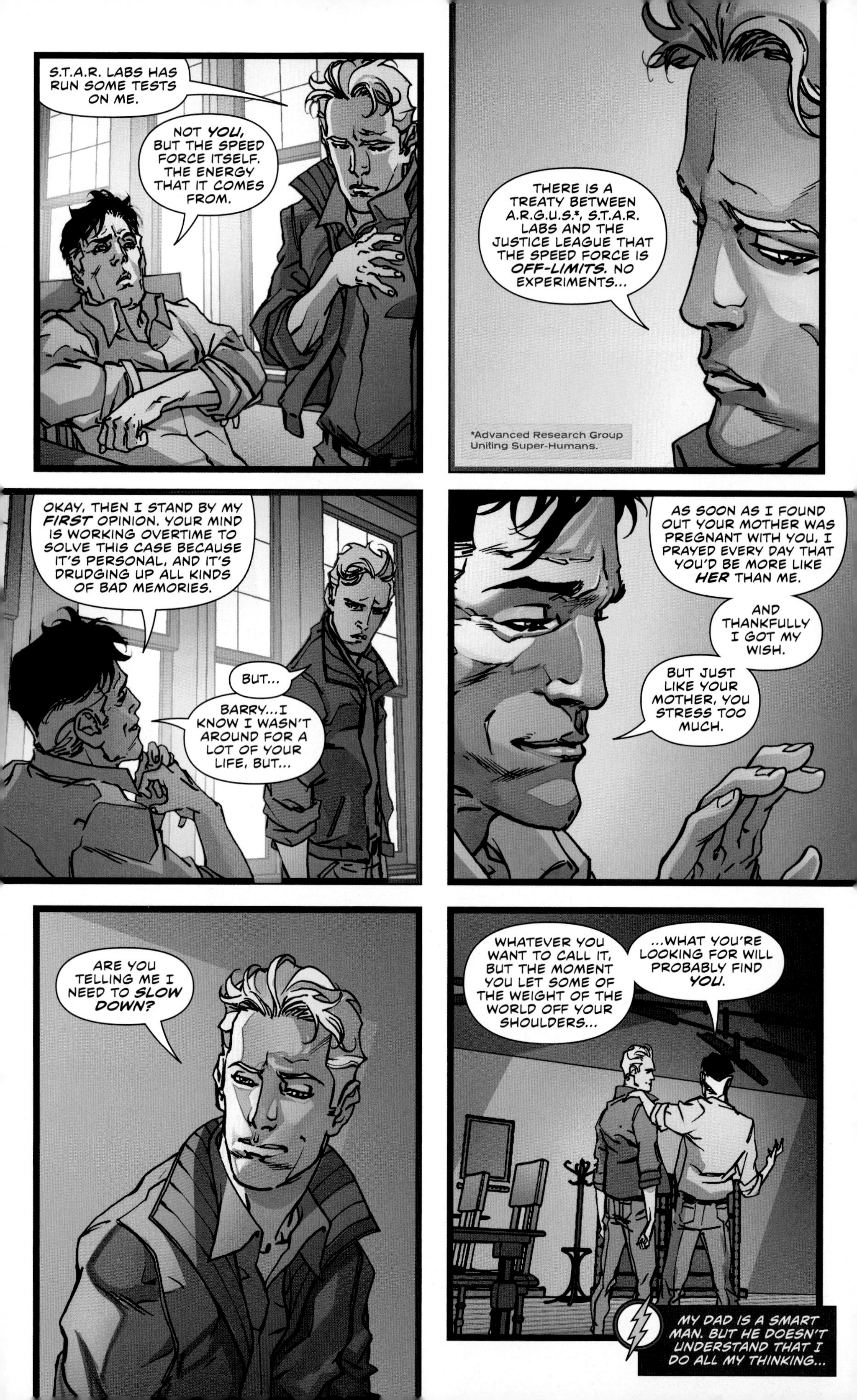
S.T.A.R. LABS HAS RUN SOME TESTS ON ME.
NOT YOU, BUT THE SPEED FORCE ITSELF. THE ENERGY THAT IT COMES FROM.
THERE IS A TREATY BETWEEN A.R.G.U.S.*, S.T.A.R. LABS AND THE JUSTICE LEAGUE THAT THE SPEED FORCE IS OFF-LIMITS. NO EXPERIMENTS...
*Advanced Research Group Uniting Super-Humans.
OKAY, THEN I STAND BY MY FIRST OPINION. YOUR MIND IS WORKING OVERTIME TO SOLVE THIS CASE BECAUSE IT'S PERSONAL, AND IT'S DRUDGING UP ALL KINDS OF BAD MEMORIES.
BUT...
BARRY...I KNOW I WASN'T AROUND FOR A LOT OF YOUR LIFE, BUT...
AS SOON AS I FOUND OUT YOUR MOTHER WAS PREGNANT WITH YOU, I PRAYED EVERY DAY THAT YOU'D BE MORE LIKE HER THAN ME.
AND THANKFULLY I GOT MY WISH.
BUT JUST LIKE YOUR MOTHER, YOU STRESS TOO MUCH.
ARE YOU TELLING ME I NEED TO SLOW DOWN?
WHATEVER YOU WANT TO CALL IT, BUT THE MOMENT YOU LET SOME OF THE WEIGHT OF THE WORLD OFF YOUR SHOULDERS...
...WHAT YOU'RE LOOKING FOR WILL PROBABLY FIND YOU.
MY DAD IS A SMART MAN. BUT HE DOESN'T UNDERSTAND THAT I DO ALL MY THINKING...

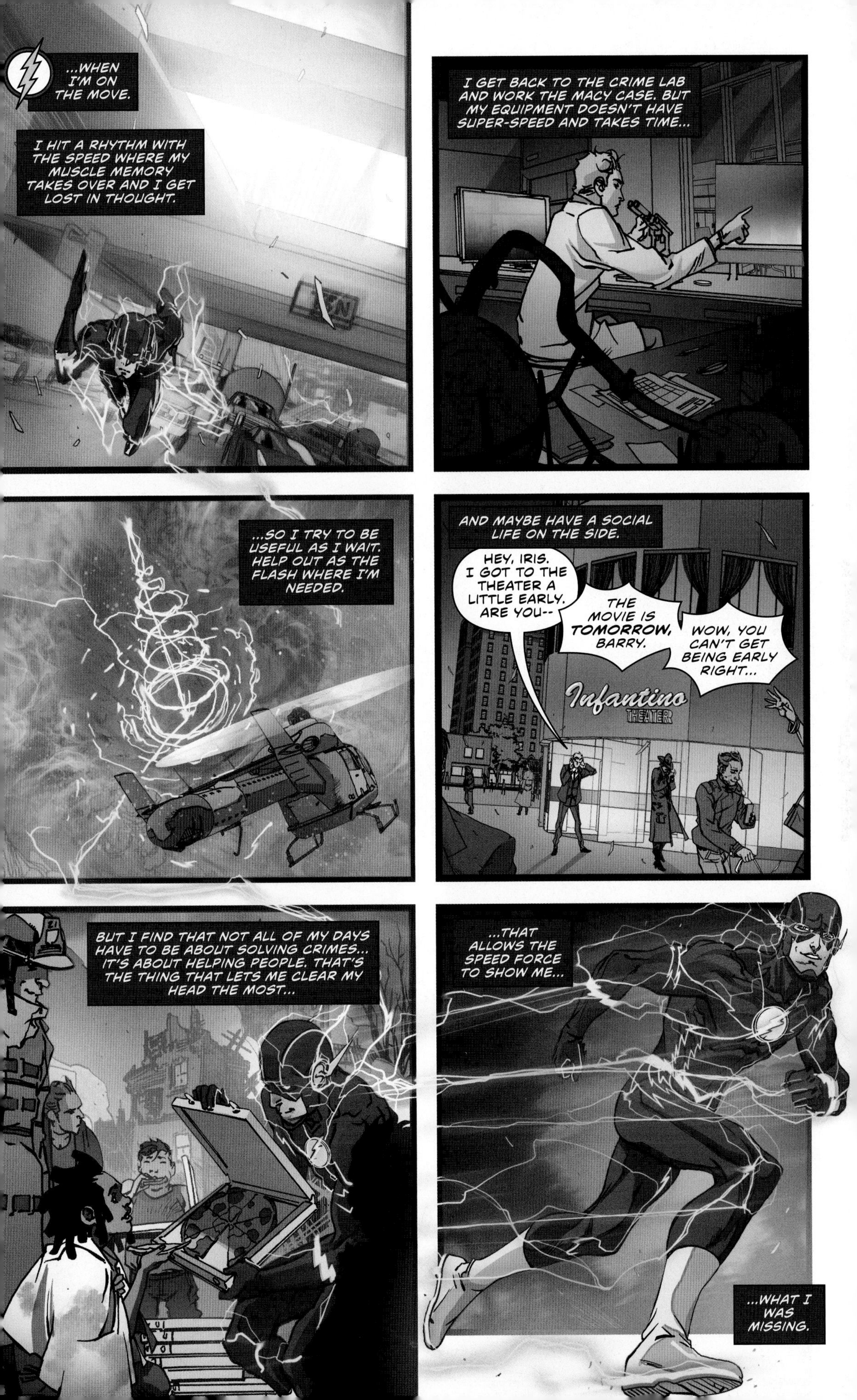
...WHEN I'M ON THE MOVE.
I HIT A RHYTHM WITH THE SPEED WHERE MY MUSCLE MEMORY TAKES OVER AND I GET LOST IN THOUGHT.
I GET BACK TO THE CRIME LAB AND WORK THE MACY CASE. BUT MY EQUIPMENT DOESN'T HAVE SUPER-SPEED AND TAKES TIME...
...SO I TRY TO BE USEFUL AS I WAIT. HELP OUT AS THE FLASH WHERE I'M NEEDED.
AND MAYBE HAVE A SOCIAL LIFE ON THE SIDE.
HEY, IRIS. I GOT TO THE THEATER A LITTLE EARLY. ARE YOU--
THE MOVIE IS TOMORROW, BARRY.
WOW, YOU CAN'T GET BEING EARLY RIGHT...
Infantino THEATER
BUT I FIND THAT NOT ALL OF MY DAYS HAVE TO BE ABOUT SOLVING CRIMES... IT'S ABOUT HELPING PEOPLE. THAT'S THE THING THAT LETS ME CLEAR MY HEAD THE MOST...
...THAT ALLOWS THE SPEED FORCE TO SHOW ME...
...WHAT I WAS MISSING.

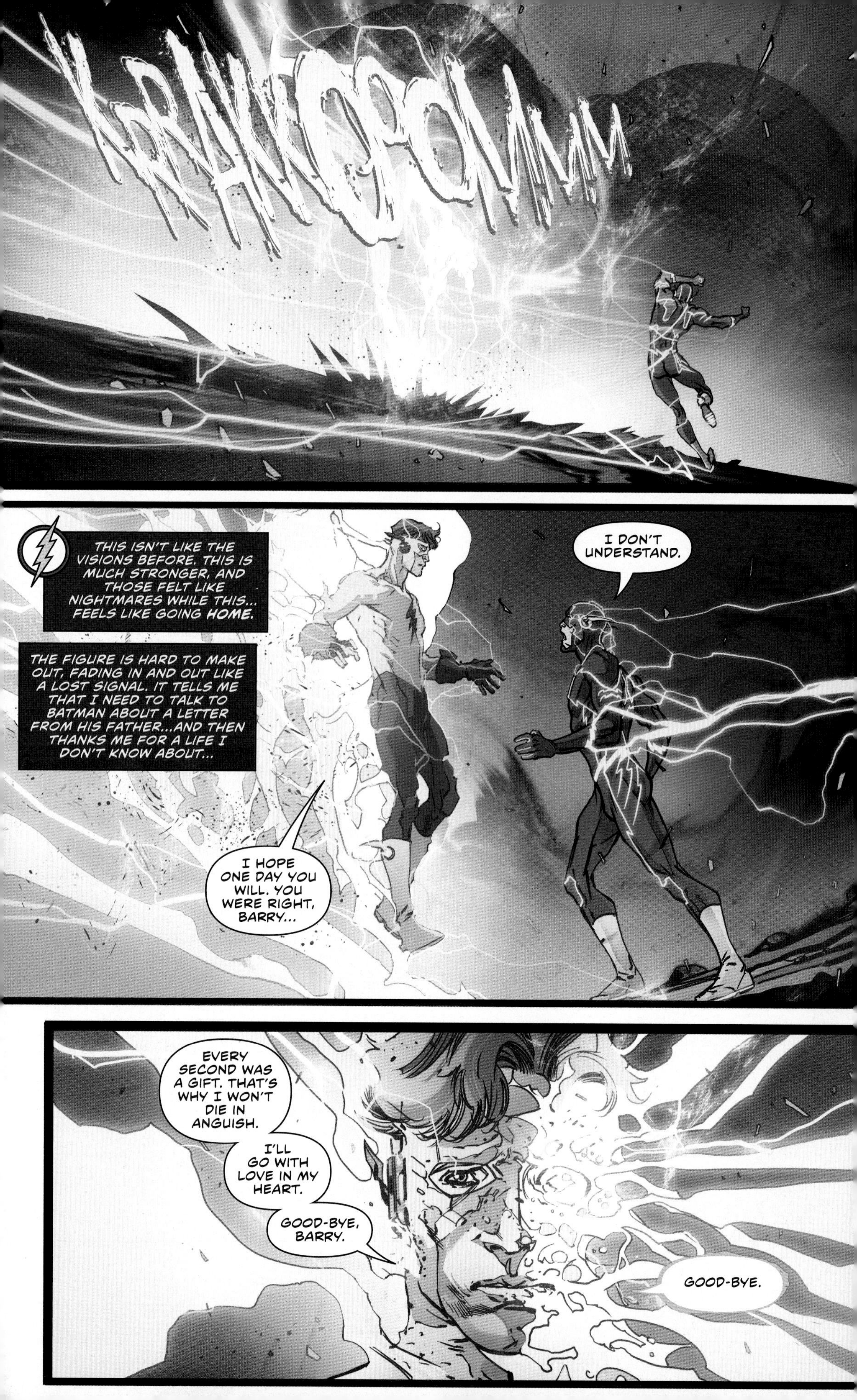
KRAKOOOMMM
THIS ISN'T LIKE THE VISIONS BEFORE. THIS IS MUCH STRONGER, AND THOSE FELT LIKE NIGHTMARES WHILE THIS... FEELS LIKE GOING **HOME**.
THE FIGURE IS HARD TO MAKE OUT, FADING IN AND OUT LIKE A LOST SIGNAL. IT TELLS ME THAT I NEED TO TALK TO BATMAN ABOUT A LETTER FROM HIS FATHER...AND THEN THANKS ME FOR A LIFE I DON'T KNOW ABOUT...
I DON'T UNDERSTAND.
I HOPE ONE DAY YOU WILL. YOU WERE RIGHT, BARRY...
EVERY SECOND WAS A GIFT. THAT'S WHY I WON'T DIE IN ANGUISH.
I'LL GO WITH LOVE IN MY HEART.
GOOD-BYE, BARRY.
GOOD-BYE.

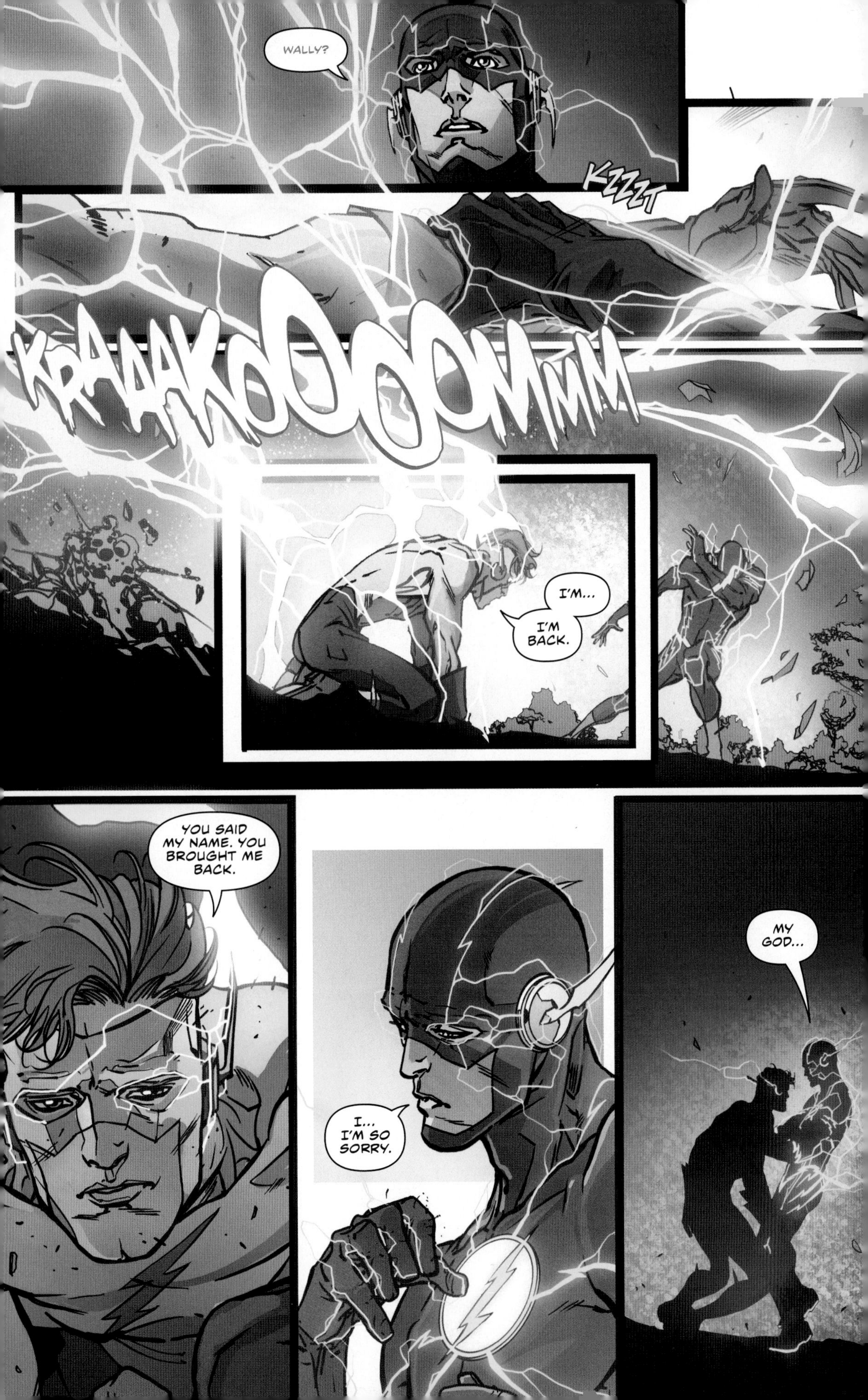
WALLY?
KZZZT
KRAAAKOOOOOMMMM
I'M...
I'M BACK.
YOU SAID MY NAME. YOU BROUGHT ME BACK.
I... I'M SO SORRY.
MY GOD...

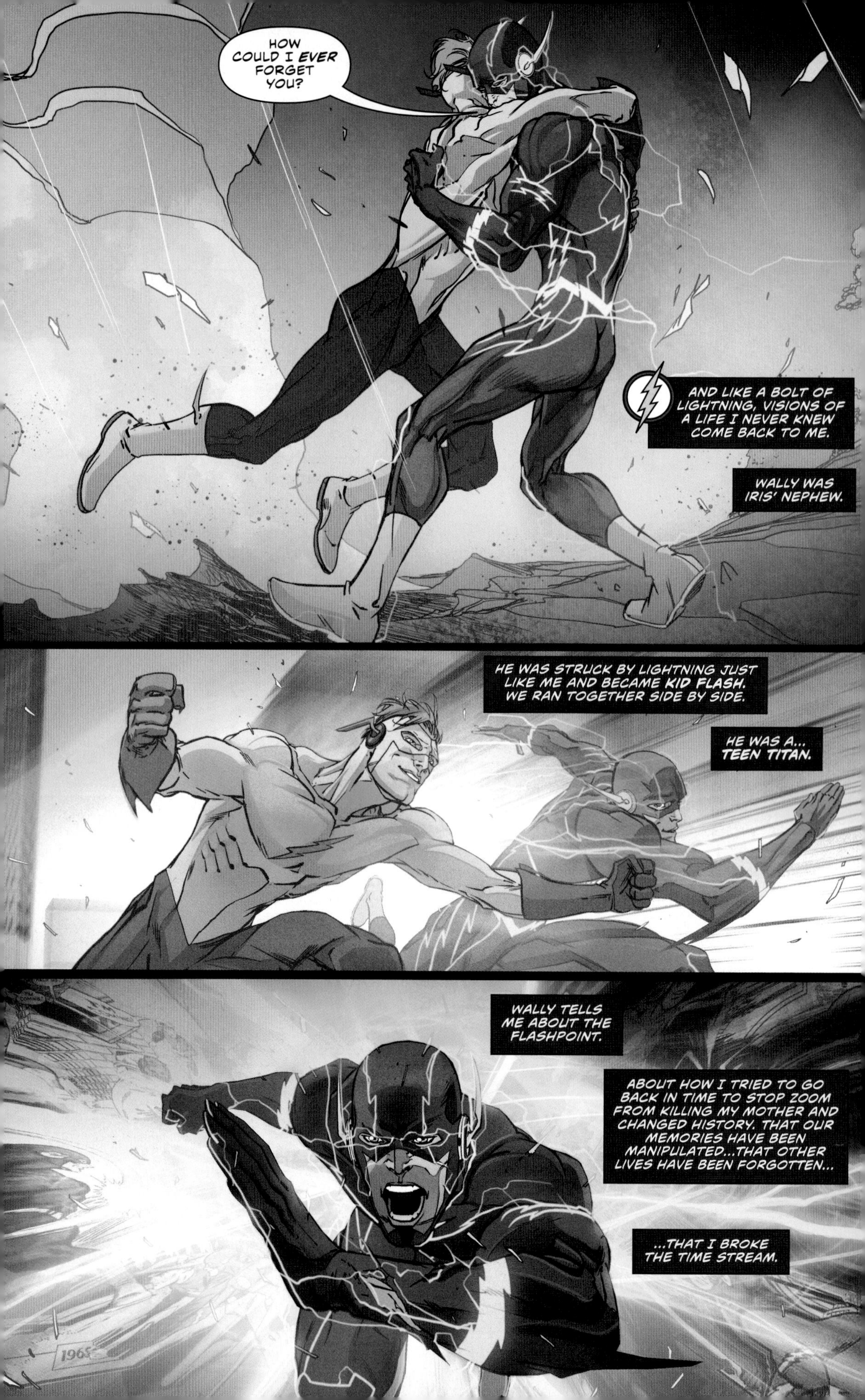
HOW COULD I EVER FORGET YOU?
AND LIKE A BOLT OF LIGHTNING, VISIONS OF A LIFE I NEVER KNEW COME BACK TO ME.
WALLY WAS IRIS' NEPHEW.
HE WAS STRUCK BY LIGHTNING JUST LIKE ME AND BECAME KID FLASH. WE RAN TOGETHER SIDE BY SIDE.
HE WAS A... TEEN TITAN.
WALLY TELLS ME ABOUT THE FLASHPOINT.
ABOUT HOW I TRIED TO GO BACK IN TIME TO STOP ZOOM FROM KILLING MY MOTHER AND CHANGED HISTORY. THAT OUR MEMORIES HAVE BEEN MANIPULATED...THAT OTHER LIVES HAVE BEEN FORGOTTEN...
...THAT I BROKE THE TIME STREAM.

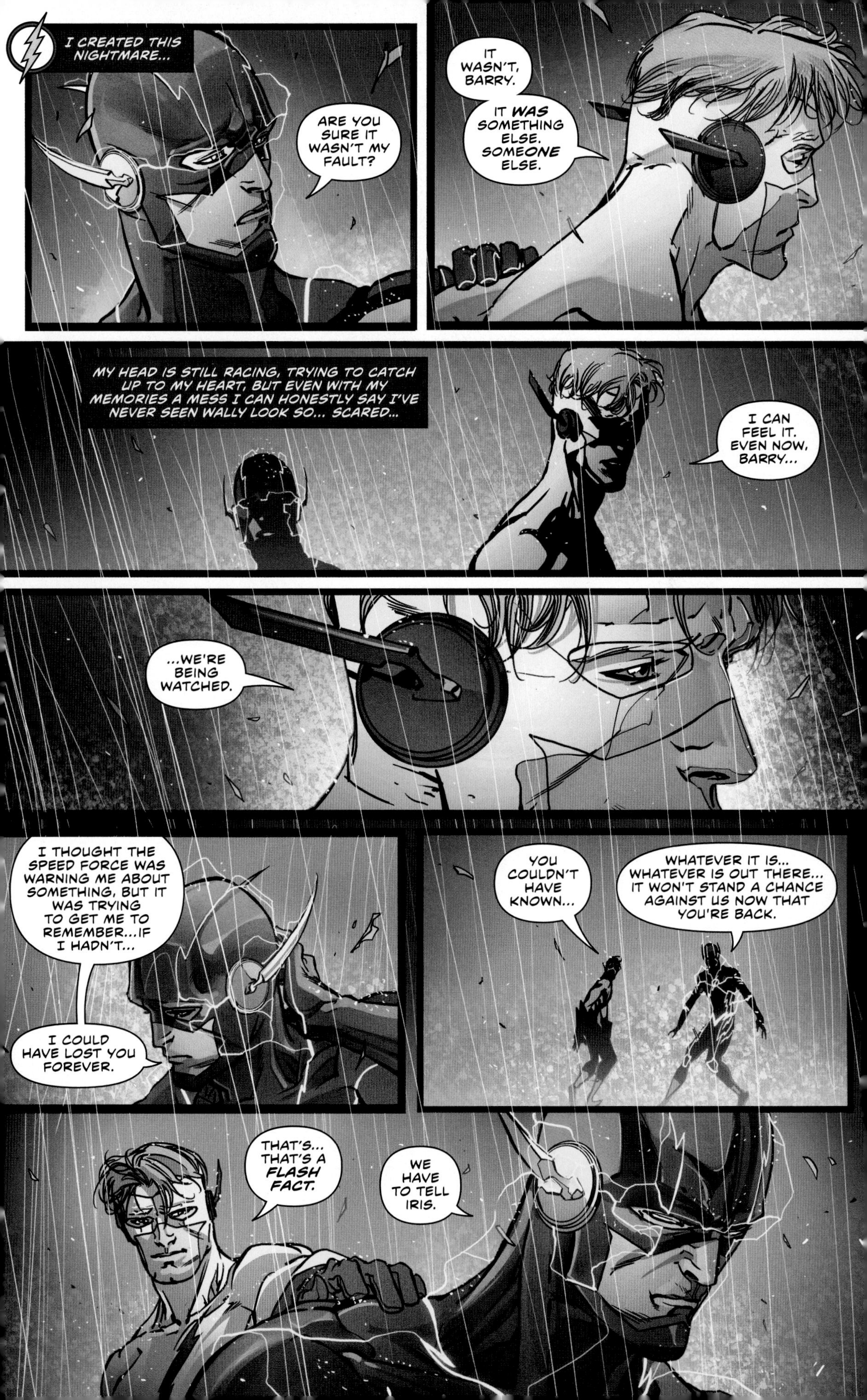

I CREATED THIS NIGHTMARE...
ARE YOU SURE IT WASN'T MY FAULT?
IT WASN'T, BARRY.
IT WAS SOMETHING ELSE. SOMEONE ELSE.
MY HEAD IS STILL RACING, TRYING TO CATCH UP TO MY HEART, BUT EVEN WITH MY MEMORIES A MESS I CAN HONESTLY SAY I'VE NEVER SEEN WALLY LOOK SO... SCARED...
I CAN FEEL IT. EVEN NOW, BARRY...
...WE'RE BEING WATCHED.
I THOUGHT THE SPEED FORCE WAS WARNING ME ABOUT SOMETHING, BUT IT WAS TRYING TO GET ME TO REMEMBER...IF I HADN'T...
I COULD HAVE LOST YOU FOREVER.
YOU COULDN'T HAVE KNOWN...
WHATEVER IT IS... WHATEVER IS OUT THERE... IT WON'T STAND A CHANCE AGAINST US NOW THAT YOU'RE BACK.
THAT'S... THAT'S A FLASH FACT.
WE HAVE TO TELL IRIS.

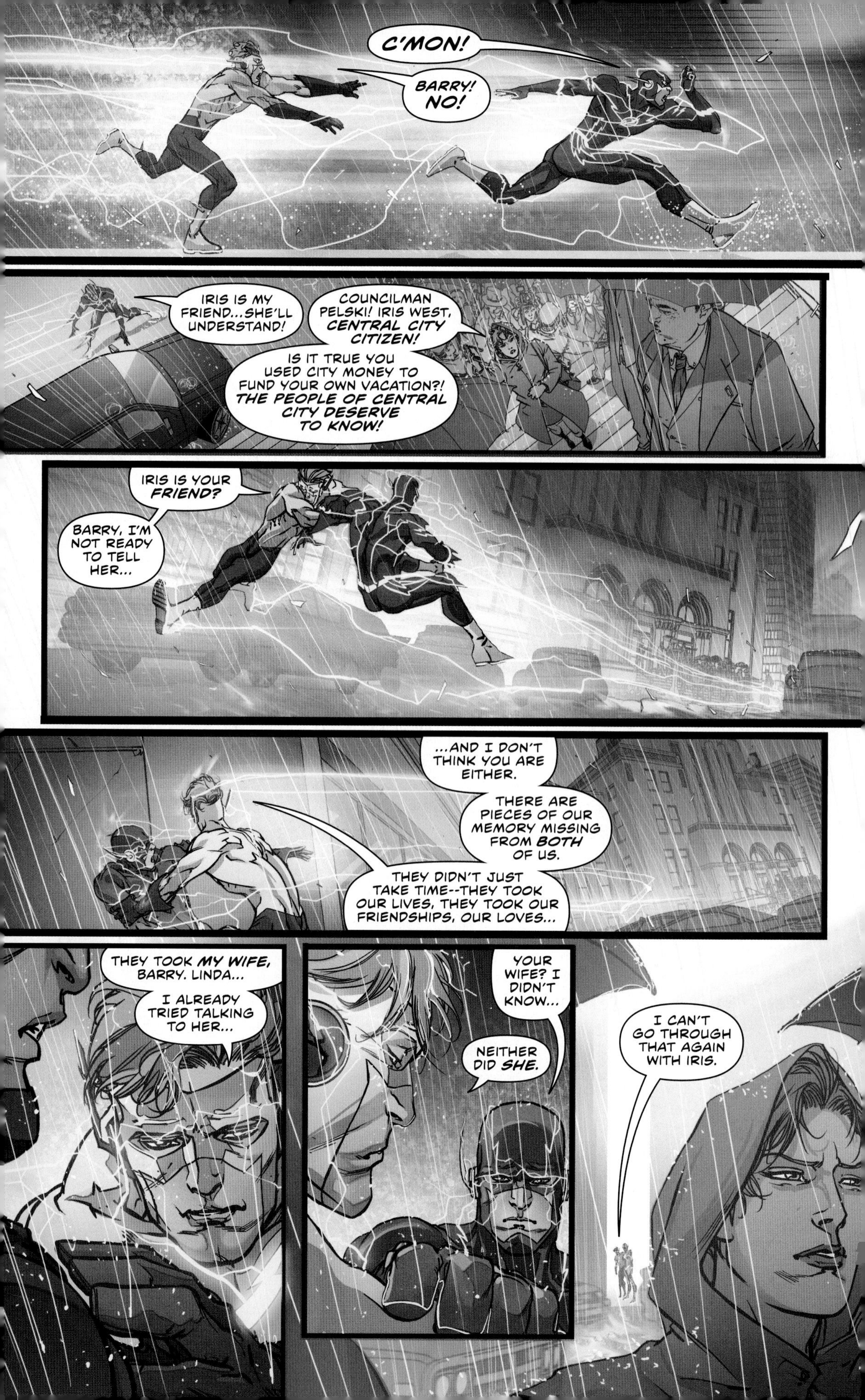
C'MON!
BARRY! NO!
IRIS IS MY FRIEND...SHE'LL UNDERSTAND!
COUNCILMAN PELSKI! IRIS WEST, CENTRAL CITY CITIZEN!
IS IT TRUE YOU USED CITY MONEY TO FUND YOUR OWN VACATION?! THE PEOPLE OF CENTRAL CITY DESERVE TO KNOW!
IRIS IS YOUR FRIEND?
BARRY, I'M NOT READY TO TELL HER...
...AND I DON'T THINK YOU ARE EITHER.
THERE ARE PIECES OF OUR MEMORY MISSING FROM BOTH OF US.
THEY DIDN'T JUST TAKE TIME--THEY TOOK OUR LIVES, THEY TOOK OUR FRIENDSHIPS, OUR LOVES...
THEY TOOK MY WIFE, BARRY. LINDA...
I ALREADY TRIED TALKING TO HER...
YOUR WIFE? I DIDN'T KNOW...
NEITHER DID SHE.
I CAN'T GO THROUGH THAT AGAIN WITH IRIS.

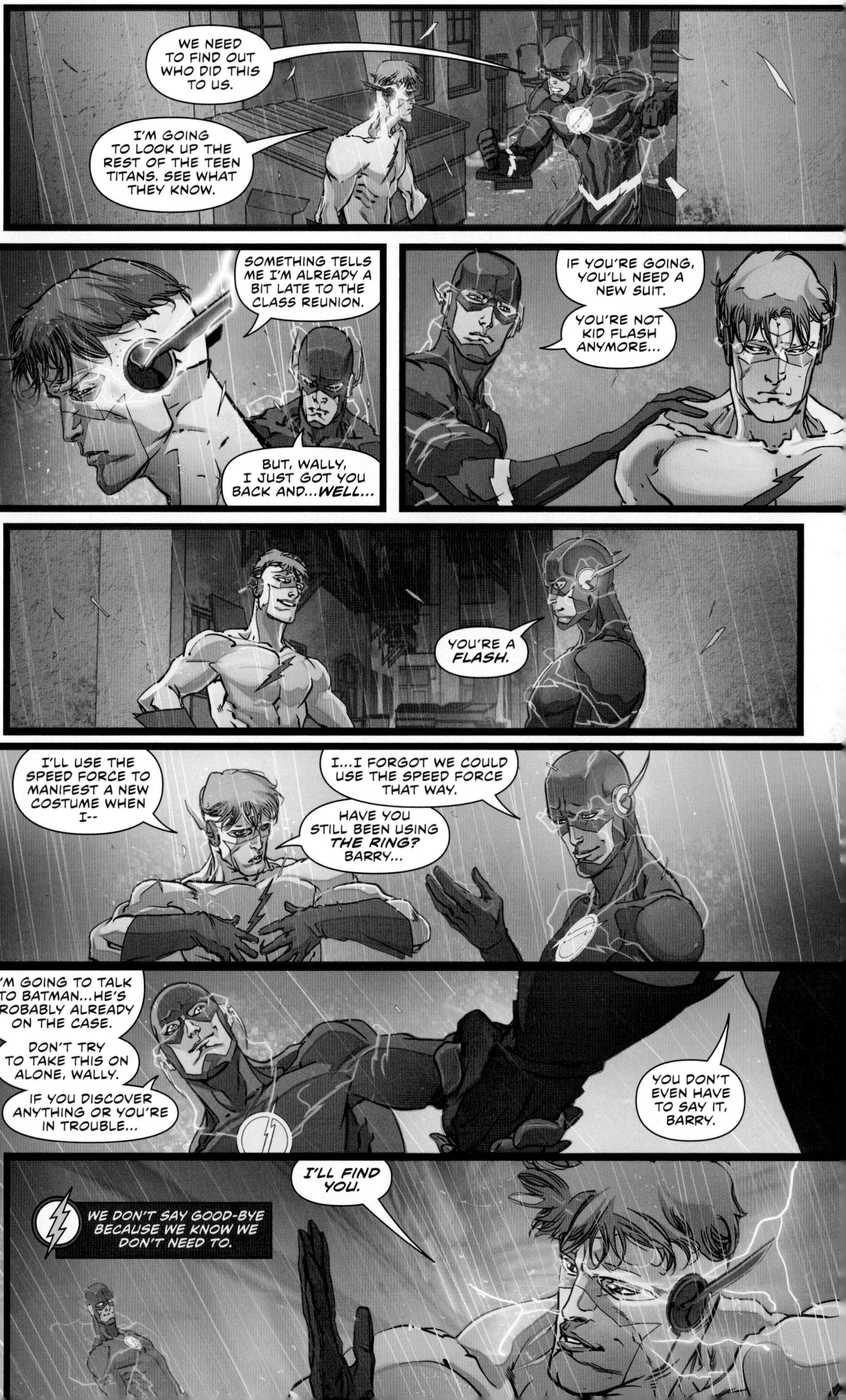
WE NEED TO FIND OUT WHO DID THIS TO US.
I'M GOING TO LOOK UP THE REST OF THE TEEN TITANS. SEE WHAT THEY KNOW.
SOMETHING TELLS ME I'M ALREADY A BIT LATE TO THE CLASS REUNION.
BUT, WALLY, I JUST GOT YOU BACK AND...WELL...
IF YOU'RE GOING, YOU'LL NEED A NEW SUIT.
YOU'RE NOT KID FLASH ANYMORE...
YOU'RE A FLASH.
I'LL USE THE SPEED FORCE TO MANIFEST A NEW COSTUME WHEN I--
I...I FORGOT WE COULD USE THE SPEED FORCE THAT WAY.
HAVE YOU STILL BEEN USING THE RING? BARRY...
I'M GOING TO TALK TO BATMAN...HE'S PROBABLY ALREADY ON THE CASE.
DON'T TRY TO TAKE THIS ON ALONE, WALLY.
IF YOU DISCOVER ANYTHING OR YOU'RE IN TROUBLE...
YOU DON'T EVEN HAVE TO SAY IT, BARRY.
I'LL FIND YOU.
WE DON'T SAY GOOD-BYE BECAUSE WE KNOW WE DON'T NEED TO.

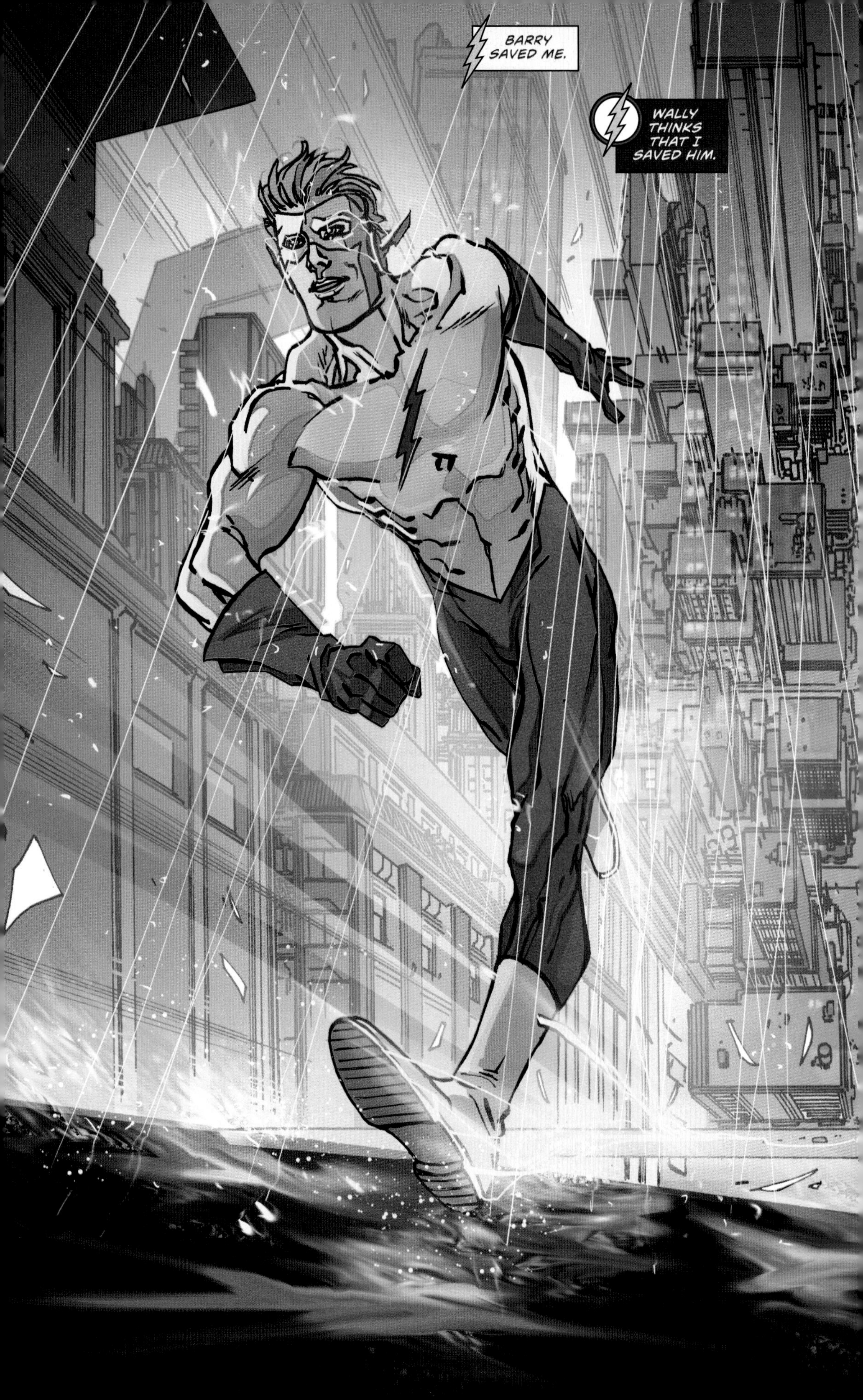
BARRY SAVED ME.
WALLY THINKS THAT I SAVED HIM.

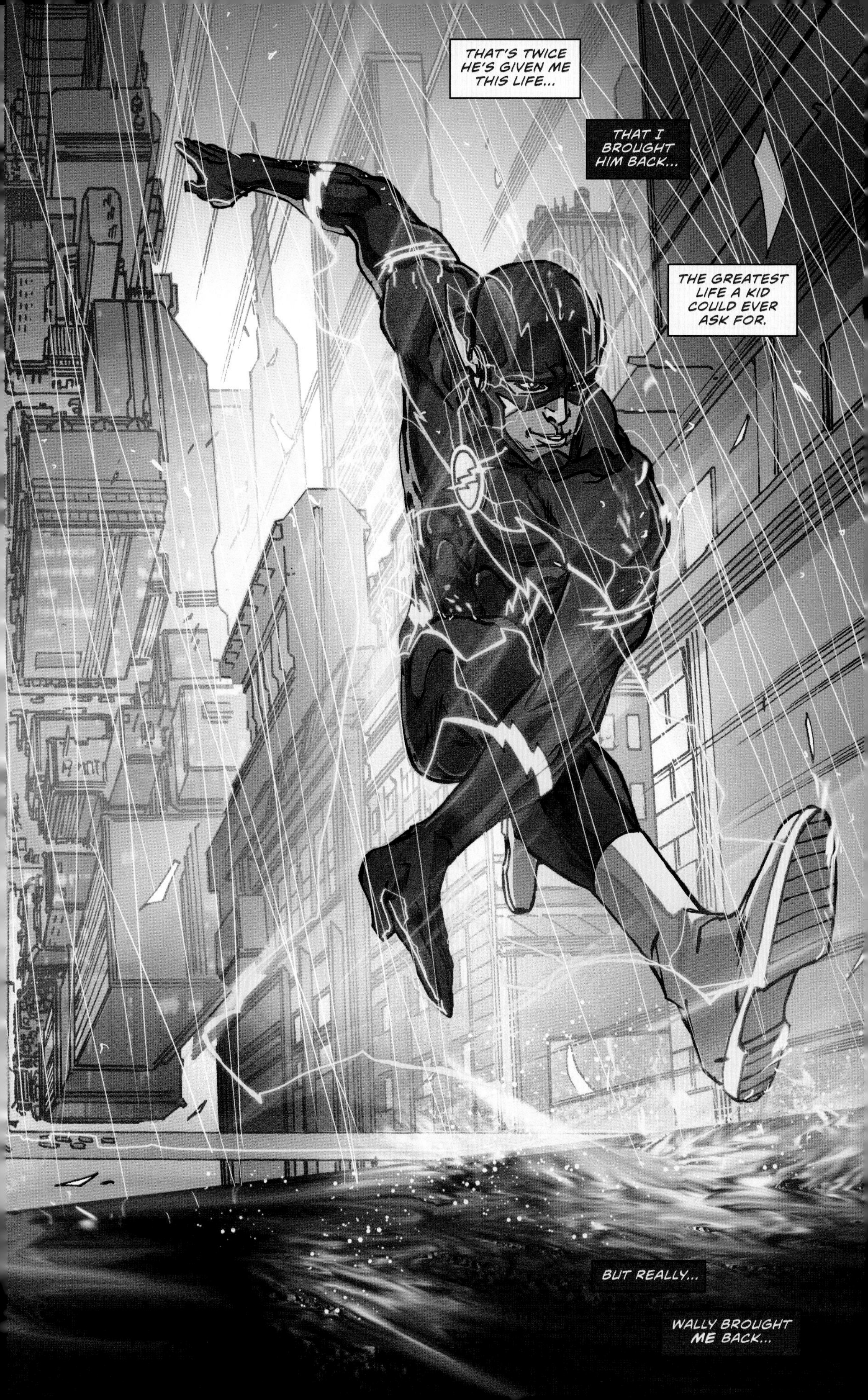
THAT'S TWICE HE'S GIVEN ME THIS LIFE...
THAT I BROUGHT HIM BACK...
THE GREATEST LIFE A KID COULD EVER ASK FOR.
BUT REALLY...
WALLY BROUGHT ME BACK...

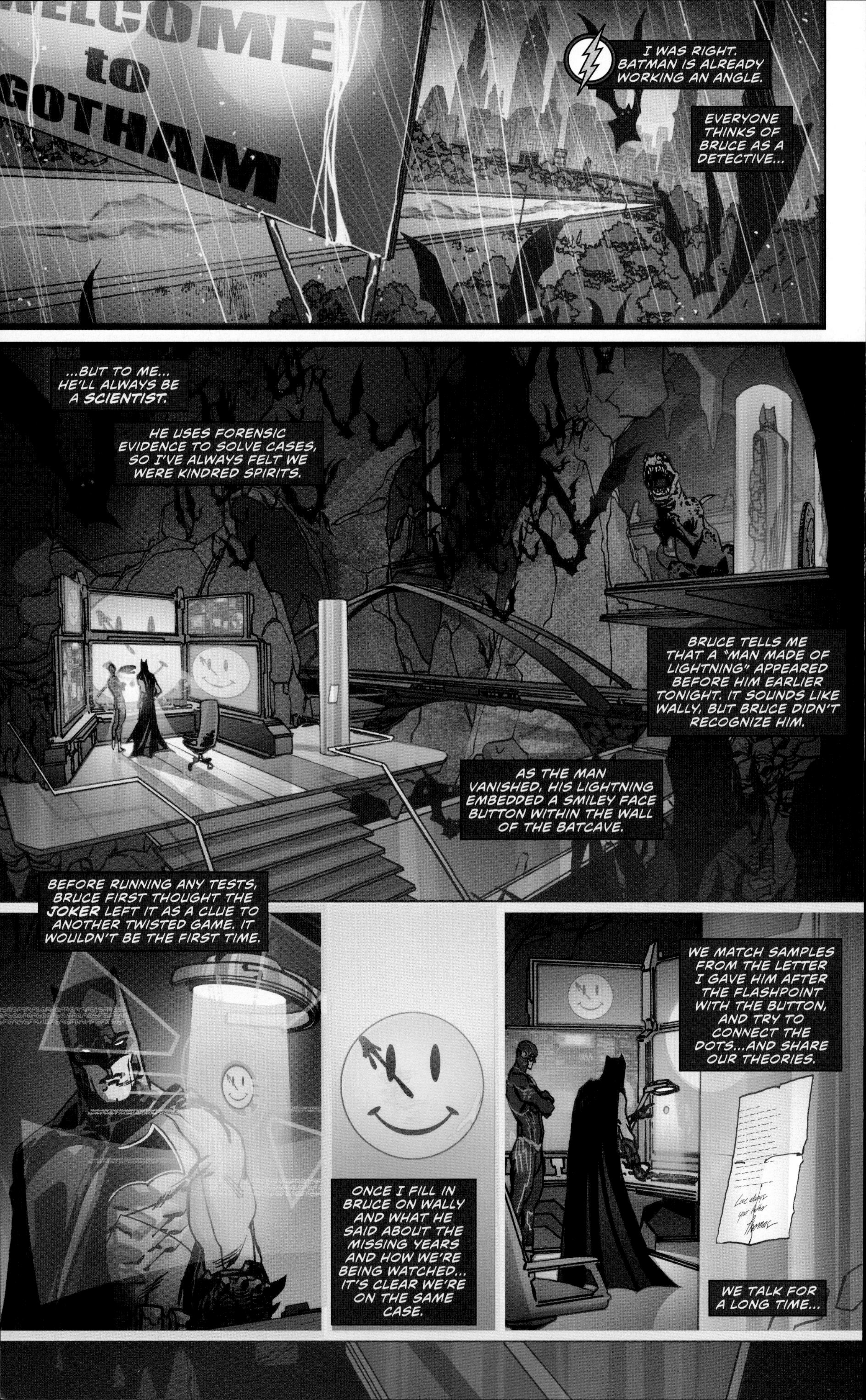
to
GOTHAM
I WAS RIGHT. BATMAN IS ALREADY WORKING AN ANGLE.
EVERYONE THINKS OF BRUCE AS A DETECTIVE...
...BUT TO ME... HE'LL ALWAYS BE A SCIENTIST.
HE USES FORENSIC EVIDENCE TO SOLVE CASES, SO I'VE ALWAYS FELT WE WERE KINDRED SPIRITS.
BRUCE TELLS ME THAT A "MAN MADE OF LIGHTNING" APPEARED BEFORE HIM EARLIER TONIGHT. IT SOUNDS LIKE WALLY, BUT BRUCE DIDN'T RECOGNIZE HIM.
AS THE MAN VANISHED, HIS LIGHTNING EMBEDDED A SMILEY FACE BUTTON WITHIN THE WALL OF THE BATCAVE.
BEFORE RUNNING ANY TESTS, BRUCE FIRST THOUGHT THE JOKER LEFT IT AS A CLUE TO ANOTHER TWISTED GAME. IT WOULDN'T BE THE FIRST TIME.
ONCE I FILL IN BRUCE ON WALLY AND WHAT HE SAID ABOUT THE MISSING YEARS AND HOW WE'RE BEING WATCHED... IT'S CLEAR WE'RE ON THE SAME CASE.
WE MATCH SAMPLES FROM THE LETTER I GAVE HIM AFTER THE FLASHPOINT WITH THE BUTTON, AND TRY TO CONNECT THE DOTS...AND SHARE OUR THEORIES.
WE TALK FOR A LONG TIME...

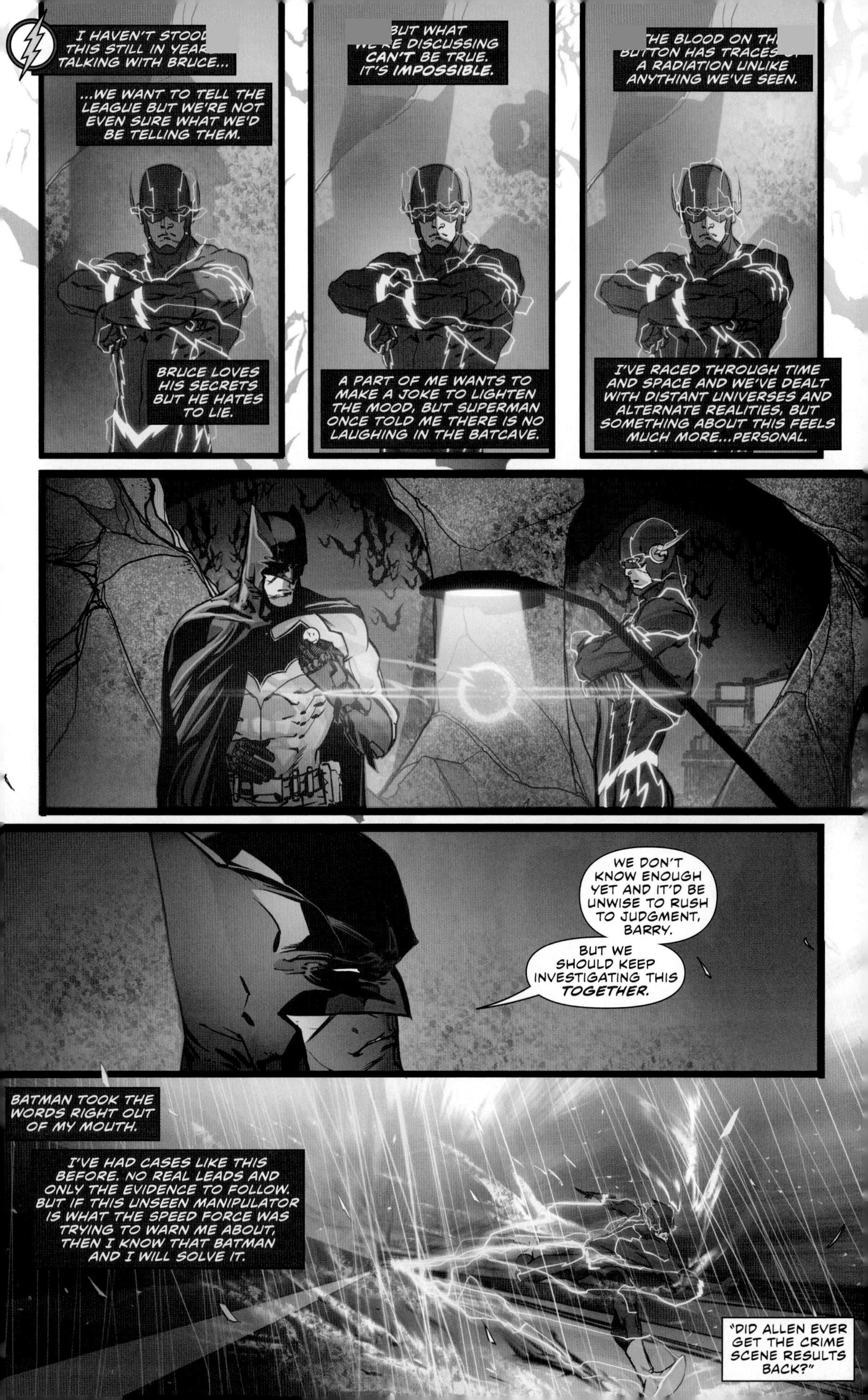
I HAVEN'T STOOD THIS STILL IN YEAR TALKING WITH BRUCE...
...WE WANT TO TELL THE LEAGUE BUT WE'RE NOT EVEN SURE WHAT WE'D BE TELLING THEM.
BRUCE LOVES HIS SECRETS BUT HE HATES TO LIE.
BUT WHAT WE'RE DISCUSSING CAN'T BE TRUE. IT'S IMPOSSIBLE.
A PART OF ME WANTS TO MAKE A JOKE TO LIGHTEN THE MOOD, BUT SUPERMAN ONCE TOLD ME THERE IS NO LAUGHING IN THE BATCAVE.
THE BLOOD ON TH BUTTON HAS TRACES A RADIATION UNLIKE ANYTHING WE'VE SEEN.
I'VE RACED THROUGH TIME AND SPACE AND WE'VE DEALT WITH DISTANT UNIVERSES AND ALTERNATE REALITIES, BUT SOMETHING ABOUT THIS FEELS MUCH MORE...PERSONAL.
WE DON'T KNOW ENOUGH YET AND IT'D BE UNWISE TO RUSH TO JUDGMENT, BARRY.
BUT WE SHOULD KEEP INVESTIGATING THIS TOGETHER.
BATMAN TOOK THE WORDS RIGHT OUT OF MY MOUTH.
I'VE HAD CASES LIKE THIS BEFORE. NO REAL LEADS AND ONLY THE EVIDENCE TO FOLLOW. BUT IF THIS UNSEEN MANIPULATOR IS WHAT THE SPEED FORCE WAS TRYING TO WARN ME ABOUT, THEN I KNOW THAT BATMAN AND I WILL SOLVE IT.
"DID ALLEN EVER GET THE CRIME SCENE RESULTS BACK?"

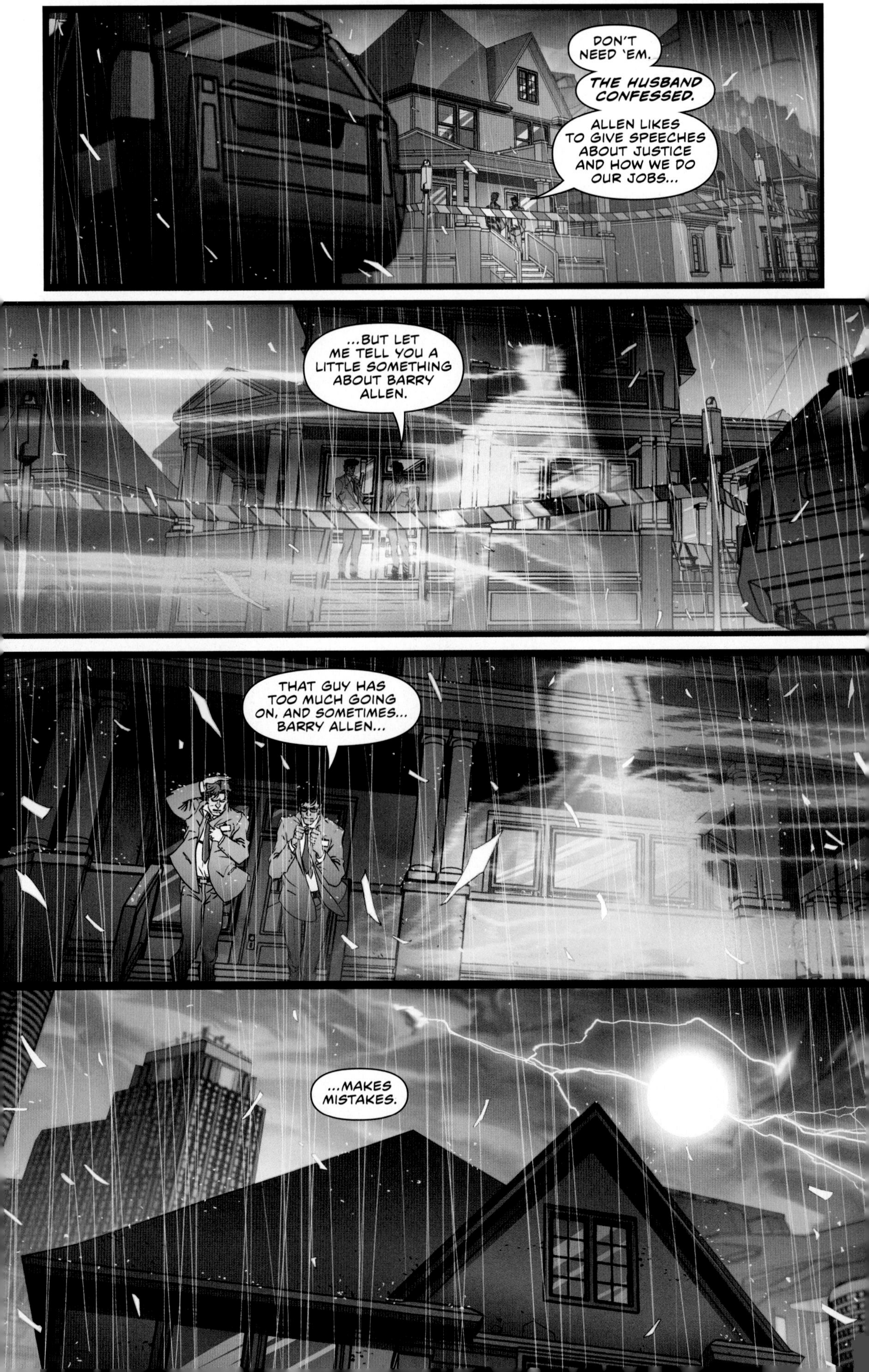
DON'T NEED 'EM.
THE HUSBAND CONFESSED.
ALLEN LIKES TO GIVE SPEECHES ABOUT JUSTICE AND HOW WE DO OUR JOBS...
...BUT LET ME TELL YOU A LITTLE SOMETHING ABOUT BARRY ALLEN.
THAT GUY HAS TOO MUCH GOING ON, AND SOMETIMES... BARRY ALLEN...
...MAKES MISTAKES.

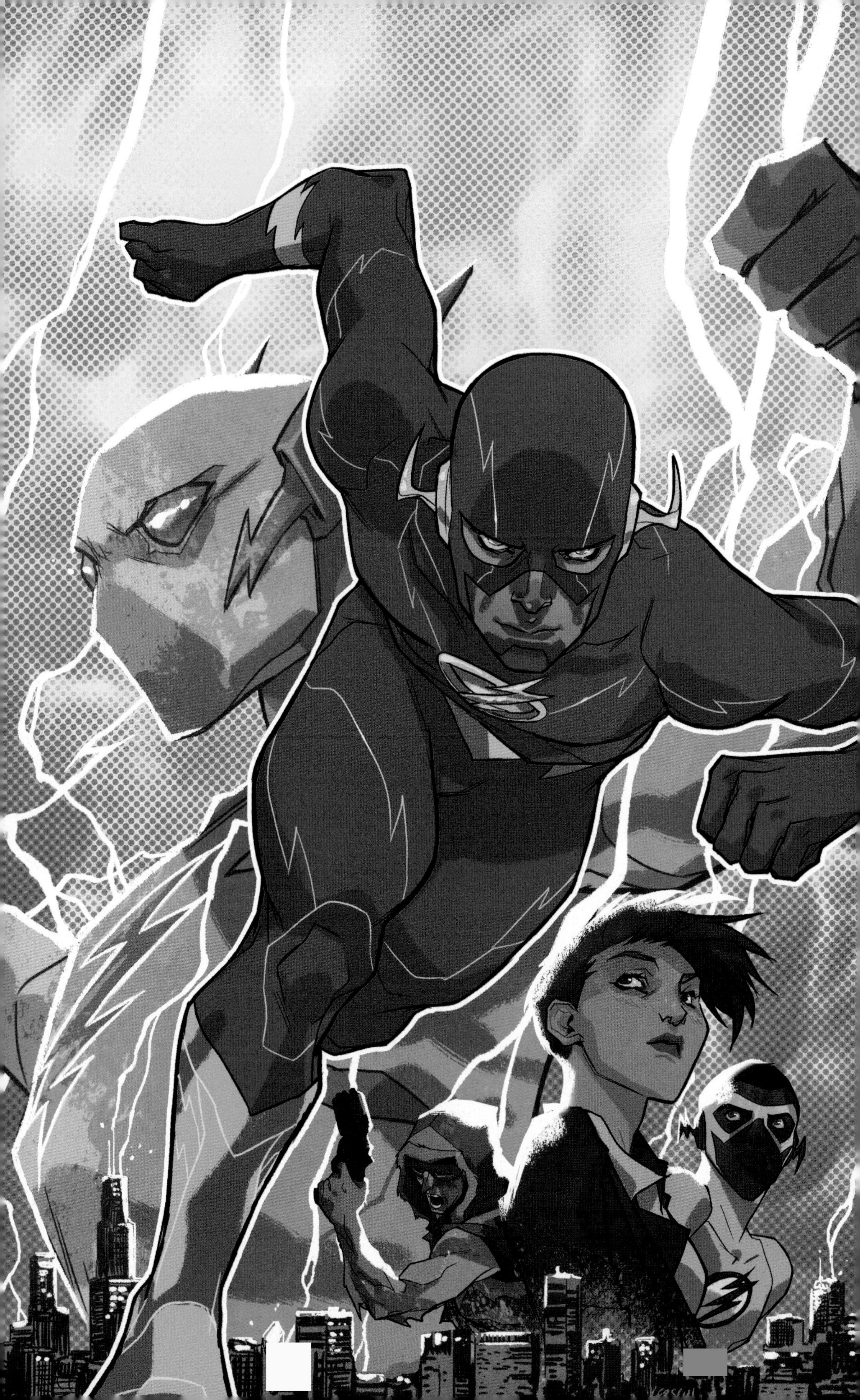

LIGHTNING STRIKES TWICE PART ONE: DEUS EX MACHINA

CARMINE DI GIANDOMENICO artist * KARL KERSCHL cover artist

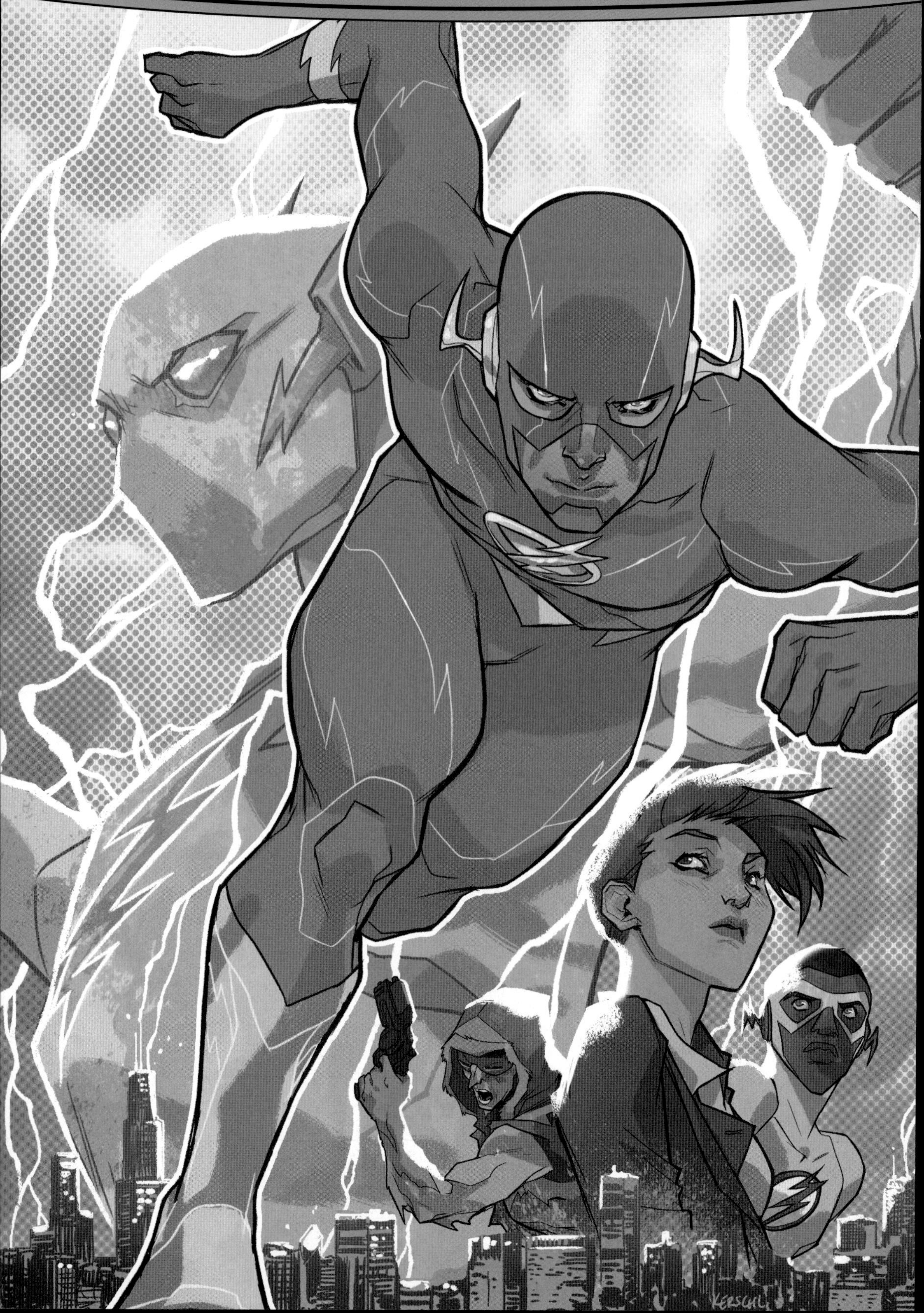

KERSCHL

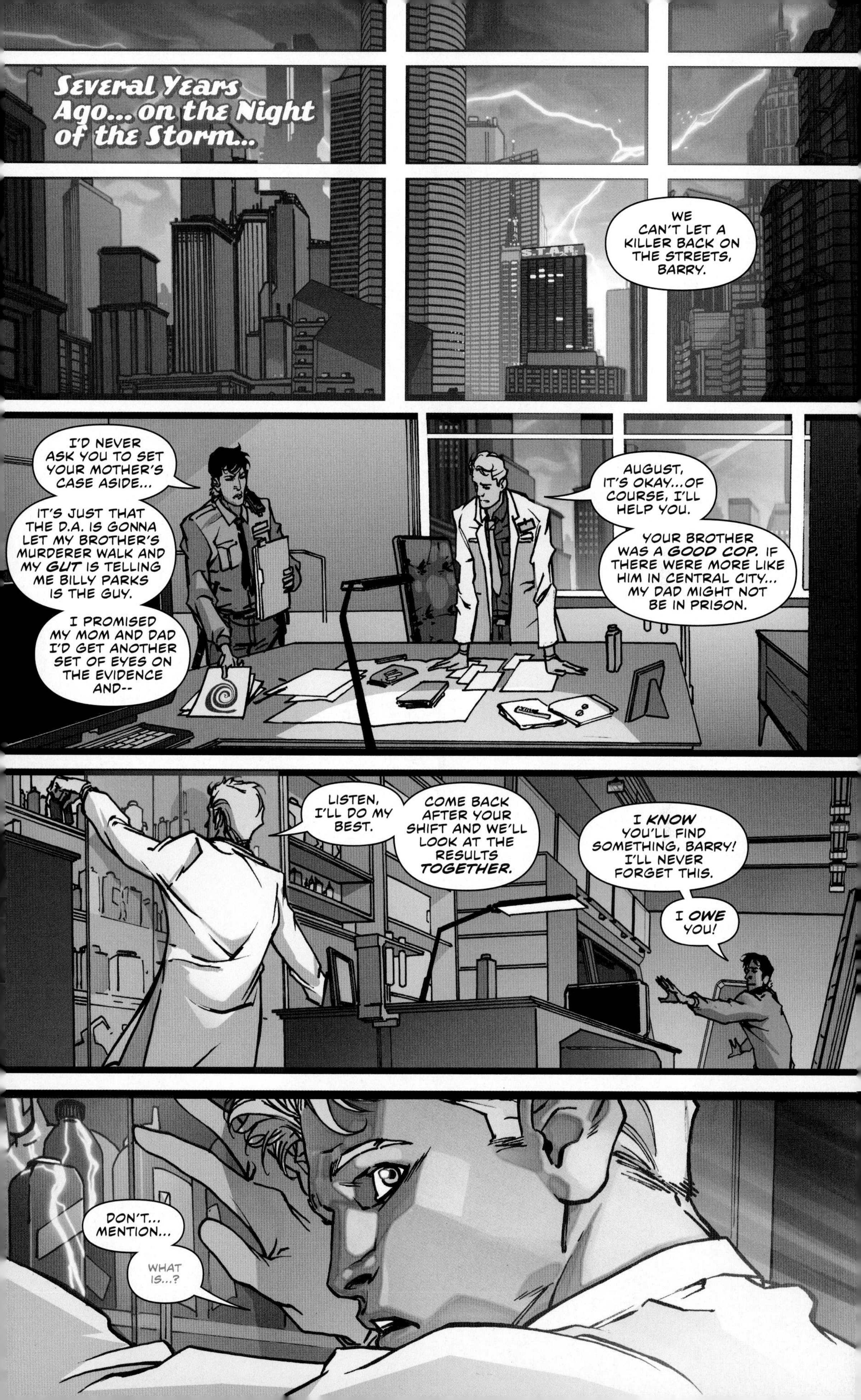
Several Years Ago... on the Night of the Storm...
S.T.A.R.
WE CAN'T LET A KILLER BACK ON THE STREETS, BARRY.
I'D NEVER ASK YOU TO SET YOUR MOTHER'S CASE ASIDE...
IT'S JUST THAT THE D.A. IS GONNA LET MY BROTHER'S MURDERER WALK AND MY GUT IS TELLING ME BILLY PARKS IS THE GUY.
I PROMISED MY MOM AND DAD I'D GET ANOTHER SET OF EYES ON THE EVIDENCE AND--
AUGUST, IT'S OKAY...OF COURSE, I'LL HELP YOU.
YOUR BROTHER WAS A GOOD COP. IF THERE WERE MORE LIKE HIM IN CENTRAL CITY... MY DAD MIGHT NOT BE IN PRISON.
LISTEN, I'LL DO MY BEST.
COME BACK AFTER YOUR SHIFT AND WE'LL LOOK AT THE RESULTS TOGETHER.
I KNOW YOU'LL FIND SOMETHING, BARRY! I'LL NEVER FORGET THIS.
I OWE YOU!
DON'T... MENTION...
WHAT IS...?

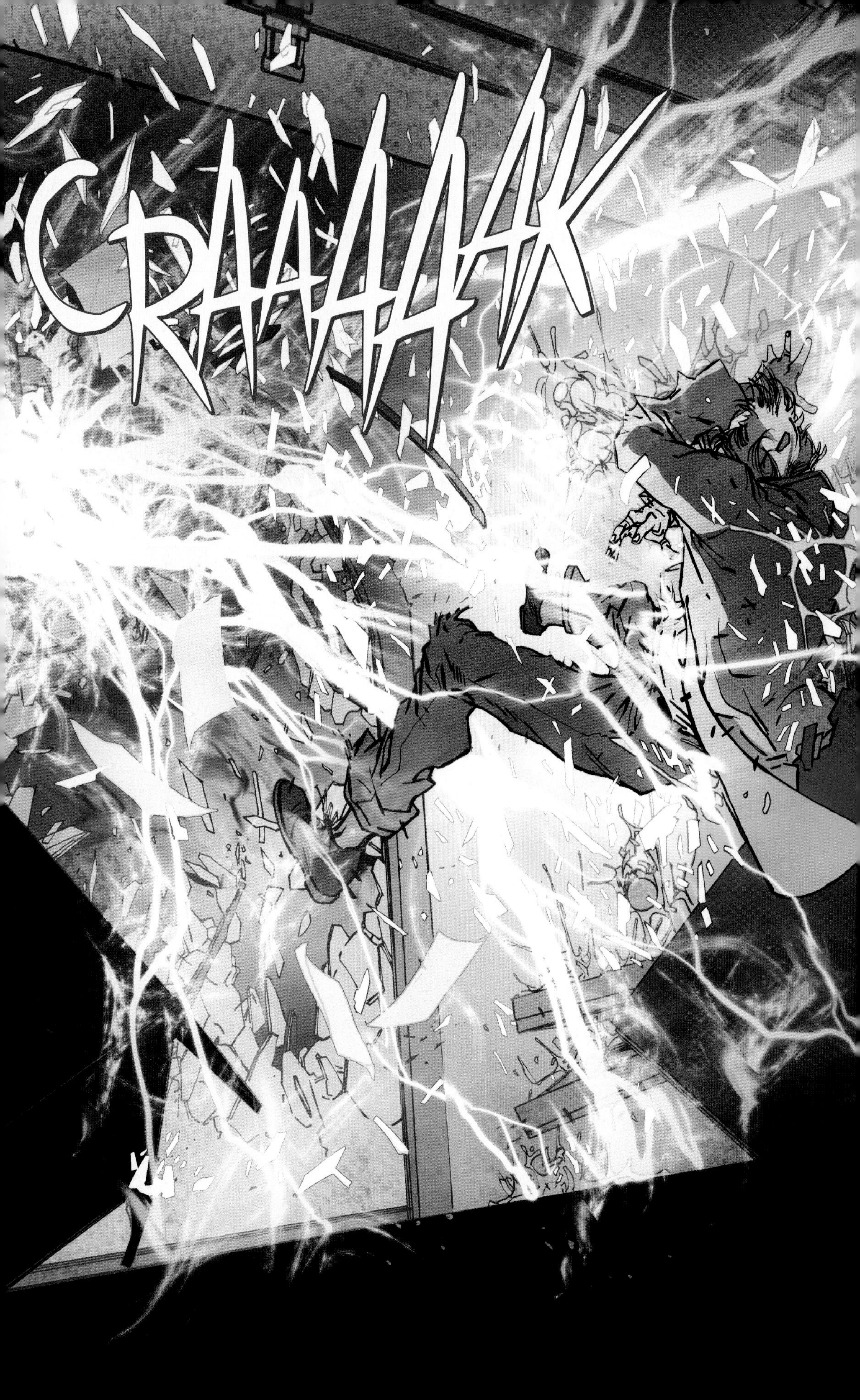
CRAAAAAK

BARRY?!

WHAT HAPPENED?! ARE YOU--?

BARRY!

OFFICER DOWN!

OFFICER DOWN!

CALL AN AMBULANCE! NOW!

YOU'RE GONNA BE OKAY. HELP IS ON THE WAY!

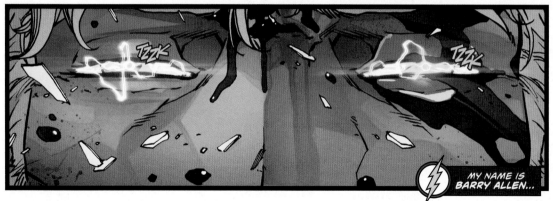

MY NAME IS BARRY ALLEN...

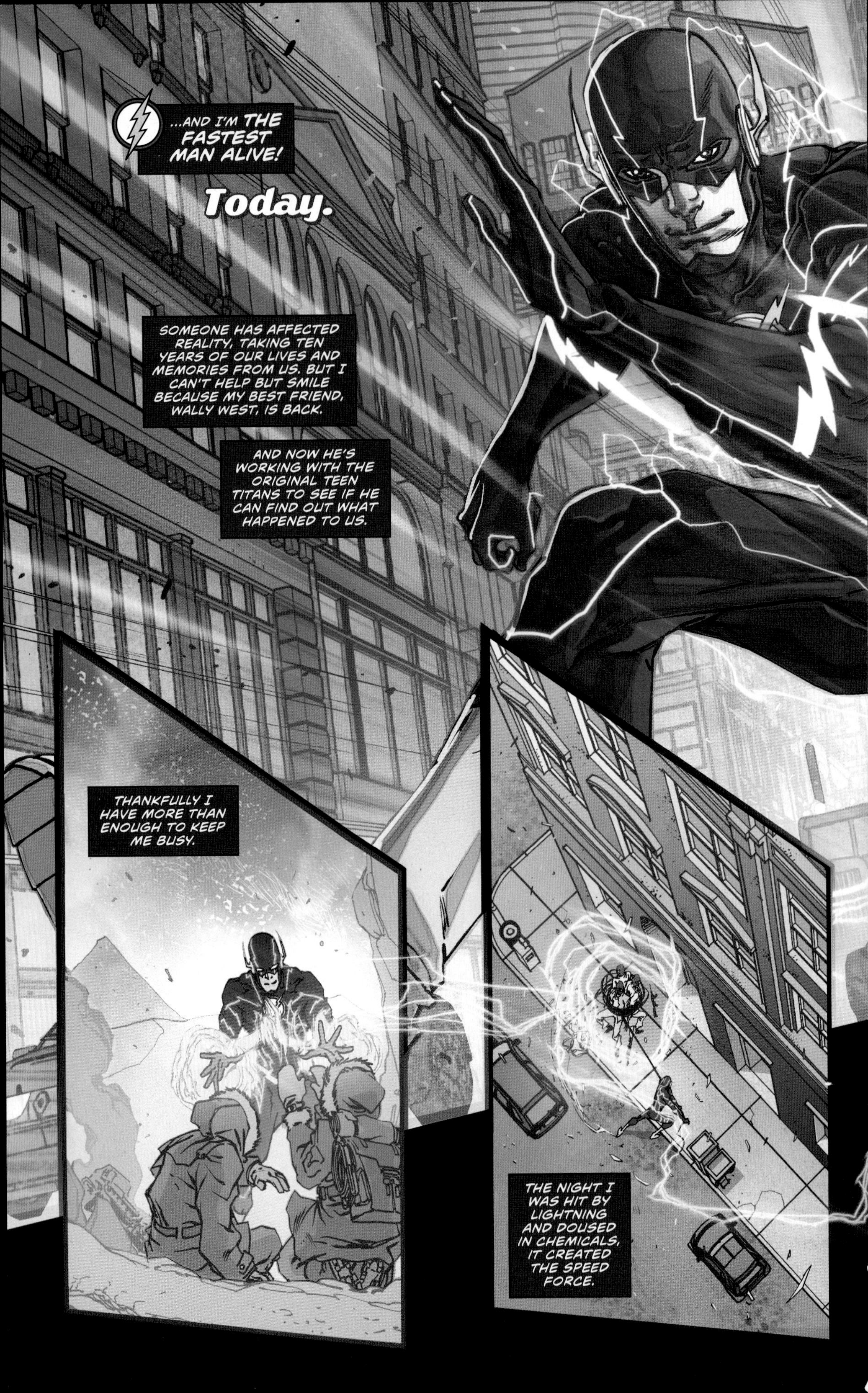
...AND I'M THE FASTEST MAN ALIVE!
Today.
SOMEONE HAS AFFECTED REALITY, TAKING TEN YEARS OF OUR LIVES AND MEMORIES FROM US. BUT I CAN'T HELP BUT SMILE BECAUSE MY BEST FRIEND, WALLY WEST, IS BACK.
AND NOW HE'S WORKING WITH THE ORIGINAL TEEN TITANS TO SEE IF HE CAN FIND OUT WHAT HAPPENED TO US.
THANKFULLY I HAVE MORE THAN ENOUGH TO KEEP ME BUSY.
THE NIGHT I WAS HIT BY LIGHTNING AND DOUSED IN CHEMICALS, IT CREATED THE SPEED FORCE.

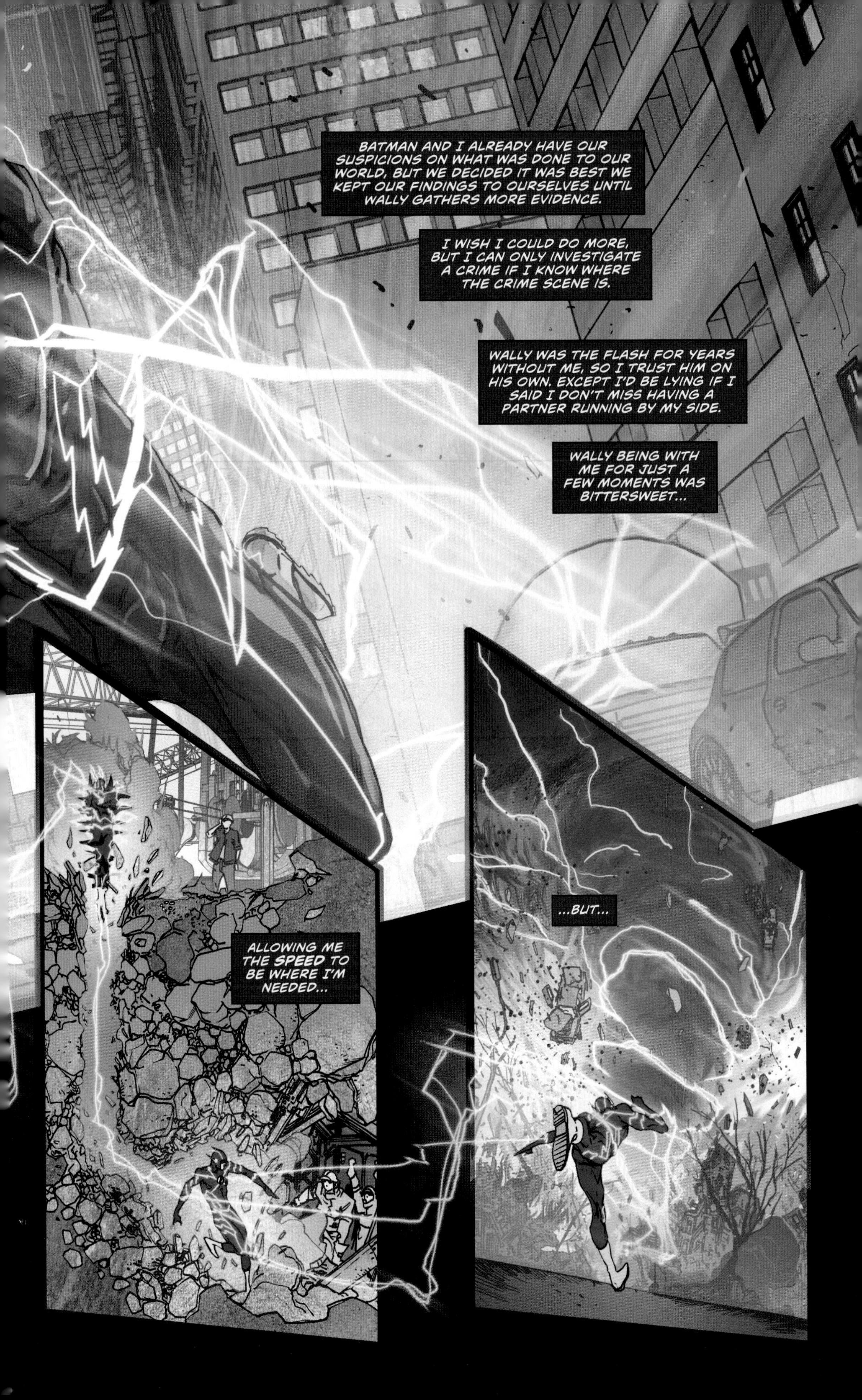
BATMAN AND I ALREADY HAVE OUR SUSPICIONS ON WHAT WAS DONE TO OUR WORLD, BUT WE DECIDED IT WAS BEST WE KEPT OUR FINDINGS TO OURSELVES UNTIL WALLY GATHERS MORE EVIDENCE.
I WISH I COULD DO MORE, BUT I CAN ONLY INVESTIGATE A CRIME IF I KNOW WHERE THE CRIME SCENE IS.
WALLY WAS THE FLASH FOR YEARS WITHOUT ME, SO I TRUST HIM ON HIS OWN. EXCEPT I'D BE LYING IF I SAID I DON'T MISS HAVING A PARTNER RUNNING BY MY SIDE.
WALLY BEING WITH ME FOR JUST A FEW MOMENTS WAS BITTERSWEET...
ALLOWING ME THE SPEED TO BE WHERE I'M NEEDED...
...BUT...

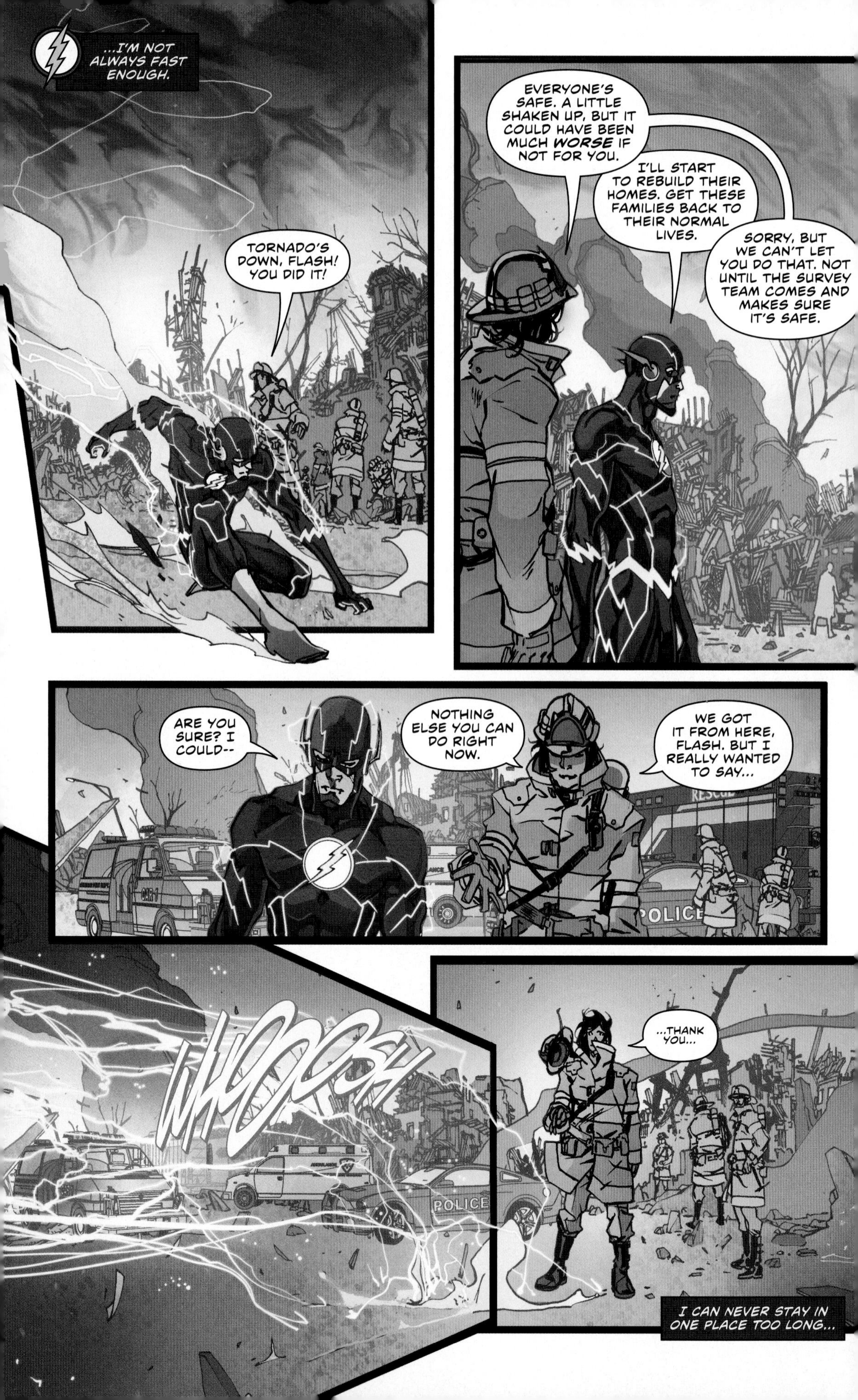

...I'M NOT ALWAYS FAST ENOUGH.
TORNADO'S DOWN, FLASH! YOU DID IT!
EVERYONE'S SAFE. A LITTLE SHAKEN UP, BUT IT COULD HAVE BEEN MUCH WORSE IF NOT FOR YOU.
I'LL START TO REBUILD THEIR HOMES. GET THESE FAMILIES BACK TO THEIR NORMAL LIVES.
SORRY, BUT WE CAN'T LET YOU DO THAT. NOT UNTIL THE SURVEY TEAM COMES AND MAKES SURE IT'S SAFE.
ARE YOU SURE? I COULD--
NOTHING ELSE YOU CAN DO RIGHT NOW.
WE GOT IT FROM HERE, FLASH. BUT I REALLY WANTED TO SAY...
POLICE
WHOOOSH
POLICE
...THANK YOU...
I CAN NEVER STAY IN ONE PLACE TOO LONG...

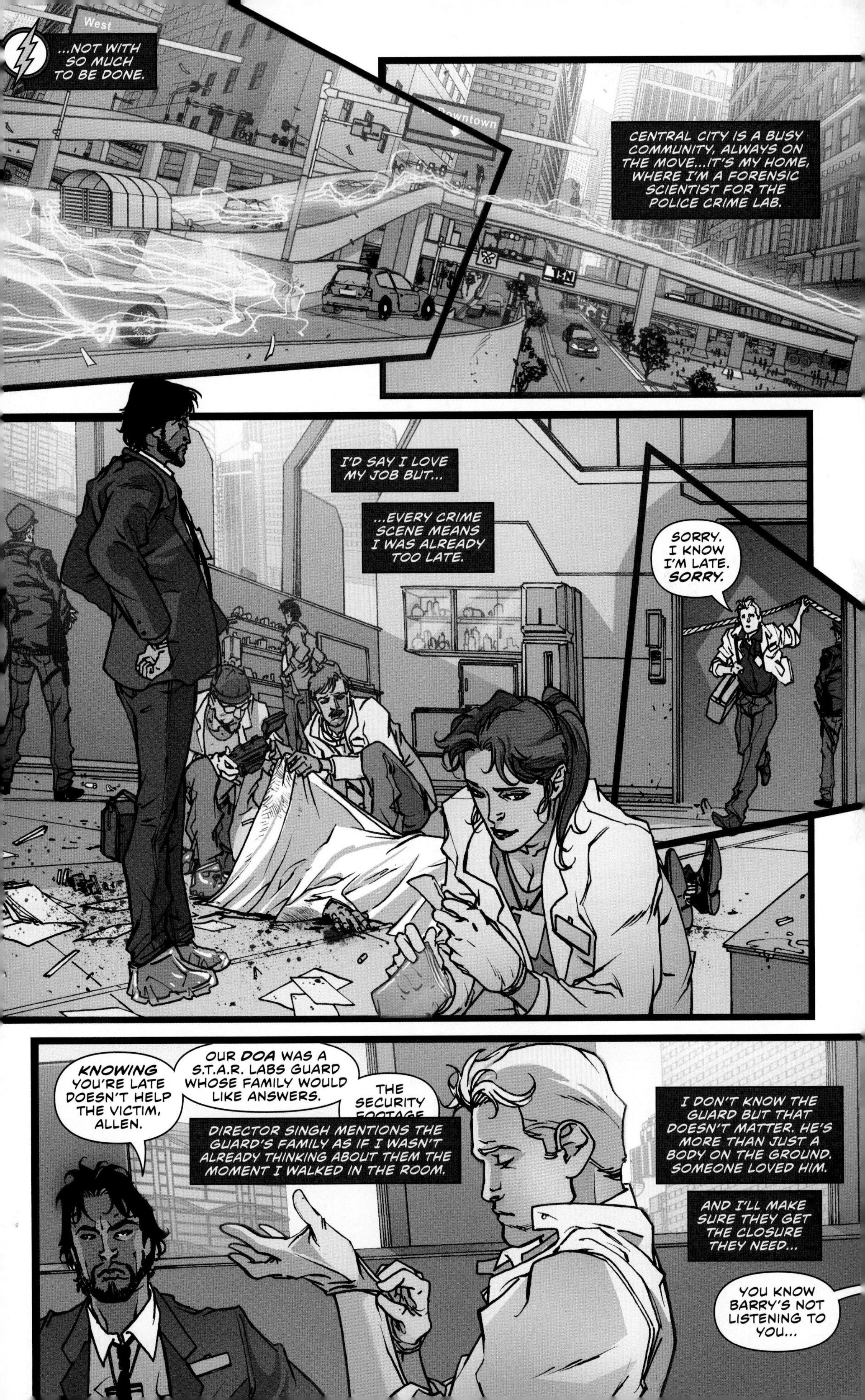
West
...NOT WITH SO MUCH TO BE DONE.
Downtown
CENTRAL CITY IS A BUSY COMMUNITY, ALWAYS ON THE MOVE...IT'S MY HOME, WHERE I'M A FORENSIC SCIENTIST FOR THE POLICE CRIME LAB.
I'D SAY I LOVE MY JOB BUT...
...EVERY CRIME SCENE MEANS I WAS ALREADY TOO LATE.
SORRY. I KNOW I'M LATE. SORRY.
KNOWING YOU'RE LATE DOESN'T HELP THE VICTIM, ALLEN.
OUR DOA WAS A S.T.A.R. LABS GUARD WHOSE FAMILY WOULD LIKE ANSWERS.
THE SECURITY
DIRECTOR SINGH MENTIONS THE GUARD'S FAMILY AS IF I WASN'T ALREADY THINKING ABOUT THEM THE MOMENT I WALKED IN THE ROOM.
I DON'T KNOW THE GUARD BUT THAT DOESN'T MATTER. HE'S MORE THAN JUST A BODY ON THE GROUND. SOMEONE LOVED HIM.
AND I'LL MAKE SURE THEY GET THE CLOSURE THEY NEED...
YOU KNOW BARRY'S NOT LISTENING TO YOU...

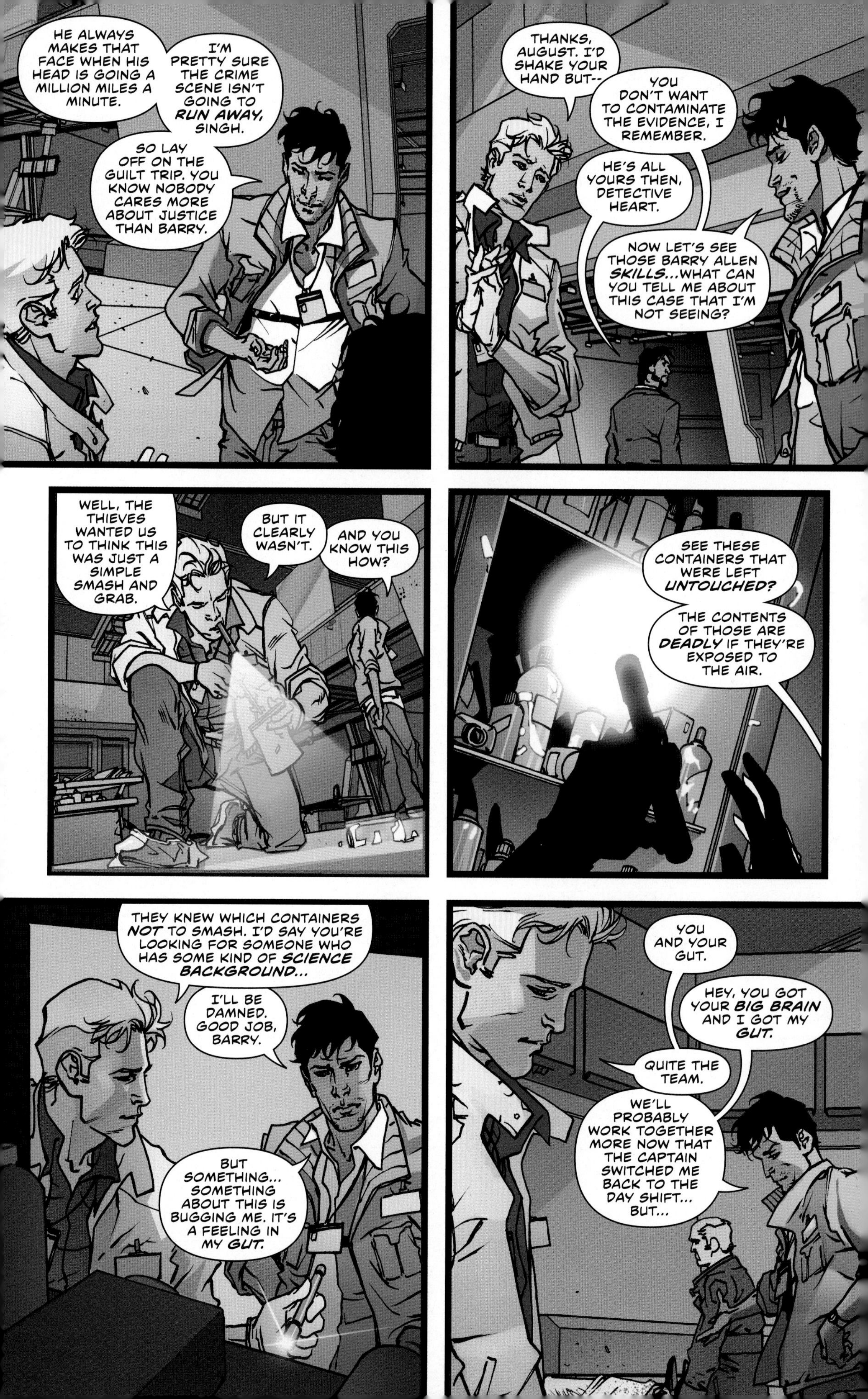
HE ALWAYS MAKES THAT FACE WHEN HIS HEAD IS GOING A MILLION MILES A MINUTE.
I'M PRETTY SURE THE CRIME SCENE ISN'T GOING TO RUN AWAY, SINGH.
SO LAY OFF ON THE GUILT TRIP. YOU KNOW NOBODY CARES MORE ABOUT JUSTICE THAN BARRY.
THANKS, AUGUST. I'D SHAKE YOUR HAND BUT--
YOU DON'T WANT TO CONTAMINATE THE EVIDENCE, I REMEMBER.
HE'S ALL YOURS THEN, DETECTIVE HEART.
NOW LET'S SEE THOSE BARRY ALLEN SKILLS...WHAT CAN YOU TELL ME ABOUT THIS CASE THAT I'M NOT SEEING?
WELL, THE THIEVES WANTED US TO THINK THIS WAS JUST A SIMPLE SMASH AND GRAB.
BUT IT CLEARLY WASN'T.
AND YOU KNOW THIS HOW?
SEE THESE CONTAINERS THAT WERE LEFT UNTOUCHED?
THE CONTENTS OF THOSE ARE DEADLY IF THEY'RE EXPOSED TO THE AIR.
THEY KNEW WHICH CONTAINERS NOT TO SMASH. I'D SAY YOU'RE LOOKING FOR SOMEONE WHO HAS SOME KIND OF SCIENCE BACKGROUND...
I'LL BE DAMNED. GOOD JOB, BARRY.
BUT SOMETHING... SOMETHING ABOUT THIS IS BUGGING ME. IT'S A FEELING IN MY GUT.
YOU AND YOUR GUT.
HEY, YOU GOT YOUR BIG BRAIN AND I GOT MY GUT.
QUITE THE TEAM.
WE'LL PROBABLY WORK TOGETHER MORE NOW THAT THE CAPTAIN SWITCHED ME BACK TO THE DAY SHIFT... BUT...

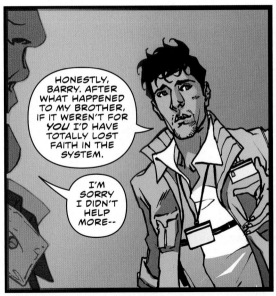

HONESTLY, BARRY. AFTER WHAT HAPPENED TO MY BROTHER, IF IT WEREN'T FOR *YOU* I'D HAVE TOTALLY LOST FAITH IN THE SYSTEM.

I'M SORRY I DIDN'T HELP MORE--

HOLD THAT THOUGHT...S.T.A.R. LABS WANTS A POLICE ESCORT FOR ONE OF THEIR TRANSPORTS TODAY AND YOURS TRULY PULLED THE *SHORT STRAW.*

ANNDDDD, I'M LATE. DAMMIT.

YOU'RE LATE? HA!

I THOUGHT *I* WAS THE ONE WHO WAS ALWAYS LATE TO--

OH NO! IRIS!

I TOLD IRIS I'D GRAB LUNCH WITH HER AND HER NEPHEW *WALLY* AT JITTERS TO HELP HIM WITH A SCHOOL PROJECT!

I'LL COVER FOR YOU, BARRY.

WOULDN'T BE THE FIRST TIME.

KRISTEN? ARE YOU A FULL CSI NOW? WHEN DID YOU GET PROMOTED?

I HAVEN'T BEEN AN INTERN FOR *MONTHS.*

BUT...

YOU NEVER NOTICED ME BEFORE, WHY START NOW?

I...

BARRY...IRIS? NEPHEW? SCHOOL PROJECT?

RIGHT! THANKS, AUGUST!

YOU BETTER HURRY. JITTERS IS ALL THE WAY *UPTOWN!*

I SHOULD HAVE STAYED AND HELPED KRISTEN WITH THE SCENE. IRIS WOULD UNDERSTAND.

BUT EVER SINCE MY OLD PROTÉGÉ KID FLASH RETURNED...

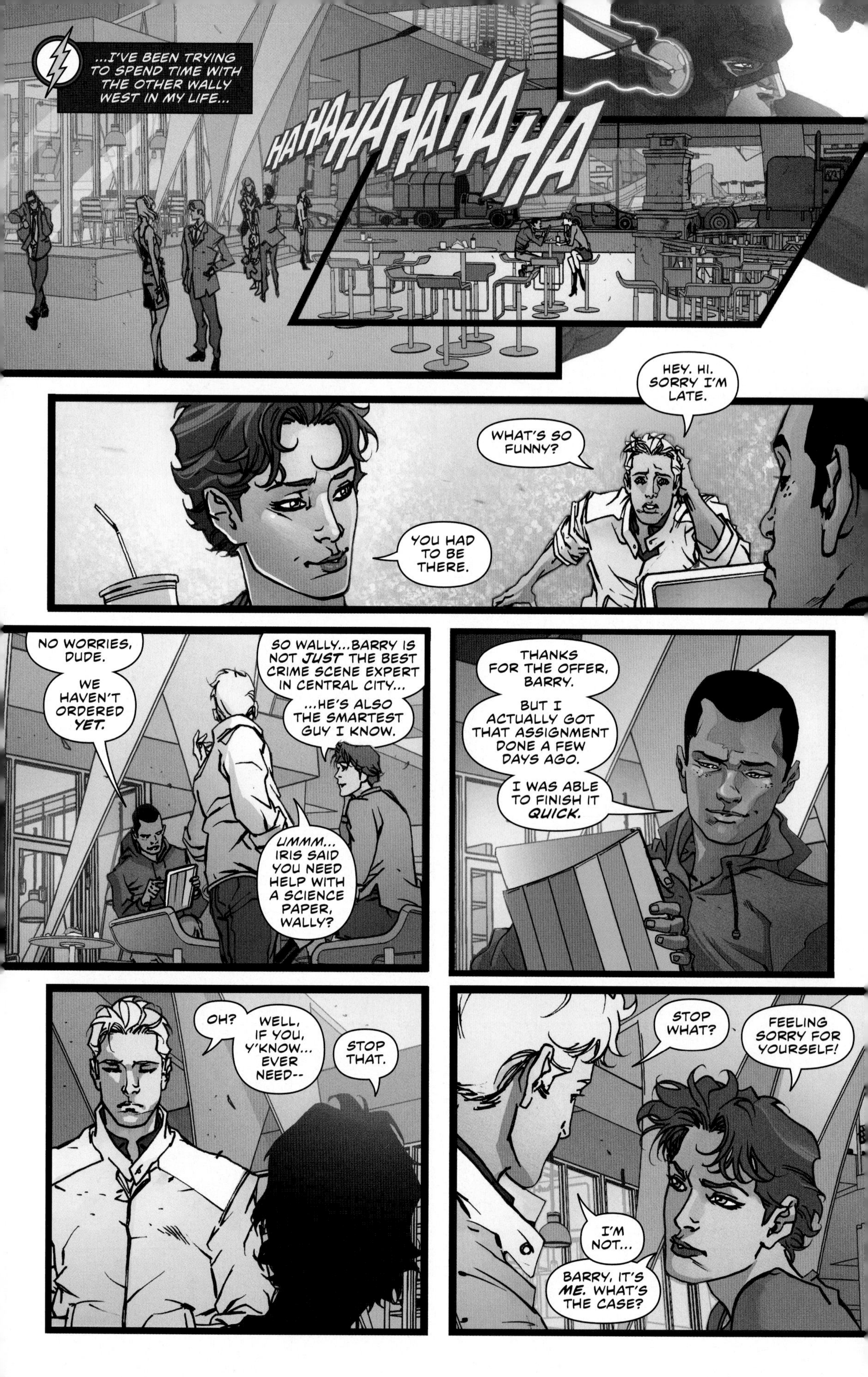
...I'VE BEEN TRYING TO SPEND TIME WITH THE OTHER WALLY WEST IN MY LIFE...
HAHAHAHAHAHAHA
HEY. HI. SORRY I'M LATE.
WHAT'S SO FUNNY?
YOU HAD TO BE THERE.
NO WORRIES, DUDE.
WE HAVEN'T ORDERED YET.
SO WALLY...BARRY IS NOT JUST THE BEST CRIME SCENE EXPERT IN CENTRAL CITY...
...HE'S ALSO THE SMARTEST GUY I KNOW.
UMMM... IRIS SAID YOU NEED HELP WITH A SCIENCE PAPER, WALLY?
THANKS FOR THE OFFER, BARRY.
BUT I ACTUALLY GOT THAT ASSIGNMENT DONE A FEW DAYS AGO.
I WAS ABLE TO FINISH IT QUICK.
OH?
WELL, IF YOU, Y'KNOW... EVER NEED--
STOP THAT.
STOP WHAT?
FEELING SORRY FOR YOURSELF!
I'M NOT...
BARRY, IT'S ME. WHAT'S THE CASE?

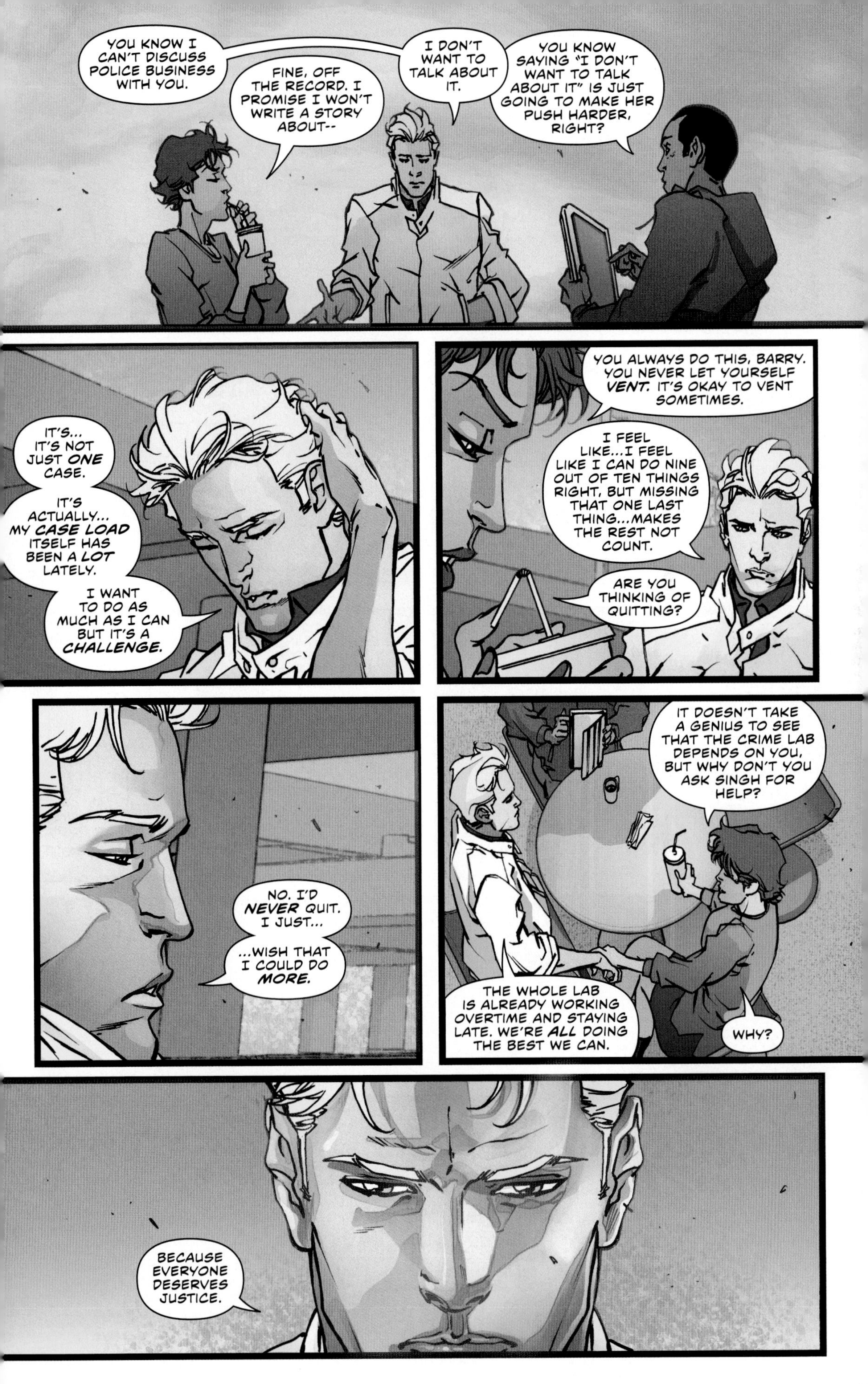
YOU KNOW I CAN'T DISCUSS POLICE BUSINESS WITH YOU.
FINE, OFF THE RECORD. I PROMISE I WON'T WRITE A STORY ABOUT--
I DON'T WANT TO TALK ABOUT IT.
YOU KNOW SAYING "I DON'T WANT TO TALK ABOUT IT" IS JUST GOING TO MAKE HER PUSH HARDER, RIGHT?
IT'S... IT'S NOT JUST ONE CASE.
IT'S ACTUALLY... MY CASE LOAD ITSELF HAS BEEN A LOT LATELY.
I WANT TO DO AS MUCH AS I CAN BUT IT'S A CHALLENGE.
YOU ALWAYS DO THIS, BARRY. YOU NEVER LET YOURSELF VENT. IT'S OKAY TO VENT SOMETIMES.
I FEEL LIKE...I FEEL LIKE I CAN DO NINE OUT OF TEN THINGS RIGHT, BUT MISSING THAT ONE LAST THING...MAKES THE REST NOT COUNT.
ARE YOU THINKING OF QUITTING?
NO. I'D NEVER QUIT. I JUST...
...WISH THAT I COULD DO MORE.
IT DOESN'T TAKE A GENIUS TO SEE THAT THE CRIME LAB DEPENDS ON YOU, BUT WHY DON'T YOU ASK SINGH FOR HELP?
THE WHOLE LAB IS ALREADY WORKING OVERTIME AND STAYING LATE. WE'RE ALL DOING THE BEST WE CAN.
WHY?
BECAUSE EVERYONE DESERVES JUSTICE.

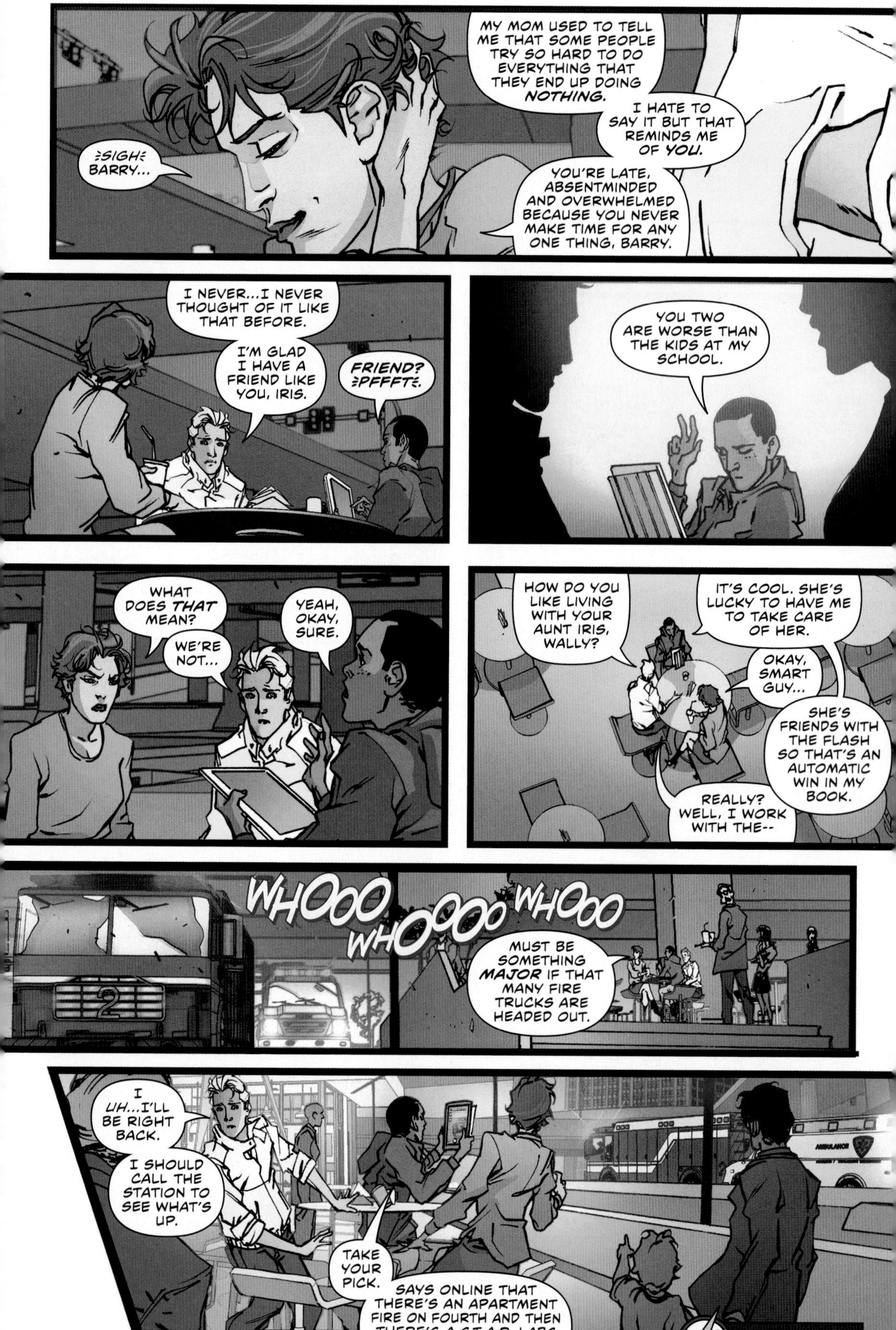
MY MOM USED TO TELL ME THAT SOME PEOPLE TRY SO HARD TO DO EVERYTHING THAT THEY END UP DOING NOTHING.
I HATE TO SAY IT BUT THAT REMINDS ME OF YOU.
SIGH BARRY...
YOU'RE LATE, ABSENTMINDED AND OVERWHELMED BECAUSE YOU NEVER MAKE TIME FOR ANY ONE THING, BARRY.
I NEVER...I NEVER THOUGHT OF IT LIKE THAT BEFORE.
I'M GLAD I HAVE A FRIEND LIKE YOU, IRIS.
FRIEND? PFFFT.
YOU TWO ARE WORSE THAN THE KIDS AT MY SCHOOL.
WHAT DOES THAT MEAN?
WE'RE NOT...
YEAH, OKAY, SURE.
HOW DO YOU LIKE LIVING WITH YOUR AUNT IRIS, WALLY?
IT'S COOL. SHE'S LUCKY TO HAVE ME TO TAKE CARE OF HER.
OKAY, SMART GUY...
SHE'S FRIENDS WITH THE FLASH SO THAT'S AN AUTOMATIC WIN IN MY BOOK.
REALLY? WELL, I WORK WITH THE--
WHOOO WHOOOOO WHOOO
2
MUST BE SOMETHING MAJOR IF THAT MANY FIRE TRUCKS ARE HEADED OUT.
I UH...I'LL BE RIGHT BACK.
I SHOULD CALL THE STATION TO SEE WHAT'S UP.
TAKE YOUR PICK.
SAYS ONLINE THAT THERE'S AN APARTMENT FIRE ON FOURTH AND THEN THERE'S A S.T.A.R. LABS TRANSPORT UNDER ATTACK ON 22ND.
IRIS IS RIGHT. I KNOW SHE IS...

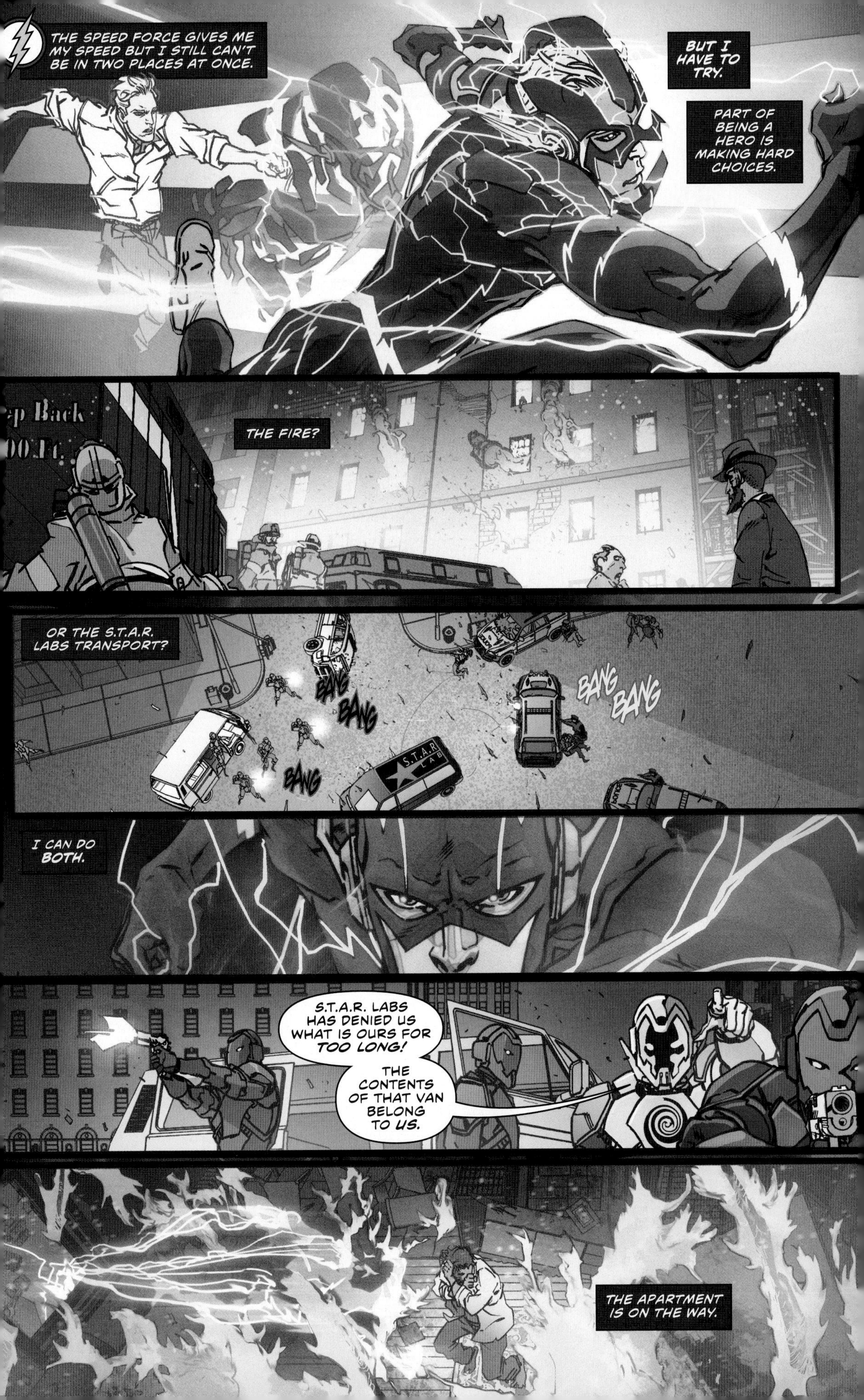

THE SPEED FORCE GIVES ME MY SPEED BUT I STILL CAN'T BE IN TWO PLACES AT ONCE.
BUT I HAVE TO TRY.
PART OF BEING A HERO IS MAKING HARD CHOICES.
THE FIRE?
OR THE S.T.A.R. LABS TRANSPORT?
BANG
BANG
BANG
BANG
BANG
S.T.A.R. LAB
I CAN DO BOTH.
S.T.A.R. LABS HAS DENIED US WHAT IS OURS FOR TOO LONG!
THE CONTENTS OF THAT VAN BELONG TO US.
THE APARTMENT IS ON THE WAY.

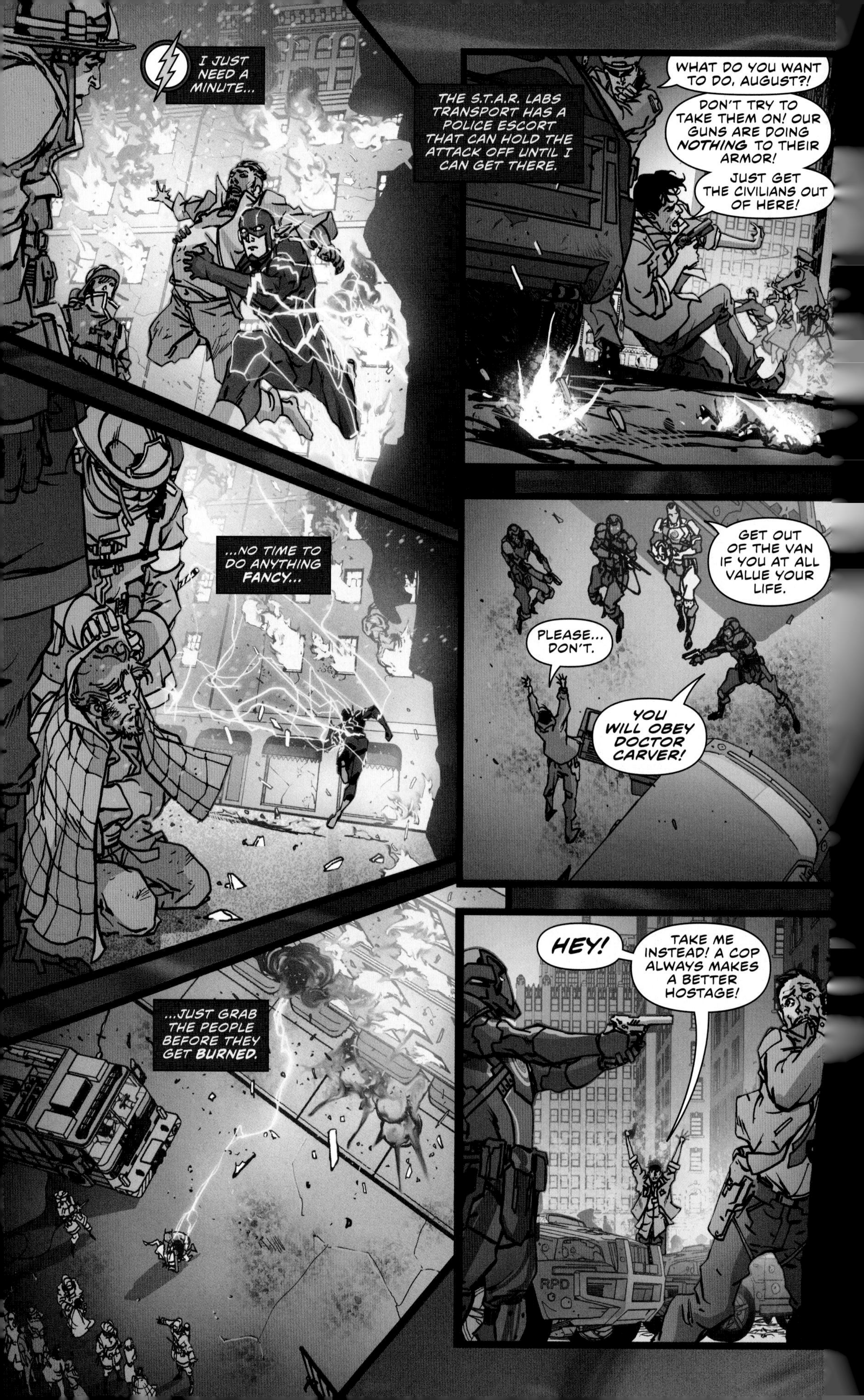

I JUST NEED A MINUTE...
THE S.T.A.R. LABS TRANSPORT HAS A POLICE ESCORT THAT CAN HOLD THE ATTACK OFF UNTIL I CAN GET THERE.
WHAT DO YOU WANT TO DO, AUGUST?!
DON'T TRY TO TAKE THEM ON! OUR GUNS ARE DOING NOTHING TO THEIR ARMOR!
JUST GET THE CIVILIANS OUT OF HERE!
...NO TIME TO DO ANYTHING FANCY...
GET OUT OF THE VAN IF YOU AT ALL VALUE YOUR LIFE.
PLEASE... DON'T.
YOU WILL OBEY DOCTOR CARVER!
...JUST GRAB THE PEOPLE BEFORE THEY GET BURNED.
HEY!
TAKE ME INSTEAD! A COP ALWAYS MAKES A BETTER HOSTAGE!
RPD

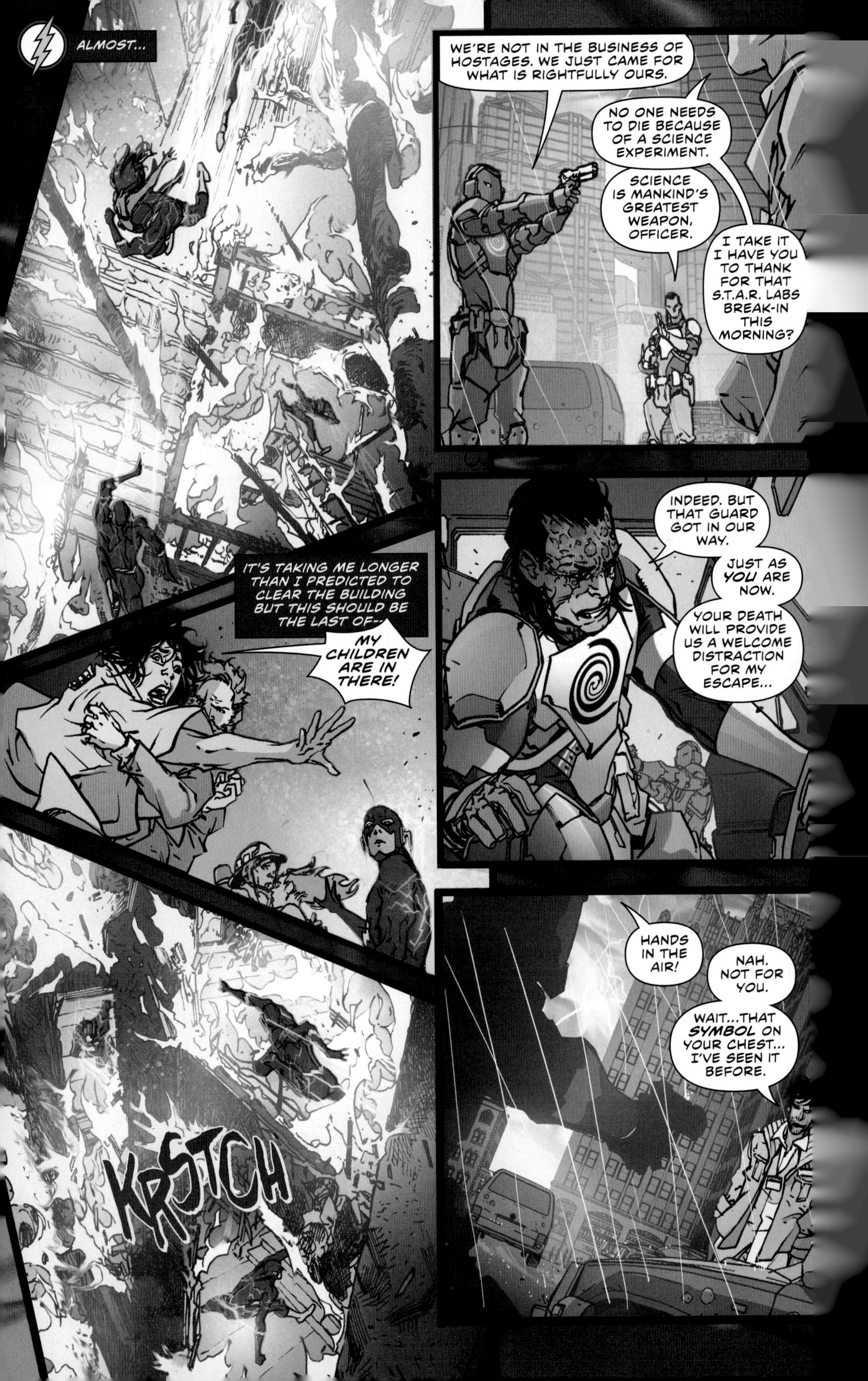
ALMOST...
WE'RE NOT IN THE BUSINESS OF HOSTAGES. WE JUST CAME FOR WHAT IS RIGHTFULLY OURS.
NO ONE NEEDS TO DIE BECAUSE OF A SCIENCE EXPERIMENT.
SCIENCE IS MANKIND'S GREATEST WEAPON, OFFICER.
I TAKE IT I HAVE YOU TO THANK FOR THAT S.T.A.R. LABS BREAK-IN THIS MORNING?
INDEED. BUT THAT GUARD GOT IN OUR WAY.
JUST AS YOU ARE NOW.
YOUR DEATH WILL PROVIDE US A WELCOME DISTRACTION FOR MY ESCAPE...
IT'S TAKING ME LONGER THAN I PREDICTED TO CLEAR THE BUILDING BUT THIS SHOULD BE THE LAST OF--
MY CHILDREN ARE IN THERE!
HANDS IN THE AIR!
NAH. NOT FOR YOU.
WAIT...THAT SYMBOL ON YOUR CHEST... I'VE SEEN IT BEFORE.
KRSTCH

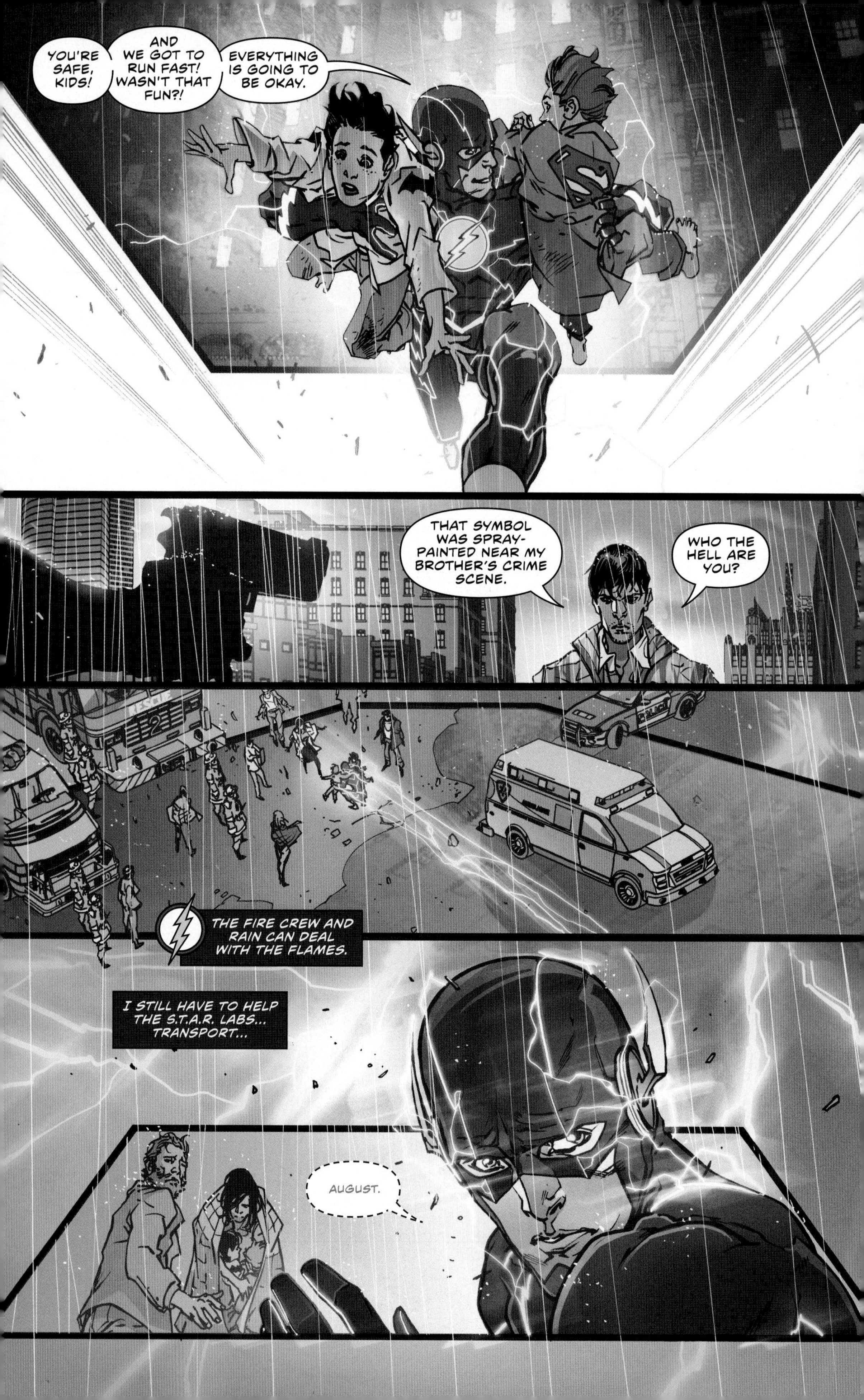
YOU'RE SAFE, KIDS!
AND WE GOT TO RUN FAST! WASN'T THAT FUN?!
EVERYTHING IS GOING TO BE OKAY.
THAT SYMBOL WAS SPRAY-PAINTED NEAR MY BROTHER'S CRIME SCENE.
WHO THE HELL ARE YOU?
RESCUE 2
POLICE
THE FIRE CREW AND RAIN CAN DEAL WITH THE FLAMES.
I STILL HAVE TO HELP THE S.T.A.R. LABS... TRANSPORT...
AUGUST.

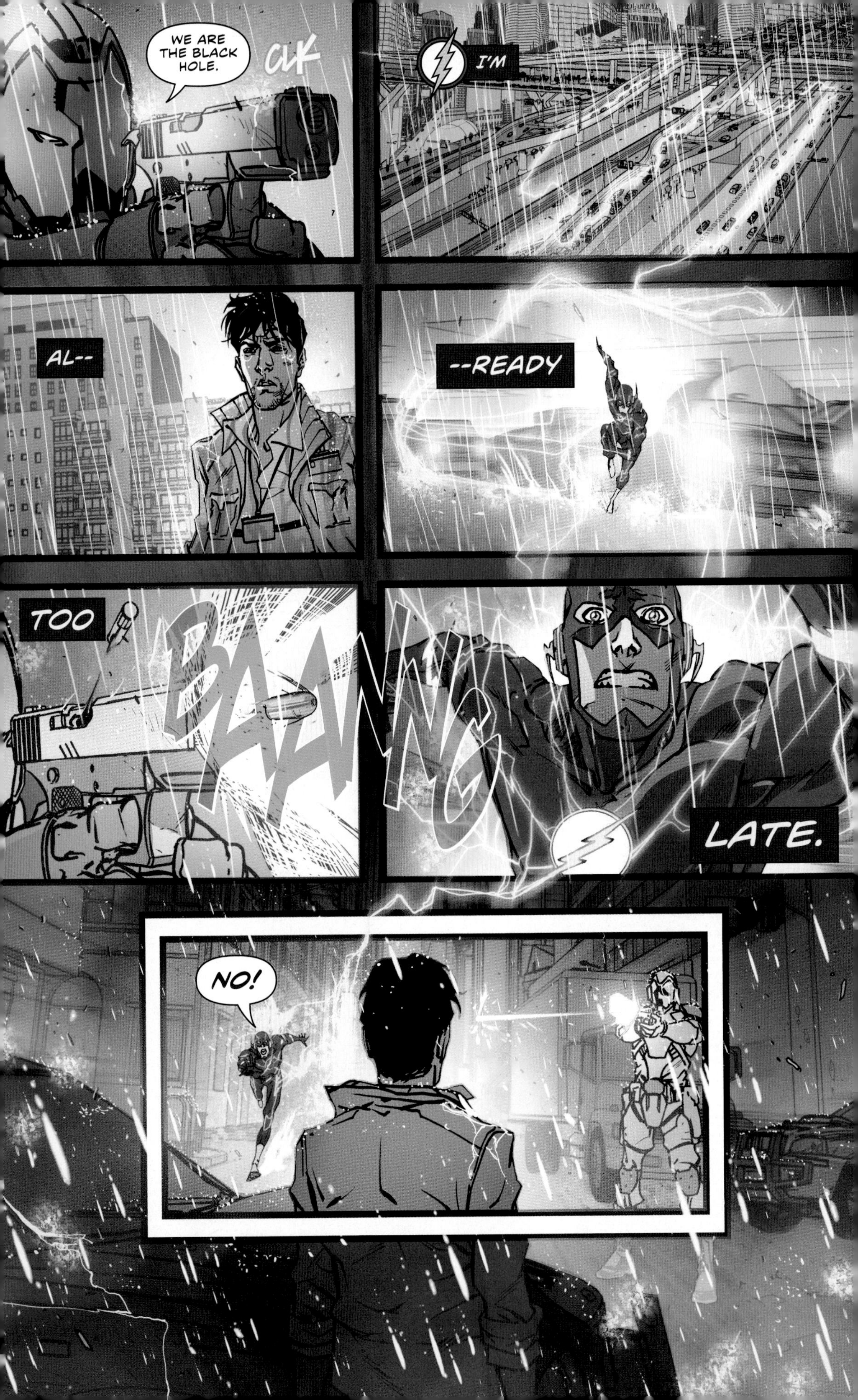
WE ARE THE BLACK HOLE.
CLK
I'M
AL--
--READY
TOO
BLAMMG
LATE.
NO!

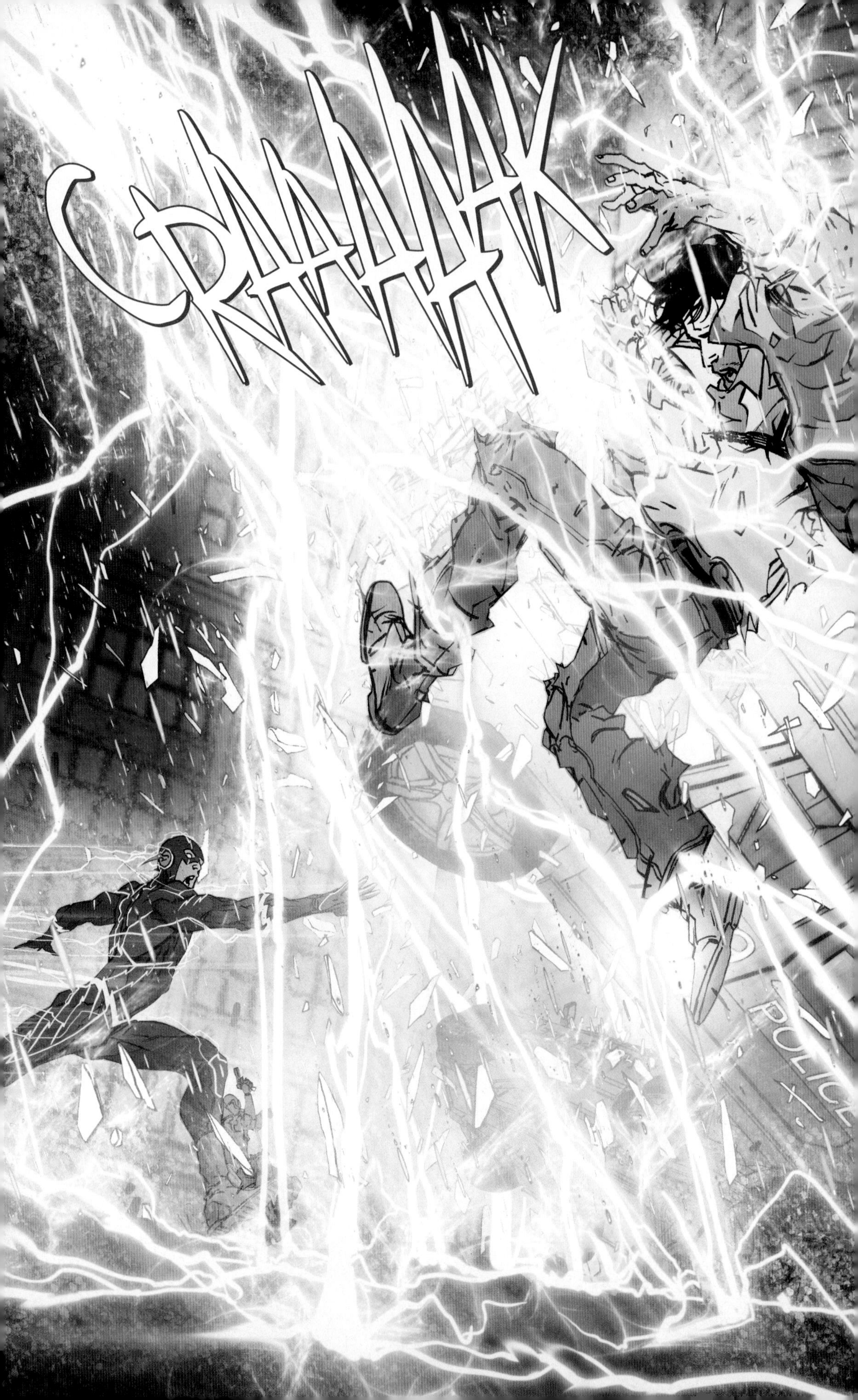
CRAAAAAK
POLICE

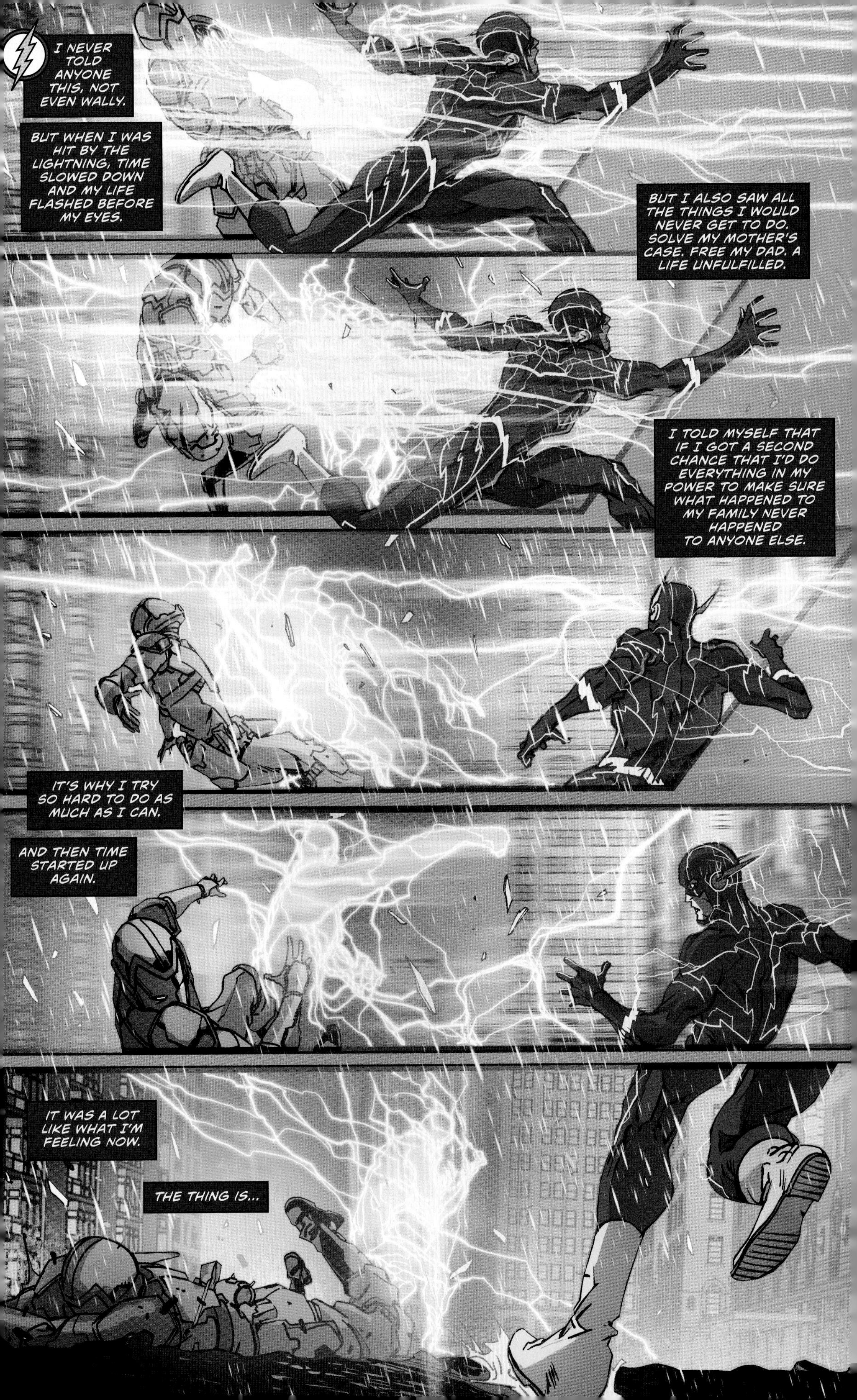
I NEVER TOLD ANYONE THIS, NOT EVEN WALLY.
BUT WHEN I WAS HIT BY THE LIGHTNING, TIME SLOWED DOWN AND MY LIFE FLASHED BEFORE MY EYES.
BUT I ALSO SAW ALL THE THINGS I WOULD NEVER GET TO DO. SOLVE MY MOTHER'S CASE. FREE MY DAD. A LIFE UNFULFILLED.
I TOLD MYSELF THAT IF I GOT A SECOND CHANCE THAT I'D DO EVERYTHING IN MY POWER TO MAKE SURE WHAT HAPPENED TO MY FAMILY NEVER HAPPENED TO ANYONE ELSE.
IT'S WHY I TRY SO HARD TO DO AS MUCH AS I CAN.
AND THEN TIME STARTED UP AGAIN.
IT WAS A LOT LIKE WHAT I'M FEELING NOW.
THE THING IS...

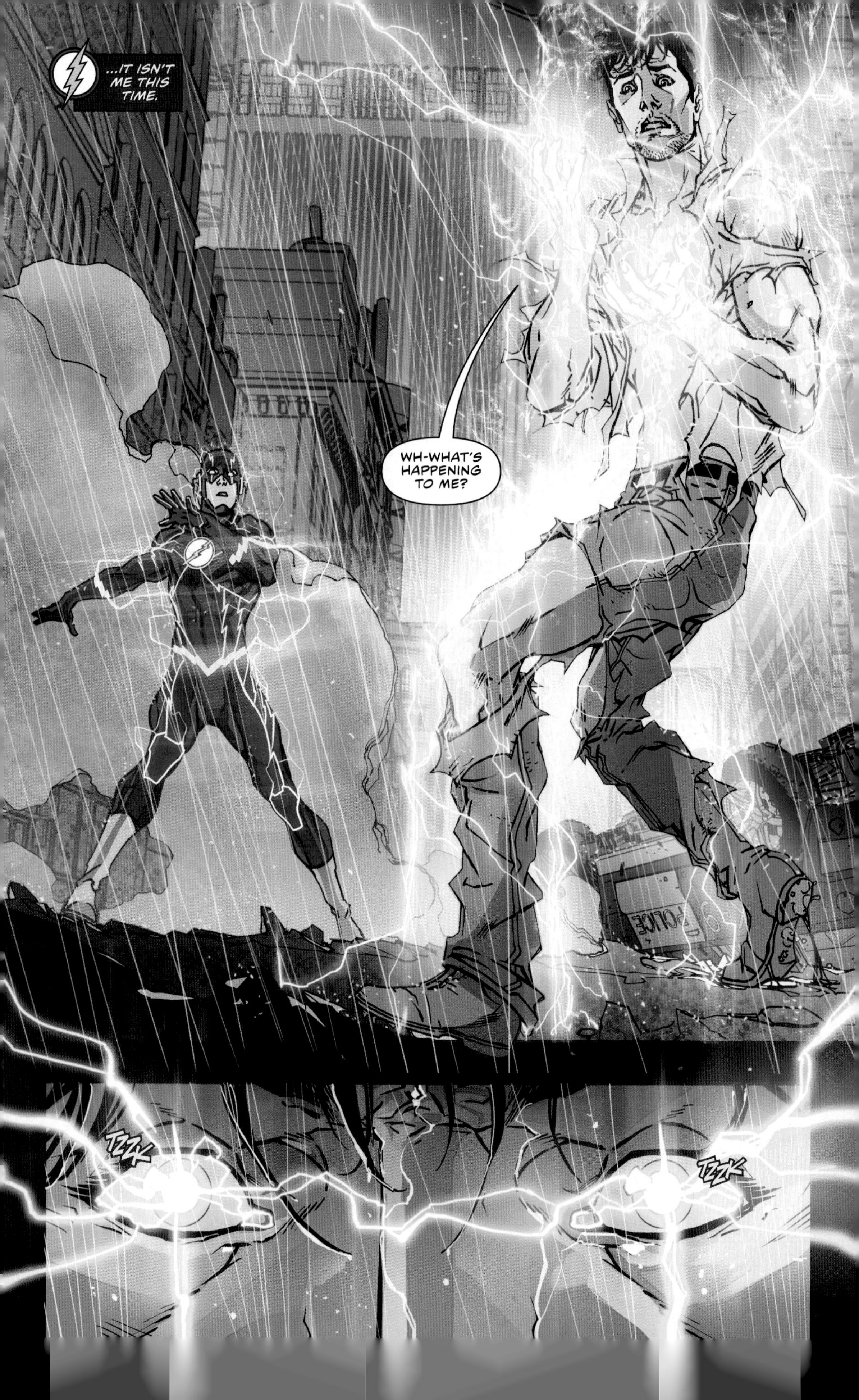
...IT ISN'T ME THIS TIME.
WH-WHAT'S HAPPENING TO ME?
POLICE
TZZK
TZZK

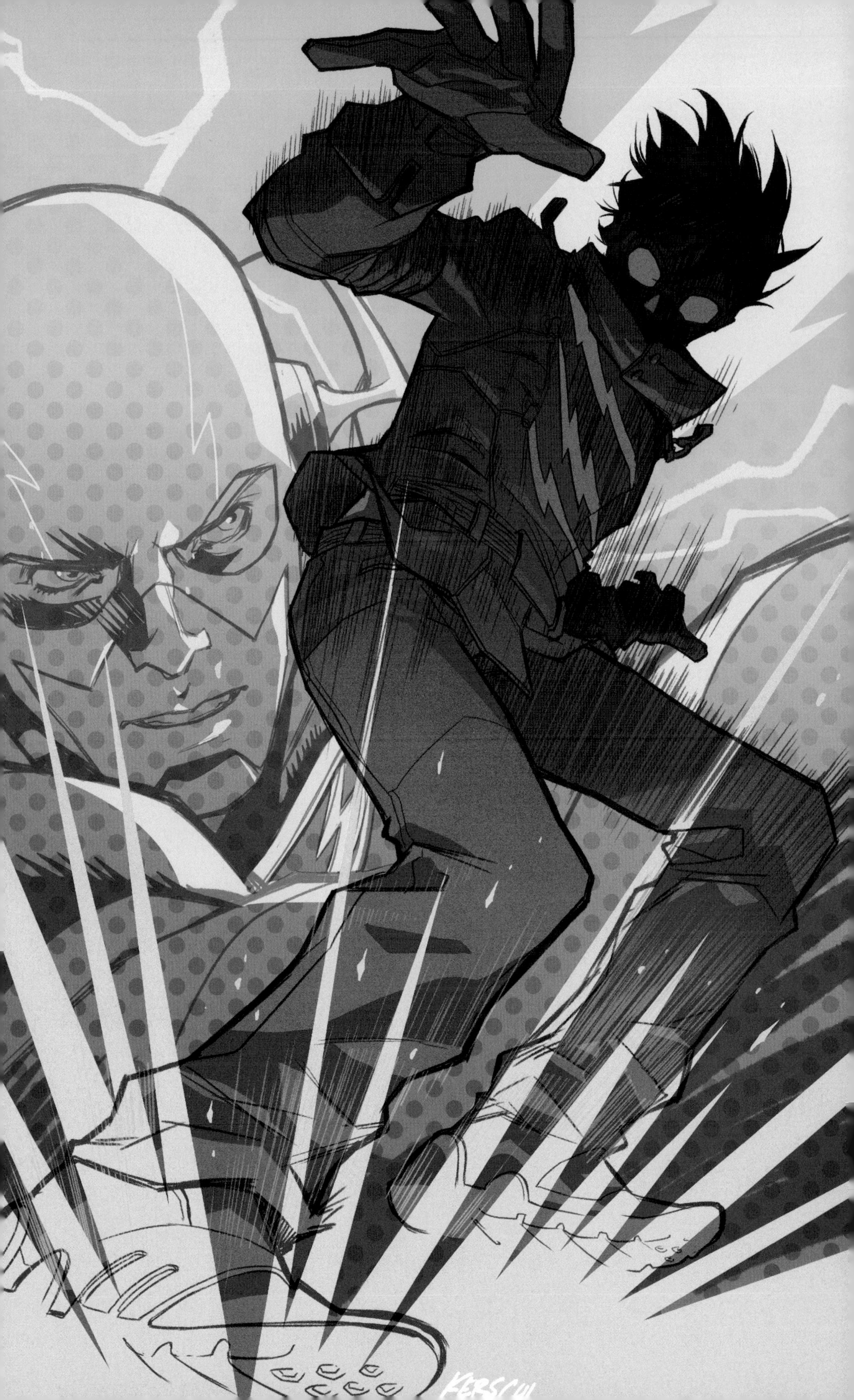

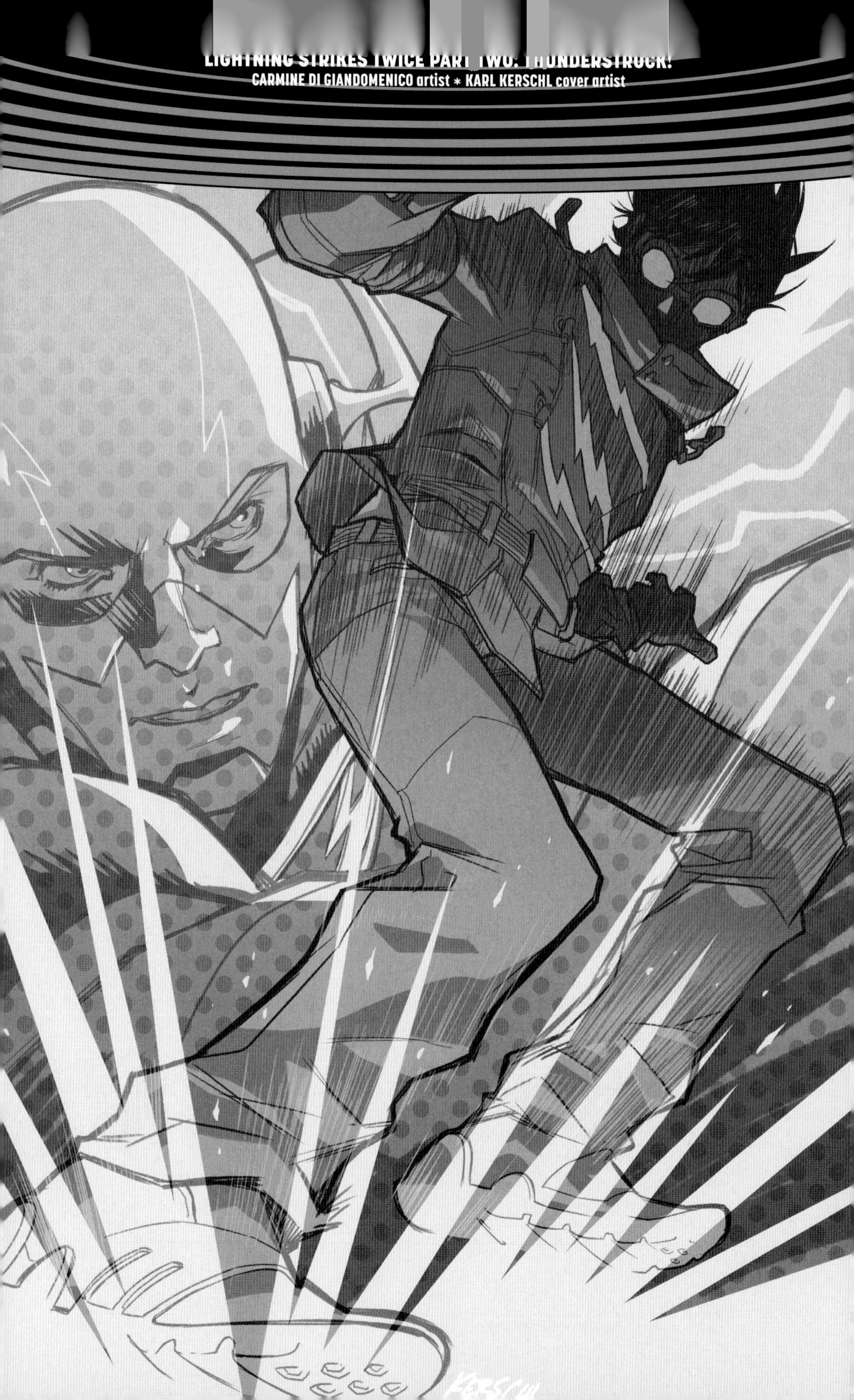
LIGHTNING STRIKES TWICE PART TWO: THUNDERSTRUCK!
CARMINE DI GIANDOMENICO artist * KARL KERSCHL cover artist

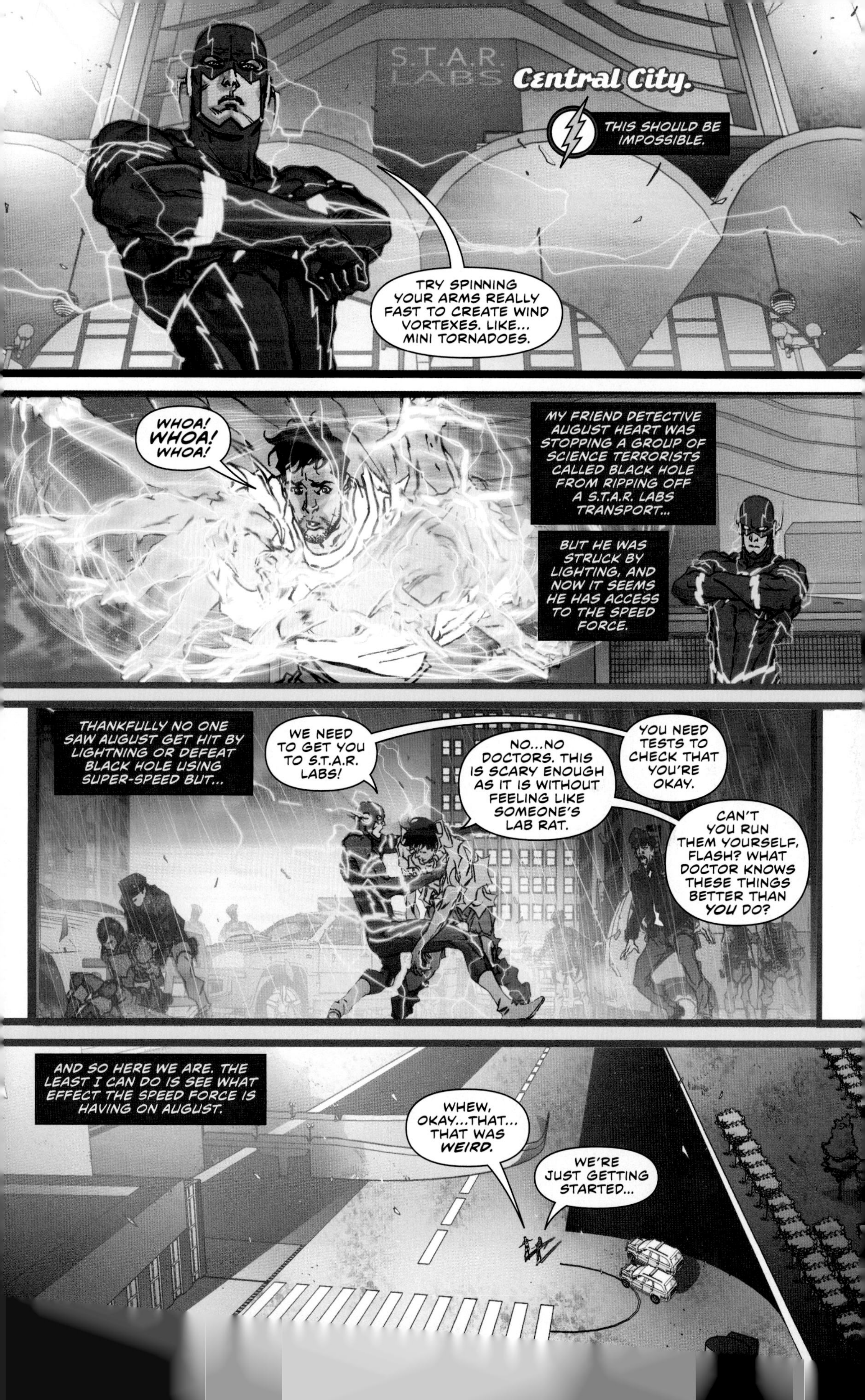
S.T.A.R. LABS
Central City.
THIS SHOULD BE IMPOSSIBLE.
TRY SPINNING YOUR ARMS REALLY FAST TO CREATE WIND VORTEXES. LIKE... MINI TORNADOES.
WHOA! WHOA! WHOA!
MY FRIEND DETECTIVE AUGUST HEART WAS STOPPING A GROUP OF SCIENCE TERRORISTS CALLED BLACK HOLE FROM RIPPING OFF A S.T.A.R. LABS TRANSPORT...
BUT HE WAS STRUCK BY LIGHTING, AND NOW IT SEEMS HE HAS ACCESS TO THE SPEED FORCE.
THANKFULLY NO ONE SAW AUGUST GET HIT BY LIGHTNING OR DEFEAT BLACK HOLE USING SUPER-SPEED BUT...
WE NEED TO GET YOU TO S.T.A.R. LABS!
YOU NEED TESTS TO CHECK THAT YOU'RE OKAY.
NO...NO DOCTORS. THIS IS SCARY ENOUGH AS IT IS WITHOUT FEELING LIKE SOMEONE'S LAB RAT.
CAN'T YOU RUN THEM YOURSELF, FLASH? WHAT DOCTOR KNOWS THESE THINGS BETTER THAN YOU DO?
AND SO HERE WE ARE. THE LEAST I CAN DO IS SEE WHAT EFFECT THE SPEED FORCE IS HAVING ON AUGUST.
WHEW, OKAY...THAT... THAT WAS WEIRD.
WE'RE JUST GETTING STARTED...

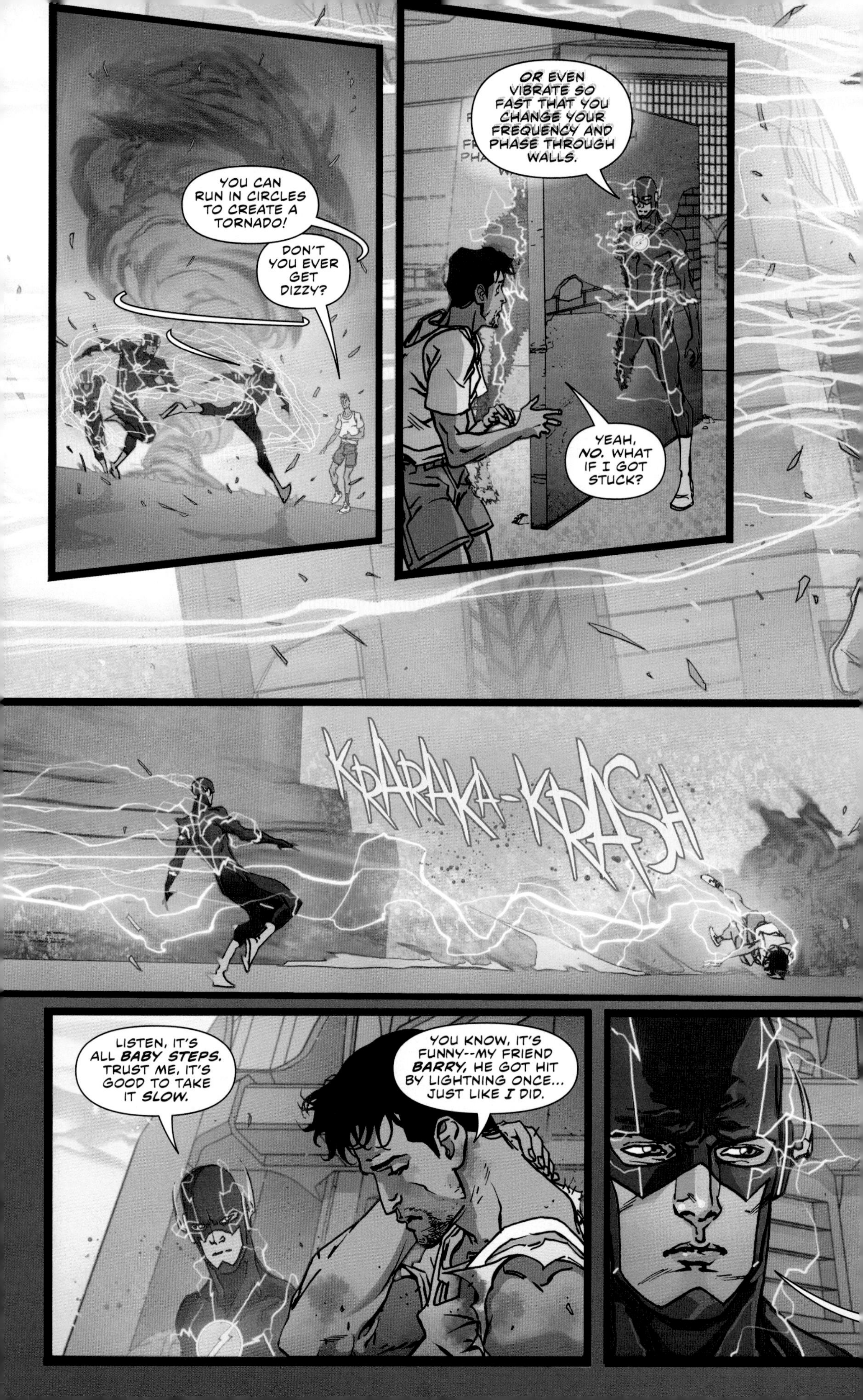
YOU CAN RUN IN CIRCLES TO CREATE A TORNADO!
DON'T YOU EVER GET DIZZY?
OR EVEN VIBRATE SO FAST THAT YOU CHANGE YOUR FREQUENCY AND PHASE THROUGH WALLS.
YEAH, NO. WHAT IF I GOT STUCK?
KRARAKA-KRASH
LISTEN, IT'S ALL BABY STEPS. TRUST ME, IT'S GOOD TO TAKE IT SLOW.
YOU KNOW, IT'S FUNNY--MY FRIEND BARRY, HE GOT HIT BY LIGHTNING ONCE... JUST LIKE I DID.

OKAY, LET'S TRY...

RUNNING!

RUN, AUGUST! HOW FAST ARE YOU?!

TKK

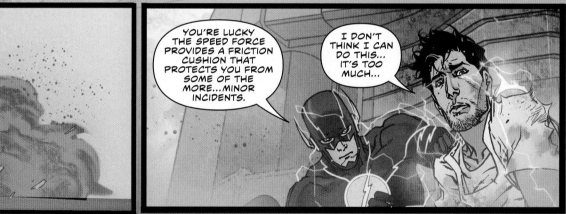

YOU'RE LUCKY THE SPEED FORCE PROVIDES A FRICTION CUSHION THAT PROTECTS YOU FROM SOME OF THE MORE...MINOR INCIDENTS.

I DON'T THINK I CAN DO THIS... IT'S TOO MUCH...

...OH? DID HE?

YEAH. I MEAN, WHAT ARE THE ODDS, RIGHT?

BILLION TO ONE.

OF COURSE YOU KNOW THE ODDS...WHAT I'M TRYING TO SAY IS THAT BARRY IS A REALLY GOOD FRIEND.

I--

SO I WANT YOU TO KNOW THAT I APPRECIATE WHAT YOU'RE DOING FOR ME HERE...

BARRY.

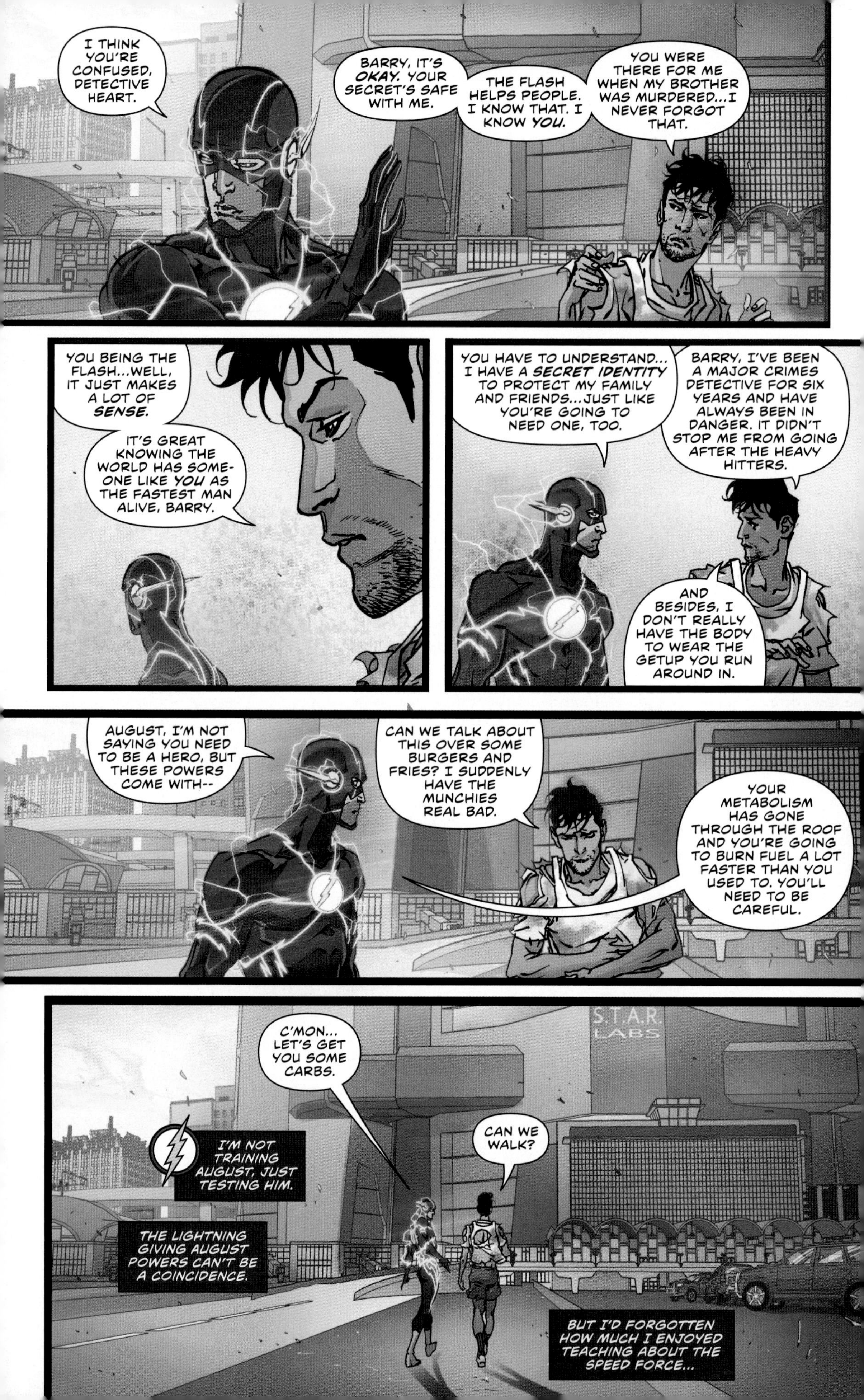
I THINK YOU'RE CONFUSED, DETECTIVE HEART.
BARRY, IT'S *OKAY.* YOUR SECRET'S SAFE WITH ME.
THE FLASH HELPS PEOPLE. I KNOW THAT. I KNOW *YOU.*
YOU WERE THERE FOR ME WHEN MY BROTHER WAS MURDERED...I NEVER FORGOT THAT.
YOU BEING THE FLASH...WELL, IT JUST MAKES A LOT OF *SENSE.*
IT'S GREAT KNOWING THE WORLD HAS SOME-ONE LIKE *YOU* AS THE FASTEST MAN ALIVE, BARRY.
YOU HAVE TO UNDERSTAND... I HAVE A *SECRET IDENTITY* TO PROTECT MY FAMILY AND FRIENDS...JUST LIKE YOU'RE GOING TO NEED ONE, TOO.
BARRY, I'VE BEEN A MAJOR CRIMES DETECTIVE FOR SIX YEARS AND HAVE ALWAYS BEEN IN DANGER. IT DIDN'T STOP ME FROM GOING AFTER THE HEAVY HITTERS.
AND BESIDES, I DON'T REALLY HAVE THE BODY TO WEAR THE GETUP YOU RUN AROUND IN.
AUGUST, I'M NOT SAYING YOU NEED TO BE A HERO, BUT THESE POWERS COME WITH--
CAN WE TALK ABOUT THIS OVER SOME BURGERS AND FRIES? I SUDDENLY HAVE THE MUNCHIES REAL BAD.
YOUR METABOLISM HAS GONE THROUGH THE ROOF AND YOU'RE GOING TO BURN FUEL A LOT FASTER THAN YOU USED TO. YOU'LL NEED TO BE CAREFUL.
S.T.A.R. LABS
C'MON... LET'S GET YOU SOME CARBS.
CAN WE WALK?
I'M NOT TRAINING AUGUST, JUST TESTING HIM.
THE LIGHTNING GIVING AUGUST POWERS CAN'T BE A COINCIDENCE.
BUT I'D FORGOTTEN HOW MUCH I ENJOYED TEACHING ABOUT THE SPEED FORCE...

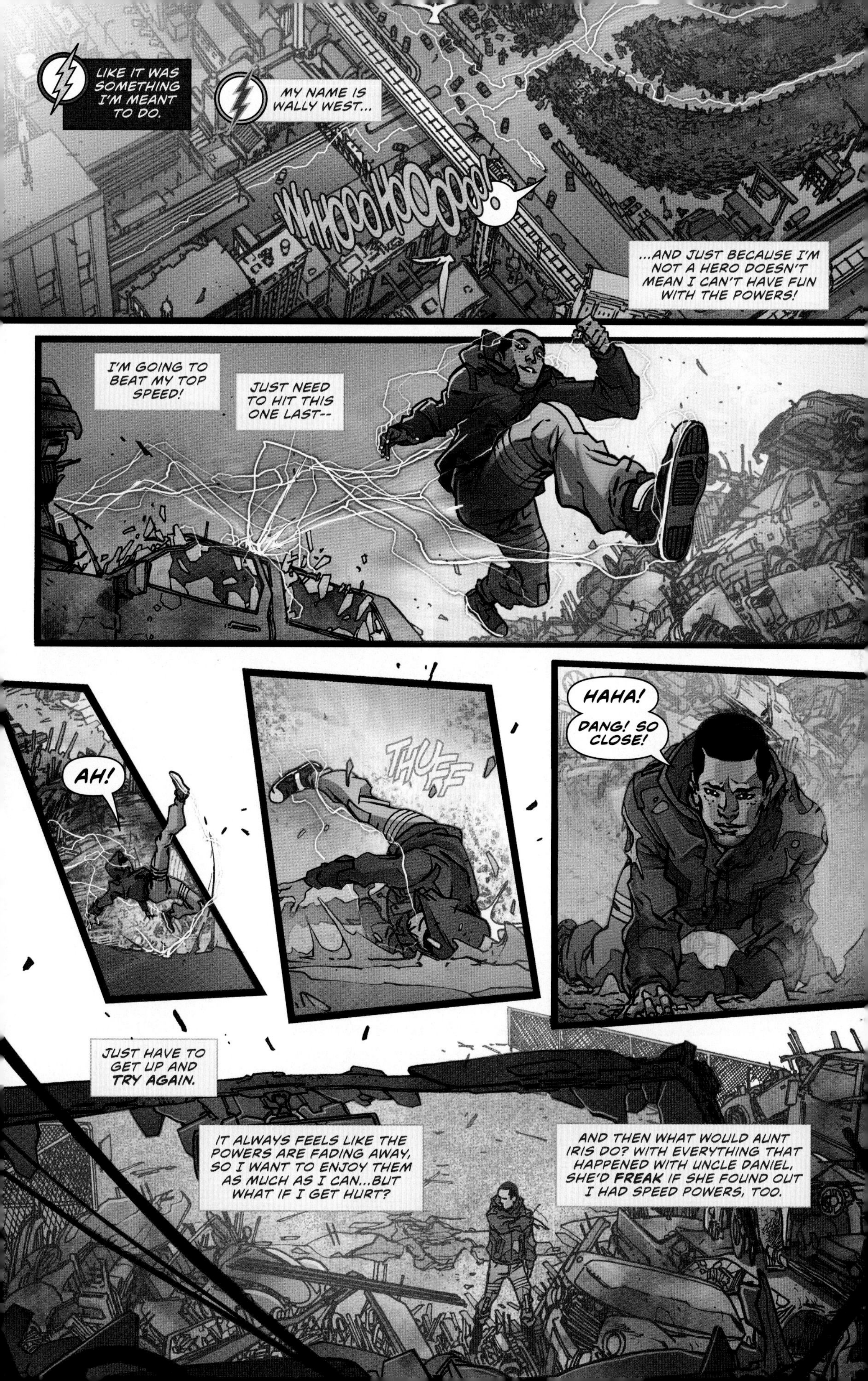
LIKE IT WAS SOMETHING I'M MEANT TO DO.
MY NAME IS WALLY WEST...
WHHOOOHOOOOO!
...AND JUST BECAUSE I'M NOT A HERO DOESN'T MEAN I CAN'T HAVE FUN WITH THE POWERS!
I'M GOING TO BEAT MY TOP SPEED!
JUST NEED TO HIT THIS ONE LAST--
AH!
THUFF
HAHA!
DANG! SO CLOSE!
JUST HAVE TO GET UP AND TRY AGAIN.
IT ALWAYS FEELS LIKE THE POWERS ARE FADING AWAY, SO I WANT TO ENJOY THEM AS MUCH AS I CAN...BUT WHAT IF I GET HURT?
AND THEN WHAT WOULD AUNT IRIS DO? WITH EVERYTHING THAT HAPPENED WITH UNCLE DANIEL, SHE'D FREAK IF SHE FOUND OUT I HAD SPEED POWERS, TOO.

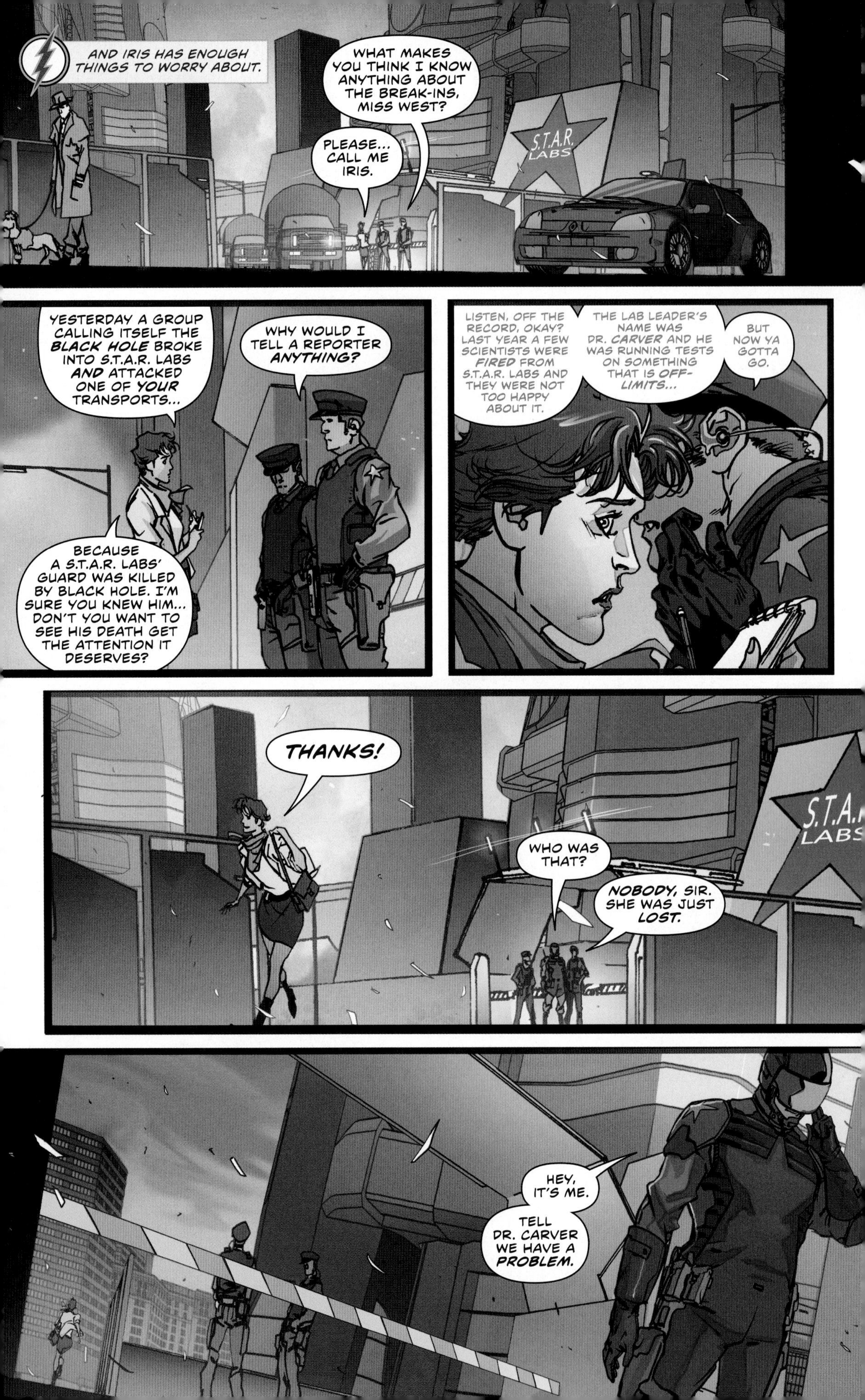
AND IRIS HAS ENOUGH THINGS TO WORRY ABOUT.
WHAT MAKES YOU THINK I KNOW ANYTHING ABOUT THE BREAK-INS, MISS WEST?
PLEASE... CALL ME IRIS.
S.T.A.R. LABS
YESTERDAY A GROUP CALLING ITSELF THE BLACK HOLE BROKE INTO S.T.A.R. LABS AND ATTACKED ONE OF YOUR TRANSPORTS...
WHY WOULD I TELL A REPORTER ANYTHING?
BECAUSE A S.T.A.R. LABS' GUARD WAS KILLED BY BLACK HOLE. I'M SURE YOU KNEW HIM... DON'T YOU WANT TO SEE HIS DEATH GET THE ATTENTION IT DESERVES?
LISTEN, OFF THE RECORD, OKAY? LAST YEAR A FEW SCIENTISTS WERE FIRED FROM S.T.A.R. LABS AND THEY WERE NOT TOO HAPPY ABOUT IT.
THE LAB LEADER'S NAME WAS DR. CARVER AND HE WAS RUNNING TESTS ON SOMETHING THAT IS OFF-LIMITS...
BUT NOW YA GOTTA GO.
THANKS!
WHO WAS THAT?
NOBODY, SIR. SHE WAS JUST LOST.
HEY, IT'S ME.
TELL DR. CARVER WE HAVE A PROBLEM.

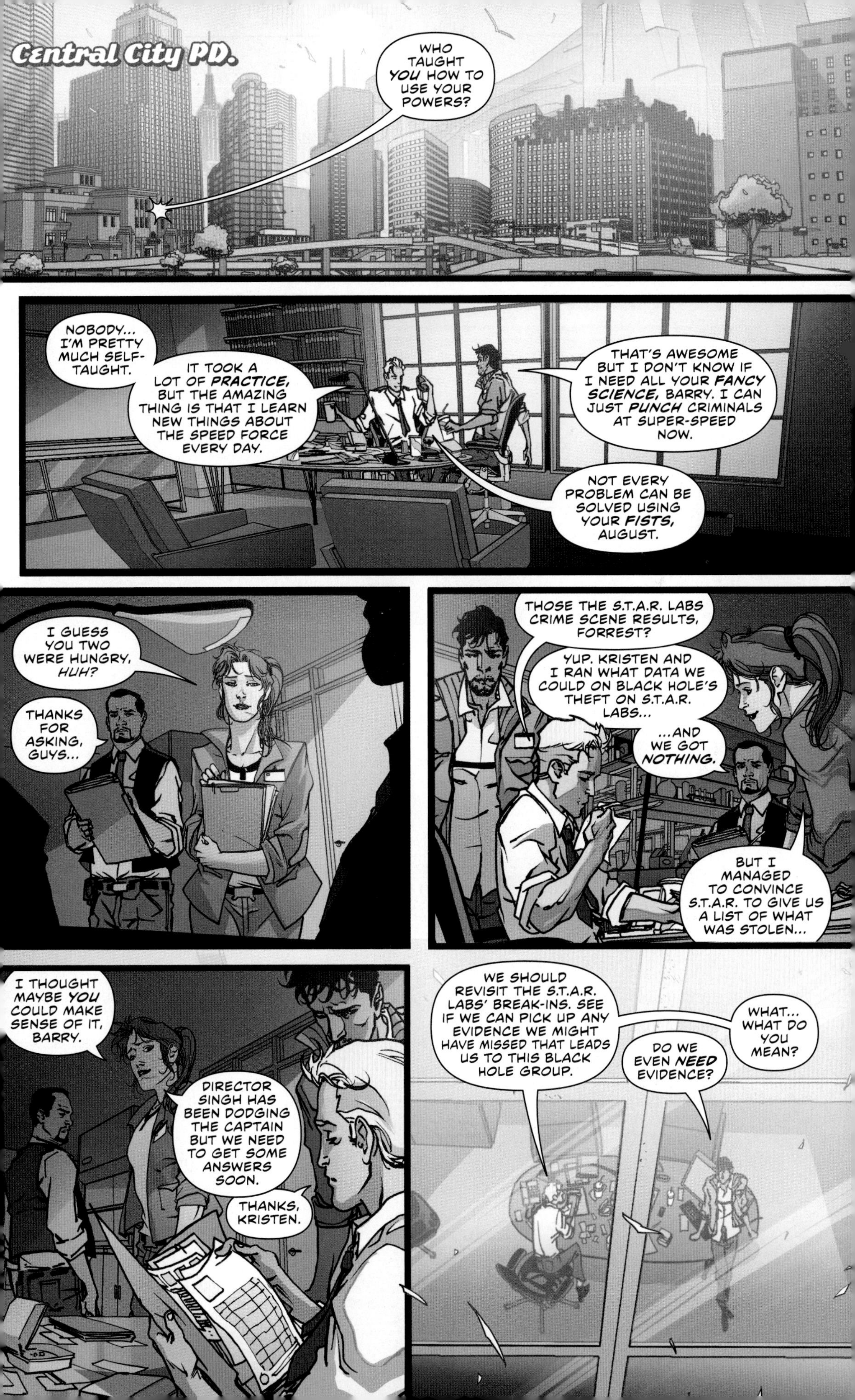
Central City PD.
WHO TAUGHT YOU HOW TO USE YOUR POWERS?
NOBODY... I'M PRETTY MUCH SELF-TAUGHT.
IT TOOK A LOT OF PRACTICE, BUT THE AMAZING THING IS THAT I LEARN NEW THINGS ABOUT THE SPEED FORCE EVERY DAY.
THAT'S AWESOME BUT I DON'T KNOW IF I NEED ALL YOUR FANCY SCIENCE, BARRY. I CAN JUST PUNCH CRIMINALS AT SUPER-SPEED NOW.
NOT EVERY PROBLEM CAN BE SOLVED USING YOUR FISTS, AUGUST.
I GUESS YOU TWO WERE HUNGRY, HUH?
THANKS FOR ASKING, GUYS...
THOSE THE S.T.A.R. LABS CRIME SCENE RESULTS, FORREST?
YUP. KRISTEN AND I RAN WHAT DATA WE COULD ON BLACK HOLE'S THEFT ON S.T.A.R. LABS...
...AND WE GOT NOTHING.
BUT I MANAGED TO CONVINCE S.T.A.R. TO GIVE US A LIST OF WHAT WAS STOLEN...
I THOUGHT MAYBE YOU COULD MAKE SENSE OF IT, BARRY.
DIRECTOR SINGH HAS BEEN DODGING THE CAPTAIN BUT WE NEED TO GET SOME ANSWERS SOON.
THANKS, KRISTEN.
WE SHOULD REVISIT THE S.T.A.R. LABS' BREAK-INS. SEE IF WE CAN PICK UP ANY EVIDENCE WE MIGHT HAVE MISSED THAT LEADS US TO THIS BLACK HOLE GROUP.
WHAT... WHAT DO YOU MEAN?
DO WE EVEN NEED EVIDENCE?

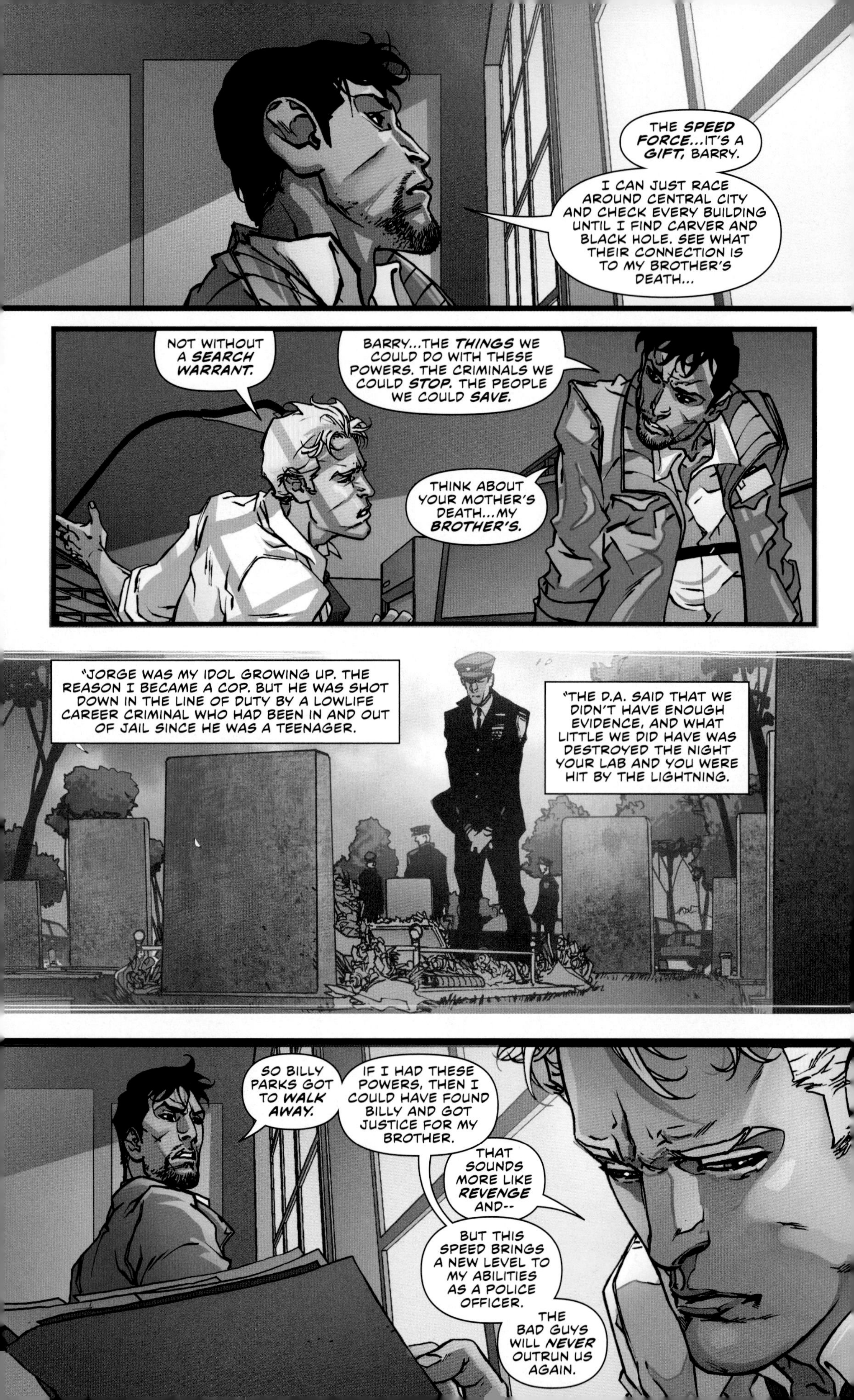
THE SPEED FORCE...IT'S A GIFT, BARRY.
I CAN JUST RACE AROUND CENTRAL CITY AND CHECK EVERY BUILDING UNTIL I FIND CARVER AND BLACK HOLE. SEE WHAT THEIR CONNECTION IS TO MY BROTHER'S DEATH...
NOT WITHOUT A SEARCH WARRANT.
BARRY...THE THINGS WE COULD DO WITH THESE POWERS. THE CRIMINALS WE COULD STOP. THE PEOPLE WE COULD SAVE.
THINK ABOUT YOUR MOTHER'S DEATH...MY BROTHER'S.
"JORGE WAS MY IDOL GROWING UP. THE REASON I BECAME A COP. BUT HE WAS SHOT DOWN IN THE LINE OF DUTY BY A LOWLIFE CAREER CRIMINAL WHO HAD BEEN IN AND OUT OF JAIL SINCE HE WAS A TEENAGER.
"THE D.A. SAID THAT WE DIDN'T HAVE ENOUGH EVIDENCE, AND WHAT LITTLE WE DID HAVE WAS DESTROYED THE NIGHT YOUR LAB AND YOU WERE HIT BY THE LIGHTNING.
SO BILLY PARKS GOT TO WALK AWAY.
IF I HAD THESE POWERS, THEN I COULD HAVE FOUND BILLY AND GOT JUSTICE FOR MY BROTHER.
THAT SOUNDS MORE LIKE REVENGE AND--
BUT THIS SPEED BRINGS A NEW LEVEL TO MY ABILITIES AS A POLICE OFFICER.
THE BAD GUYS WILL NEVER OUTRUN US AGAIN.

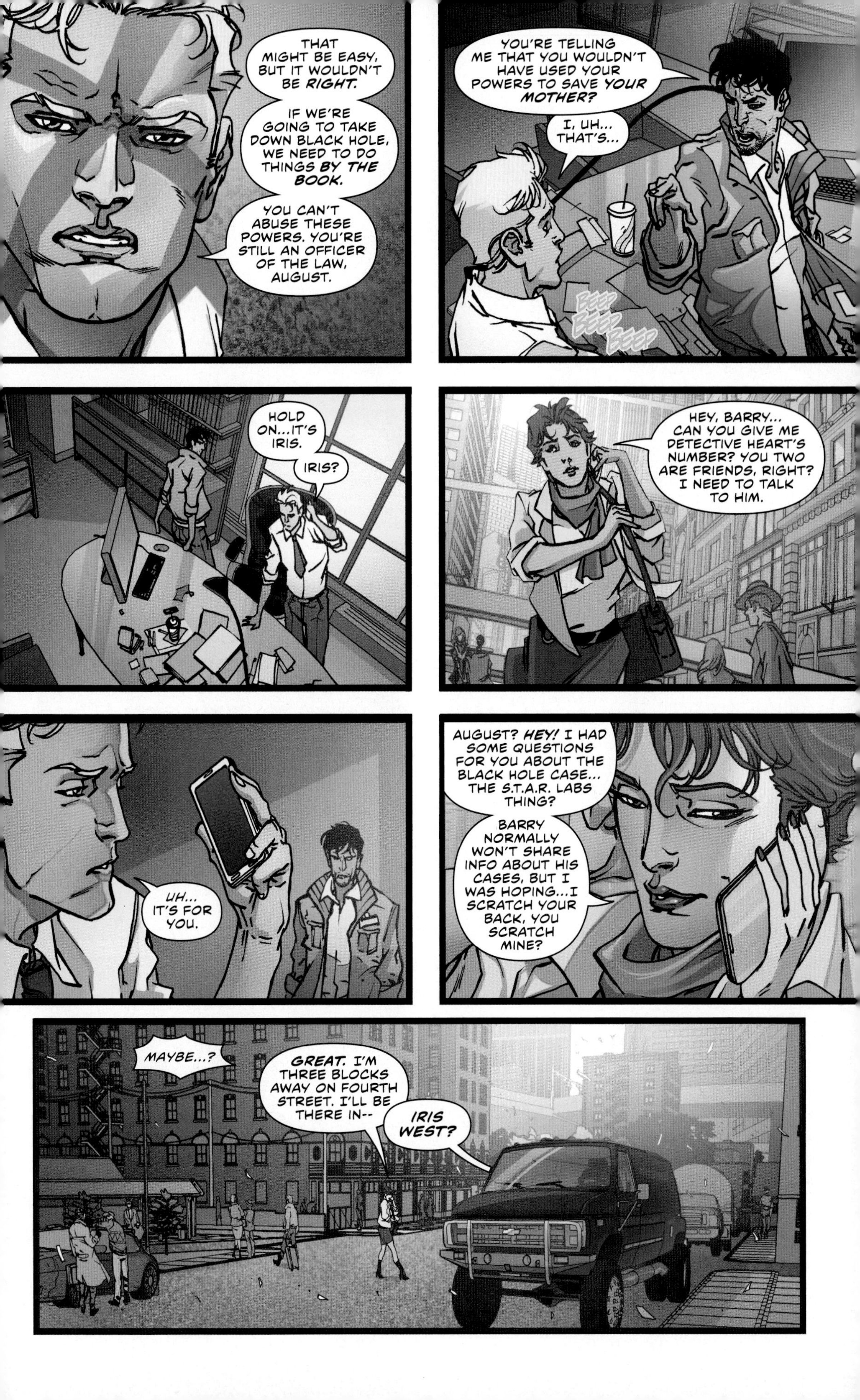
THAT MIGHT BE EASY, BUT IT WOULDN'T BE RIGHT.
IF WE'RE GOING TO TAKE DOWN BLACK HOLE, WE NEED TO DO THINGS BY THE BOOK.
YOU CAN'T ABUSE THESE POWERS. YOU'RE STILL AN OFFICER OF THE LAW, AUGUST.
YOU'RE TELLING ME THAT YOU WOULDN'T HAVE USED YOUR POWERS TO SAVE YOUR MOTHER?
I, UH... THAT'S...
BEEP BEEP BEEP
HOLD ON...IT'S IRIS.
IRIS?
HEY, BARRY... CAN YOU GIVE ME DETECTIVE HEART'S NUMBER? YOU TWO ARE FRIENDS, RIGHT? I NEED TO TALK TO HIM.
UH... IT'S FOR YOU.
AUGUST? HEY! I HAD SOME QUESTIONS FOR YOU ABOUT THE BLACK HOLE CASE... THE S.T.A.R. LABS THING?
BARRY NORMALLY WON'T SHARE INFO ABOUT HIS CASES, BUT I WAS HOPING...I SCRATCH YOUR BACK, YOU SCRATCH MINE?
MAYBE...?
GREAT. I'M THREE BLOCKS AWAY ON FOURTH STREET. I'LL BE THERE IN--
IRIS WEST?

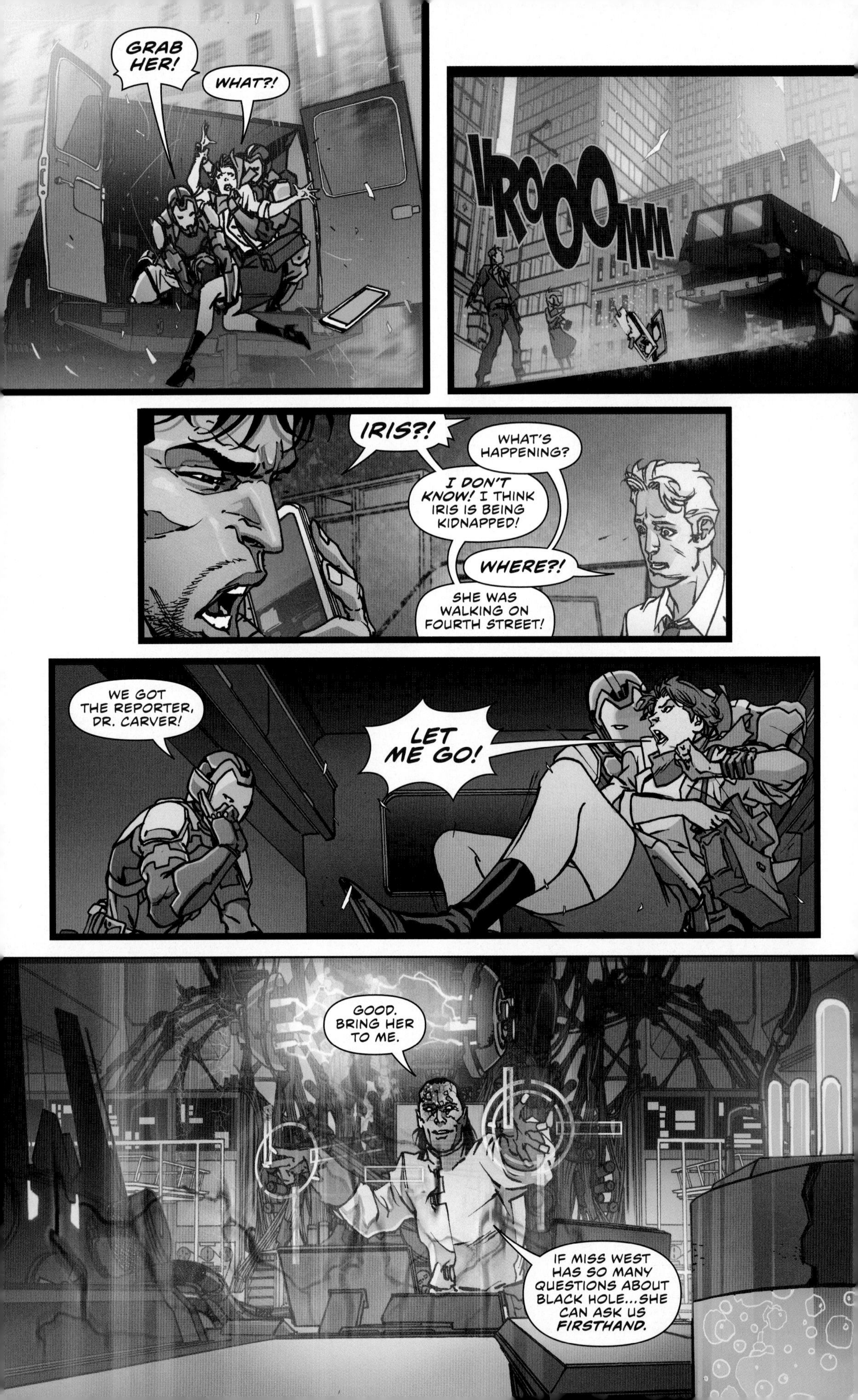
GRAB HER!
WHAT?!
VROOOMM
IRIS?!
WHAT'S HAPPENING?
I DON'T KNOW! I THINK IRIS IS BEING KIDNAPPED!
WHERE?!
SHE WAS WALKING ON FOURTH STREET!
WE GOT THE REPORTER, DR. CARVER!
LET ME GO!
GOOD. BRING HER TO ME.
IF MISS WEST HAS SO MANY QUESTIONS ABOUT BLACK HOLE...SHE CAN ASK US FIRSTHAND.

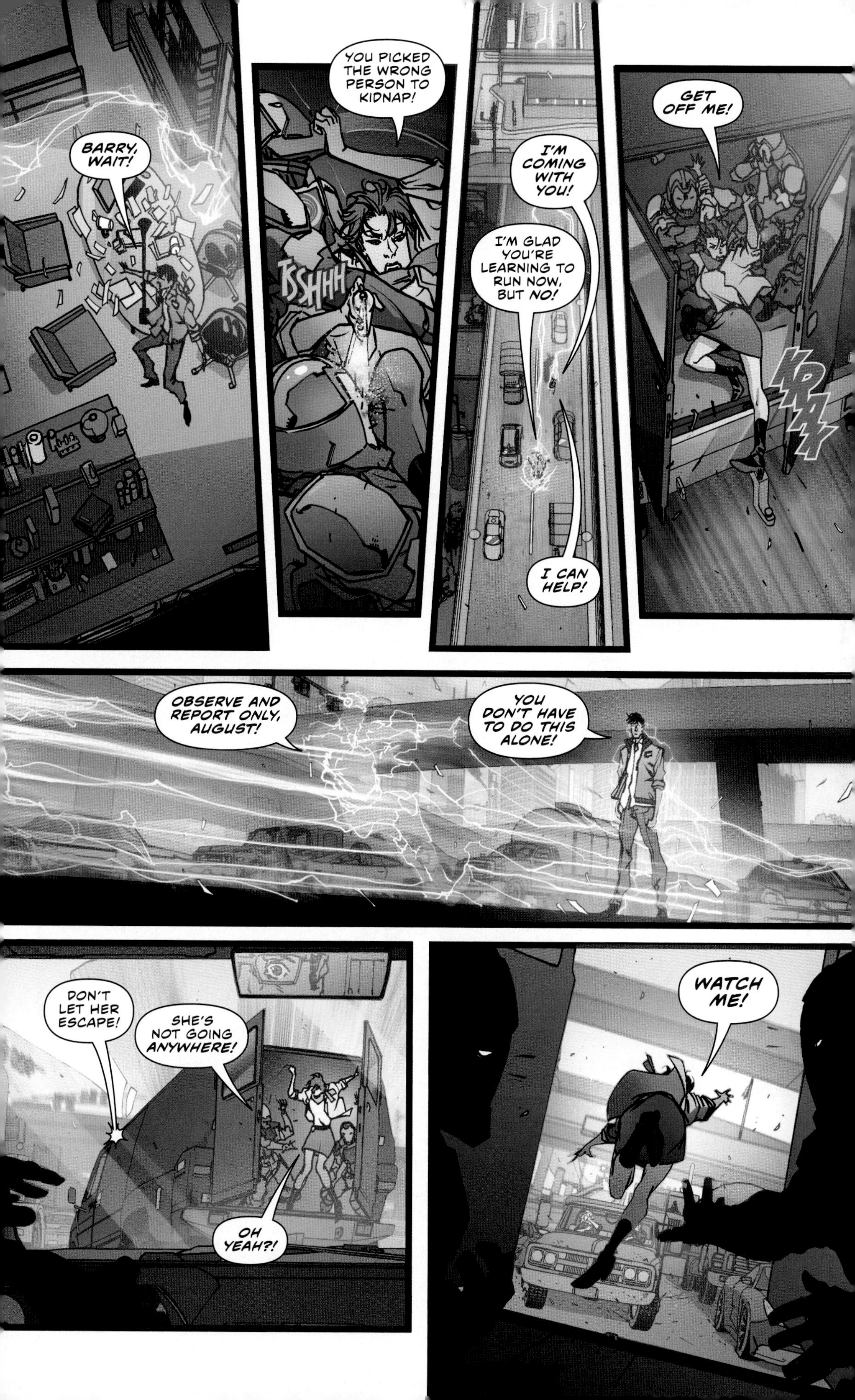
BARRY, WAIT!
YOU PICKED THE WRONG PERSON TO KIDNAP!
TSSHHH
I'M COMING WITH YOU!
I'M GLAD YOU'RE LEARNING TO RUN NOW, BUT NO!
I CAN HELP!
GET OFF ME!
KRAK
OBSERVE AND REPORT ONLY, AUGUST!
YOU DON'T HAVE TO DO THIS ALONE!
DON'T LET HER ESCAPE!
SHE'S NOT GOING ANYWHERE!
OH YEAH?!
WATCH ME!

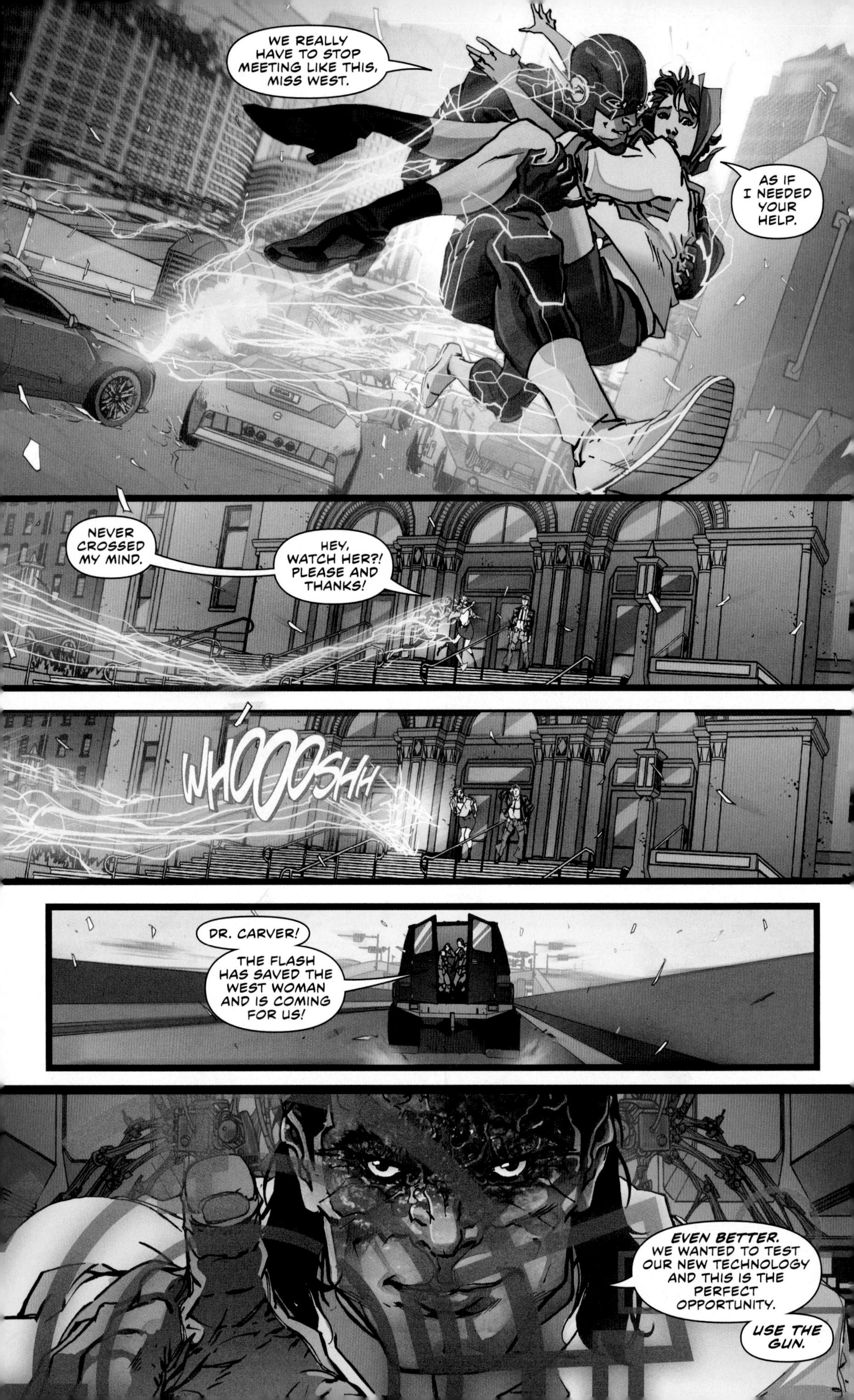
WE REALLY HAVE TO STOP MEETING LIKE THIS, MISS WEST.
AS IF I NEEDED YOUR HELP.
NEVER CROSSED MY MIND.
HEY, WATCH HER?! PLEASE AND THANKS!
WHOOOOSHH
DR. CARVER!
THE FLASH HAS SAVED THE WEST WOMAN AND IS COMING FOR US!
EVEN BETTER. WE WANTED TO TEST OUR NEW TECHNOLOGY AND THIS IS THE PERFECT OPPORTUNITY.
USE THE GUN.

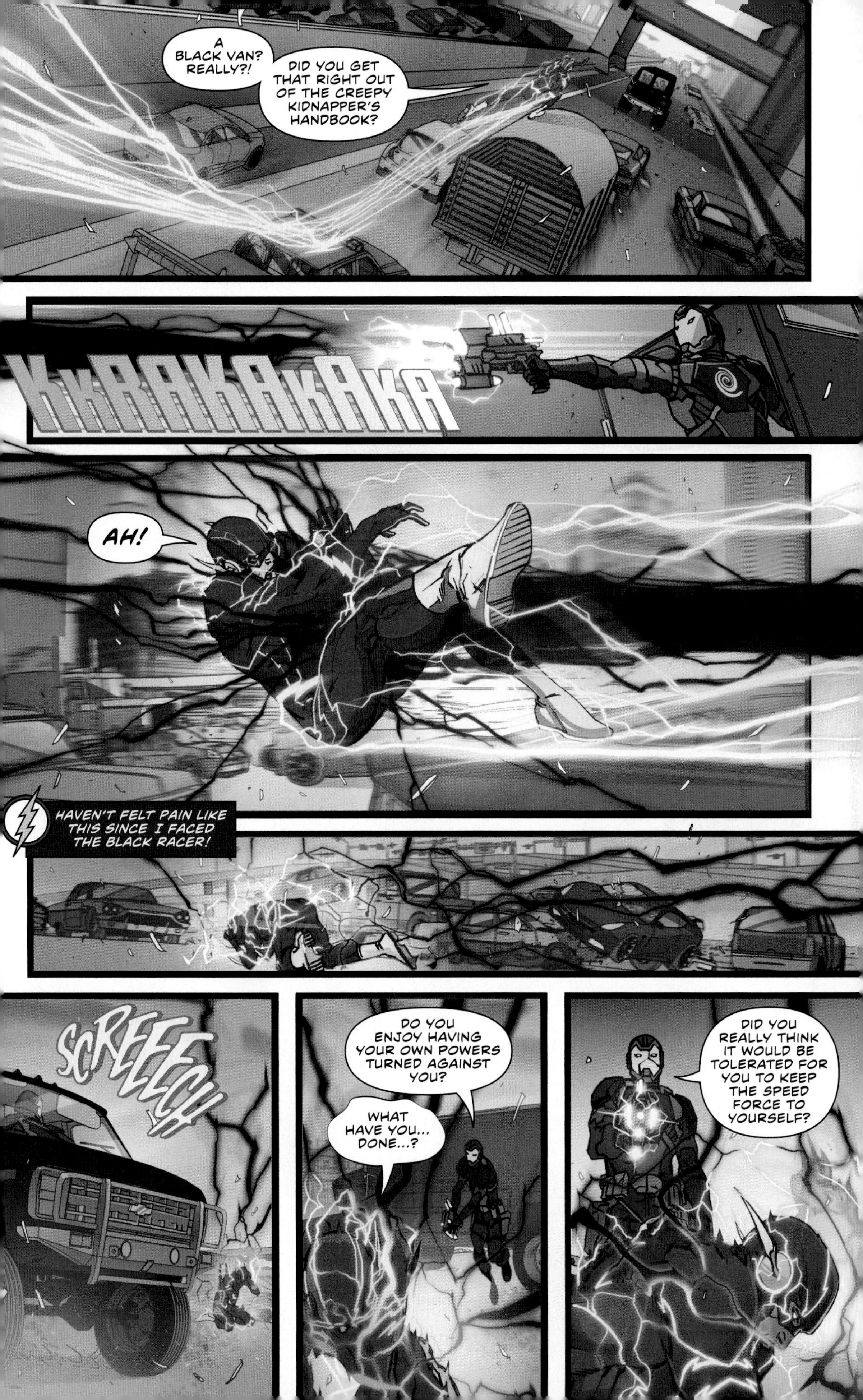
A BLACK VAN? REALLY?!
DID YOU GET THAT RIGHT OUT OF THE CREEPY KIDNAPPER'S HANDBOOK?
KKRAKAKAKAKA
AH!
HAVEN'T FELT PAIN LIKE THIS SINCE I FACED THE BLACK RACER!
SCREEECH
DO YOU ENJOY HAVING YOUR OWN POWERS TURNED AGAINST YOU?
WHAT HAVE YOU... DONE...?
DID YOU REALLY THINK IT WOULD BE TOLERATED FOR YOU TO KEEP THE SPEED FORCE TO YOURSELF?

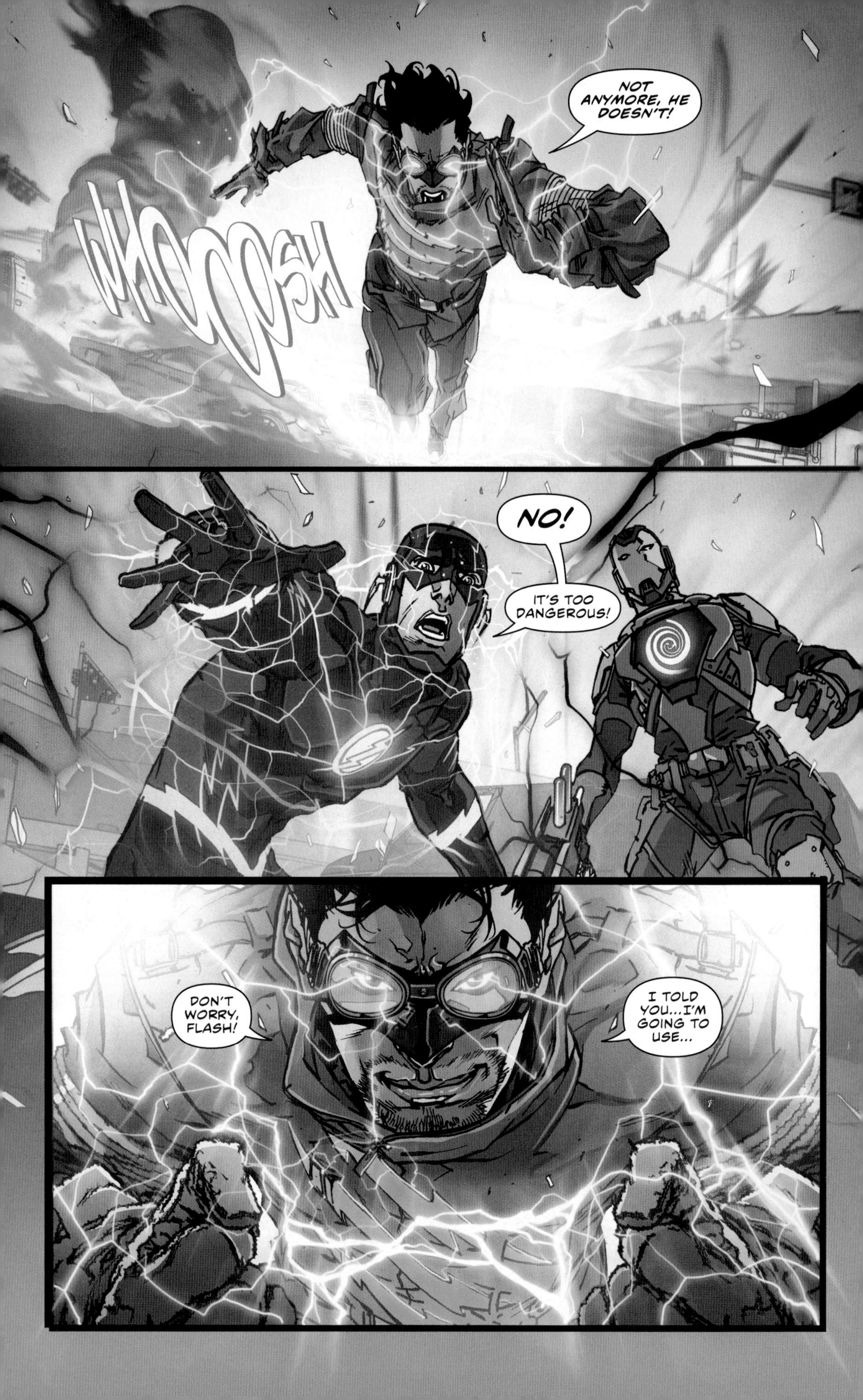
NOT ANYMORE, HE DOESN'T!
WHOOOSH
NO!
IT'S TOO DANGEROUS!
DON'T WORRY, FLASH!
I TOLD YOU...I'M GOING TO USE...

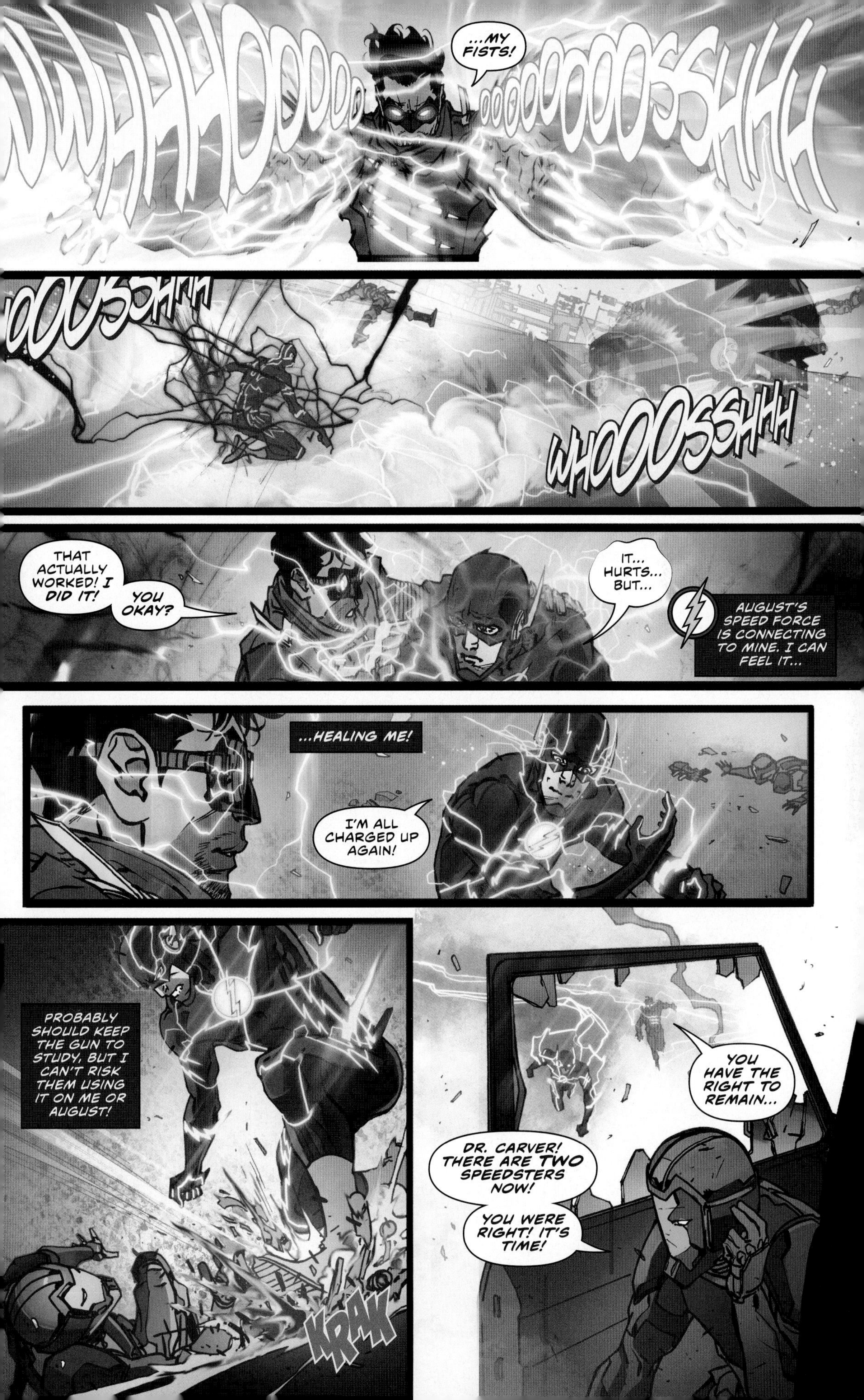
NWAHHOOOOD
...MY FISTS!
OOOOOOOOOSSHHH
OOOSSHHH
WHOOOOSSHHH
THAT ACTUALLY WORKED! I DID IT!
YOU OKAY?
IT... HURTS... BUT...
AUGUST'S SPEED FORCE IS CONNECTING TO MINE. I CAN FEEL IT...
...HEALING ME!
I'M ALL CHARGED UP AGAIN!
PROBABLY SHOULD KEEP THE GUN TO STUDY, BUT I CAN'T RISK THEM USING IT ON ME OR AUGUST!
KRAK
YOU HAVE THE RIGHT TO REMAIN...
DR. CARVER! THERE ARE TWO SPEEDSTERS NOW!
YOU WERE RIGHT! IT'S TIME!

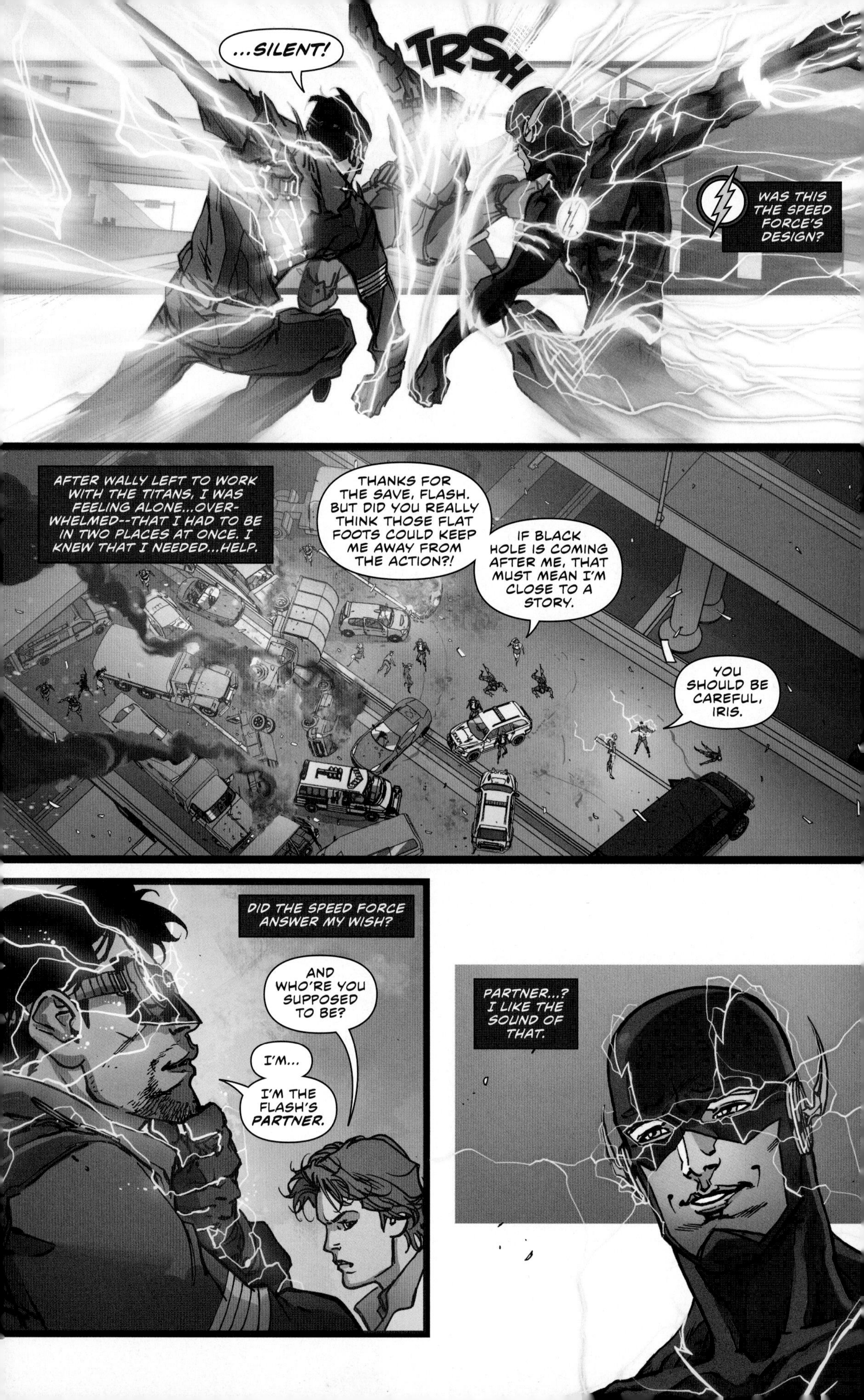
...SILENT!
TRSH
WAS THIS THE SPEED FORCE'S DESIGN?
AFTER WALLY LEFT TO WORK WITH THE TITANS, I WAS FEELING ALONE...OVER-WHELMED--THAT I HAD TO BE IN TWO PLACES AT ONCE. I KNEW THAT I NEEDED...HELP.
THANKS FOR THE SAVE, FLASH. BUT DID YOU REALLY THINK THOSE FLAT FOOTS COULD KEEP ME AWAY FROM THE ACTION?!
IF BLACK HOLE IS COMING AFTER ME, THAT MUST MEAN I'M CLOSE TO A STORY.
YOU SHOULD BE CAREFUL, IRIS.
DID THE SPEED FORCE ANSWER MY WISH?
AND WHO'RE YOU SUPPOSED TO BE?
I'M...
I'M THE FLASH'S PARTNER.
PARTNER...? I LIKE THE SOUND OF THAT.

RUMBLE RUMBLE RUMBLE

WHEN THE OLDER WALLY WAS HIT BY LIGHTNING, I THOUGHT THEN THAT MAYBE I CALLED ON THE SPEED FORCE TO GIVE HIM HIS POWERS.

IS THIS HAPPENING NOW BECAUSE OF WALLY'S RETURN, OR BECAUSE I MISSED HAVING A PARTNER?

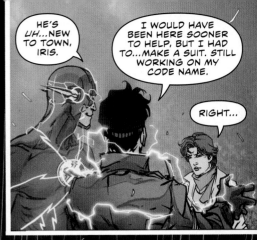

HE'S *UH*...NEW TO TOWN, IRIS.

I WOULD HAVE BEEN HERE SOONER TO HELP, BUT I HAD TO...MAKE A SUIT. STILL WORKING ON MY CODE NAME.

RIGHT...

RUMBLE RUMBLE RUMBLE

I THOUGHT YOU *WEREN'T* GOING TO HAVE A SECRET IDENTITY?

MAYBE YOU'RE JUST A GOOD TEACHER, FLASH.

NICE SUIT.

NOW THAT WE HAVE A FEW MORE OF THE BLACK HOLE AGENTS IN CUSTODY WE CAN--

WAIT...DO YOU FEEL THAT?

THOOM-RUMBLE

WHERE DID THAT STORM COME FROM?!

I DON'T KNOW BUT...

IT LOOKS JUST LIKE THE STORM FROM YESTERDAY...

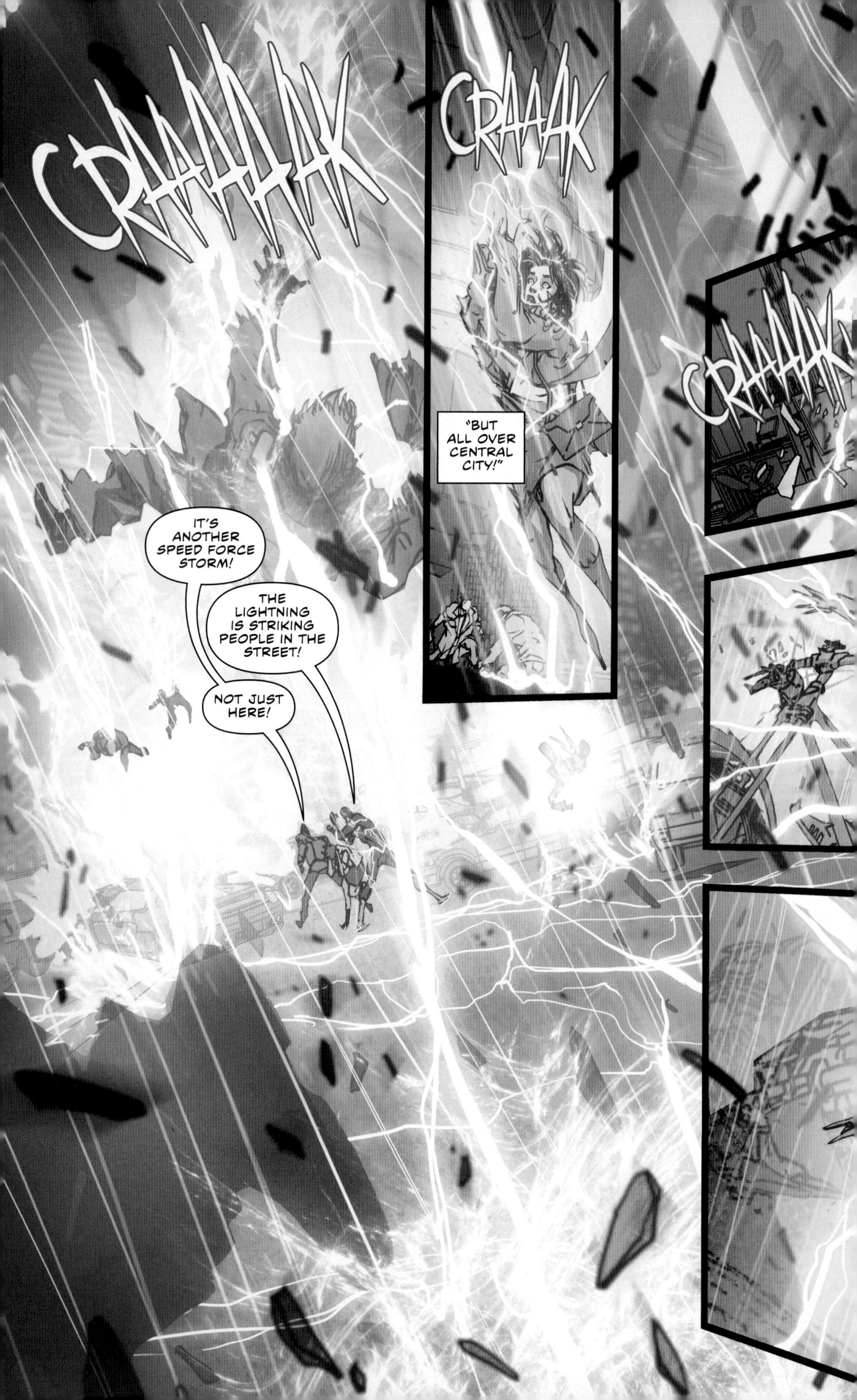
CRAAAAAK
IT'S ANOTHER SPEED FORCE STORM!
THE LIGHTNING IS STRIKING PEOPLE IN THE STREET!
NOT JUST HERE!
CRAAAK
"BUT ALL OVER CENTRAL CITY!"
CRAAAK

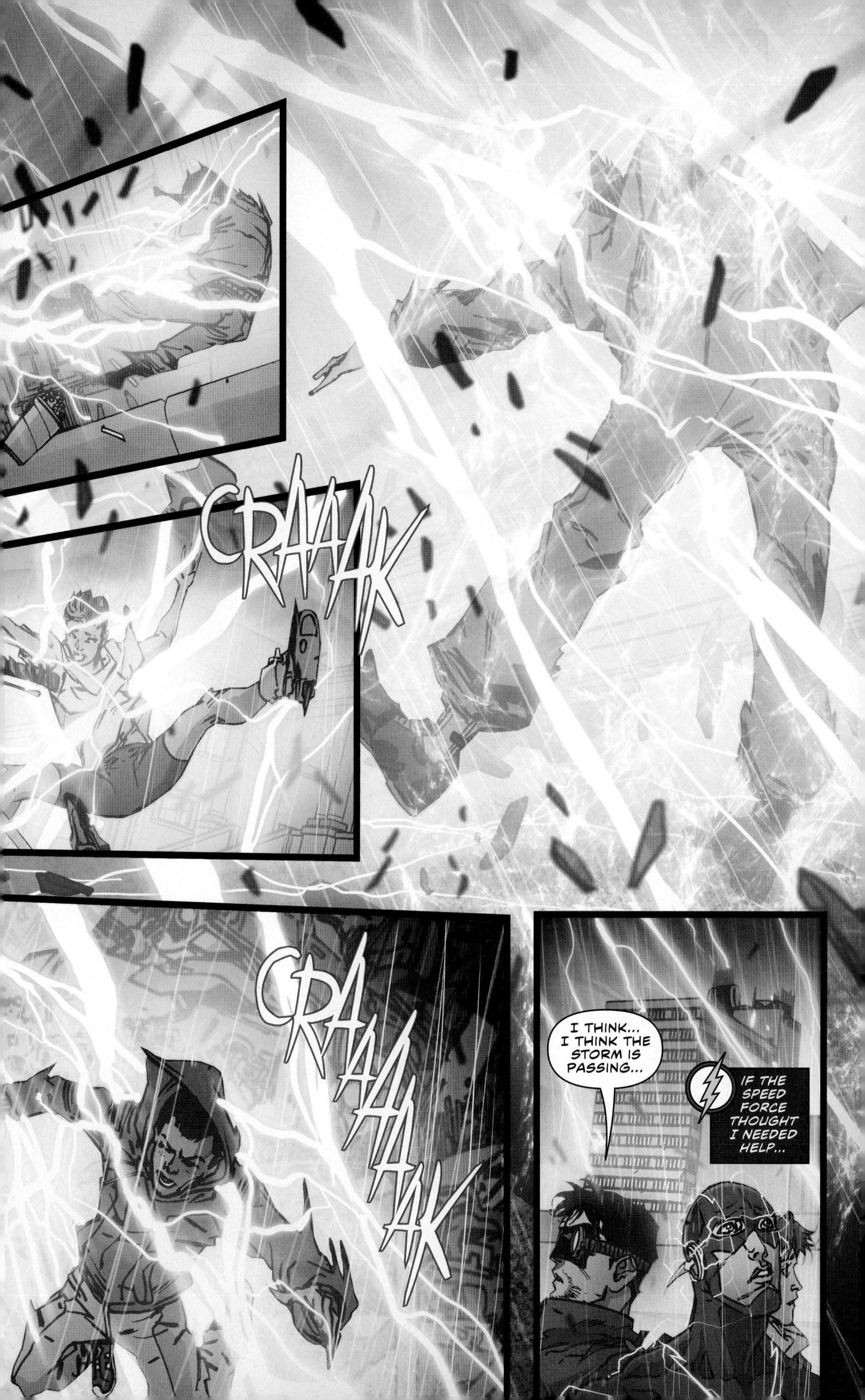
CRAAAK
CRAAAAAAK
I THINK... I THINK THE STORM IS PASSING...
IF THE SPEED FORCE THOUGHT I NEEDED HELP...

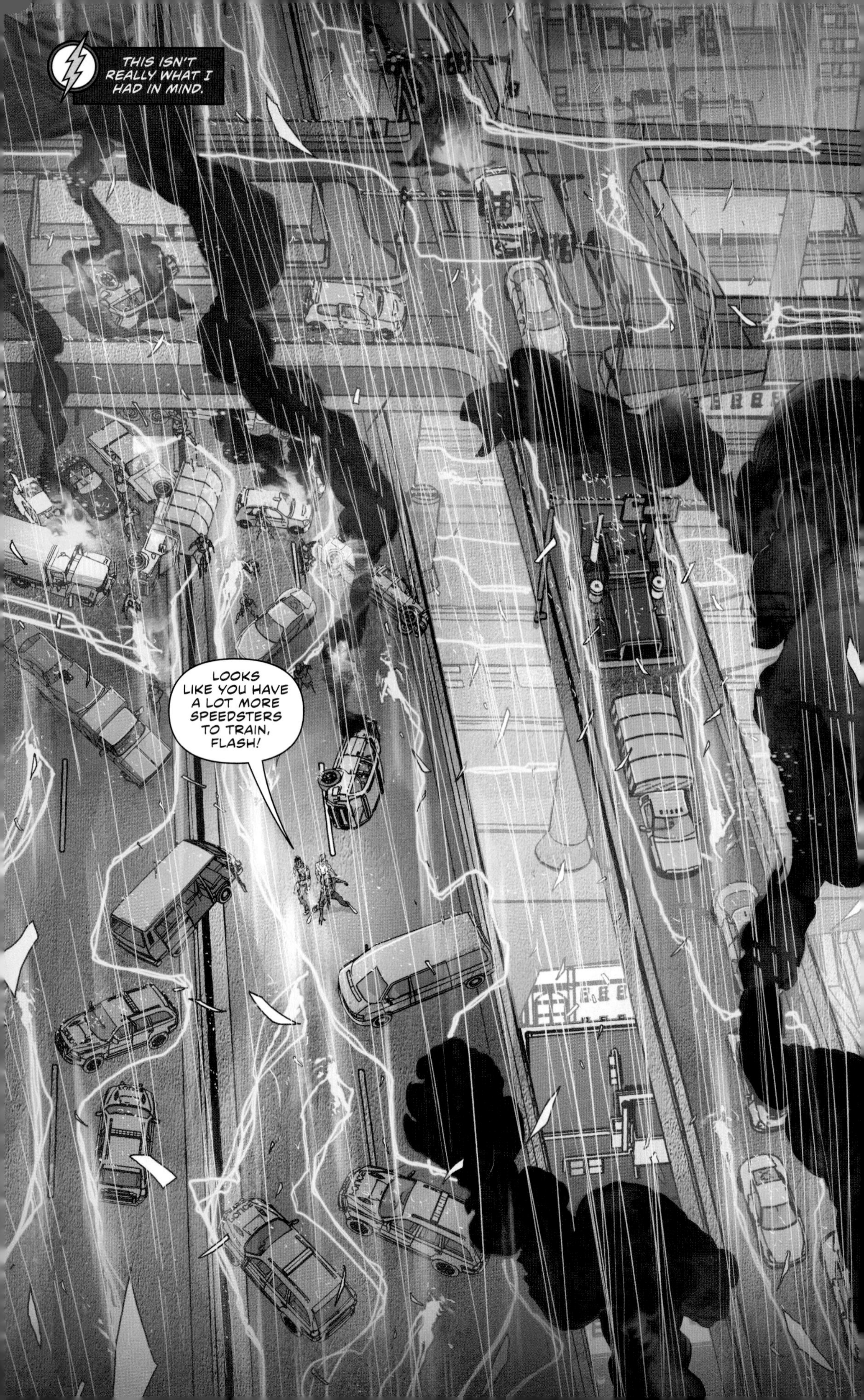
THIS ISN'T REALLY WHAT I HAD IN MIND.
LOOKS LIKE YOU HAVE A LOT MORE SPEEDSTERS TO TRAIN, FLASH!

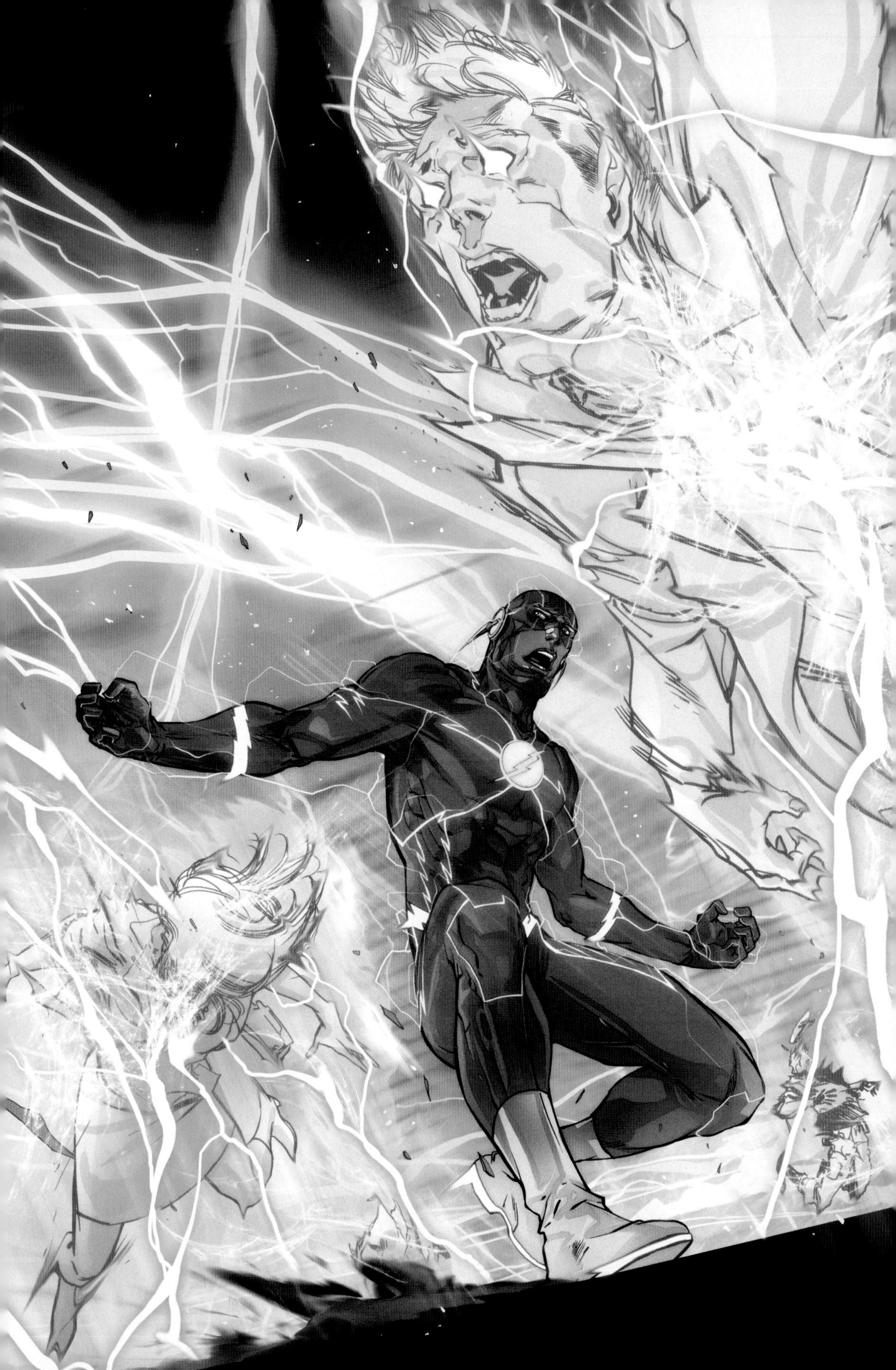

SPEED CITY

CARMINE DI GIANDOMENICO artist/cover

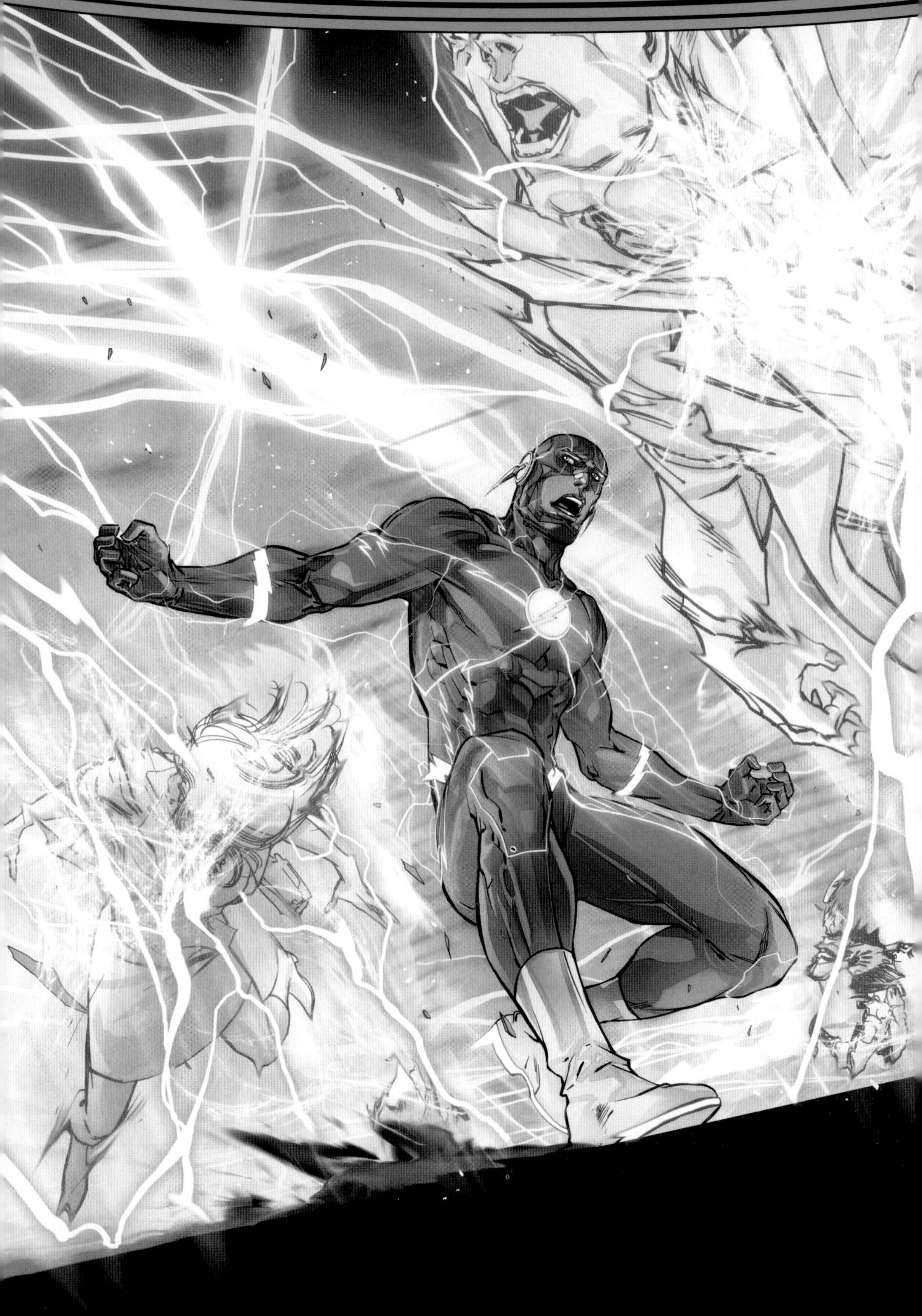

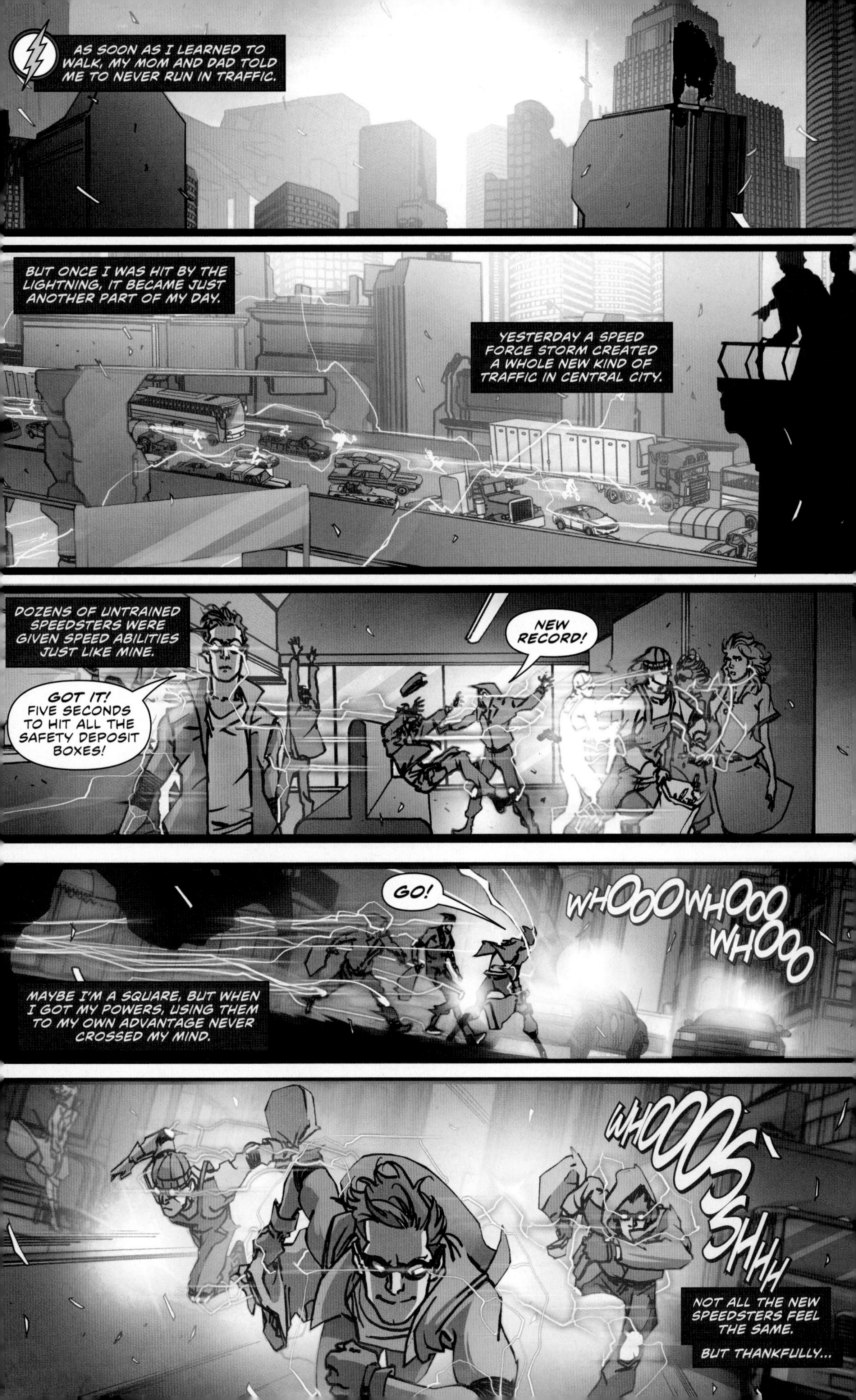
AS SOON AS I LEARNED TO WALK, MY MOM AND DAD TOLD ME TO NEVER RUN IN TRAFFIC.
BUT ONCE I WAS HIT BY THE LIGHTNING, IT BECAME JUST ANOTHER PART OF MY DAY.
YESTERDAY A SPEED FORCE STORM CREATED A WHOLE NEW KIND OF TRAFFIC IN CENTRAL CITY.
DOZENS OF UNTRAINED SPEEDSTERS WERE GIVEN SPEED ABILITIES JUST LIKE MINE.
GOT IT! FIVE SECONDS TO HIT ALL THE SAFETY DEPOSIT BOXES!
NEW RECORD!
GO!
WHOOOWHOOO WHOOO
MAYBE I'M A SQUARE, BUT WHEN I GOT MY POWERS, USING THEM TO MY OWN ADVANTAGE NEVER CROSSED MY MIND.
WHOOOSHHH
NOT ALL THE NEW SPEEDSTERS FEEL THE SAME.
BUT THANKFULLY...

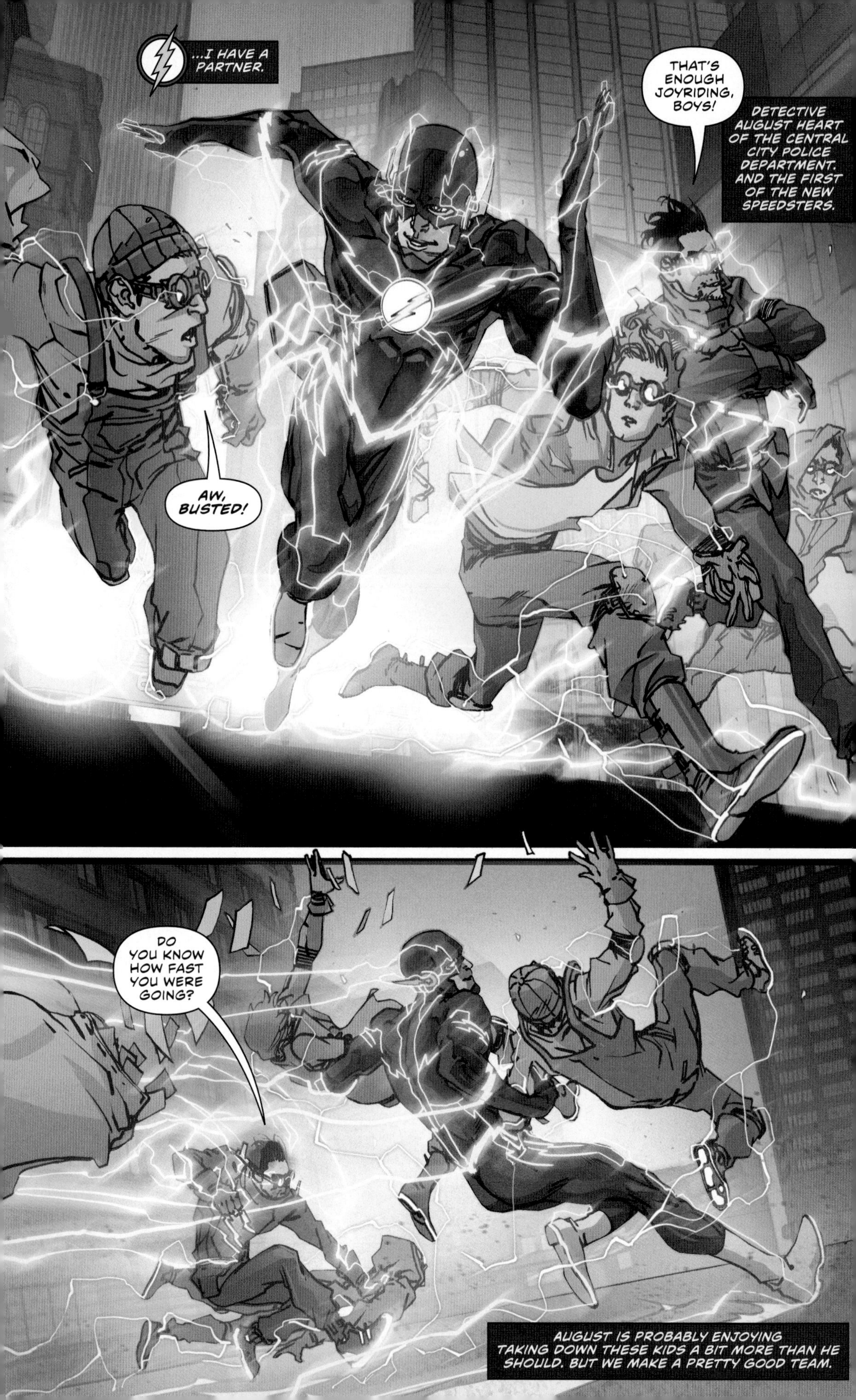
...I HAVE A PARTNER.
THAT'S ENOUGH JOYRIDING, BOYS!
DETECTIVE AUGUST HEART OF THE CENTRAL CITY POLICE DEPARTMENT. AND THE FIRST OF THE NEW SPEEDSTERS.
AW, BUSTED!
DO YOU KNOW HOW FAST YOU WERE GOING?
AUGUST IS PROBABLY ENJOYING TAKING DOWN THESE KIDS A BIT MORE THAN HE SHOULD. BUT WE MAKE A PRETTY GOOD TEAM.

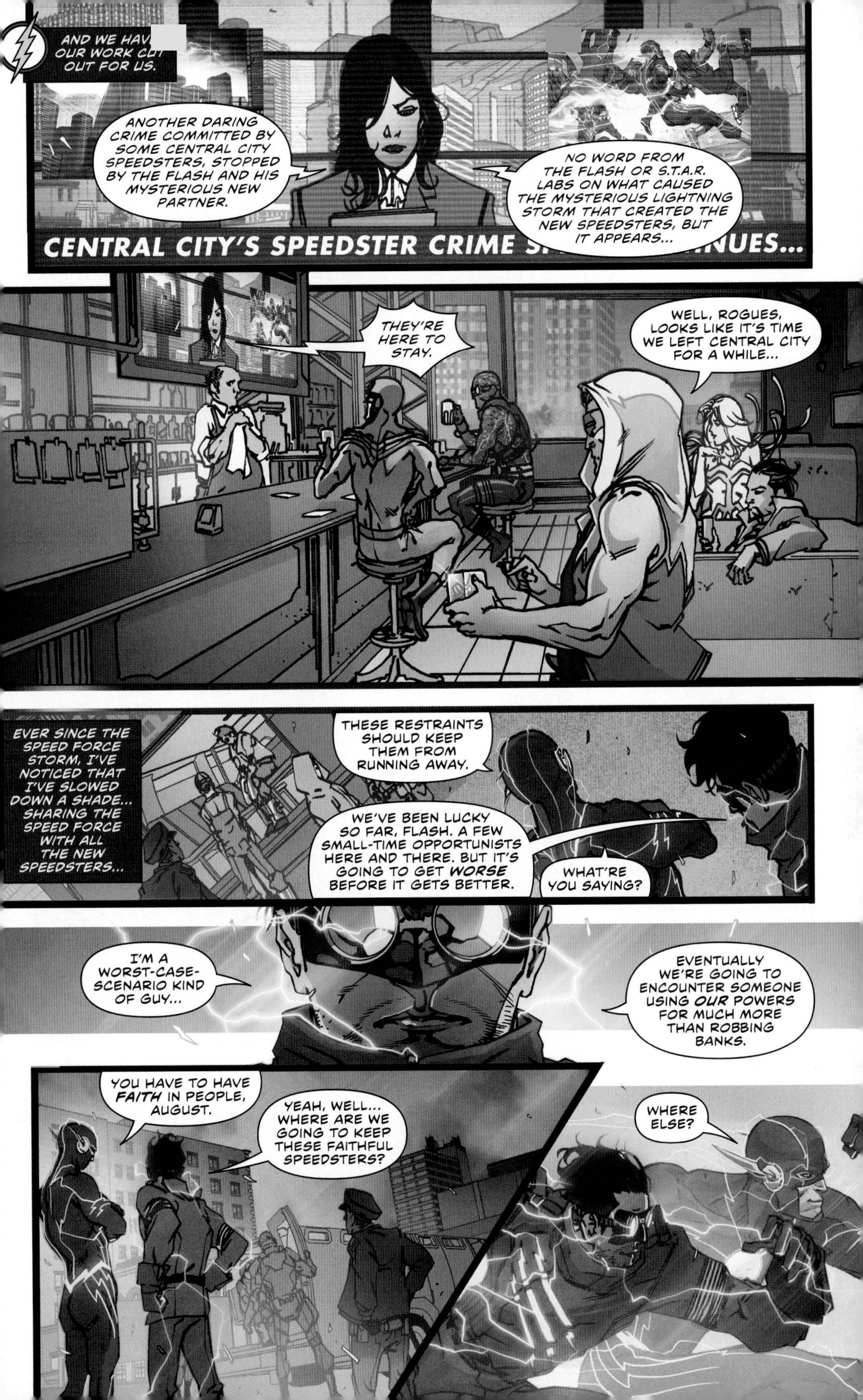
AND WE HAV OUR WORK CU OUT FOR US.
ANOTHER DARING CRIME COMMITTED BY SOME CENTRAL CITY SPEEDSTERS, STOPPED BY THE FLASH AND HIS MYSTERIOUS NEW PARTNER.
NO WORD FROM THE FLASH OR S.T.A.R. LABS ON WHAT CAUSED THE MYSTERIOUS LIGHTNING STORM THAT CREATED THE NEW SPEEDSTERS, BUT IT APPEARS...
CENTRAL CITY'S SPEEDSTER CRIME S INUES...
THEY'RE HERE TO STAY.
WELL, ROGUES, LOOKS LIKE IT'S TIME WE LEFT CENTRAL CITY FOR A WHILE...
EVER SINCE THE SPEED FORCE STORM, I'VE NOTICED THAT I'VE SLOWED DOWN A SHADE... SHARING THE SPEED FORCE WITH ALL THE NEW SPEEDSTERS...
THESE RESTRAINTS SHOULD KEEP THEM FROM RUNNING AWAY.
WE'VE BEEN LUCKY SO FAR, FLASH. A FEW SMALL-TIME OPPORTUNISTS HERE AND THERE. BUT IT'S GOING TO GET WORSE BEFORE IT GETS BETTER.
WHAT'RE YOU SAYING?
I'M A WORST-CASE-SCENARIO KIND OF GUY...
EVENTUALLY WE'RE GOING TO ENCOUNTER SOMEONE USING OUR POWERS FOR MUCH MORE THAN ROBBING BANKS.
YOU HAVE TO HAVE FAITH IN PEOPLE, AUGUST.
YEAH, WELL... WHERE ARE WE GOING TO KEEP THESE FAITHFUL SPEEDSTERS?
WHERE ELSE?

EVERY TIME I SAVE THE CITY THERE IS TALK OF CREATING A MUSEUM IN MY HONOR, BUT I ALWAYS SAY NO BECAUSE I DON'T DO THIS TO COLLECT TROPHIES.

BUT IRON HEIGHTS...IS A TESTAMENT TO MY LOSSES.

MY MOTHER'S KILLER USED TO CALL HIMSELF PROFESSOR ZOOM... BUT NOW EOBARD THAWNE CALLS THIS PRISON "HOME."

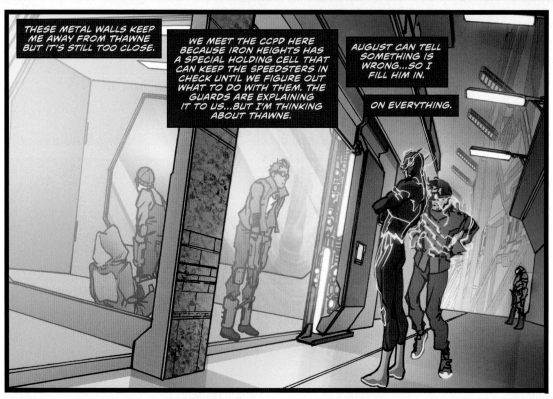

THESE METAL WALLS KEEP ME AWAY FROM THAWNE BUT IT'S STILL TOO CLOSE.

WE MEET THE CCPD HERE BECAUSE IRON HEIGHTS HAS A SPECIAL HOLDING CELL THAT CAN KEEP THE SPEEDSTERS IN CHECK UNTIL WE FIGURE OUT WHAT TO DO WITH THEM. THE GUARDS ARE EXPLAINING IT TO US...BUT I'M THINKING ABOUT THAWNE.

AUGUST CAN TELL SOMETHING IS WRONG...SO I FILL HIM IN.

ON EVERYTHING.

HOLY...THAT IS *CRAZY.* ZOOM DID ALL THAT JUST TO MAKE YOU SUFFER?

I KNEW THAT THAWNE MURDERED YOUR MOTHER, BUT I HAD NO IDEA...

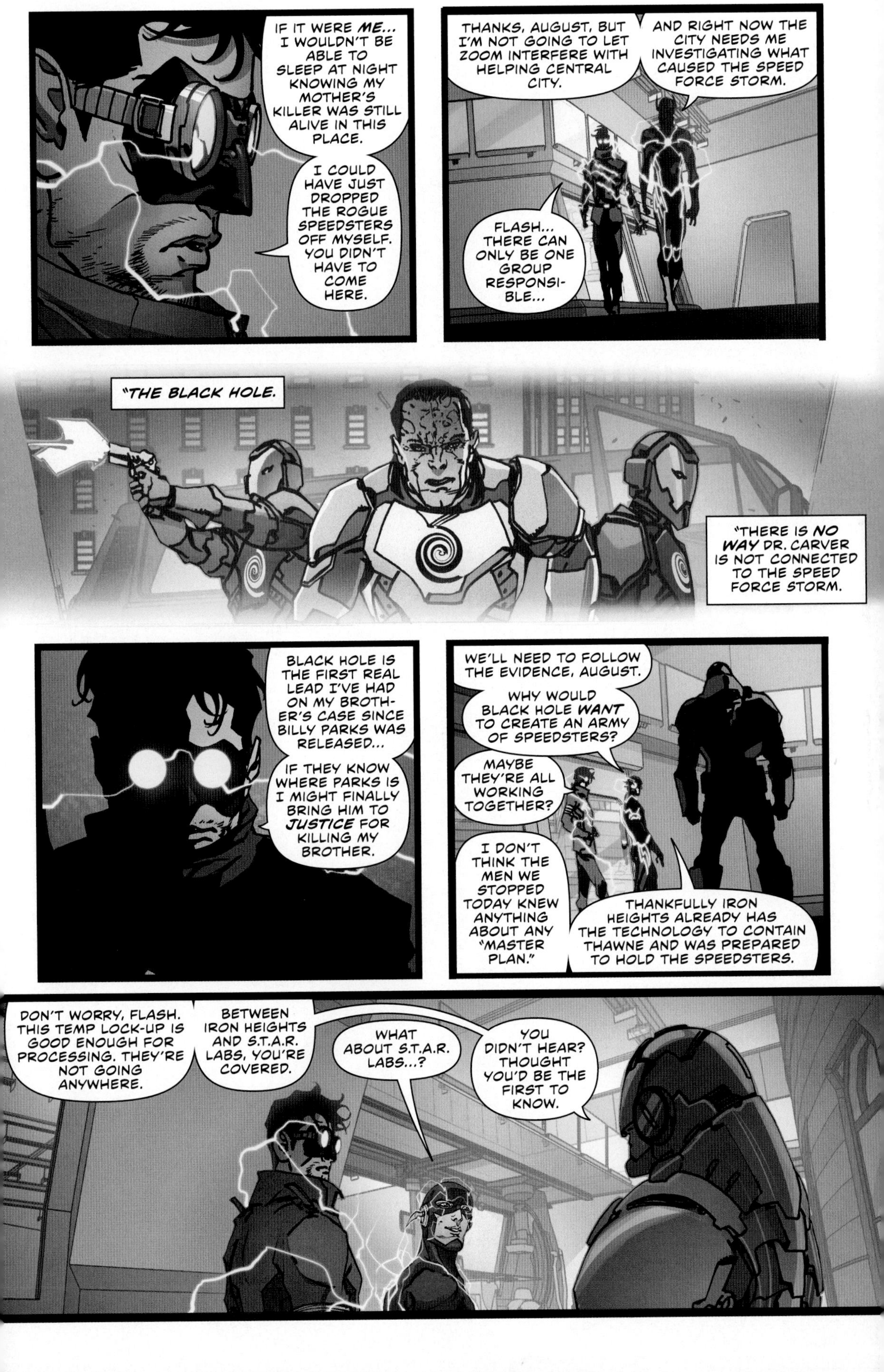
IF IT WERE *ME*... I WOULDN'T BE ABLE TO SLEEP AT NIGHT KNOWING MY MOTHER'S KILLER WAS STILL ALIVE IN THIS PLACE.
I COULD HAVE JUST DROPPED THE ROGUE SPEEDSTERS OFF MYSELF. YOU DIDN'T HAVE TO COME HERE.
THANKS, AUGUST, BUT I'M NOT GOING TO LET ZOOM INTERFERE WITH HELPING CENTRAL CITY.
AND RIGHT NOW THE CITY NEEDS ME INVESTIGATING WHAT CAUSED THE SPEED FORCE STORM.
FLASH... THERE CAN ONLY BE ONE GROUP RESPONSIBLE...
"*THE BLACK HOLE.*
"THERE IS *NO WAY* DR. CARVER IS NOT CONNECTED TO THE SPEED FORCE STORM.
BLACK HOLE IS THE FIRST REAL LEAD I'VE HAD ON MY BROTHER'S CASE SINCE BILLY PARKS WAS RELEASED...
IF THEY KNOW WHERE PARKS IS I MIGHT FINALLY BRING HIM TO *JUSTICE* FOR KILLING MY BROTHER.
WE'LL NEED TO FOLLOW THE EVIDENCE, AUGUST.
WHY WOULD BLACK HOLE *WANT* TO CREATE AN ARMY OF SPEEDSTERS?
MAYBE THEY'RE ALL WORKING TOGETHER?
I DON'T THINK THE MEN WE STOPPED TODAY KNEW ANYTHING ABOUT ANY "MASTER PLAN."
THANKFULLY IRON HEIGHTS ALREADY HAS THE TECHNOLOGY TO CONTAIN THAWNE AND WAS PREPARED TO HOLD THE SPEEDSTERS.
DON'T WORRY, FLASH. THIS TEMP LOCK-UP IS GOOD ENOUGH FOR PROCESSING. THEY'RE NOT GOING ANYWHERE.
BETWEEN IRON HEIGHTS AND S.T.A.R. LABS, YOU'RE COVERED.
WHAT ABOUT S.T.A.R. LABS...?
YOU DIDN'T HEAR? THOUGHT YOU'D BE THE FIRST TO KNOW.

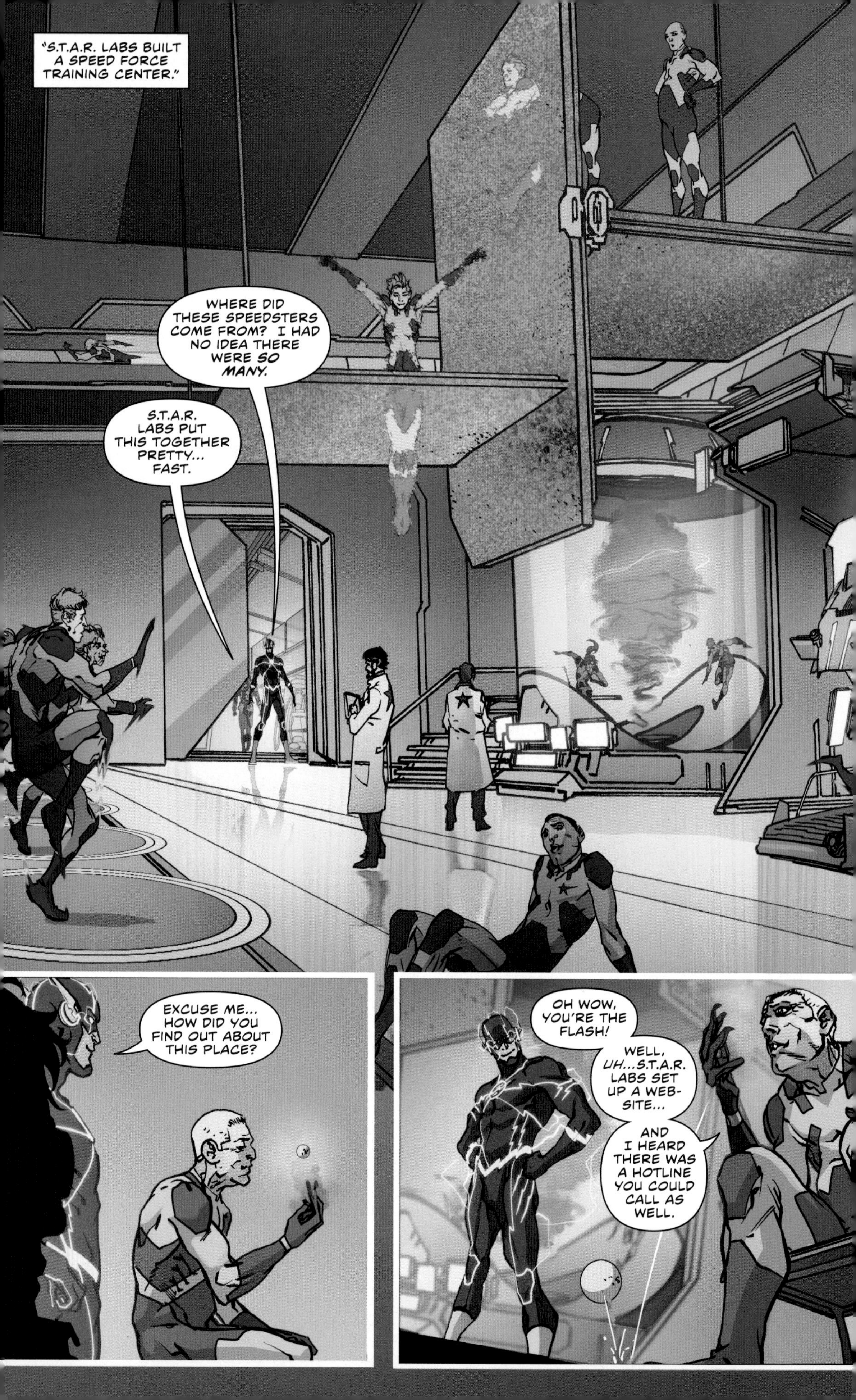
"S.T.A.R. LABS BUILT A SPEED FORCE TRAINING CENTER."
WHERE DID THESE SPEEDSTERS COME FROM? I HAD NO IDEA THERE WERE *SO MANY.*
S.T.A.R. LABS PUT THIS TOGETHER PRETTY... FAST.
EXCUSE ME... HOW DID YOU FIND OUT ABOUT THIS PLACE?
OH WOW, YOU'RE THE FLASH!
WELL, *UH*...S.T.A.R. LABS SET UP A WEB-SITE...
AND I HEARD THERE WAS A HOTLINE YOU COULD CALL AS WELL.

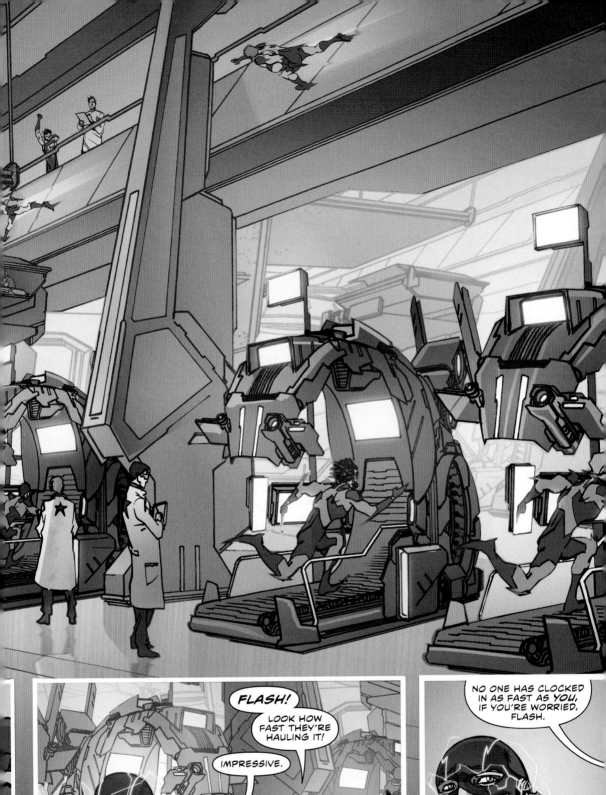

FLASH! LOOK HOW FAST THEY'RE HAULING IT!

IMPRESSIVE.

NO ONE HAS CLOCKED IN AS FAST AS *YOU*, IF YOU'RE WORRIED, FLASH.

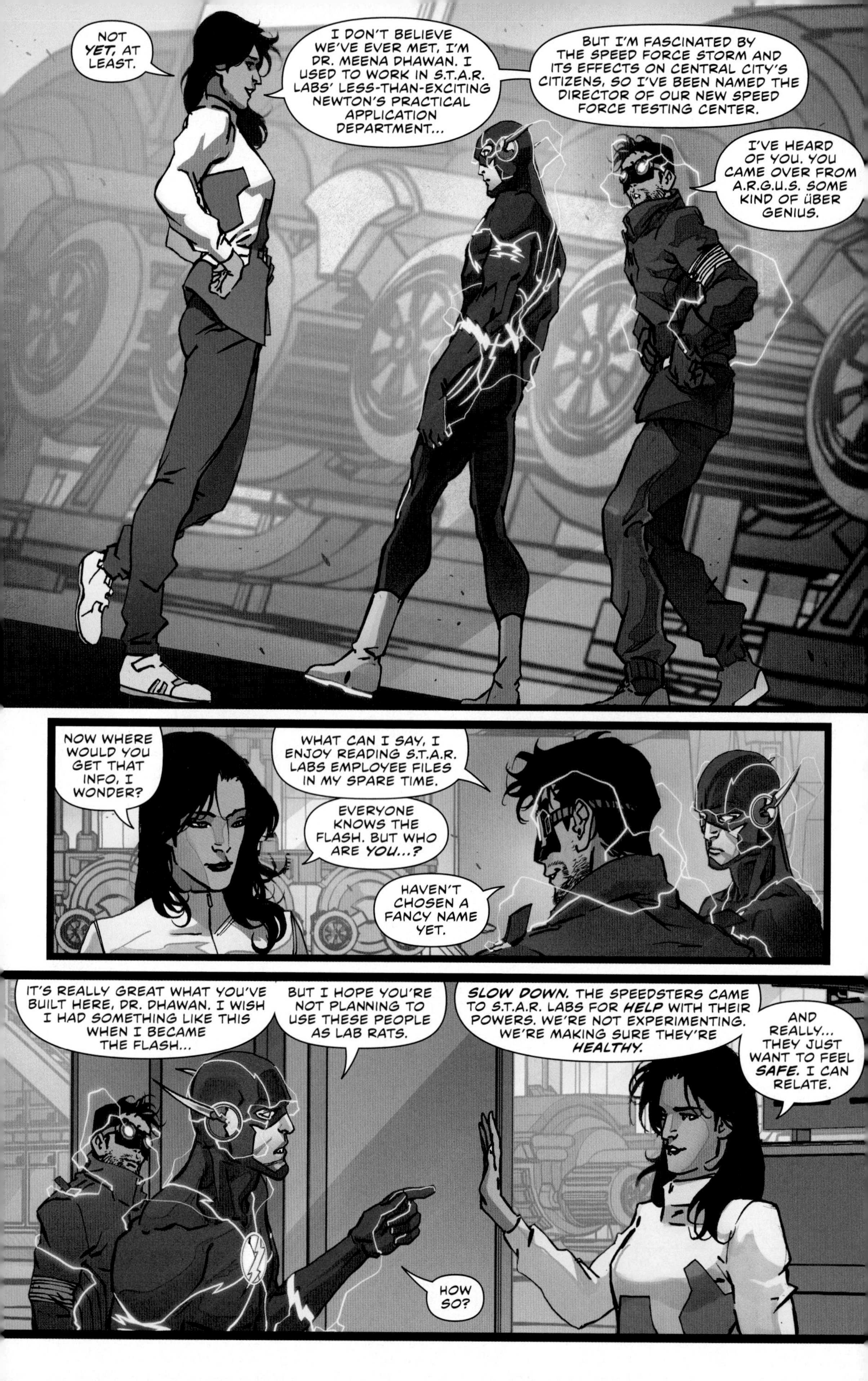
NOT YET, AT LEAST.
I DON'T BELIEVE WE'VE EVER MET, I'M DR. MEENA DHAWAN. I USED TO WORK IN S.T.A.R. LABS' LESS-THAN-EXCITING NEWTON'S PRACTICAL APPLICATION DEPARTMENT...
BUT I'M FASCINATED BY THE SPEED FORCE STORM AND ITS EFFECTS ON CENTRAL CITY'S CITIZENS, SO I'VE BEEN NAMED THE DIRECTOR OF OUR NEW SPEED FORCE TESTING CENTER.
I'VE HEARD OF YOU. YOU CAME OVER FROM A.R.G.U.S. SOME KIND OF ÜBER GENIUS.
NOW WHERE WOULD YOU GET THAT INFO, I WONDER?
WHAT CAN I SAY, I ENJOY READING S.T.A.R. LABS EMPLOYEE FILES IN MY SPARE TIME.
EVERYONE KNOWS THE FLASH. BUT WHO ARE YOU...?
HAVEN'T CHOSEN A FANCY NAME YET.
IT'S REALLY GREAT WHAT YOU'VE BUILT HERE, DR. DHAWAN. I WISH I HAD SOMETHING LIKE THIS WHEN I BECAME THE FLASH...
BUT I HOPE YOU'RE NOT PLANNING TO USE THESE PEOPLE AS LAB RATS.
SLOW DOWN. THE SPEEDSTERS CAME TO S.T.A.R. LABS FOR HELP WITH THEIR POWERS. WE'RE NOT EXPERIMENTING. WE'RE MAKING SURE THEY'RE HEALTHY.
AND REALLY... THEY JUST WANT TO FEEL SAFE. I CAN RELATE.
HOW SO?

BECAUSE...

...I JUST RAN TO KEYSTONE CITY AND BACK.

FFFtt

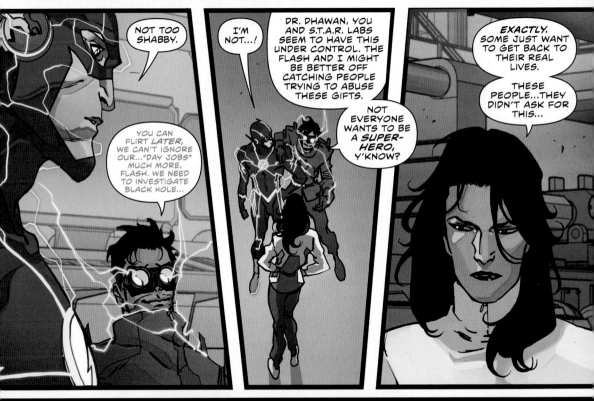

NOT TOO SHABBY.

I'M NOT...!

DR. DHAWAN, YOU AND S.T.A.R. LABS SEEM TO HAVE THIS UNDER CONTROL. THE FLASH AND I MIGHT BE BETTER OFF CATCHING PEOPLE TRYING TO ABUSE THESE GIFTS.

NOT EVERYONE WANTS TO BE A SUPER-HERO, Y'KNOW?

EXACTLY. SOME JUST WANT TO GET BACK TO THEIR REAL LIVES.

THESE PEOPLE...THEY DIDN'T ASK FOR THIS...

YOU CAN FLIRT LATER, WE CAN'T IGNORE OUR..."DAY JOBS" MUCH MORE, FLASH. WE NEED TO INVESTIGATE BLACK HOLE...

LET ME SHOW YOU SOMETHING.

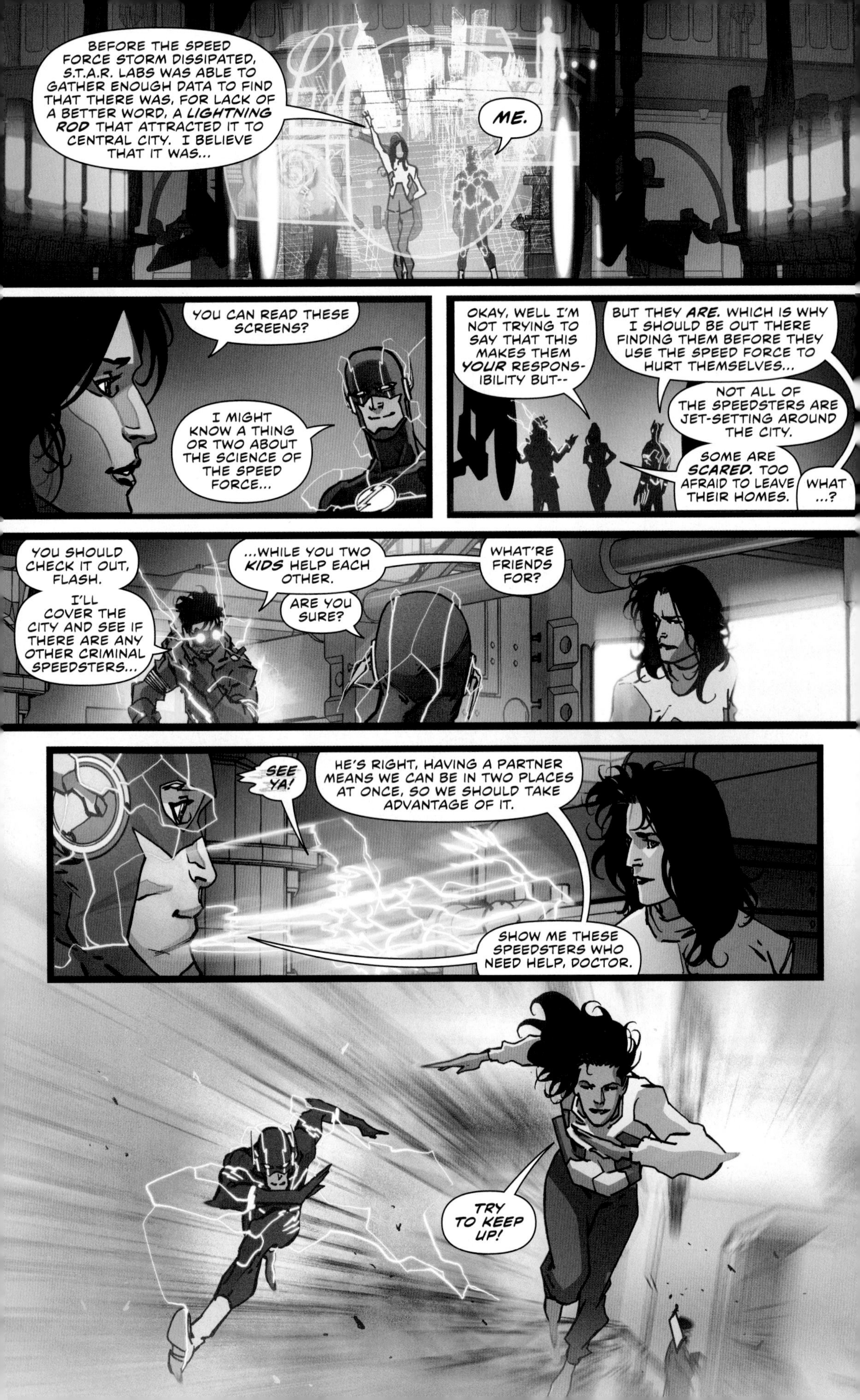
BEFORE THE SPEED FORCE STORM DISSIPATED, S.T.A.R. LABS WAS ABLE TO GATHER ENOUGH DATA TO FIND THAT THERE WAS, FOR LACK OF A BETTER WORD, A LIGHTNING ROD THAT ATTRACTED IT TO CENTRAL CITY. I BELIEVE THAT IT WAS...
ME.
YOU CAN READ THESE SCREENS?
I MIGHT KNOW A THING OR TWO ABOUT THE SCIENCE OF THE SPEED FORCE...
OKAY, WELL I'M NOT TRYING TO SAY THAT THIS MAKES THEM YOUR RESPONSIBILITY BUT--
BUT THEY ARE. WHICH IS WHY I SHOULD BE OUT THERE FINDING THEM BEFORE THEY USE THE SPEED FORCE TO HURT THEMSELVES...
NOT ALL OF THE SPEEDSTERS ARE JET-SETTING AROUND THE CITY.
SOME ARE SCARED. TOO AFRAID TO LEAVE THEIR HOMES.
WHAT ...?
YOU SHOULD CHECK IT OUT, FLASH.
I'LL COVER THE CITY AND SEE IF THERE ARE ANY OTHER CRIMINAL SPEEDSTERS...
...WHILE YOU TWO KIDS HELP EACH OTHER.
ARE YOU SURE?
WHAT'RE FRIENDS FOR?
SEE YA!
HE'S RIGHT, HAVING A PARTNER MEANS WE CAN BE IN TWO PLACES AT ONCE, SO WE SHOULD TAKE ADVANTAGE OF IT.
SHOW ME THESE SPEEDSTERS WHO NEED HELP, DOCTOR.
TRY TO KEEP UP!

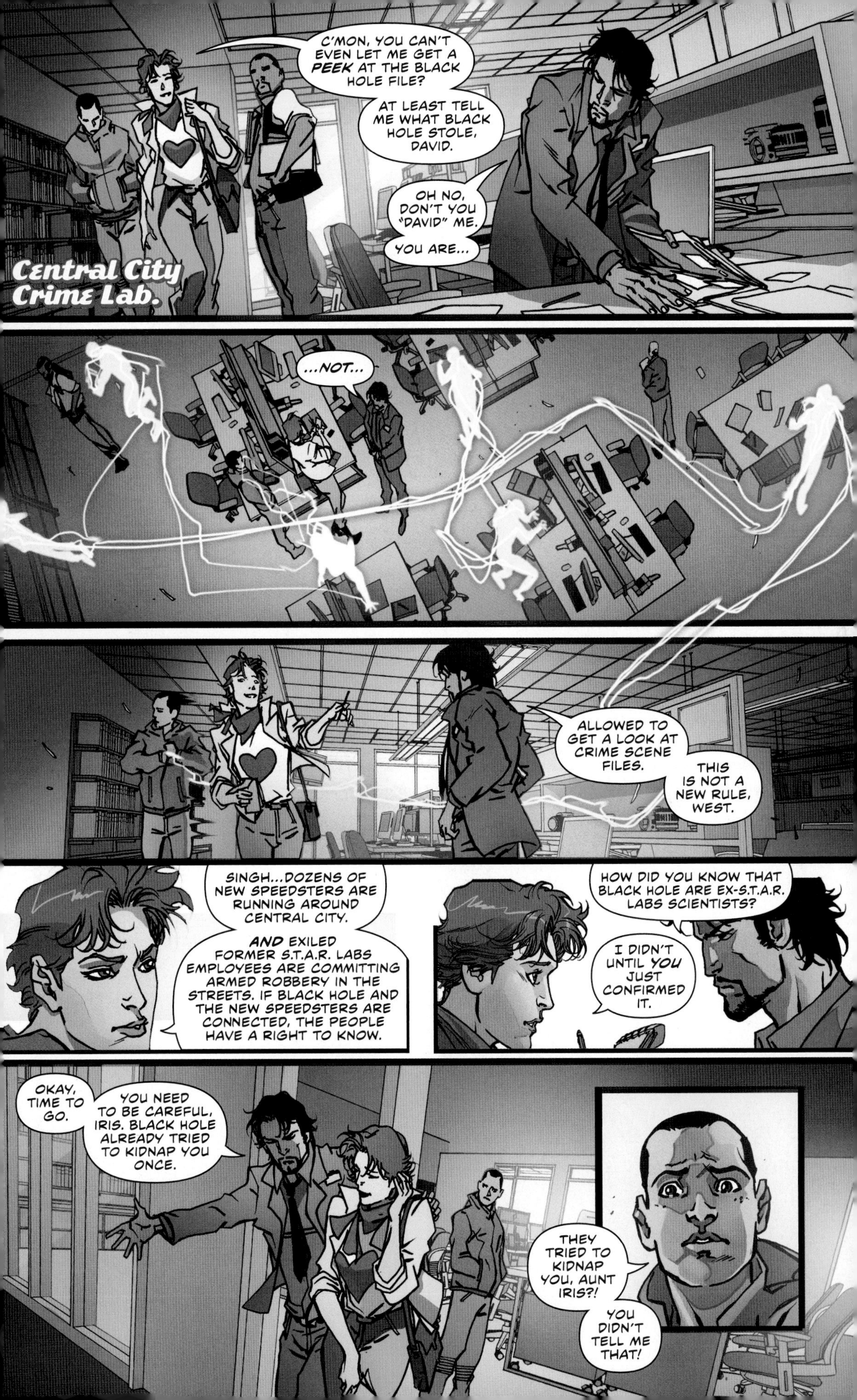
Central City Crime Lab.
C'MON, YOU CAN'T EVEN LET ME GET A PEEK AT THE BLACK HOLE FILE?
AT LEAST TELL ME WHAT BLACK HOLE STOLE, DAVID.
OH NO, DON'T YOU "DAVID" ME.
YOU ARE...
...NOT...
ALLOWED TO GET A LOOK AT CRIME SCENE FILES.
THIS IS NOT A NEW RULE, WEST.
SINGH...DOZENS OF NEW SPEEDSTERS ARE RUNNING AROUND CENTRAL CITY.
AND EXILED FORMER S.T.A.R. LABS EMPLOYEES ARE COMMITTING ARMED ROBBERY IN THE STREETS. IF BLACK HOLE AND THE NEW SPEEDSTERS ARE CONNECTED, THE PEOPLE HAVE A RIGHT TO KNOW.
HOW DID YOU KNOW THAT BLACK HOLE ARE EX-S.T.A.R. LABS SCIENTISTS?
I DIDN'T UNTIL YOU JUST CONFIRMED IT.
OKAY, TIME TO GO.
YOU NEED TO BE CAREFUL, IRIS. BLACK HOLE ALREADY TRIED TO KIDNAP YOU ONCE.
THEY TRIED TO KIDNAP YOU, AUNT IRIS?!
YOU DIDN'T TELL ME THAT!

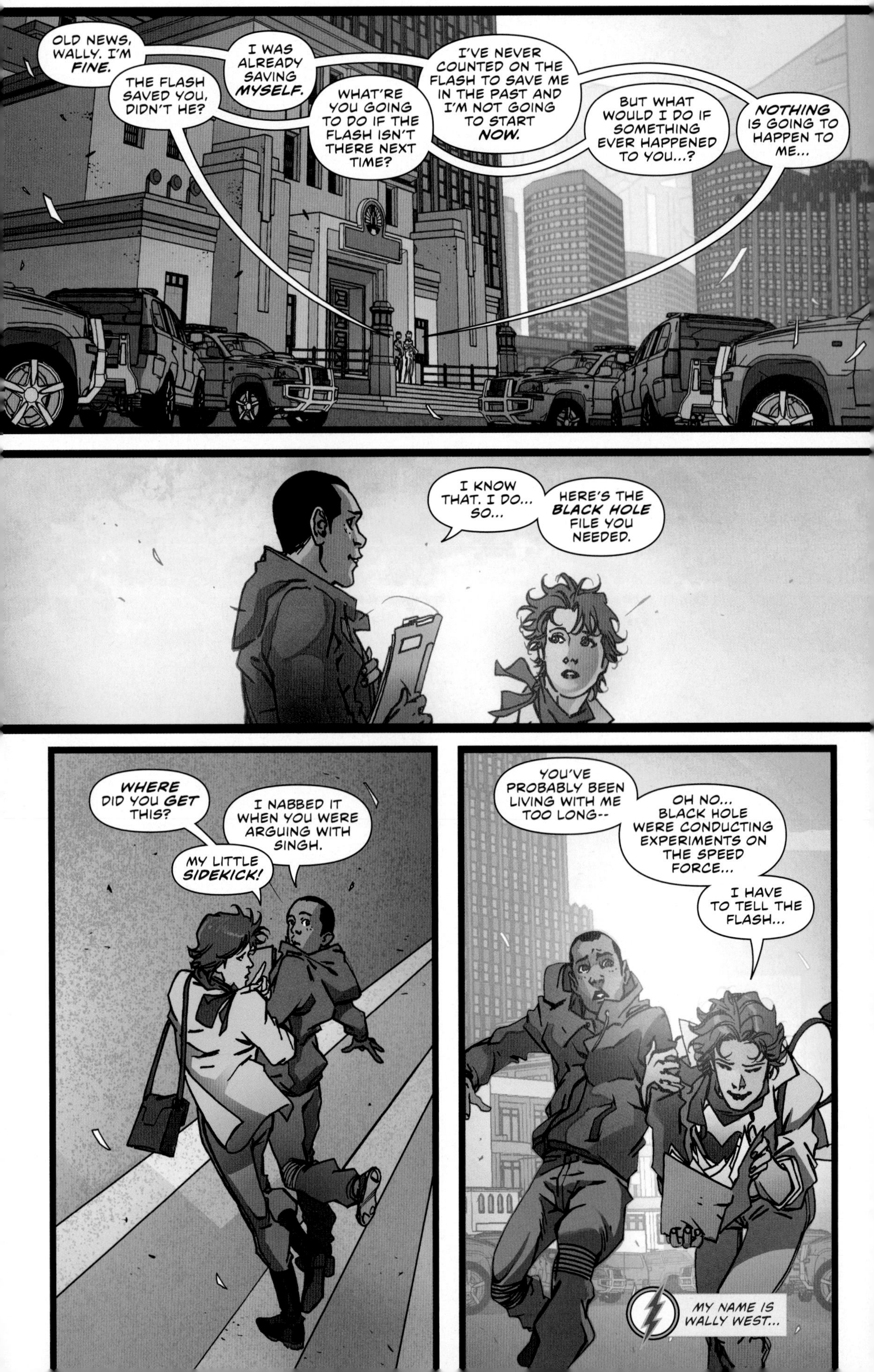
OLD NEWS, WALLY. I'M FINE.
THE FLASH SAVED YOU, DIDN'T HE?
I WAS ALREADY SAVING MYSELF.
WHAT'RE YOU GOING TO DO IF THE FLASH ISN'T THERE NEXT TIME?
I'VE NEVER COUNTED ON THE FLASH TO SAVE ME IN THE PAST AND I'M NOT GOING TO START NOW.
BUT WHAT WOULD I DO IF SOMETHING EVER HAPPENED TO YOU...?
NOTHING IS GOING TO HAPPEN TO ME...
I KNOW THAT. I DO... SO...
HERE'S THE BLACK HOLE FILE YOU NEEDED.
WHERE DID YOU GET THIS?
I NABBED IT WHEN YOU WERE ARGUING WITH SINGH.
MY LITTLE SIDEKICK!
YOU'VE PROBABLY BEEN LIVING WITH ME TOO LONG--
OH NO... BLACK HOLE WERE CONDUCTING EXPERIMENTS ON THE SPEED FORCE...
I HAVE TO TELL THE FLASH...
MY NAME IS WALLY WEST...

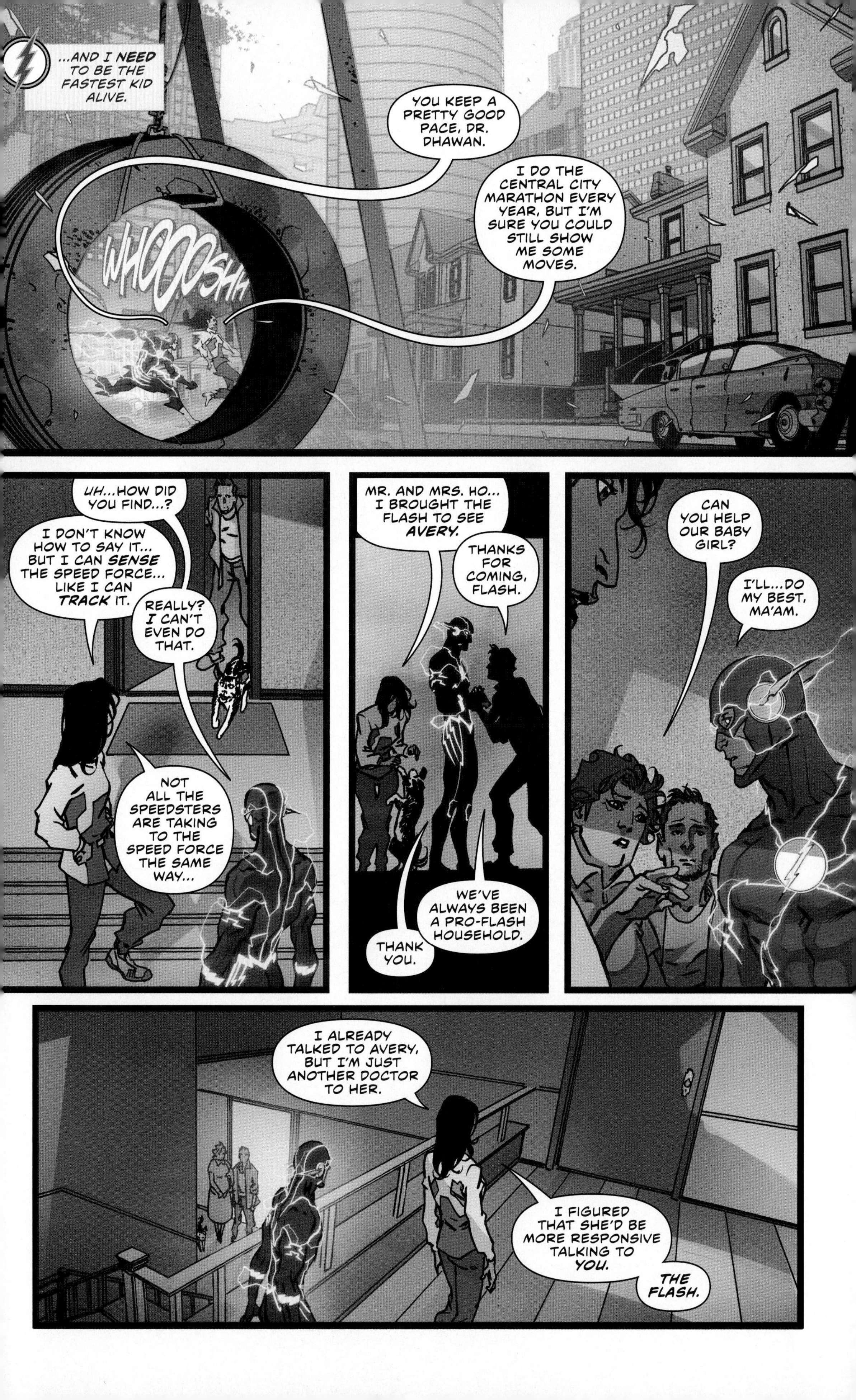
...AND I NEED TO BE THE FASTEST KID ALIVE.
WHOOOSHH
YOU KEEP A PRETTY GOOD PACE, DR. DHAWAN.
I DO THE CENTRAL CITY MARATHON EVERY YEAR, BUT I'M SURE YOU COULD STILL SHOW ME SOME MOVES.
UH...HOW DID YOU FIND...?
I DON'T KNOW HOW TO SAY IT... BUT I CAN SENSE THE SPEED FORCE... LIKE I CAN TRACK IT.
REALLY? I CAN'T EVEN DO THAT.
NOT ALL THE SPEEDSTERS ARE TAKING TO THE SPEED FORCE THE SAME WAY...
MR. AND MRS. HO... I BROUGHT THE FLASH TO SEE AVERY.
THANKS FOR COMING, FLASH.
WE'VE ALWAYS BEEN A PRO-FLASH HOUSEHOLD.
THANK YOU.
CAN YOU HELP OUR BABY GIRL?
I'LL...DO MY BEST, MA'AM.
I ALREADY TALKED TO AVERY, BUT I'M JUST ANOTHER DOCTOR TO HER.
I FIGURED THAT SHE'D BE MORE RESPONSIVE TALKING TO YOU.
THE FLASH.

WWWWRRRRRR

WOW, THE FLASH IS IN MY BEDROOM. OH MY GOD OH MY GOD OH MY GOD. I HOPE I LIVE LONG ENOUGH TO POST THIS ON INSTRAGRAM.

I TRIED TO GET HER TO TAKE SOME DEEP BREATHS, BUT--

IT'S NOT HER BREATHING THAT'S THE PROBLEM, DOCTOR.

AVERY...DR. DHAWAN TELLS ME THAT YOU CAN'T SLOW DOWN?

OH MY GOD, FLASH. I'M SO *SCARED*. WHAT IF I CAN'T STOP MOVING AND I'M STUCK LIKE THIS FOR THE REST OF MY LIFE AND THEN I'LL LOSE ALL MY *FRIENDS* BECAUSE THEY'LL THINK I'M DIFFERENT AND WEIRD AND NOT ABLE TO HANG OUT ANY-MORE I DON'T THINK I COULD HANDLE THAT KIND OF *REJECTION* AND--

I HEAR YOU, AVERY. I'VE BEEN THERE BEFORE. IT'S REALLY EASY TO SPIRAL WHEN YOUR MIND IS RACING LIKE THIS.

BUT I'M GOING TO SHOW YOU A SIMPLE *TRICK* TO GROUND YOURSELF, OKAY?

I WANT YOU TO TRY TO MAKE A *FIST*. CAN YOU DO THAT?

I THINK I CAN.

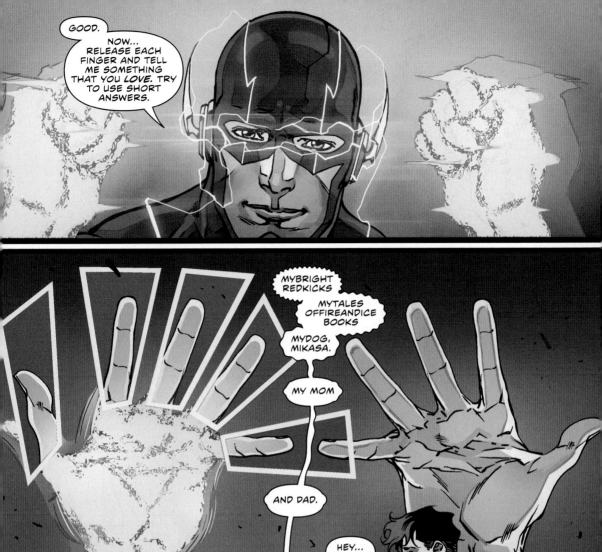

GOOD. NOW... RELEASE EACH FINGER AND TELL ME SOMETHING THAT YOU *LOVE*. TRY TO USE SHORT ANSWERS.

MY BRIGHT RED KICKS

MY TALES OF FIRE AND DICE BOOKS

MY DOG, MIKASA.

MY MOM

AND DAD.

HEY... COOL!

THANKS!

IT WAS ALL YOU.

AN *EMOTIONAL* ANSWER FOR A SCIENCE PROBLEM?

MY HEAD HAS GOTTEN A BIT LOST IN THE SPEED FORCE BEFORE...I FIND REMEMBERING THINGS YOU *LOVE* HELPS YOU STAY GROUNDED.

I'LL HAVE TO REMEMBER THAT.

AVERY...I KNOW YOU'RE AFRAID THAT PEOPLE WILL THINK YOU'RE DIFFERENT BECAUSE OF YOUR SPEED, BUT DIFFERENT CAN BE *AMAZING* AND S.T.A.R. LABS WANTS TO HELP YOU...

YOU DON'T *HAVE* TO COME WITH US. IT'S *YOUR* CHOICE.

BUT ISN'T S.T.A.R. LABS JUST A BUNCH OF *DOCTORS*? NOT SURE IF THAT'S SOMETHING I'M INTO.

BUT IF YOU *DO* DECIDE TO COME WITH US...

WE CAN RUN THERE...

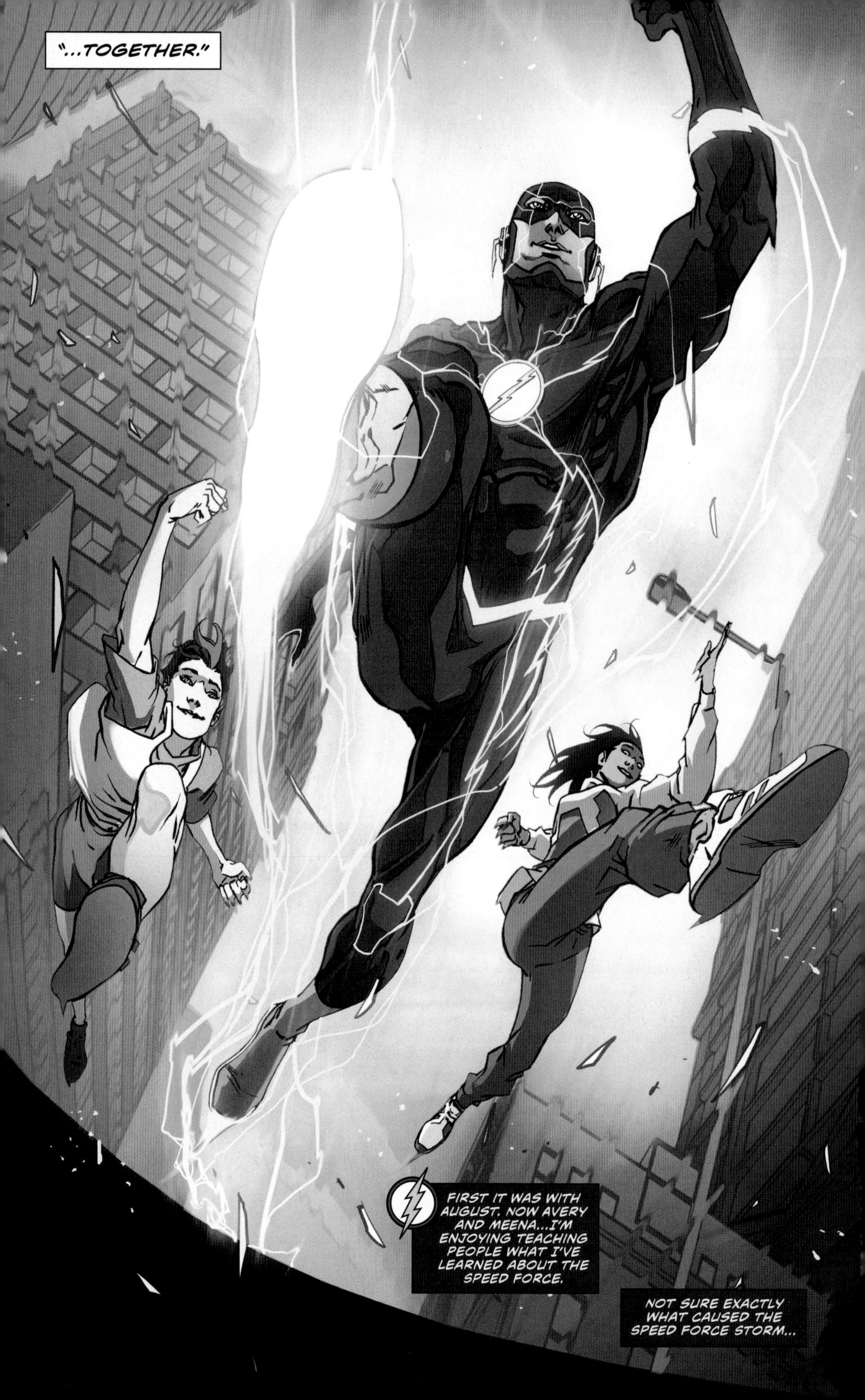
"...TOGETHER."
FIRST IT WAS WITH AUGUST. NOW AVERY AND MEENA...I'M ENJOYING TEACHING PEOPLE WHAT I'VE LEARNED ABOUT THE SPEED FORCE.
NOT SURE EXACTLY WHAT CAUSED THE SPEED FORCE STORM...

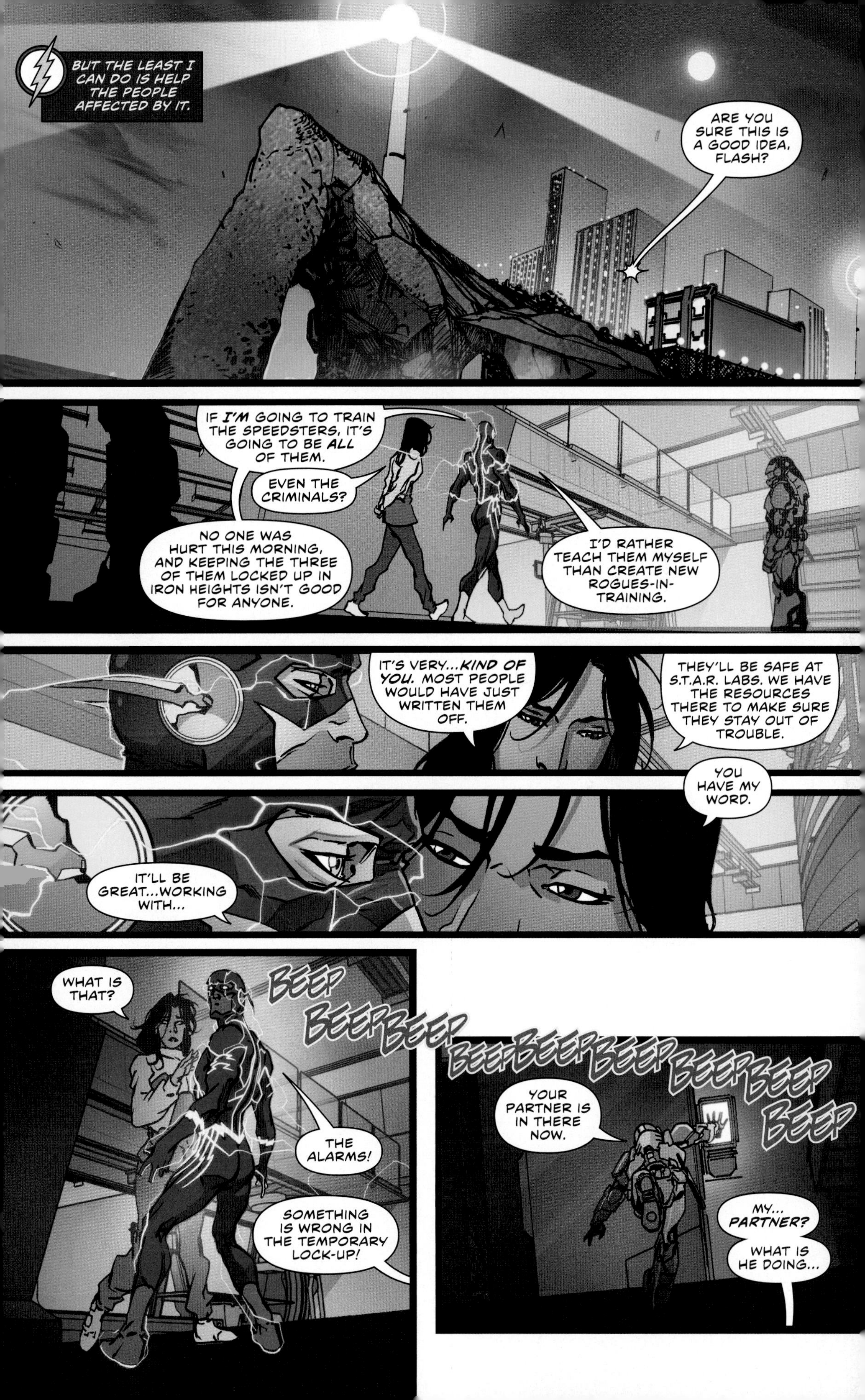
BUT THE LEAST I CAN DO IS HELP THE PEOPLE AFFECTED BY IT.
ARE YOU SURE THIS IS A GOOD IDEA, FLASH?
IF I'M GOING TO TRAIN THE SPEEDSTERS, IT'S GOING TO BE ALL OF THEM.
EVEN THE CRIMINALS?
NO ONE WAS HURT THIS MORNING, AND KEEPING THE THREE OF THEM LOCKED UP IN IRON HEIGHTS ISN'T GOOD FOR ANYONE.
I'D RATHER TEACH THEM MYSELF THAN CREATE NEW ROGUES-IN-TRAINING.
IT'S VERY...KIND OF YOU. MOST PEOPLE WOULD HAVE JUST WRITTEN THEM OFF.
THEY'LL BE SAFE AT S.T.A.R. LABS. WE HAVE THE RESOURCES THERE TO MAKE SURE THEY STAY OUT OF TROUBLE.
YOU HAVE MY WORD.
IT'LL BE GREAT...WORKING WITH...
WHAT IS THAT?
BEEP BEEP BEEP BEEP BEEP BEEP BEEP BEEP BEEP
THE ALARMS!
SOMETHING IS WRONG IN THE TEMPORARY LOCK-UP!
YOUR PARTNER IS IN THERE NOW.
MY... PARTNER?
WHAT IS HE DOING...

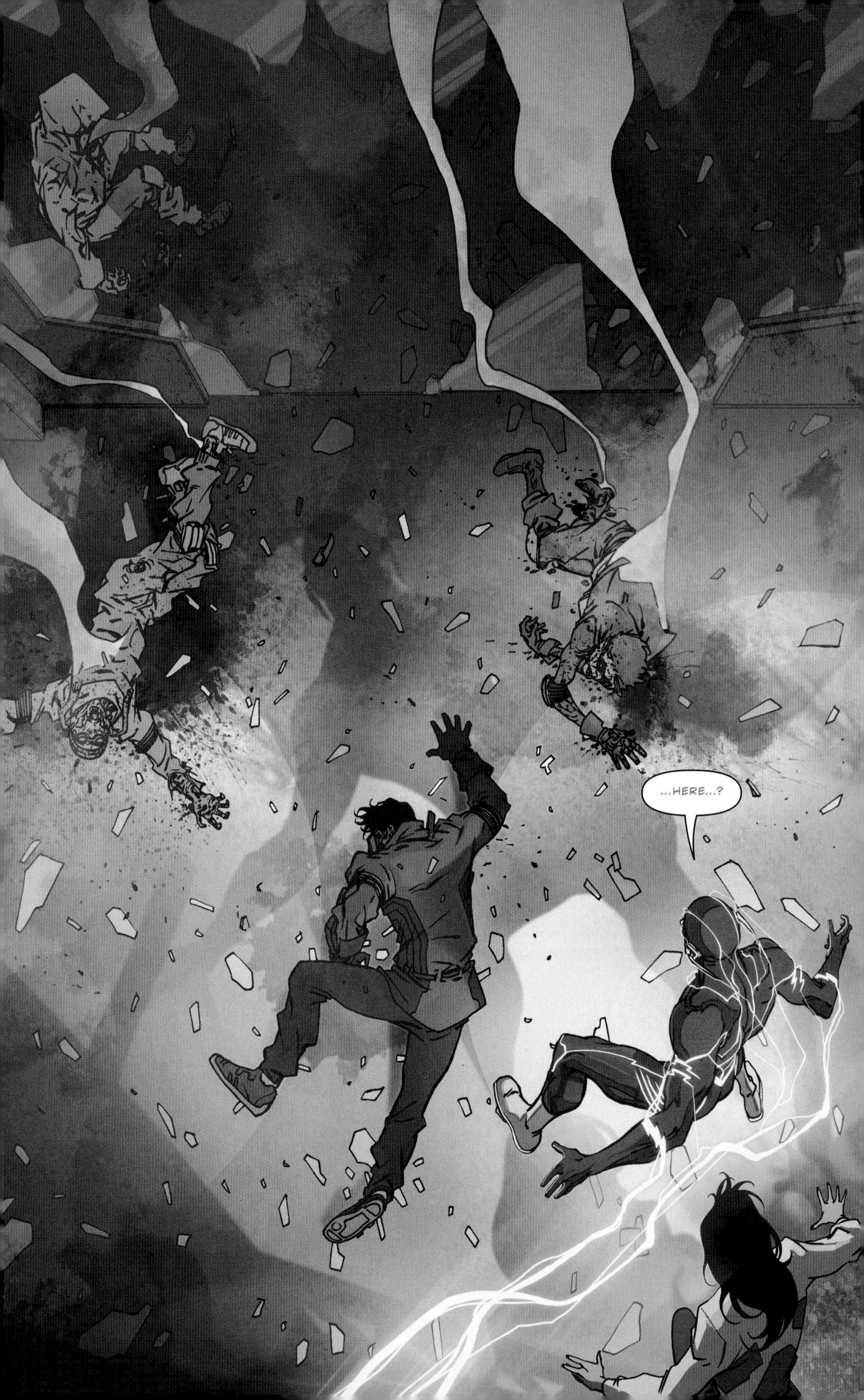
...HERE...?

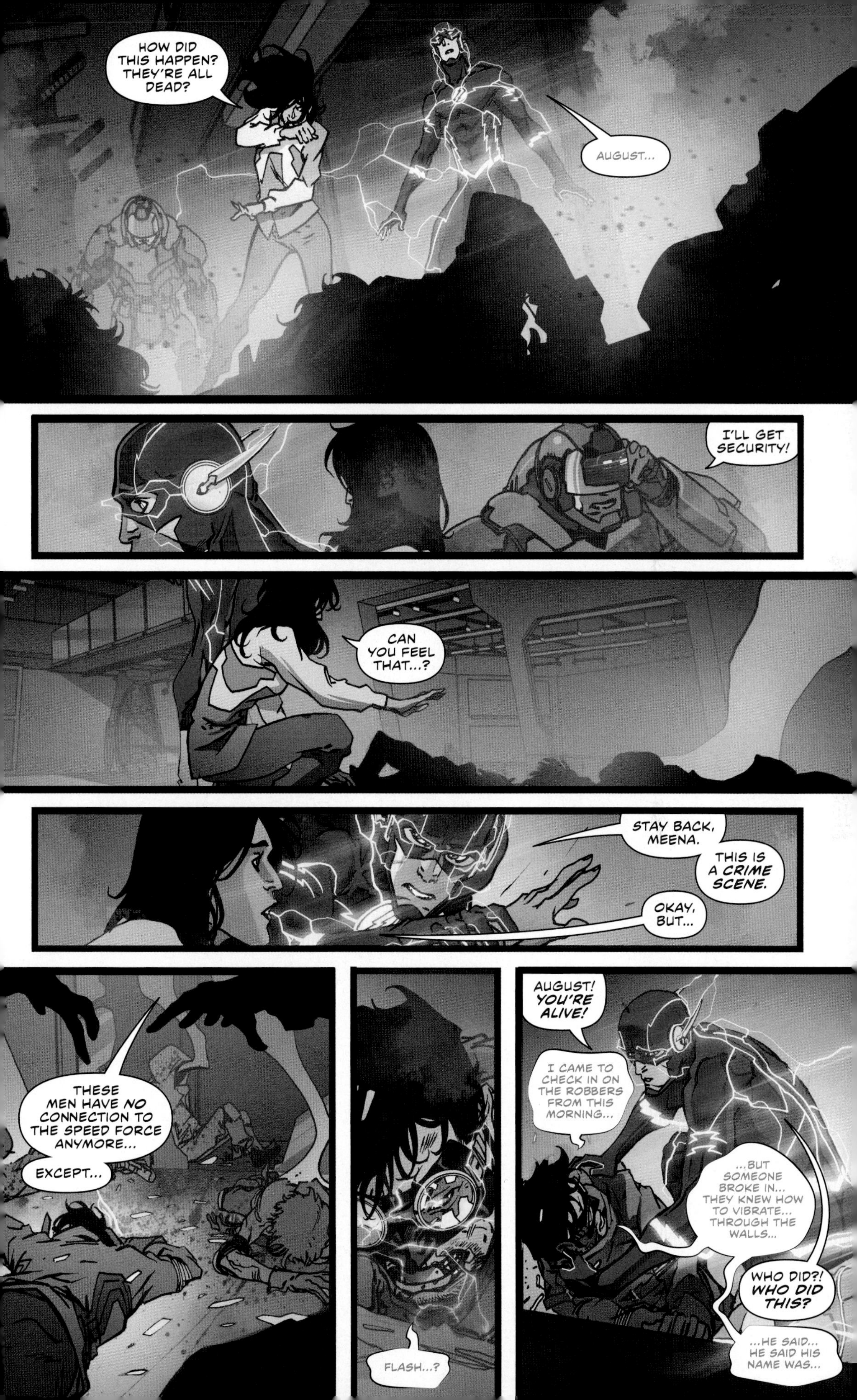
HOW DID THIS HAPPEN? THEY'RE ALL DEAD?
AUGUST...
I'LL GET SECURITY!
CAN YOU FEEL THAT...?
STAY BACK, MEENA.
THIS IS A CRIME SCENE.
OKAY, BUT...
THESE MEN HAVE NO CONNECTION TO THE SPEED FORCE ANYMORE...
EXCEPT...
FLASH...?
AUGUST! YOU'RE ALIVE!
I CAME TO CHECK IN ON THE ROBBERS FROM THIS MORNING...
...BUT SOMEONE BROKE IN... THEY KNEW HOW TO VIBRATE... THROUGH THE WALLS...
WHO DID?! WHO DID THIS?
...HE SAID... HE SAID HIS NAME WAS...

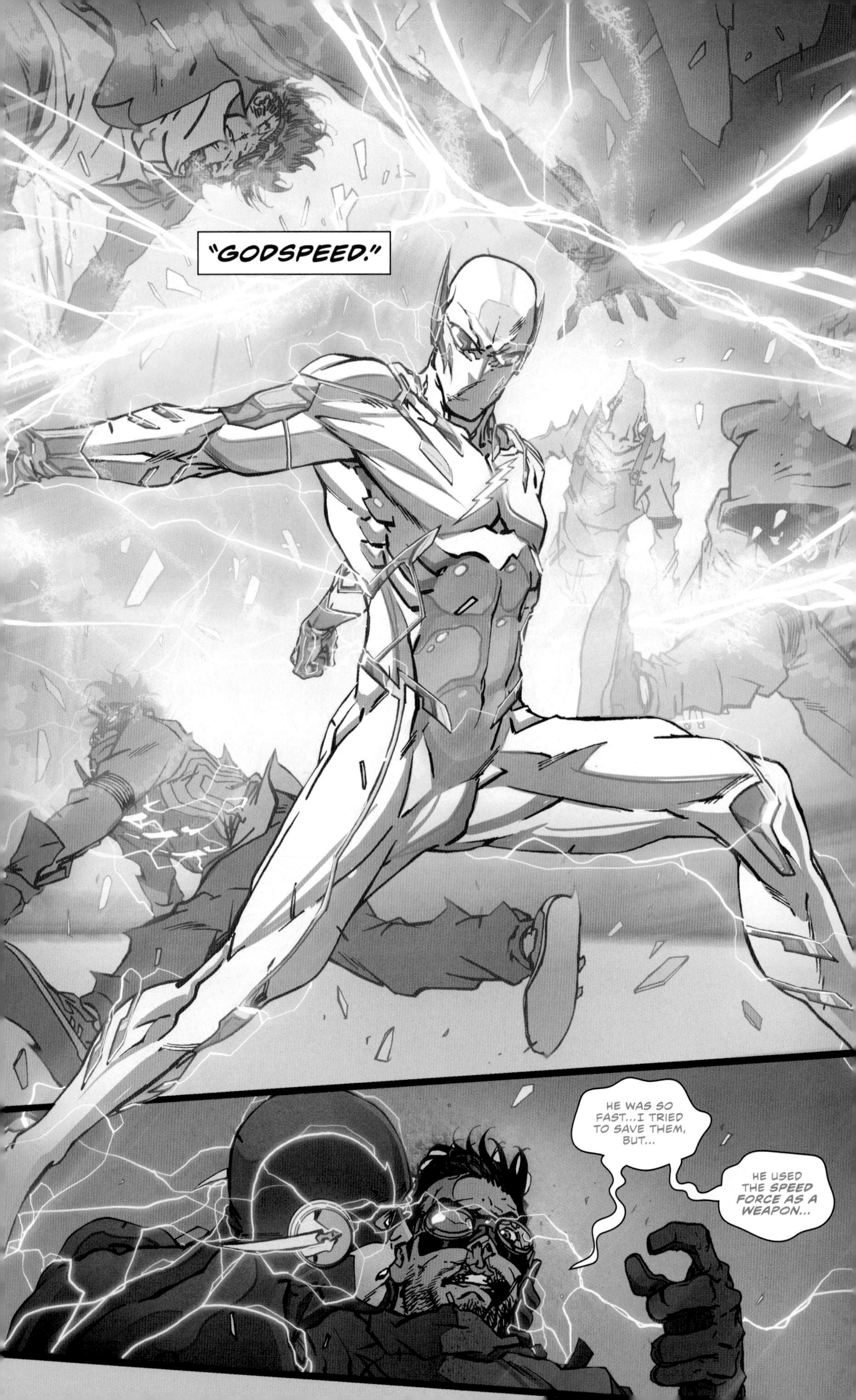
"GODSPEED."
HE WAS SO FAST...I TRIED TO SAVE THEM, BUT...
HE USED THE *SPEED FORCE* AS A WEAPON...

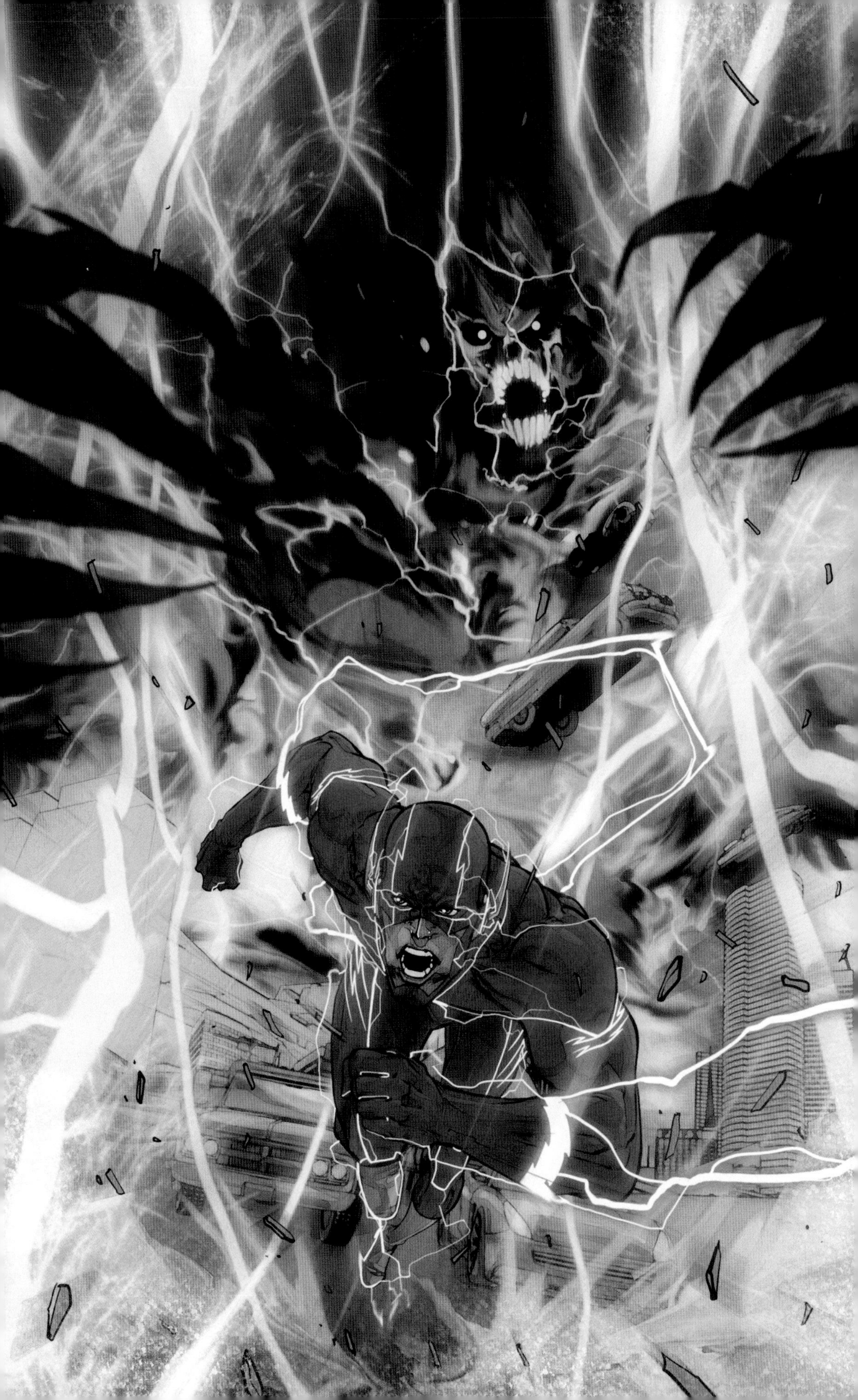

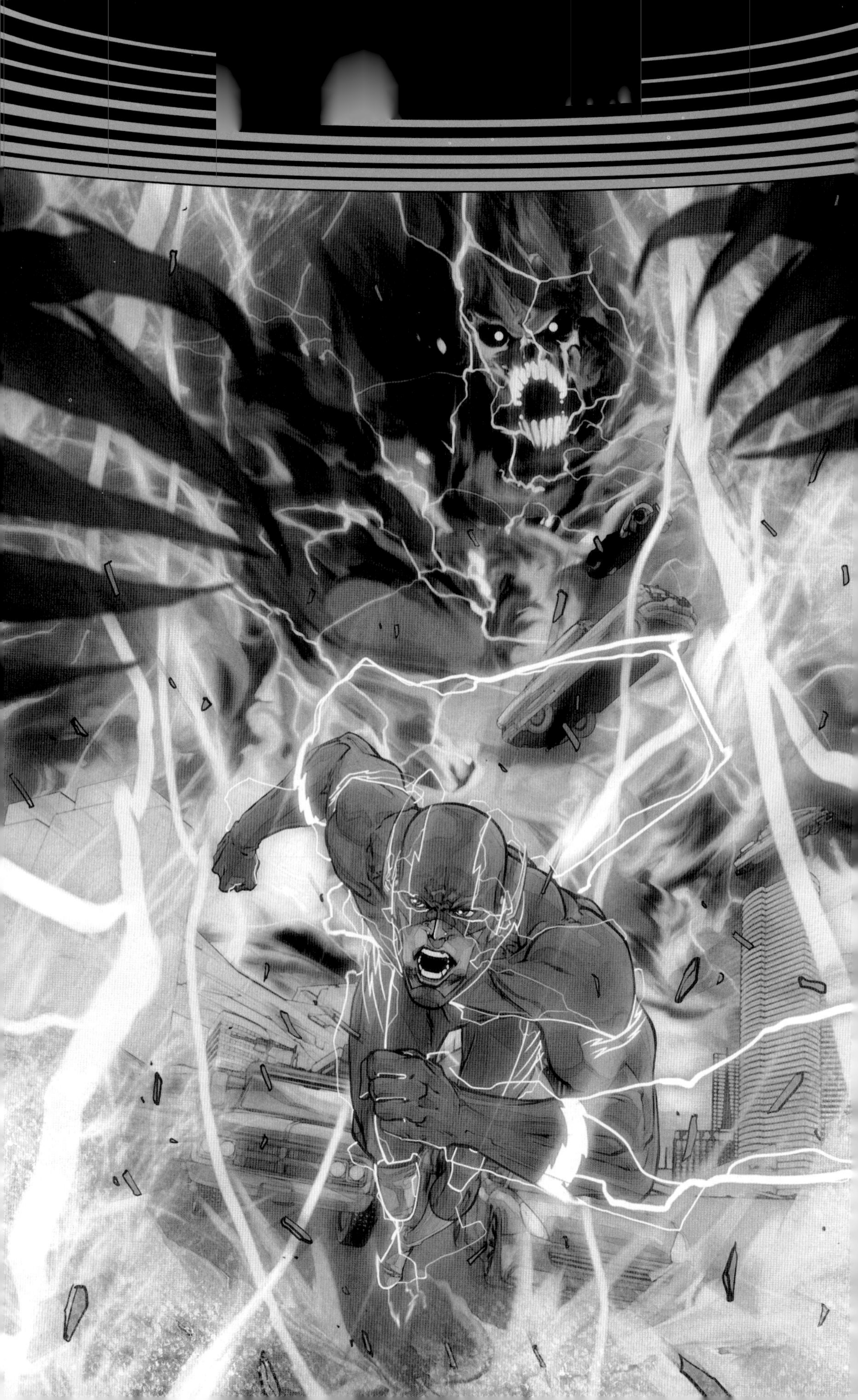

EVER SINCE THE NIGHT I WAS STRUCK BY LIGHTNING, I'VE BEEN LIVING TWO LIVES.

BARRY ALLEN, FORENSIC SCIENTIST WORKING FOR THE CENTRAL CITY CRIME LAB.

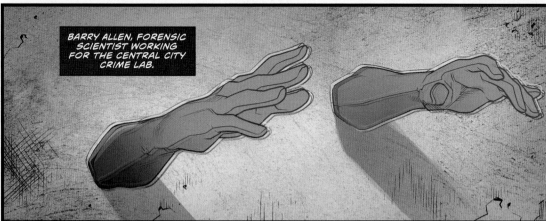

AND BARRY ALLEN, THE FLASH. THE FASTEST MAN ALIVE.

BUT NOW THERE IS ALSO...

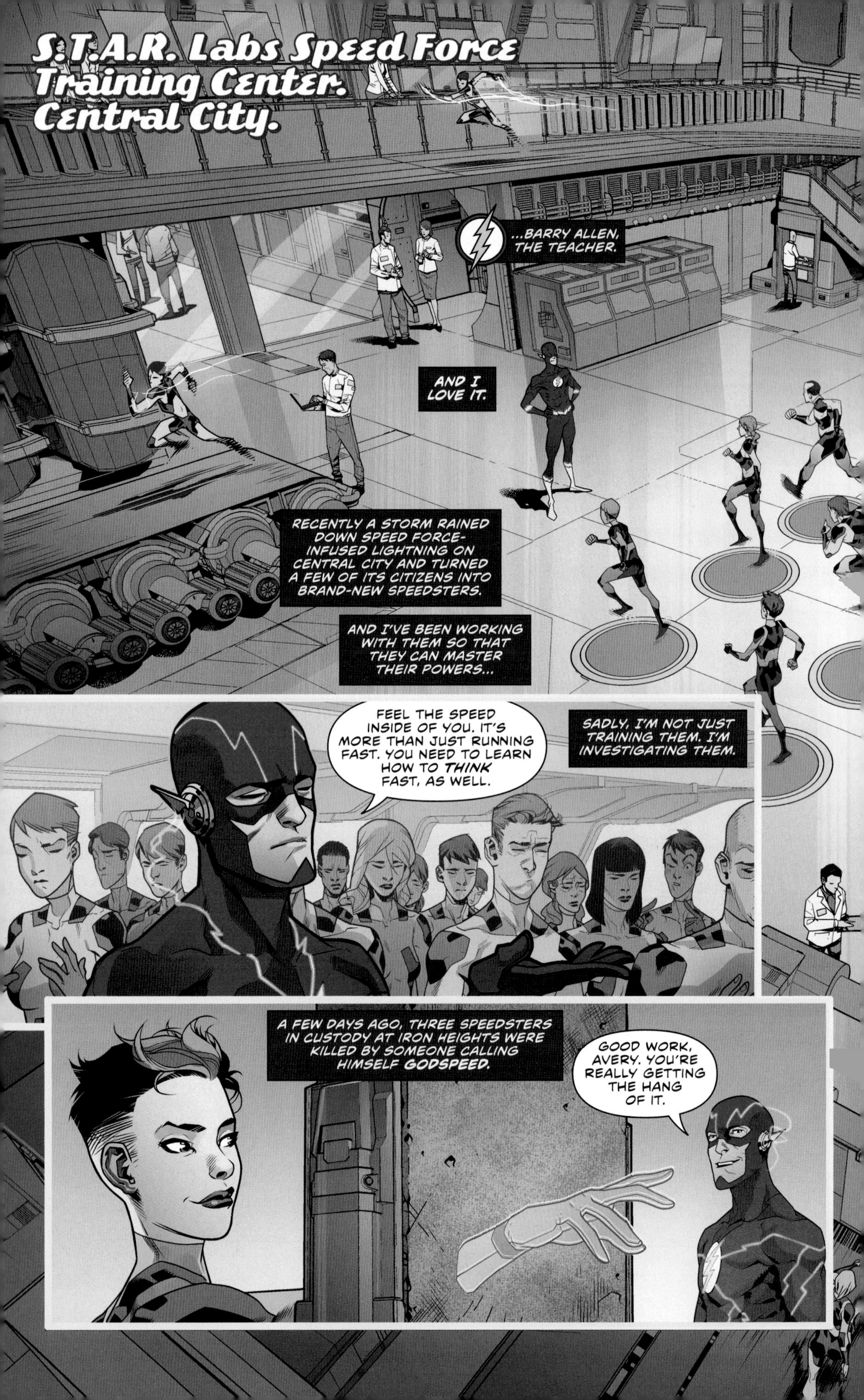
S.T.A.R. Labs Speed Force Training Center. Central City.
...BARRY ALLEN, THE TEACHER.
AND I LOVE IT.
RECENTLY A STORM RAINED DOWN SPEED FORCE-INFUSED LIGHTNING ON CENTRAL CITY AND TURNED A FEW OF ITS CITIZENS INTO BRAND-NEW SPEEDSTERS.
AND I'VE BEEN WORKING WITH THEM SO THAT THEY CAN MASTER THEIR POWERS...
FEEL THE SPEED INSIDE OF YOU. IT'S MORE THAN JUST RUNNING FAST. YOU NEED TO LEARN HOW TO THINK FAST, AS WELL.
SADLY, I'M NOT JUST TRAINING THEM. I'M INVESTIGATING THEM.
A FEW DAYS AGO, THREE SPEEDSTERS IN CUSTODY AT IRON HEIGHTS WERE KILLED BY SOMEONE CALLING HIMSELF GODSPEED.
GOOD WORK, AVERY. YOU'RE REALLY GETTING THE HANG OF IT.

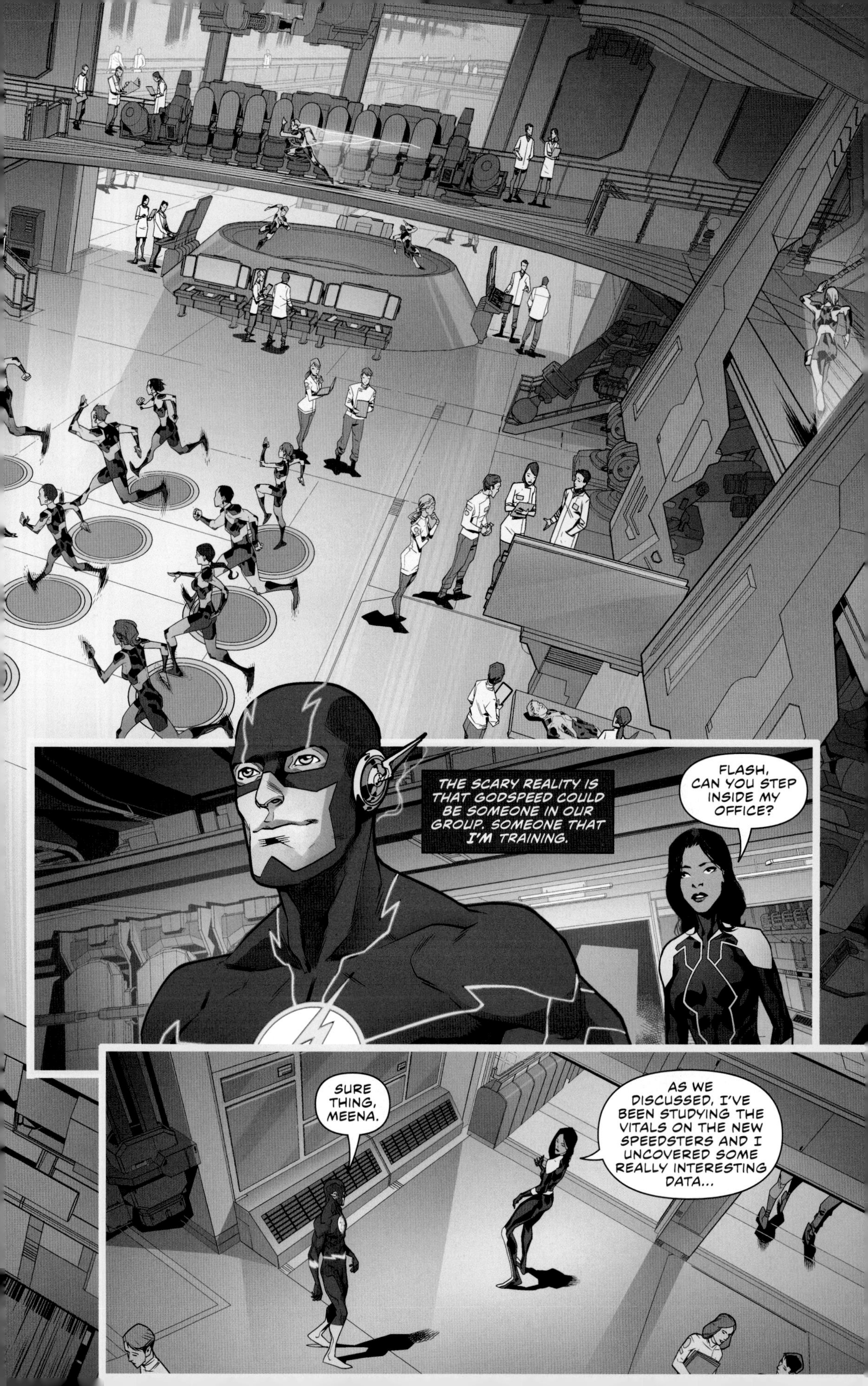
THE SCARY REALITY IS THAT GODSPEED COULD BE SOMEONE IN OUR GROUP. SOMEONE THAT I'M TRAINING.
FLASH, CAN YOU STEP INSIDE MY OFFICE?
SURE THING, MEENA.
AS WE DISCUSSED, I'VE BEEN STUDYING THE VITALS ON THE NEW SPEEDSTERS AND I UNCOVERED SOME REALLY INTERESTING DATA...

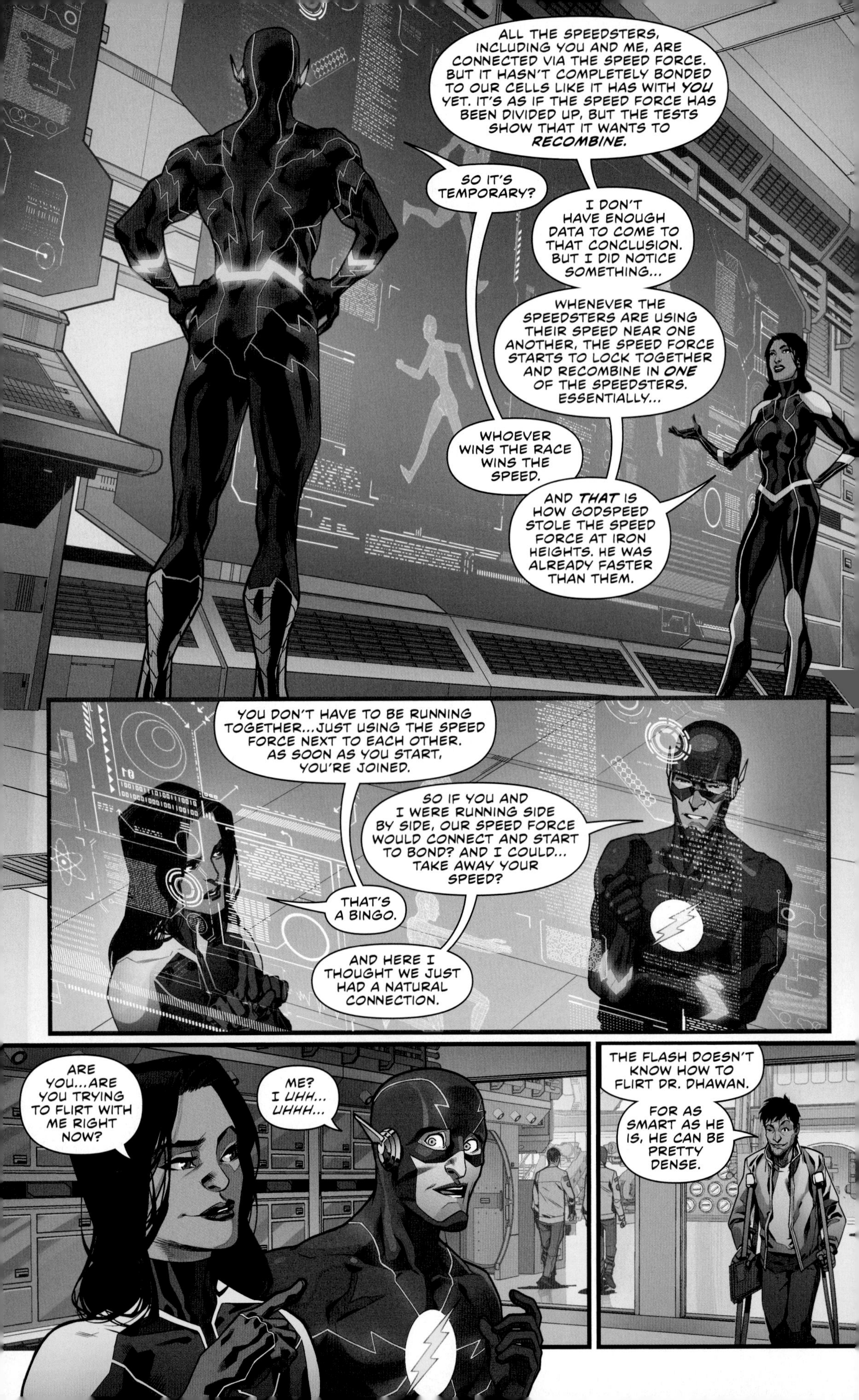
ALL THE SPEEDSTERS, INCLUDING YOU AND ME, ARE CONNECTED VIA THE SPEED FORCE. BUT IT HASN'T COMPLETELY BONDED TO OUR CELLS LIKE IT HAS WITH *YOU* YET. IT'S AS IF THE SPEED FORCE HAS BEEN DIVIDED UP, BUT THE TESTS SHOW THAT IT WANTS TO ***RECOMBINE.***
SO IT'S TEMPORARY?
I DON'T HAVE ENOUGH DATA TO COME TO THAT CONCLUSION. BUT I DID NOTICE SOMETHING...
WHENEVER THE SPEEDSTERS ARE USING THEIR SPEED NEAR ONE ANOTHER, THE SPEED FORCE STARTS TO LOCK TOGETHER AND RECOMBINE IN *ONE* OF THE SPEEDSTERS. ESSENTIALLY...
WHOEVER WINS THE RACE WINS THE SPEED.
AND ***THAT*** IS HOW GODSPEED STOLE THE SPEED FORCE AT IRON HEIGHTS. HE WAS ALREADY FASTER THAN THEM.
YOU DON'T HAVE TO BE RUNNING TOGETHER...JUST USING THE SPEED FORCE NEXT TO EACH OTHER. AS SOON AS YOU START, YOU'RE JOINED.
SO IF YOU AND I WERE RUNNING SIDE BY SIDE, OUR SPEED FORCE WOULD CONNECT AND START TO BOND? AND I COULD... TAKE AWAY YOUR SPEED?
THAT'S A BINGO.
AND HERE I THOUGHT WE JUST HAD A NATURAL CONNECTION.
ARE YOU...ARE YOU TRYING TO FLIRT WITH ME RIGHT NOW?
ME? I *UHH... UHHH...*
THE FLASH DOESN'T KNOW HOW TO FLIRT DR. DHAWAN.
FOR AS SMART AS HE IS, HE CAN BE PRETTY DENSE.

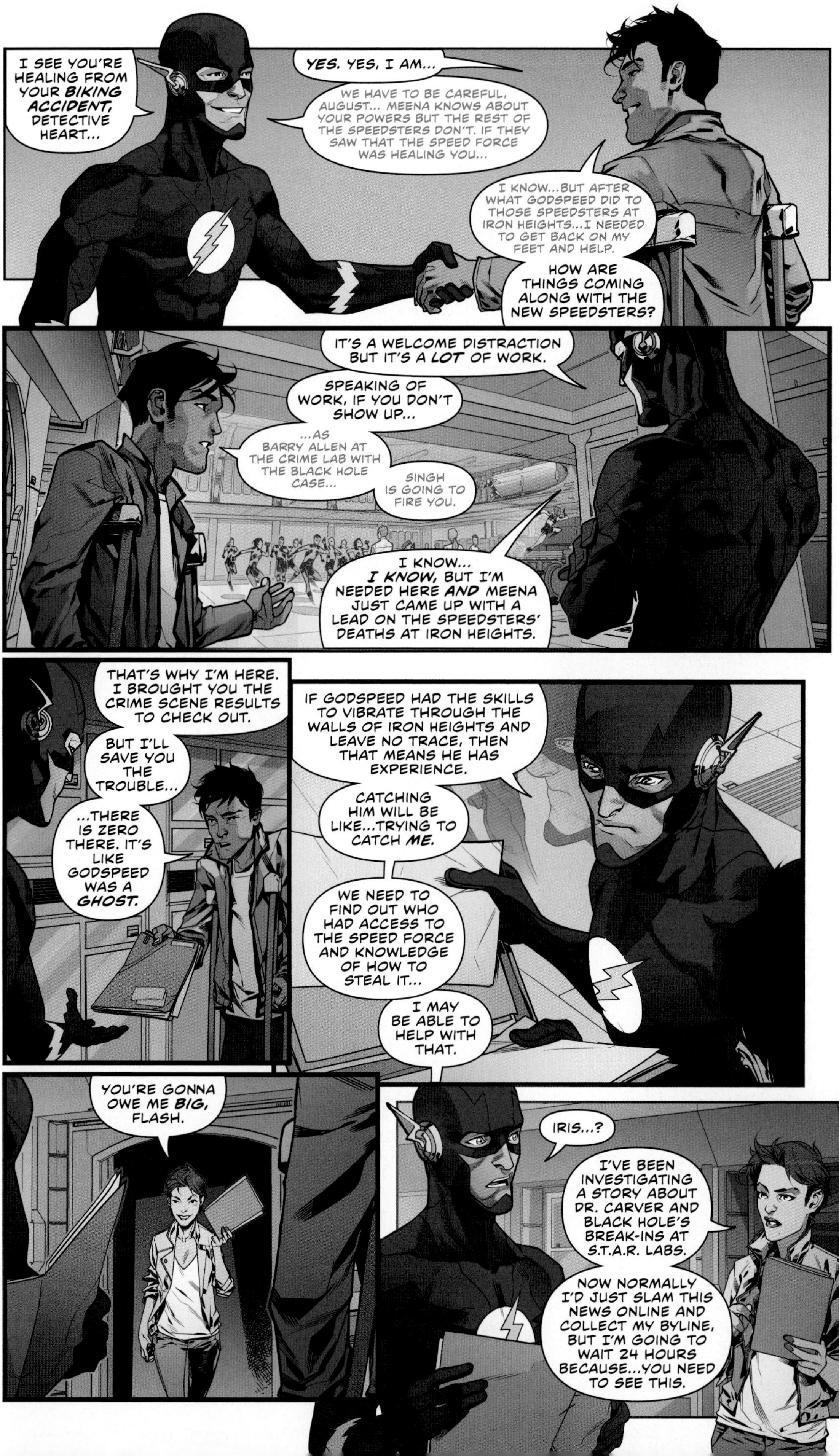
I SEE YOU'RE HEALING FROM YOUR BIKING ACCIDENT, DETECTIVE HEART...
YES. YES, I AM...
WE HAVE TO BE CAREFUL, AUGUST... MEENA KNOWS ABOUT YOUR POWERS BUT THE REST OF THE SPEEDSTERS DON'T. IF THEY SAW THAT THE SPEED FORCE WAS HEALING YOU...
I KNOW...BUT AFTER WHAT GODSPEED DID TO THOSE SPEEDSTERS AT IRON HEIGHTS...I NEEDED TO GET BACK ON MY FEET AND HELP.
HOW ARE THINGS COMING ALONG WITH THE NEW SPEEDSTERS?
IT'S A WELCOME DISTRACTION BUT IT'S A LOT OF WORK.
SPEAKING OF WORK, IF YOU DON'T SHOW UP...
...AS BARRY ALLEN AT THE CRIME LAB WITH THE BLACK HOLE CASE...
SINGH IS GOING TO FIRE YOU.
I KNOW... I KNOW, BUT I'M NEEDED HERE AND MEENA JUST CAME UP WITH A LEAD ON THE SPEEDSTERS' DEATHS AT IRON HEIGHTS.
THAT'S WHY I'M HERE. I BROUGHT YOU THE CRIME SCENE RESULTS TO CHECK OUT.
BUT I'LL SAVE YOU THE TROUBLE...
...THERE IS ZERO THERE. IT'S LIKE GODSPEED WAS A GHOST.
IF GODSPEED HAD THE SKILLS TO VIBRATE THROUGH THE WALLS OF IRON HEIGHTS AND LEAVE NO TRACE, THEN THAT MEANS HE HAS EXPERIENCE.
CATCHING HIM WILL BE LIKE...TRYING TO CATCH ME.
WE NEED TO FIND OUT WHO HAD ACCESS TO THE SPEED FORCE AND KNOWLEDGE OF HOW TO STEAL IT...
I MAY BE ABLE TO HELP WITH THAT.
YOU'RE GONNA OWE ME BIG, FLASH.
IRIS...?
I'VE BEEN INVESTIGATING A STORY ABOUT DR. CARVER AND BLACK HOLE'S BREAK-INS AT S.T.A.R. LABS.
NOW NORMALLY I'D JUST SLAM THIS NEWS ONLINE AND COLLECT MY BYLINE, BUT I'M GOING TO WAIT 24 HOURS BECAUSE...YOU NEED TO SEE THIS.

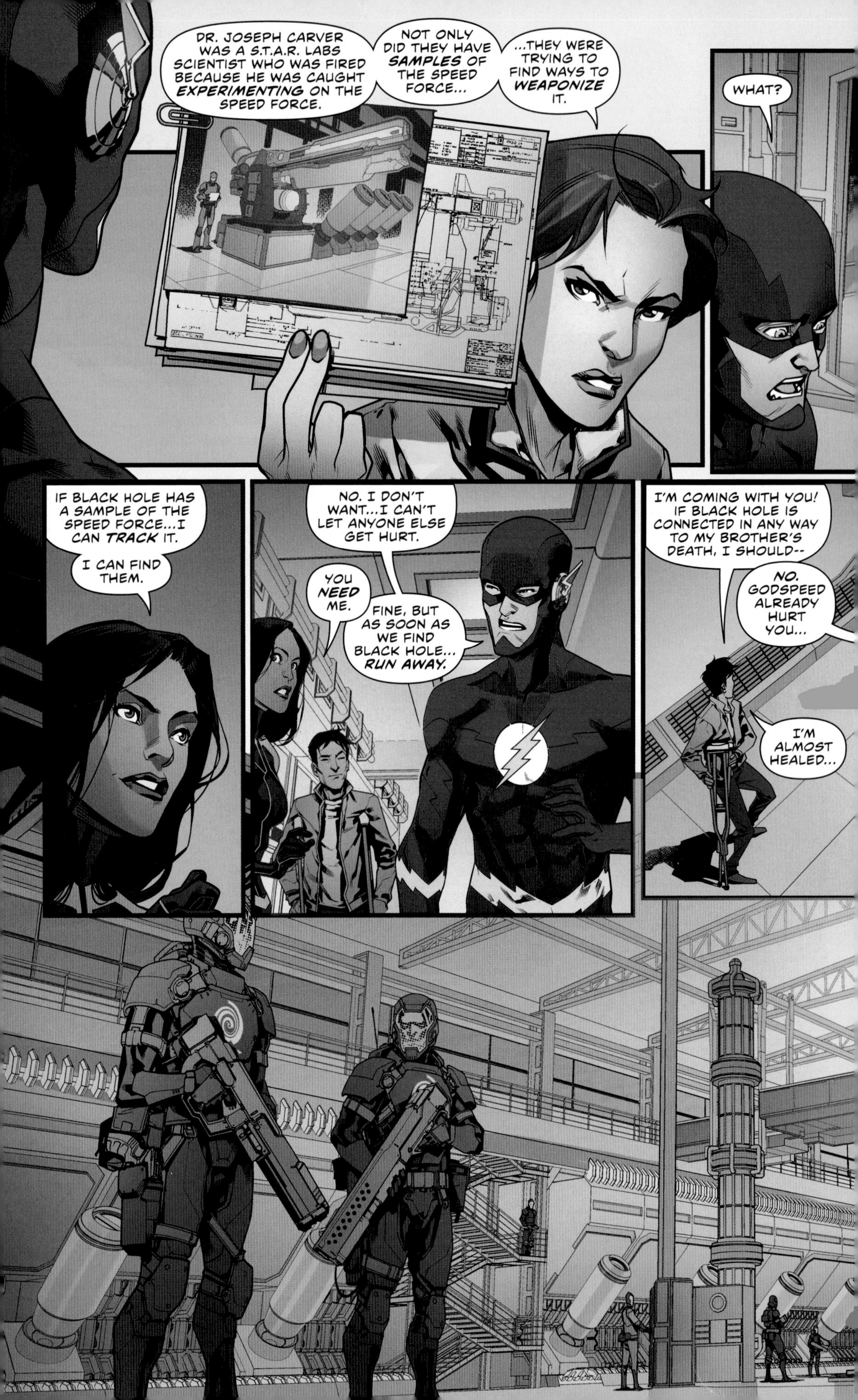

DR. JOSEPH CARVER WAS A S.T.A.R. LABS SCIENTIST WHO WAS FIRED BECAUSE HE WAS CAUGHT EXPERIMENTING ON THE SPEED FORCE.
NOT ONLY DID THEY HAVE SAMPLES OF THE SPEED FORCE...
...THEY WERE TRYING TO FIND WAYS TO WEAPONIZE IT.
WHAT?
IF BLACK HOLE HAS A SAMPLE OF THE SPEED FORCE...I CAN TRACK IT.
I CAN FIND THEM.
NO. I DON'T WANT...I CAN'T LET ANYONE ELSE GET HURT.
YOU NEED ME.
FINE, BUT AS SOON AS WE FIND BLACK HOLE... RUN AWAY.
I'M COMING WITH YOU! IF BLACK HOLE IS CONNECTED IN ANY WAY TO MY BROTHER'S DEATH, I SHOULD--
NO. GODSPEED ALREADY HURT YOU...
I'M ALMOST HEALED...

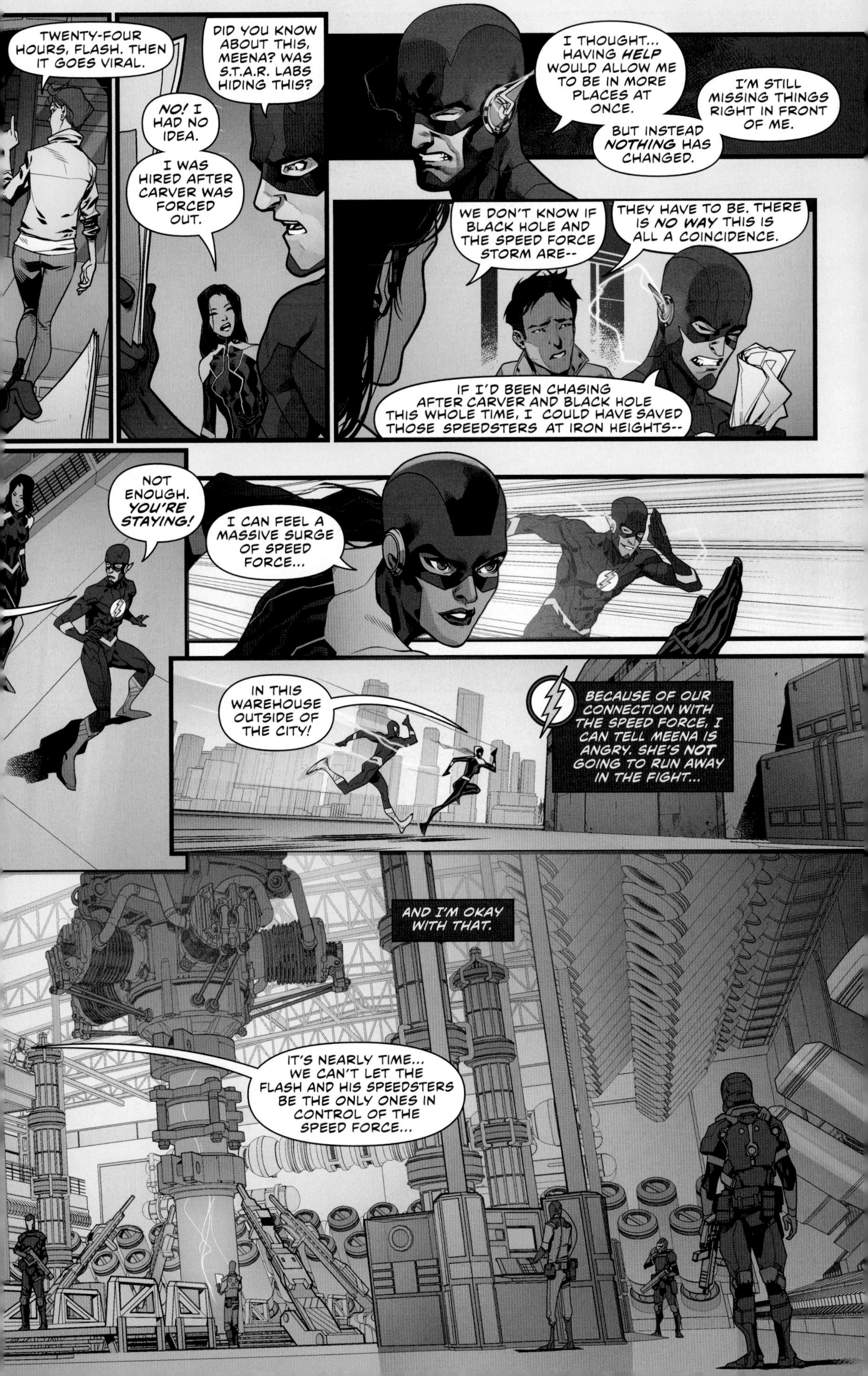

TWENTY-FOUR HOURS, FLASH. THEN IT GOES VIRAL.
DID YOU KNOW ABOUT THIS, MEENA? WAS S.T.A.R. LABS HIDING THIS?
NO! I HAD NO IDEA.
I WAS HIRED AFTER CARVER WAS FORCED OUT.
I THOUGHT... HAVING HELP WOULD ALLOW ME TO BE IN MORE PLACES AT ONCE.
BUT INSTEAD NOTHING HAS CHANGED.
I'M STILL MISSING THINGS RIGHT IN FRONT OF ME.
WE DON'T KNOW IF BLACK HOLE AND THE SPEED FORCE STORM ARE--
THEY HAVE TO BE. THERE IS NO WAY THIS IS ALL A COINCIDENCE.
IF I'D BEEN CHASING AFTER CARVER AND BLACK HOLE THIS WHOLE TIME, I COULD HAVE SAVED THOSE SPEEDSTERS AT IRON HEIGHTS--
NOT ENOUGH. YOU'RE STAYING!
I CAN FEEL A MASSIVE SURGE OF SPEED FORCE...
IN THIS WAREHOUSE OUTSIDE OF THE CITY!
BECAUSE OF OUR CONNECTION WITH THE SPEED FORCE, I CAN TELL MEENA IS ANGRY. SHE'S NOT GOING TO RUN AWAY IN THE FIGHT...
AND I'M OKAY WITH THAT.
IT'S NEARLY TIME... WE CAN'T LET THE FLASH AND HIS SPEEDSTERS BE THE ONLY ONES IN CONTROL OF THE SPEED FORCE...

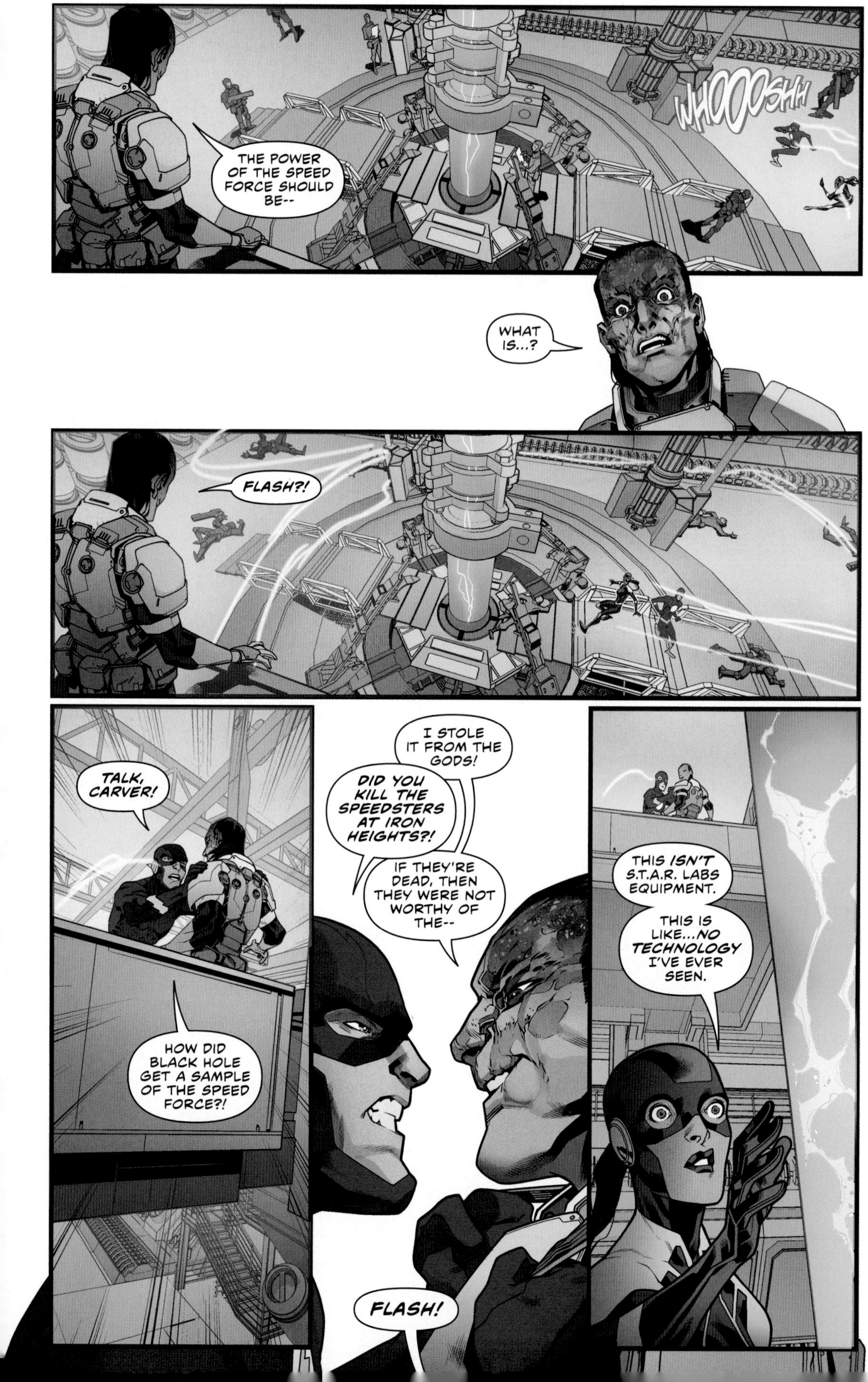
THE POWER OF THE SPEED FORCE SHOULD BE--
WHOOOSHH
WHAT IS...?
FLASH?!
TALK, CARVER!
DID YOU KILL THE SPEEDSTERS AT IRON HEIGHTS?!
I STOLE IT FROM THE GODS!
IF THEY'RE DEAD, THEN THEY WERE NOT WORTHY OF THE--
HOW DID BLACK HOLE GET A SAMPLE OF THE SPEED FORCE?!
THIS ISN'T S.T.A.R. LABS EQUIPMENT.
THIS IS LIKE...NO TECHNOLOGY I'VE EVER SEEN.
FLASH!

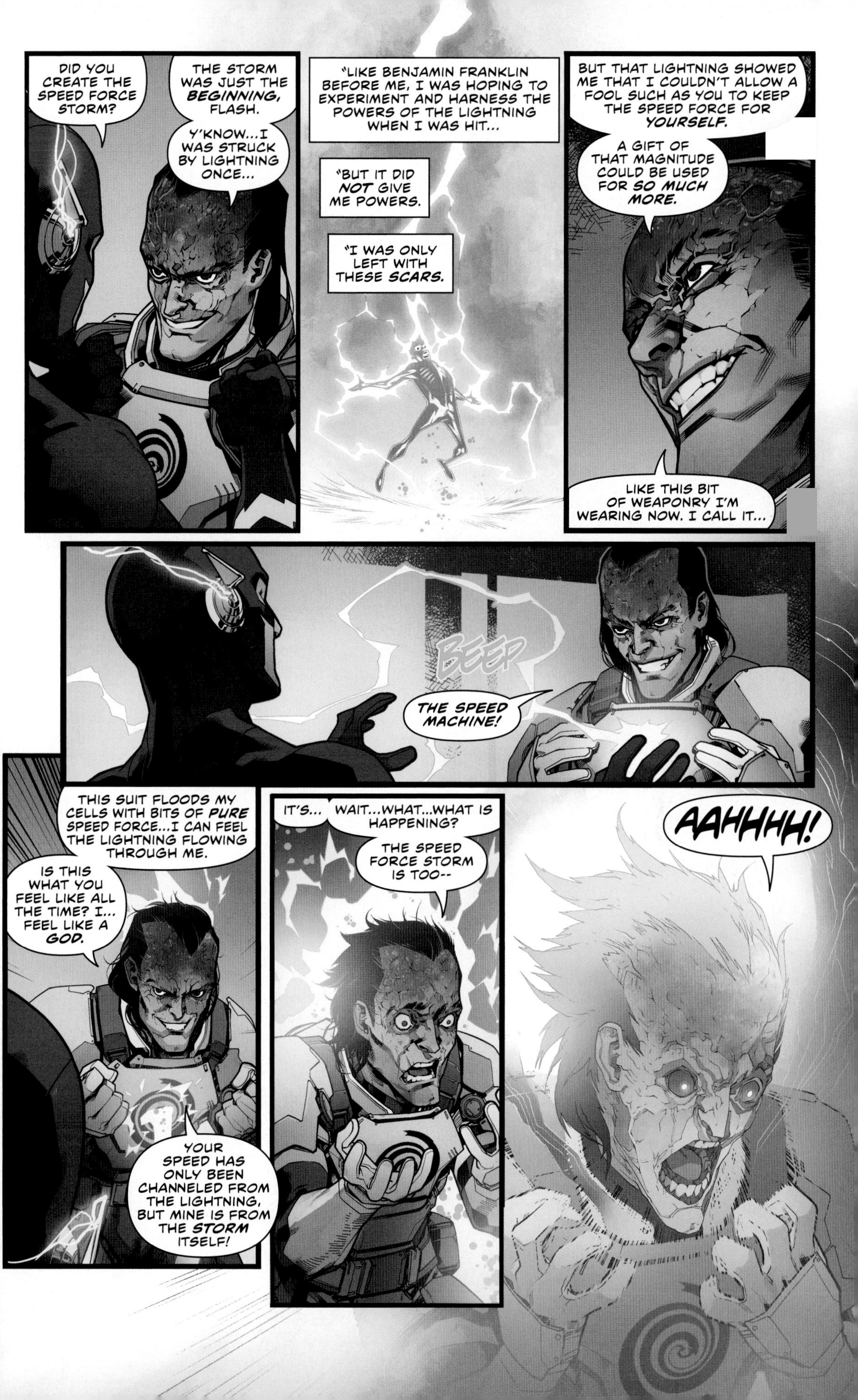
DID YOU CREATE THE SPEED FORCE STORM?
THE STORM WAS JUST THE *BEGINNING,* FLASH.
Y'KNOW...I WAS STRUCK BY LIGHTNING ONCE...
"LIKE BENJAMIN FRANKLIN BEFORE ME, I WAS HOPING TO EXPERIMENT AND HARNESS THE POWERS OF THE LIGHTNING WHEN I WAS HIT...
"BUT IT DID *NOT* GIVE ME POWERS.
"I WAS ONLY LEFT WITH THESE *SCARS.*
BUT THAT LIGHTNING SHOWED ME THAT I COULDN'T ALLOW A FOOL SUCH AS YOU TO KEEP THE SPEED FORCE FOR *YOURSELF.*
A GIFT OF THAT MAGNITUDE COULD BE USED FOR *SO MUCH MORE.*
LIKE THIS BIT OF WEAPONRY I'M WEARING NOW. I CALL IT...
BEEP
THE SPEED MACHINE!
THIS SUIT FLOODS MY CELLS WITH BITS OF *PURE* SPEED FORCE...I CAN FEEL THE LIGHTNING FLOWING THROUGH ME.
IS THIS WHAT YOU FEEL LIKE ALL THE TIME? I... FEEL LIKE A *GOD.*
YOUR SPEED HAS ONLY BEEN CHANNELED FROM THE LIGHTNING, BUT MINE IS FROM THE *STORM* ITSELF!
IT'S...
WAIT...WHAT...WHAT IS HAPPENING?
THE SPEED FORCE STORM IS TOO--
AAHHHH!

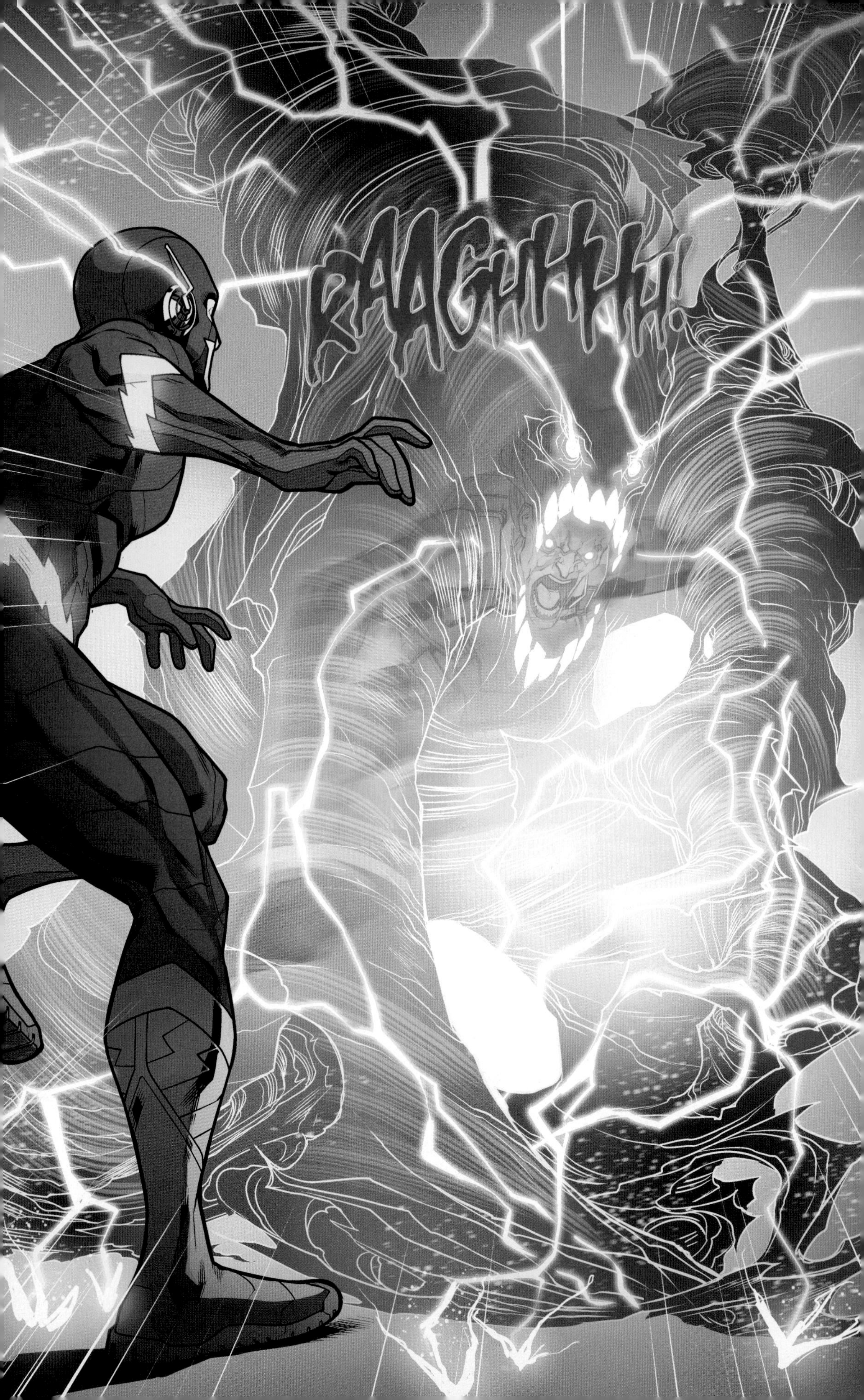
RAAGHHHH!

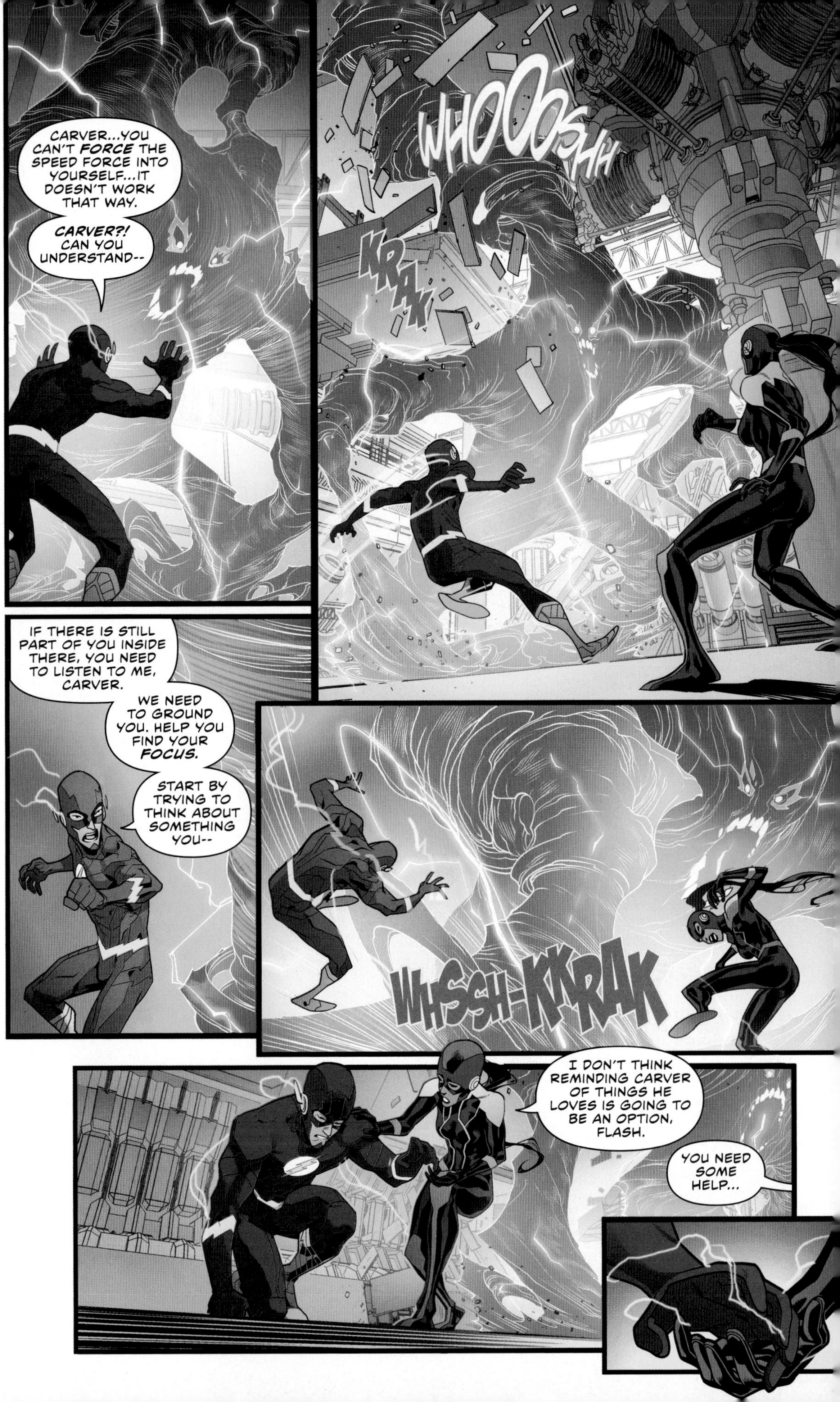

CARVER...YOU CAN'T FORCE THE SPEED FORCE INTO YOURSELF...IT DOESN'T WORK THAT WAY.
CARVER?! CAN YOU UNDERSTAND--
WHOOOOSHH
KRAK
IF THERE IS STILL PART OF YOU INSIDE THERE, YOU NEED TO LISTEN TO ME, CARVER.
WE NEED TO GROUND YOU. HELP YOU FIND YOUR FOCUS.
START BY TRYING TO THINK ABOUT SOMETHING YOU--
WHSSH-KKRAK
I DON'T THINK REMINDING CARVER OF THINGS HE LOVES IS GOING TO BE AN OPTION, FLASH.
YOU NEED SOME HELP...

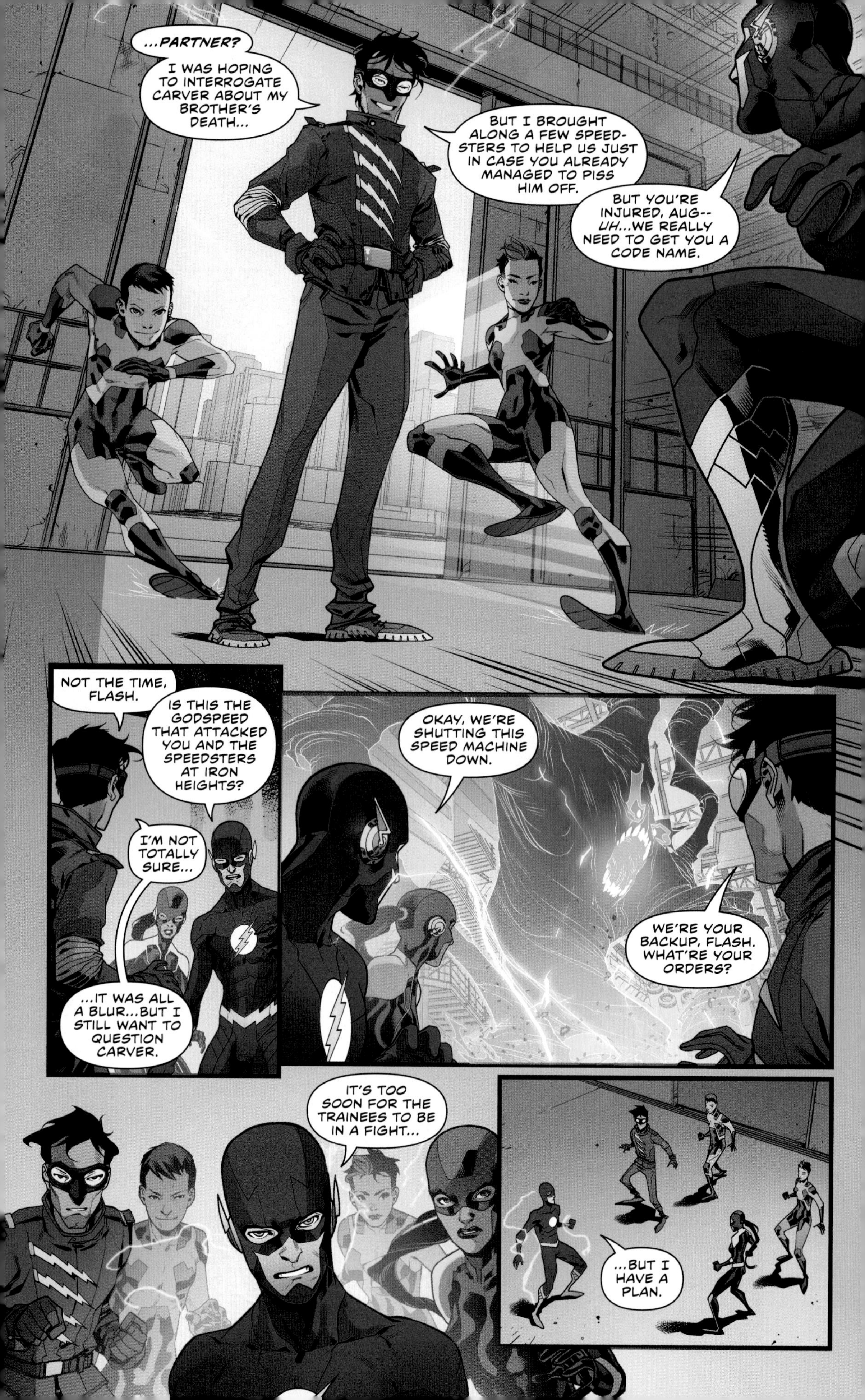
...PARTNER?
I WAS HOPING TO INTERROGATE CARVER ABOUT MY BROTHER'S DEATH...
BUT I BROUGHT ALONG A FEW SPEEDSTERS TO HELP US JUST IN CASE YOU ALREADY MANAGED TO PISS HIM OFF.
BUT YOU'RE INJURED, AUG-- *UH*...WE REALLY NEED TO GET YOU A CODE NAME.
NOT THE TIME, FLASH.
IS THIS THE GODSPEED THAT ATTACKED YOU AND THE SPEEDSTERS AT IRON HEIGHTS?
I'M NOT TOTALLY SURE...
...IT WAS ALL A BLUR...BUT I STILL WANT TO QUESTION CARVER.
OKAY, WE'RE SHUTTING THIS SPEED MACHINE DOWN.
WE'RE YOUR BACKUP, FLASH. WHAT'RE YOUR ORDERS?
IT'S TOO SOON FOR THE TRAINEES TO BE IN A FIGHT...
...BUT I HAVE A PLAN.

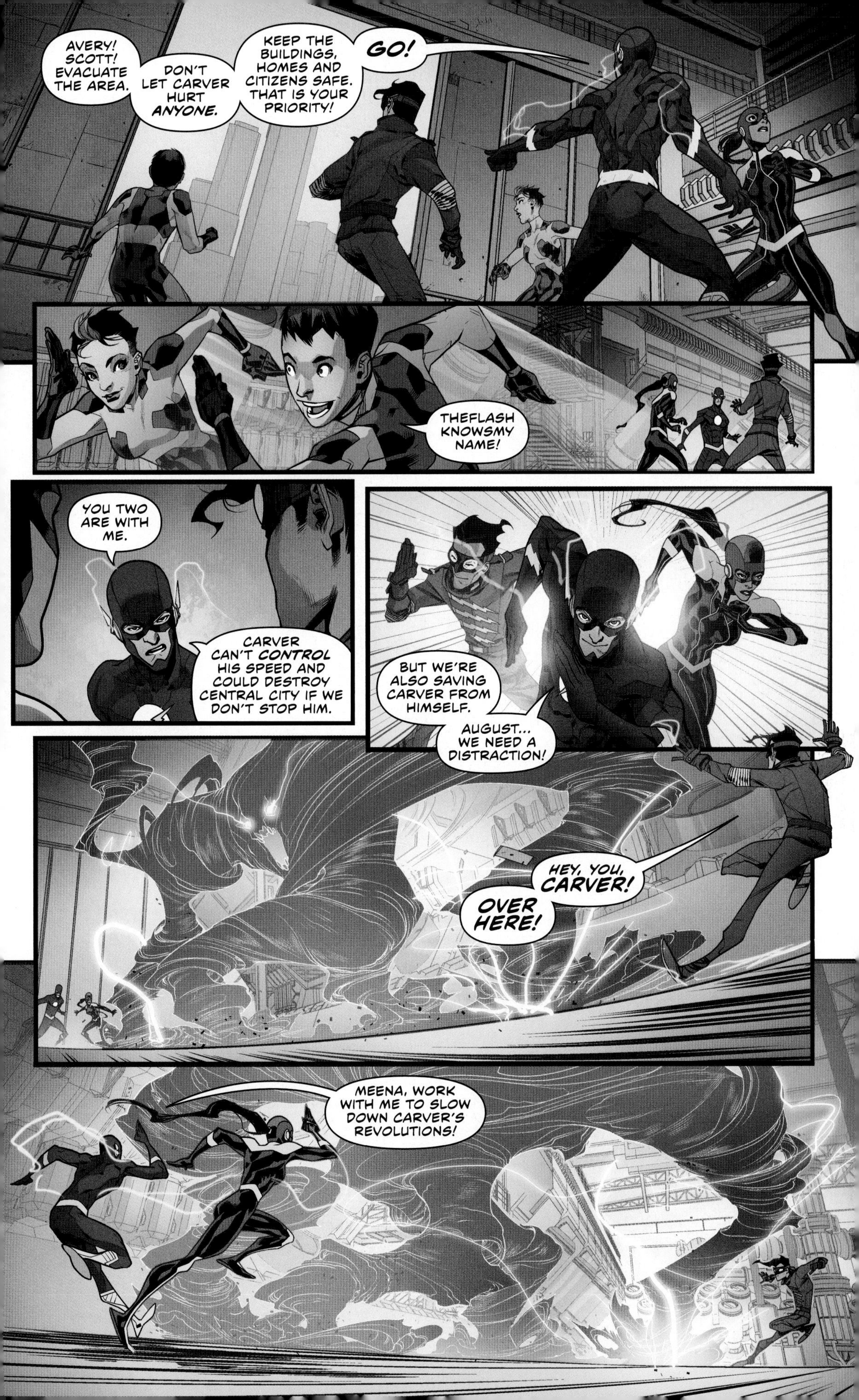
AVERY! SCOTT! EVACUATE THE AREA.
DON'T LET CARVER HURT ANYONE.
KEEP THE BUILDINGS, HOMES AND CITIZENS SAFE. THAT IS YOUR PRIORITY!
GO!
THEFLASH KNOWSMY NAME!
YOU TWO ARE WITH ME.
CARVER CAN'T CONTROL HIS SPEED AND COULD DESTROY CENTRAL CITY IF WE DON'T STOP HIM.
BUT WE'RE ALSO SAVING CARVER FROM HIMSELF.
AUGUST... WE NEED A DISTRACTION!
HEY, YOU, CARVER!
OVER HERE!
MEENA, WORK WITH ME TO SLOW DOWN CARVER'S REVOLUTIONS!

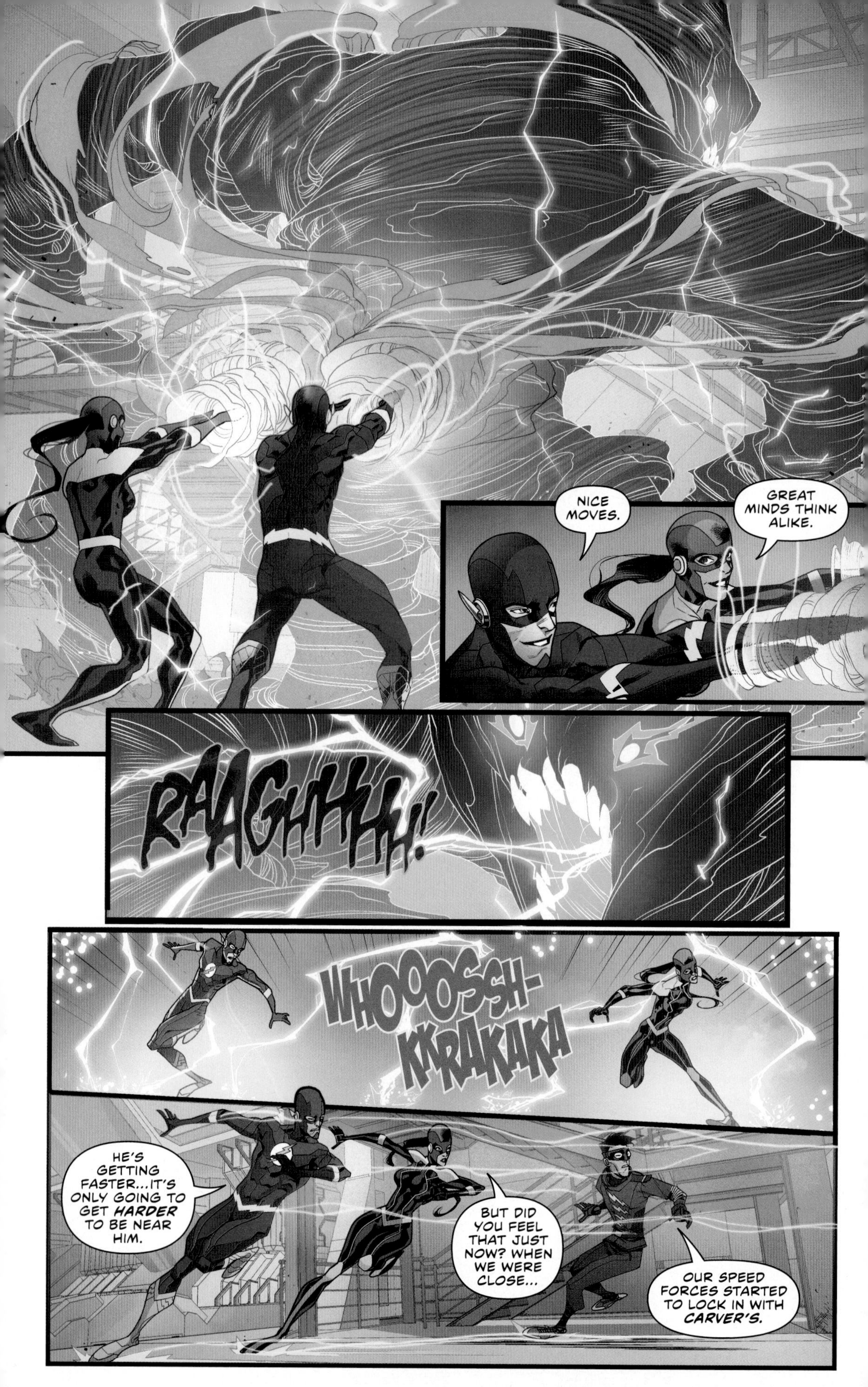
NICE MOVES.
GREAT MINDS THINK ALIKE.
RAAGHHHHH!
WHOOOSSH-KKRAKAKA
HE'S GETTING FASTER...IT'S ONLY GOING TO GET *HARDER* TO BE NEAR HIM.
BUT DID YOU FEEL THAT JUST NOW? WHEN WE WERE CLOSE...
OUR SPEED FORCES STARTED TO LOCK IN WITH *CARVER'S*.

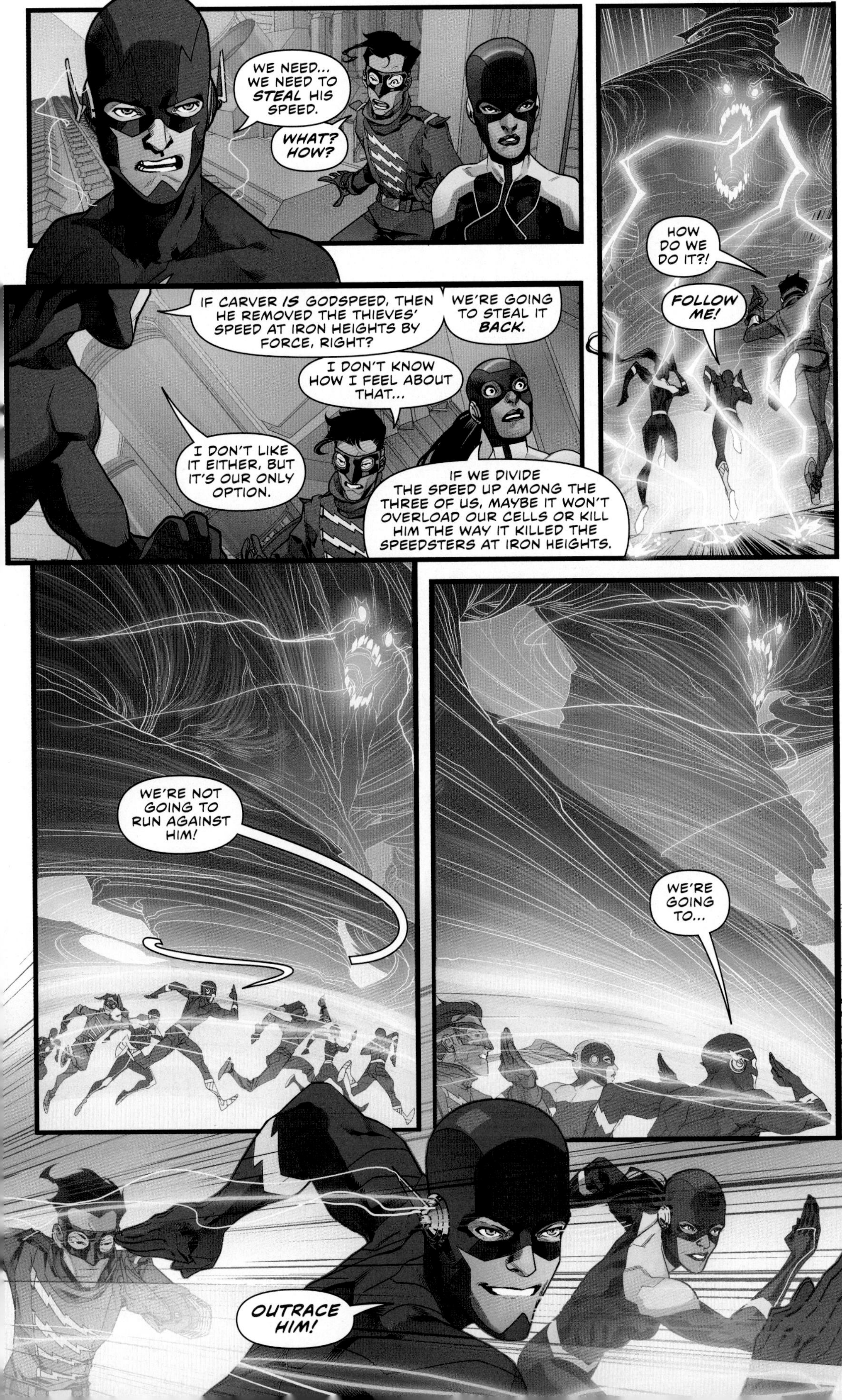
WE NEED... WE NEED TO STEAL HIS SPEED.
WHAT? HOW?
IF CARVER IS GODSPEED, THEN HE REMOVED THE THIEVES' SPEED AT IRON HEIGHTS BY FORCE, RIGHT?
WE'RE GOING TO STEAL IT BACK.
I DON'T KNOW HOW I FEEL ABOUT THAT...
I DON'T LIKE IT EITHER, BUT IT'S OUR ONLY OPTION.
IF WE DIVIDE THE SPEED UP AMONG THE THREE OF US, MAYBE IT WON'T OVERLOAD OUR CELLS OR KILL HIM THE WAY IT KILLED THE SPEEDSTERS AT IRON HEIGHTS.
HOW DO WE DO IT?!
FOLLOW ME!
WE'RE NOT GOING TO RUN AGAINST HIM!
WE'RE GOING TO...
OUTRACE HIM!

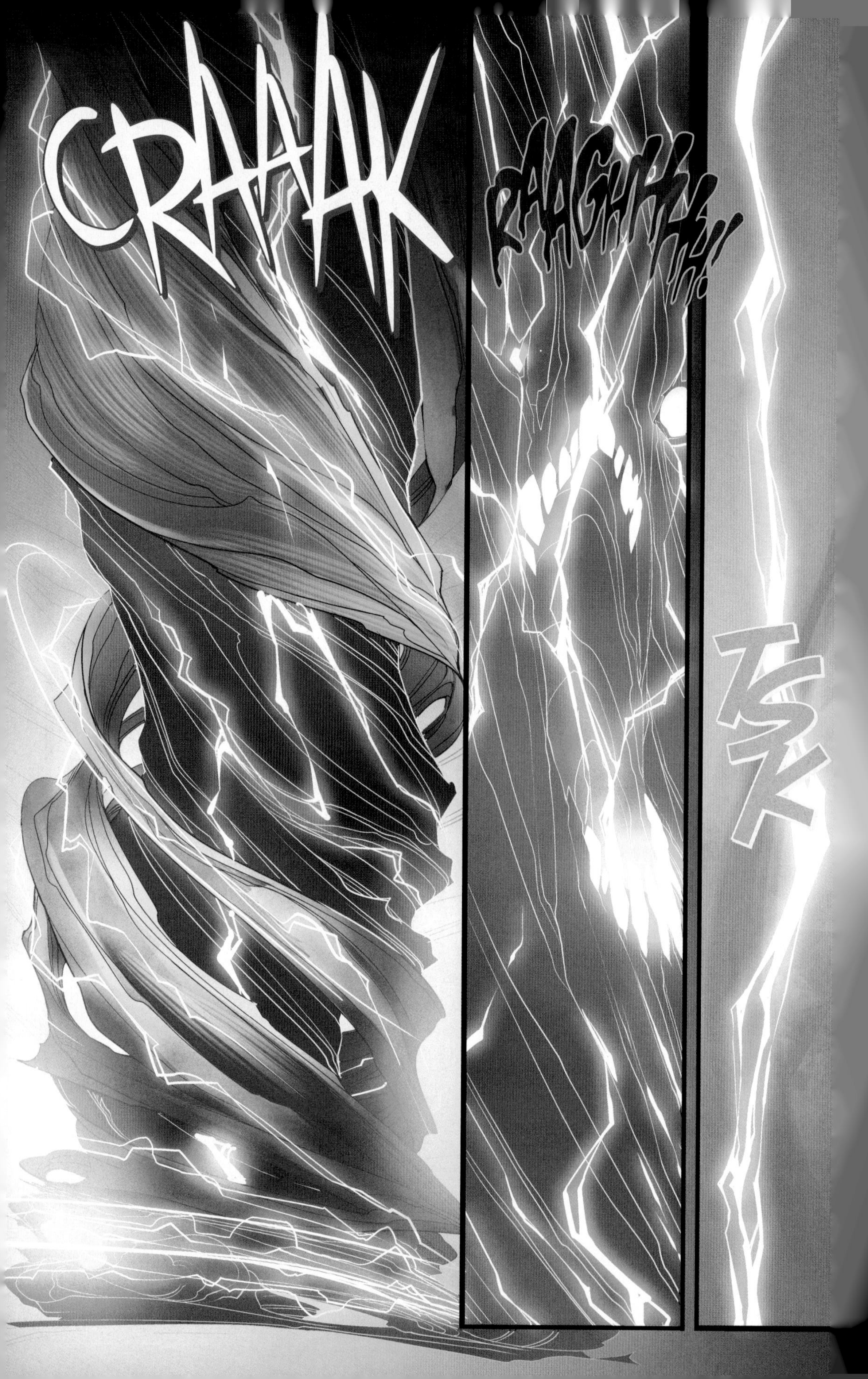
CRAAAK
RAAGHHH!!
TSSK

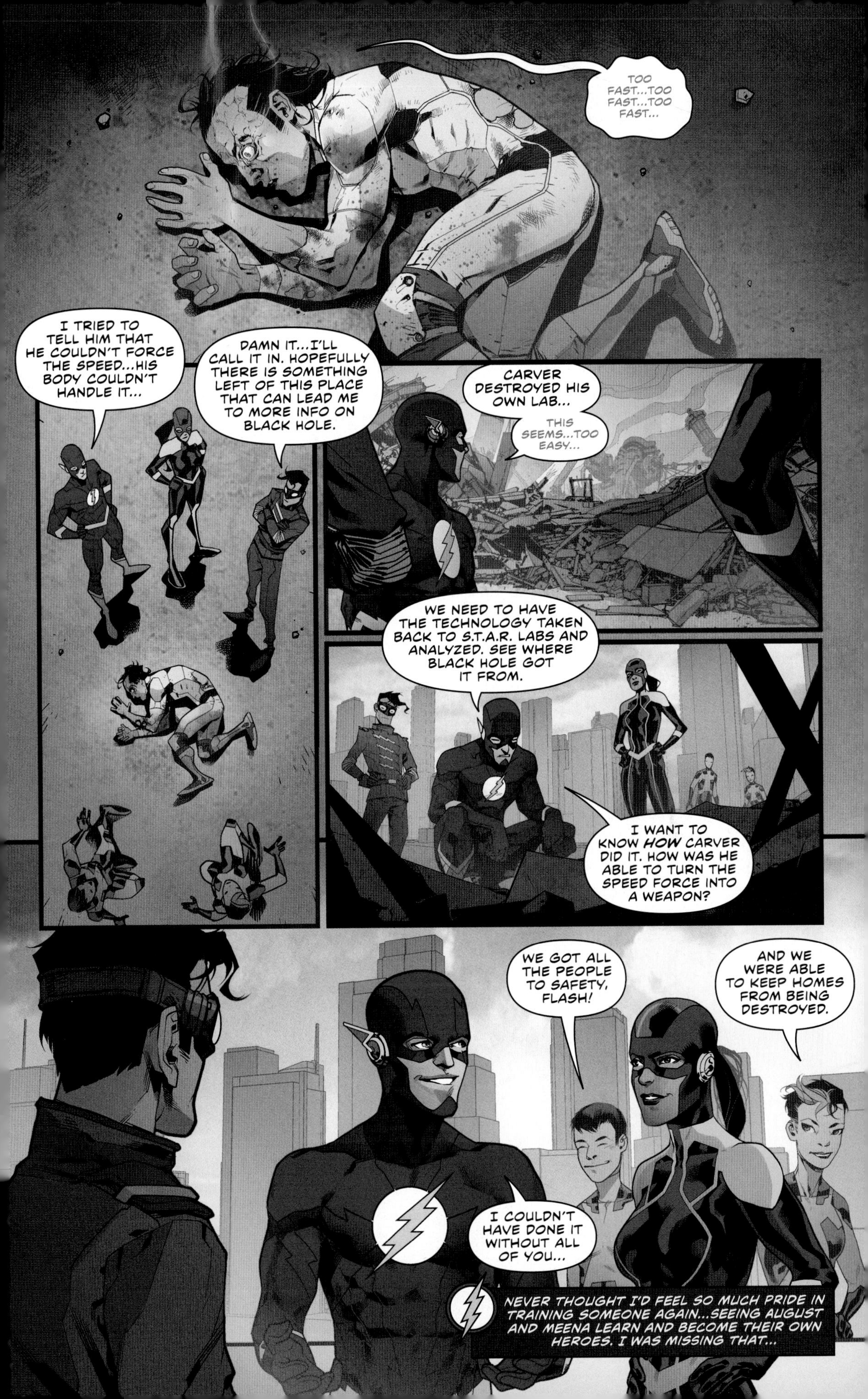
TOO FAST...TOO FAST...TOO FAST...
I TRIED TO TELL HIM THAT HE COULDN'T FORCE THE SPEED...HIS BODY COULDN'T HANDLE IT...
DAMN IT...I'LL CALL IT IN. HOPEFULLY THERE IS SOMETHING LEFT OF THIS PLACE THAT CAN LEAD ME TO MORE INFO ON BLACK HOLE.
CARVER DESTROYED HIS OWN LAB...
THIS SEEMS...TOO EASY...
WE NEED TO HAVE THE TECHNOLOGY TAKEN BACK TO S.T.A.R. LABS AND ANALYZED. SEE WHERE BLACK HOLE GOT IT FROM.
I WANT TO KNOW *HOW* CARVER DID IT. HOW WAS HE ABLE TO TURN THE SPEED FORCE INTO A WEAPON?
WE GOT ALL THE PEOPLE TO SAFETY, FLASH!
AND WE WERE ABLE TO KEEP HOMES FROM BEING DESTROYED.
I COULDN'T HAVE DONE IT WITHOUT ALL OF YOU...
NEVER THOUGHT I'D FEEL SO MUCH PRIDE IN TRAINING SOMEONE AGAIN...SEEING AUGUST AND MEENA LEARN AND BECOME THEIR OWN HEROES. I WAS MISSING THAT...

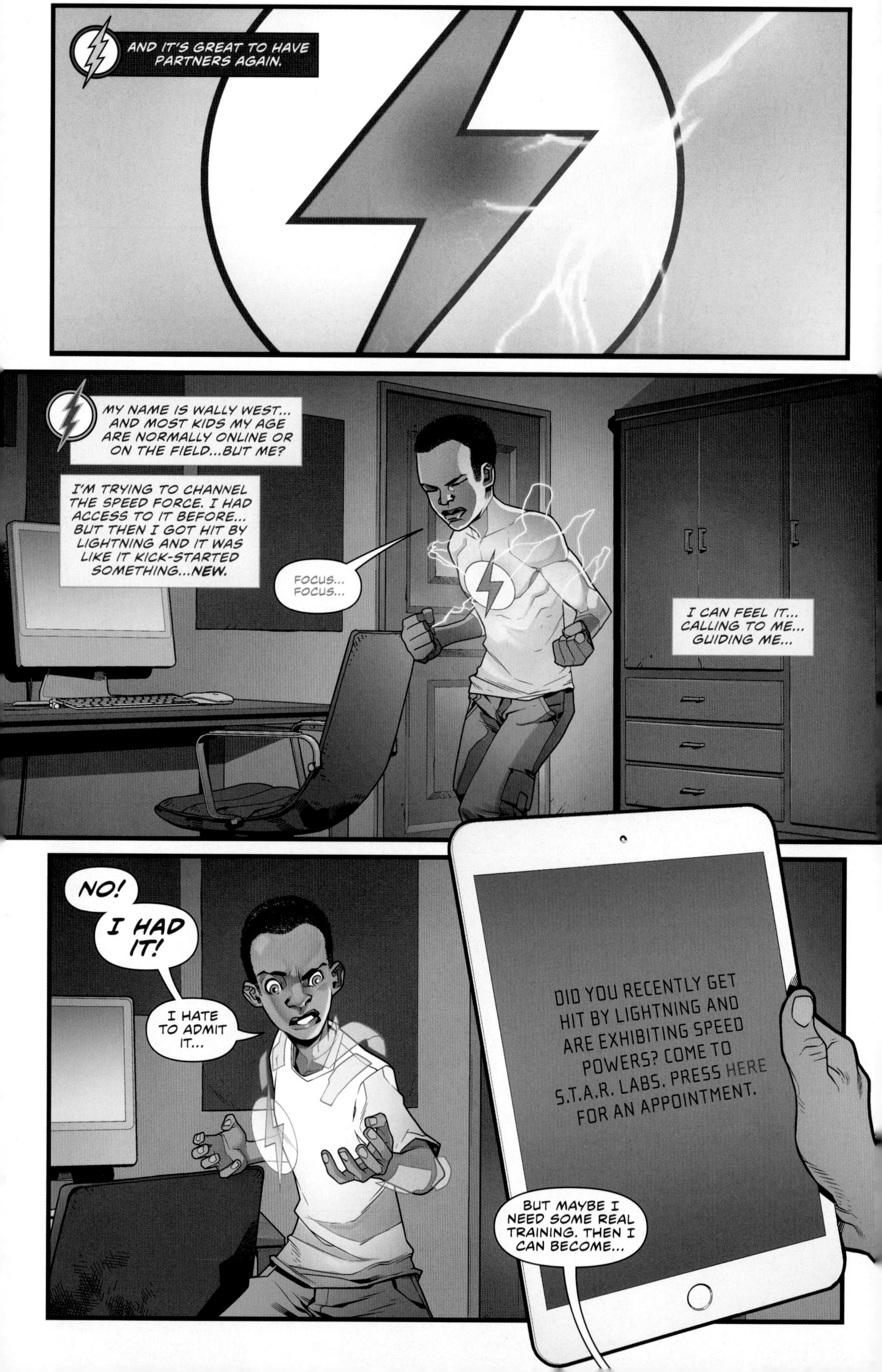

AND IT'S GREAT TO HAVE PARTNERS AGAIN.
MY NAME IS WALLY WEST... AND MOST KIDS MY AGE ARE NORMALLY ONLINE OR ON THE FIELD...BUT ME?
I'M TRYING TO CHANNEL THE SPEED FORCE. I HAD ACCESS TO IT BEFORE... BUT THEN I GOT HIT BY LIGHTNING AND IT WAS LIKE IT KICK-STARTED SOMETHING...NEW.
FOCUS... FOCUS...
I CAN FEEL IT... CALLING TO ME... GUIDING ME...
NO!
I HAD IT!
I HATE TO ADMIT IT...
DID YOU RECENTLY GET HIT BY LIGHTNING AND ARE EXHIBITING SPEED POWERS? COME TO S.T.A.R. LABS. PRESS HERE FOR AN APPOINTMENT.
BUT MAYBE I NEED SOME REAL TRAINING. THEN I CAN BECOME...

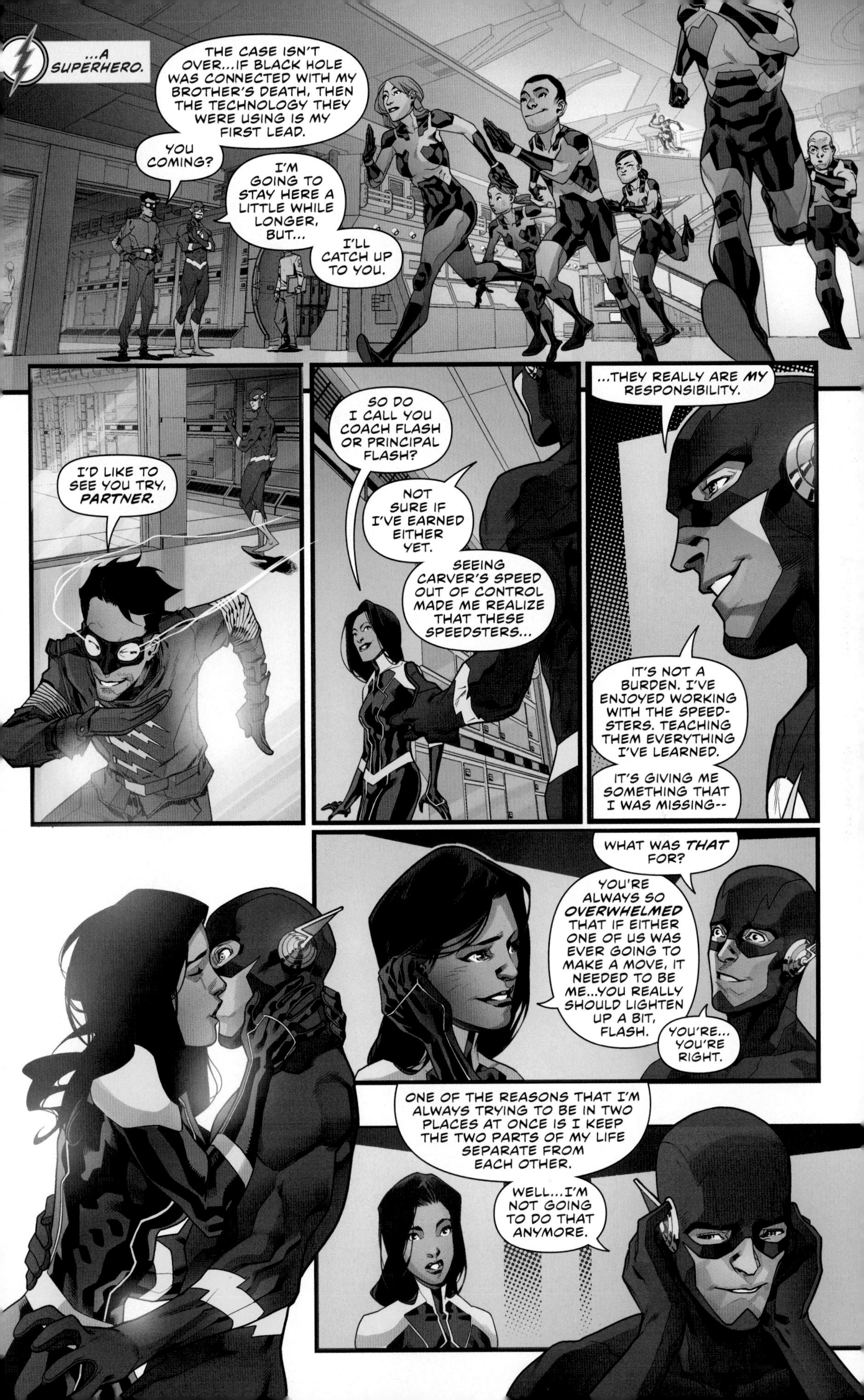
...A SUPERHERO.
THE CASE ISN'T OVER...IF BLACK HOLE WAS CONNECTED WITH MY BROTHER'S DEATH, THEN THE TECHNOLOGY THEY WERE USING IS MY FIRST LEAD.
YOU COMING?
I'M GOING TO STAY HERE A LITTLE WHILE LONGER, BUT...
I'LL CATCH UP TO YOU.
I'D LIKE TO SEE YOU TRY, PARTNER.
SO DO I CALL YOU COACH FLASH OR PRINCIPAL FLASH?
NOT SURE IF I'VE EARNED EITHER YET.
SEEING CARVER'S SPEED OUT OF CONTROL MADE ME REALIZE THAT THESE SPEEDSTERS...
...THEY REALLY ARE MY RESPONSIBILITY.
IT'S NOT A BURDEN. I'VE ENJOYED WORKING WITH THE SPEEDSTERS. TEACHING THEM EVERYTHING I'VE LEARNED.
IT'S GIVING ME SOMETHING THAT I WAS MISSING--
WHAT WAS THAT FOR?
YOU'RE ALWAYS SO OVERWHELMED THAT IF EITHER ONE OF US WAS EVER GOING TO MAKE A MOVE, IT NEEDED TO BE ME...YOU REALLY SHOULD LIGHTEN UP A BIT, FLASH.
YOU'RE... YOU'RE RIGHT.
ONE OF THE REASONS THAT I'M ALWAYS TRYING TO BE IN TWO PLACES AT ONCE IS I KEEP THE TWO PARTS OF MY LIFE SEPARATE FROM EACH OTHER.
WELL...I'M NOT GOING TO DO THAT ANYMORE.

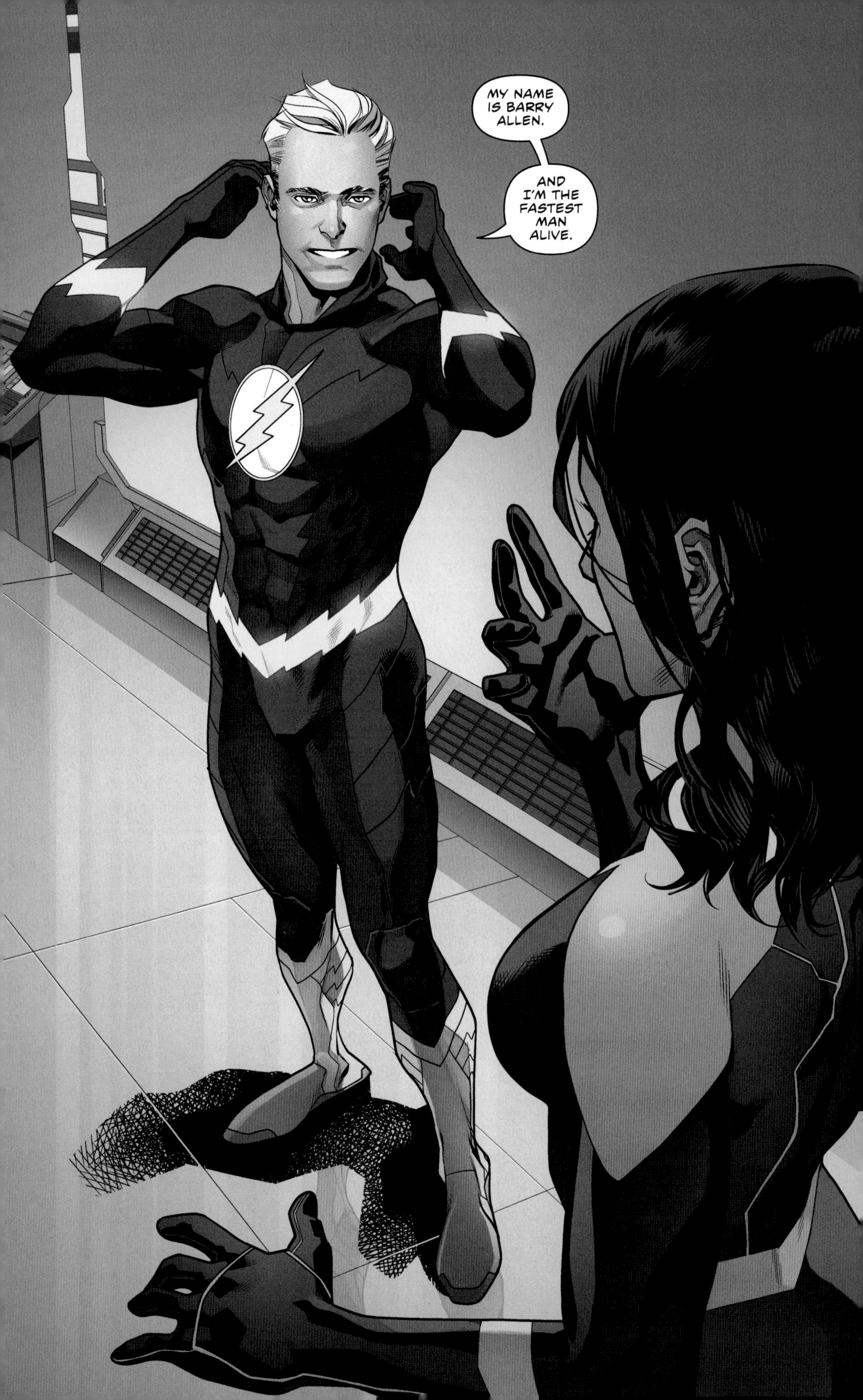
MY NAME IS BARRY ALLEN.
AND I'M THE FASTEST MAN ALIVE.

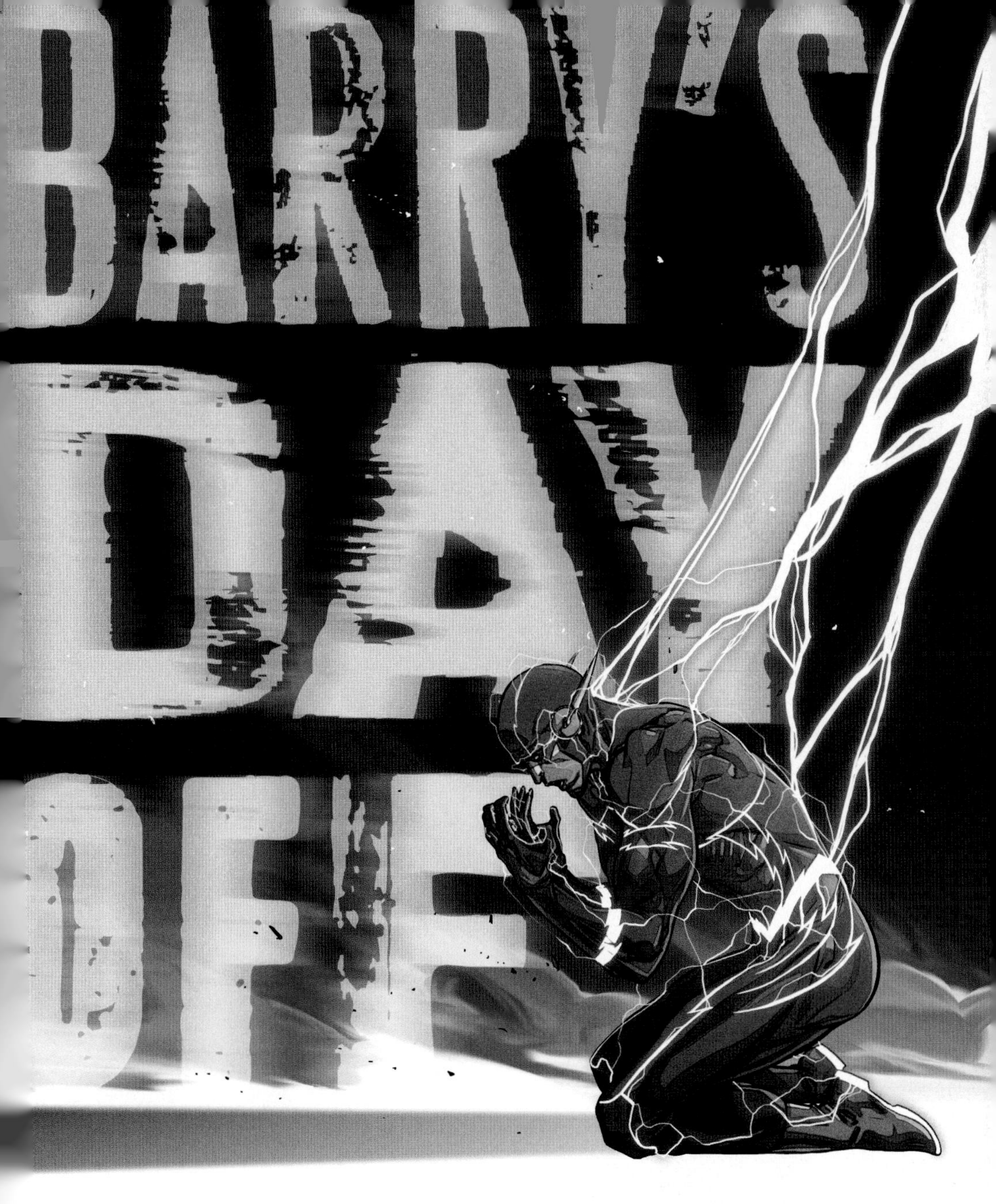
BARRY'S
DAY
OFF

BARRY ALLEN'S DAY OFF

FELIPE WATANABE penciller * ANDREW CURRIE and OCLAIR ALBERT inkers * CARMINE Di GIANDOMENICO cover artist

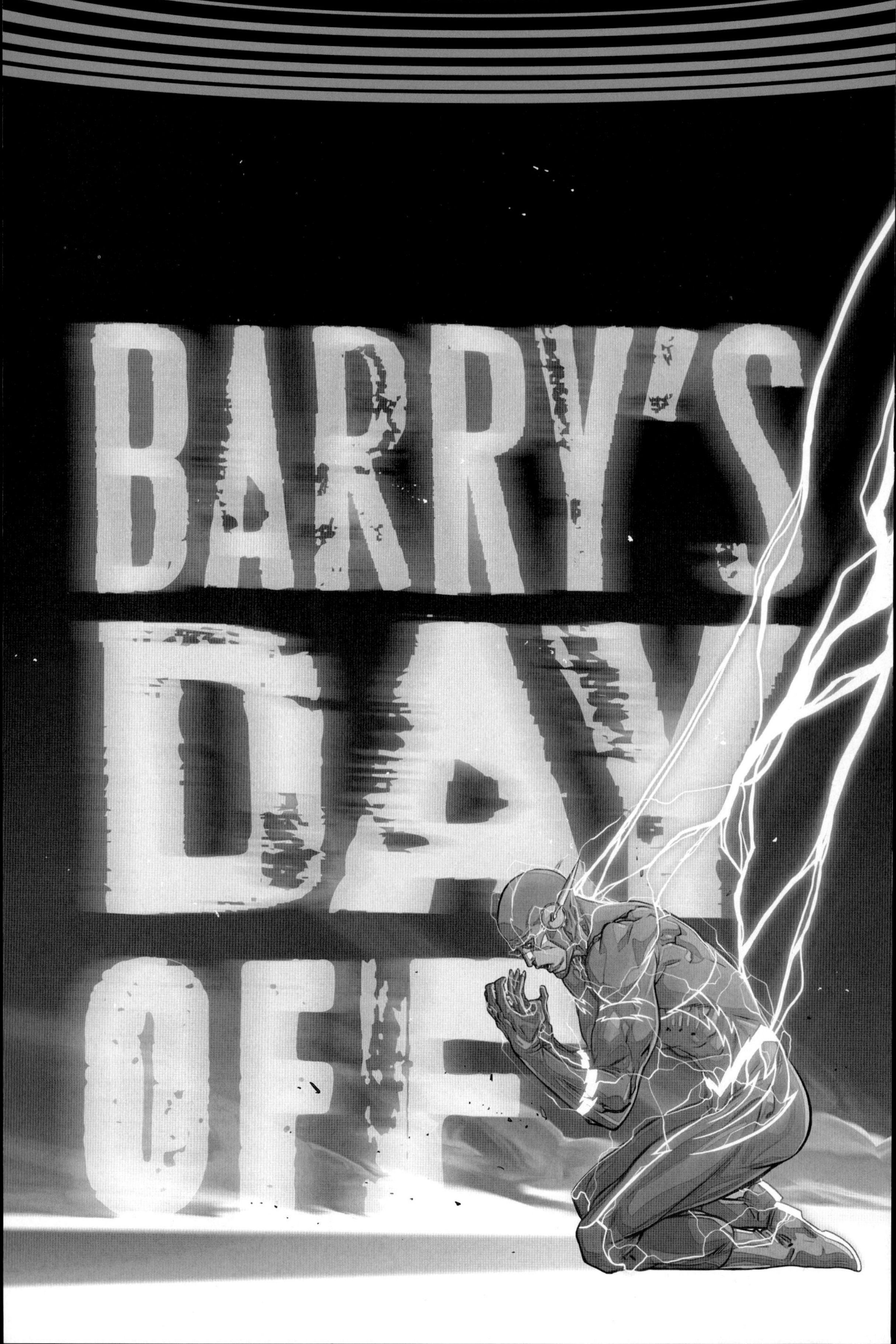
BARRY'S
DAY
OFF

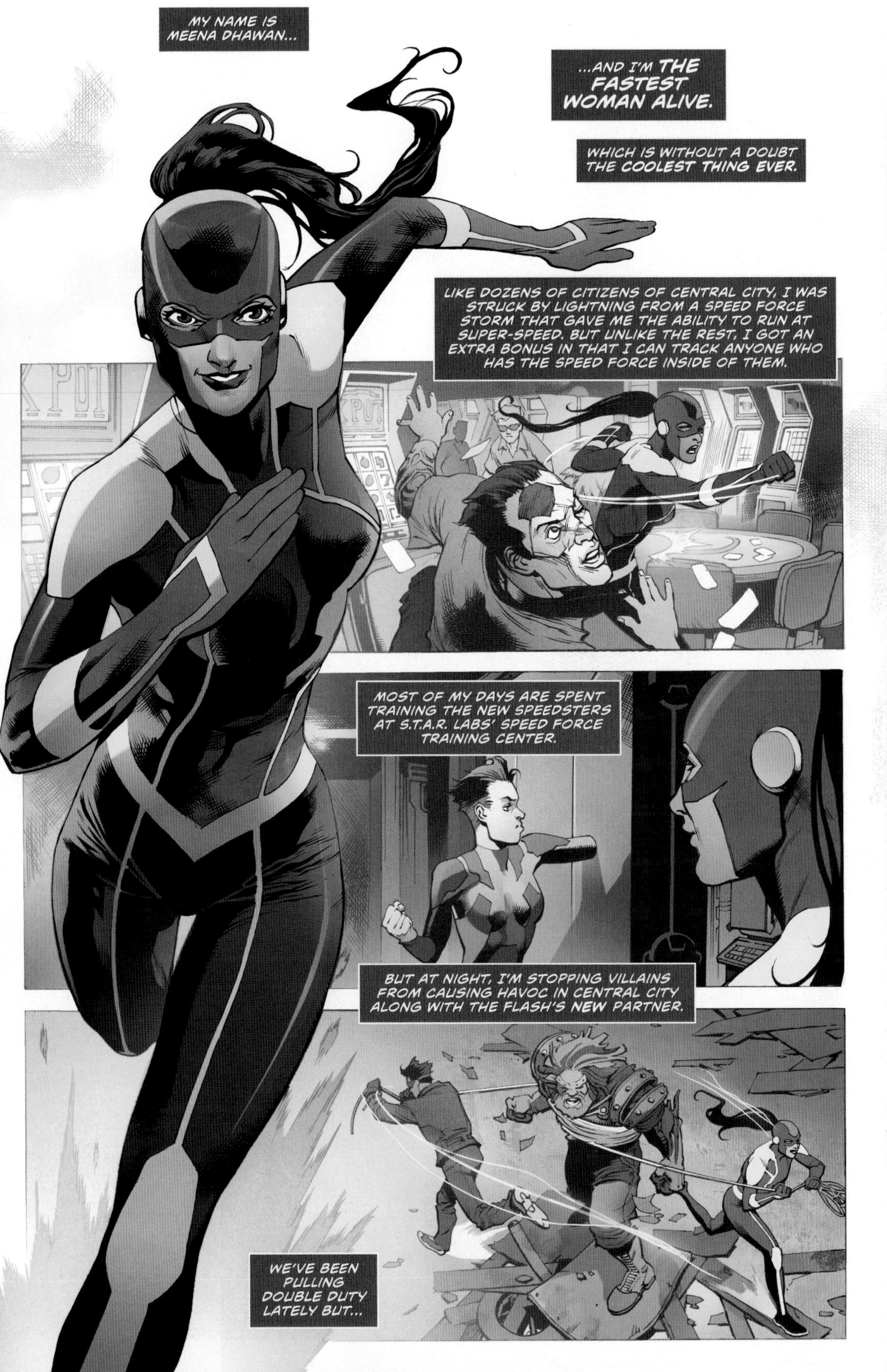
MY NAME IS MEENA DHAWAN...
...AND I'M THE FASTEST WOMAN ALIVE.
WHICH IS WITHOUT A DOUBT THE COOLEST THING EVER.
LIKE DOZENS OF CITIZENS OF CENTRAL CITY, I WAS STRUCK BY LIGHTNING FROM A SPEED FORCE STORM THAT GAVE ME THE ABILITY TO RUN AT SUPER-SPEED. BUT UNLIKE THE REST, I GOT AN EXTRA BONUS IN THAT I CAN TRACK ANYONE WHO HAS THE SPEED FORCE INSIDE OF THEM.
MOST OF MY DAYS ARE SPENT TRAINING THE NEW SPEEDSTERS AT S.T.A.R. LABS' SPEED FORCE TRAINING CENTER.
BUT AT NIGHT, I'M STOPPING VILLAINS FROM CAUSING HAVOC IN CENTRAL CITY ALONG WITH THE FLASH'S NEW PARTNER.
WE'VE BEEN PULLING DOUBLE DUTY LATELY BUT...

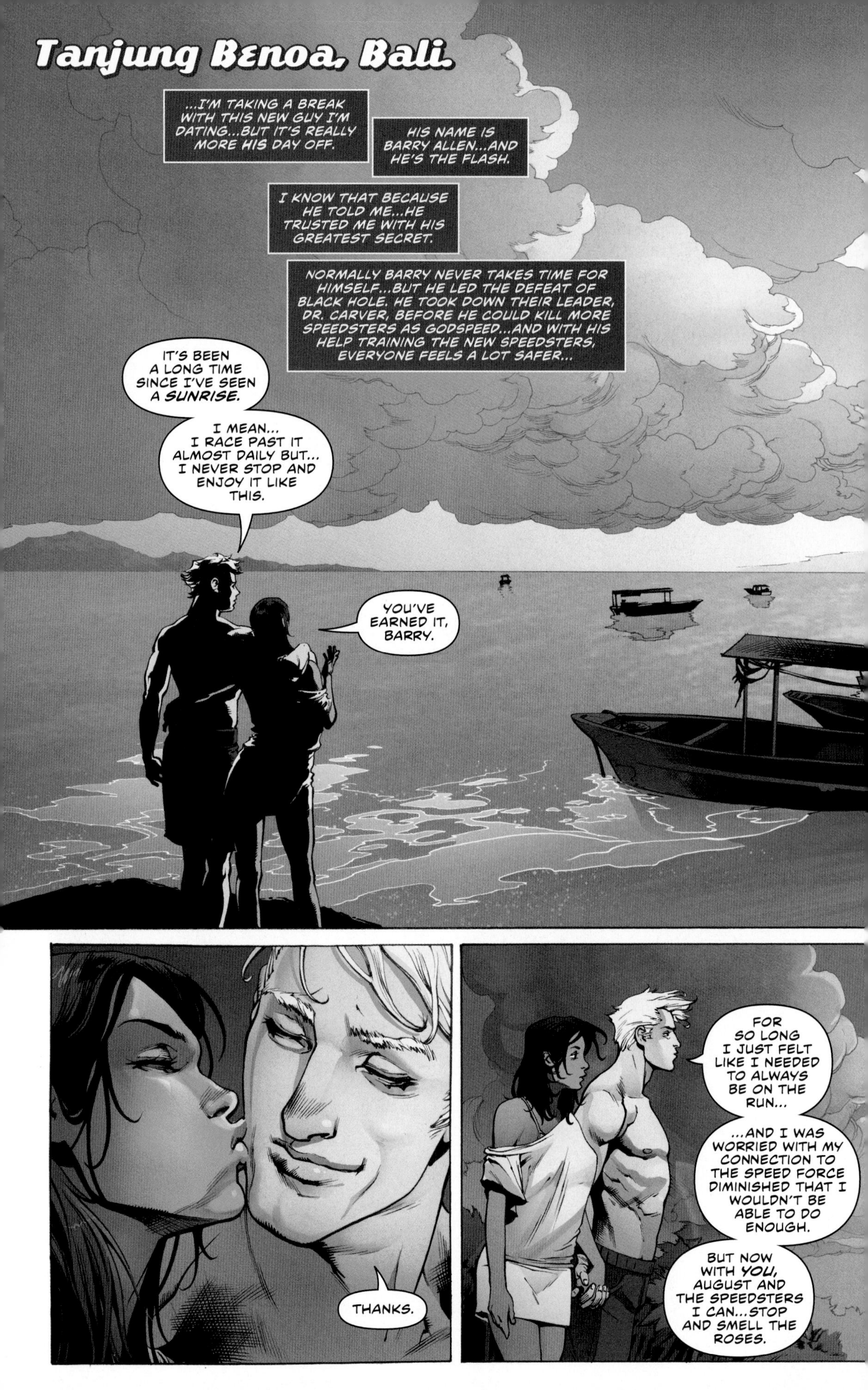
Tanjung Benoa, Bali.
...I'M TAKING A BREAK WITH THIS NEW GUY I'M DATING...BUT IT'S REALLY MORE HIS DAY OFF.
HIS NAME IS BARRY ALLEN...AND HE'S THE FLASH.
I KNOW THAT BECAUSE HE TOLD ME...HE TRUSTED ME WITH HIS GREATEST SECRET.
NORMALLY BARRY NEVER TAKES TIME FOR HIMSELF...BUT HE LED THE DEFEAT OF BLACK HOLE. HE TOOK DOWN THEIR LEADER, DR. CARVER, BEFORE HE COULD KILL MORE SPEEDSTERS AS GODSPEED...AND WITH HIS HELP TRAINING THE NEW SPEEDSTERS, EVERYONE FEELS A LOT SAFER...
IT'S BEEN A LONG TIME SINCE I'VE SEEN A SUNRISE.
I MEAN... I RACE PAST IT ALMOST DAILY BUT... I NEVER STOP AND ENJOY IT LIKE THIS.
YOU'VE EARNED IT, BARRY.
THANKS.
FOR SO LONG I JUST FELT LIKE I NEEDED TO ALWAYS BE ON THE RUN...
...AND I WAS WORRIED WITH MY CONNECTION TO THE SPEED FORCE DIMINISHED THAT I WOULDN'T BE ABLE TO DO ENOUGH.
BUT NOW WITH YOU, AUGUST AND THE SPEEDSTERS I CAN...STOP AND SMELL THE ROSES.

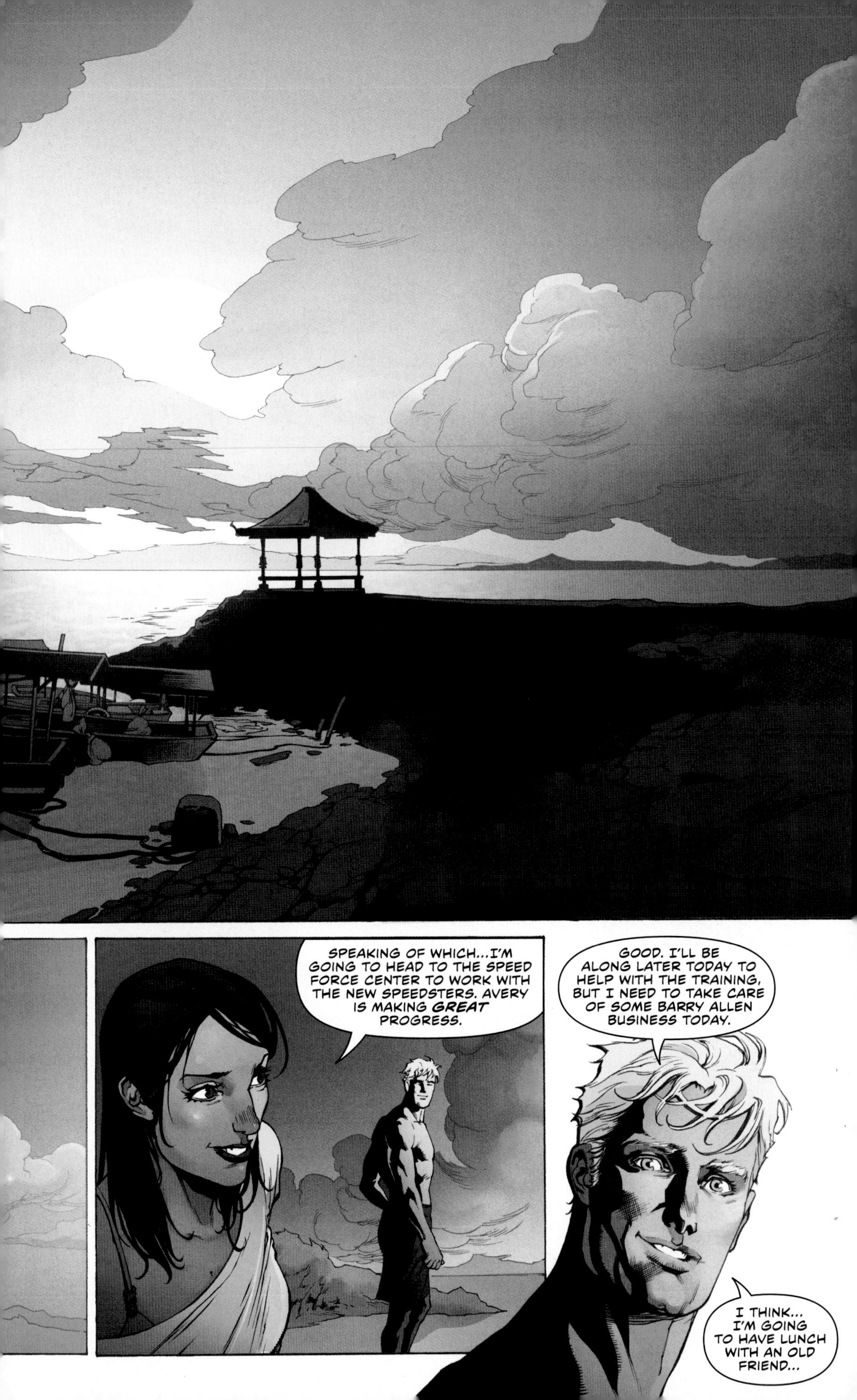
SPEAKING OF WHICH...I'M GOING TO HEAD TO THE SPEED FORCE CENTER TO WORK WITH THE NEW SPEEDSTERS. AVERY IS MAKING GREAT PROGRESS.
GOOD. I'LL BE ALONG LATER TODAY TO HELP WITH THE TRAINING, BUT I NEED TO TAKE CARE OF SOME BARRY ALLEN BUSINESS TODAY.
I THINK... I'M GOING TO HAVE LUNCH WITH AN OLD FRIEND...

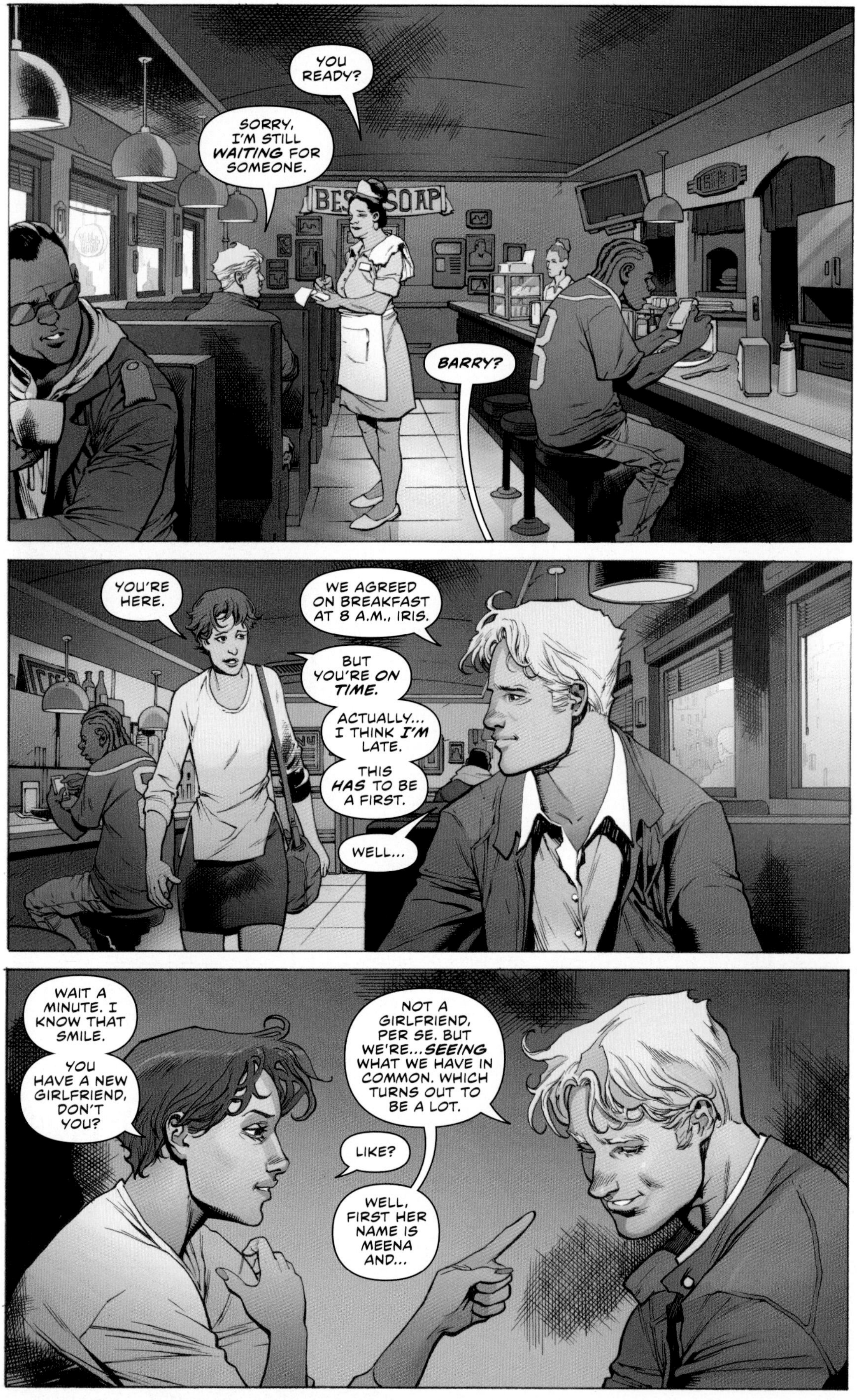
YOU READY?
SORRY, I'M STILL *WAITING* FOR SOMEONE.
BARRY?
YOU'RE HERE.
WE AGREED ON BREAKFAST AT 8 A.M., IRIS.
BUT YOU'RE *ON TIME.*
ACTUALLY... I THINK *I'M* LATE.
THIS *HAS* TO BE A FIRST.
WELL...
WAIT A MINUTE. I KNOW THAT SMILE.
YOU HAVE A NEW GIRLFRIEND, DON'T YOU?
NOT A GIRLFRIEND, PER SE. BUT WE'RE...*SEEING* WHAT WE HAVE IN COMMON. WHICH TURNS OUT TO BE A LOT.
LIKE?
WELL, FIRST HER NAME IS MEENA AND...

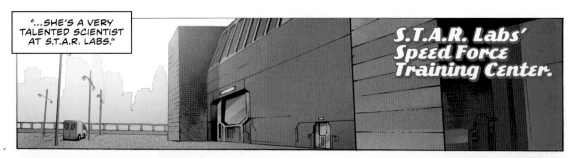

"...SHE'S A VERY TALENTED SCIENTIST AT S.T.A.R. LABS."

S.T.A.R. Labs' Speed Force Training Center.

THE SPEEDSTERS DOING WELL?

DETECTIVE AUGUST HEART WAS THE FIRST TO BE HIT BY THE LIGHTNING AND IS THE FLASH'S NEWEST PARTNER. WE DON'T ALWAYS SEE EYE TO EYE, BUT I CAN TELL HE'S A GOOD MAN WHO CARES ABOUT THE SPEEDSTERS.

EXCELLENT.

TODAY WE MIGHT EVEN PRACTICE CATCHING **BULLETS** AT SUPER-SPEED.

YOU'RE JOKING...TELL ME YOU'RE **JOKING?**

IF THEY'RE ALL GOING TO USE THE SPEED FORCE TO BE **SUPERHEROES,** THEY'RE GOING TO NEED TO BE READY TO RACE INTO DANGER.

THAT MEANS SOMETIMES THEY'RE GONNA GET SHOT AT...OR WORSE.

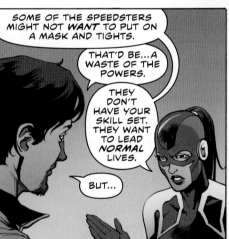

SOME OF THE SPEEDSTERS MIGHT NOT **WANT** TO PUT ON A MASK AND TIGHTS.

THAT'D BE...A WASTE OF THE POWERS.

THEY DON'T HAVE YOUR SKILL SET. THEY WANT TO LEAD **NORMAL** LIVES.

BUT...

HOLD ON...THERE IS SOMEONE OUTSIDE...

"...A **SPEEDSTER.**"

HERE YOU ARE, WALLY...DO YOU GO INSIDE AND LEARN ABOUT THE SPEED FORCE...?

NO...I **CAN'T.**

IF AUNT IRIS FOUND OUT, SHE'D BE TOO WORRIED.

WHERE YA GOING, KID?

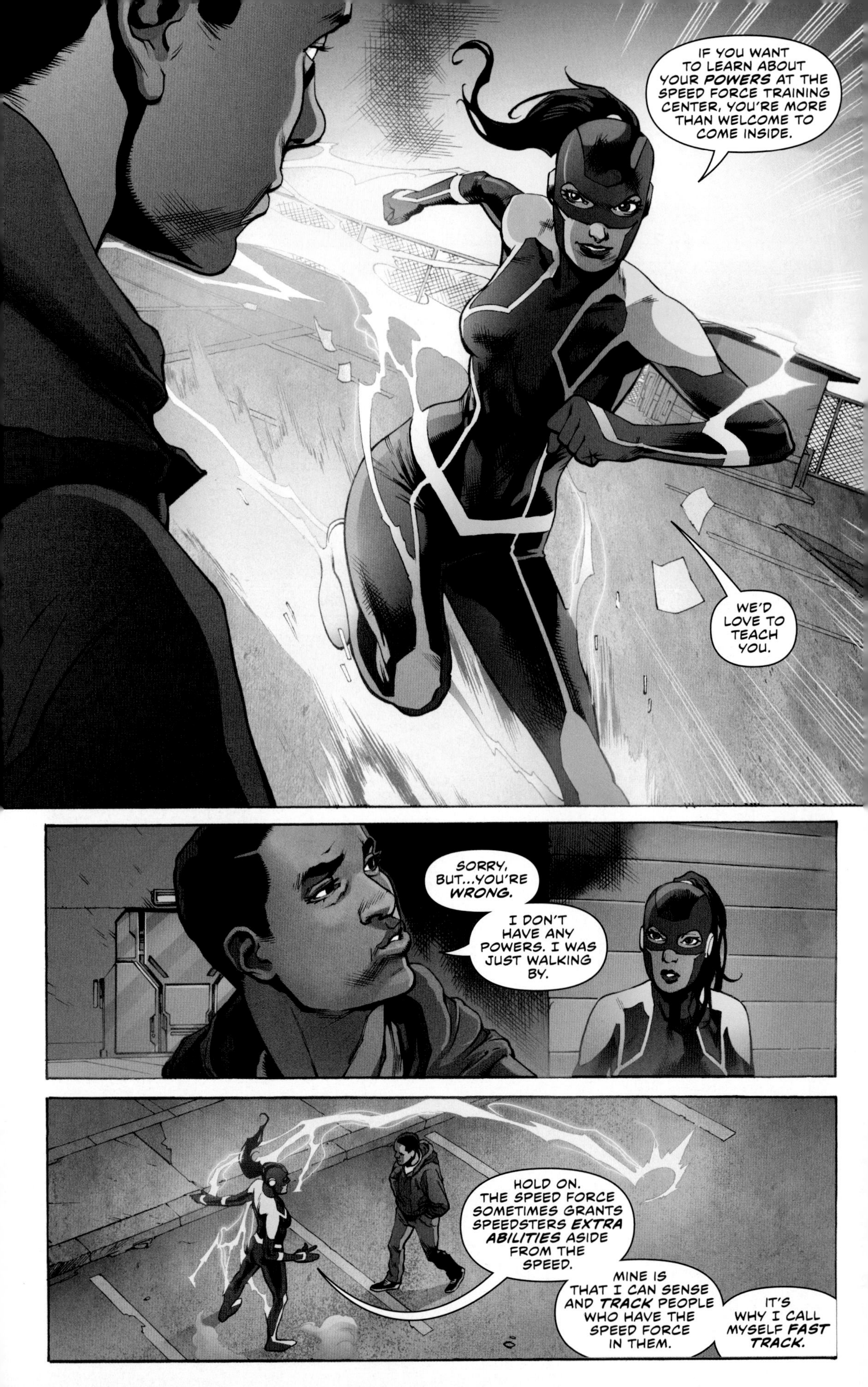
IF YOU WANT TO LEARN ABOUT YOUR *POWERS* AT THE SPEED FORCE TRAINING CENTER, YOU'RE MORE THAN WELCOME TO COME INSIDE.
WE'D LOVE TO TEACH YOU.
SORRY, BUT...YOU'RE *WRONG.*
I DON'T HAVE ANY POWERS. I WAS JUST WALKING BY.
HOLD ON. THE SPEED FORCE SOMETIMES GRANTS SPEEDSTERS *EXTRA ABILITIES* ASIDE FROM THE SPEED.
MINE IS THAT I CAN SENSE AND *TRACK* PEOPLE WHO HAVE THE SPEED FORCE IN THEM.
IT'S WHY I CALL MYSELF *FAST TRACK.*

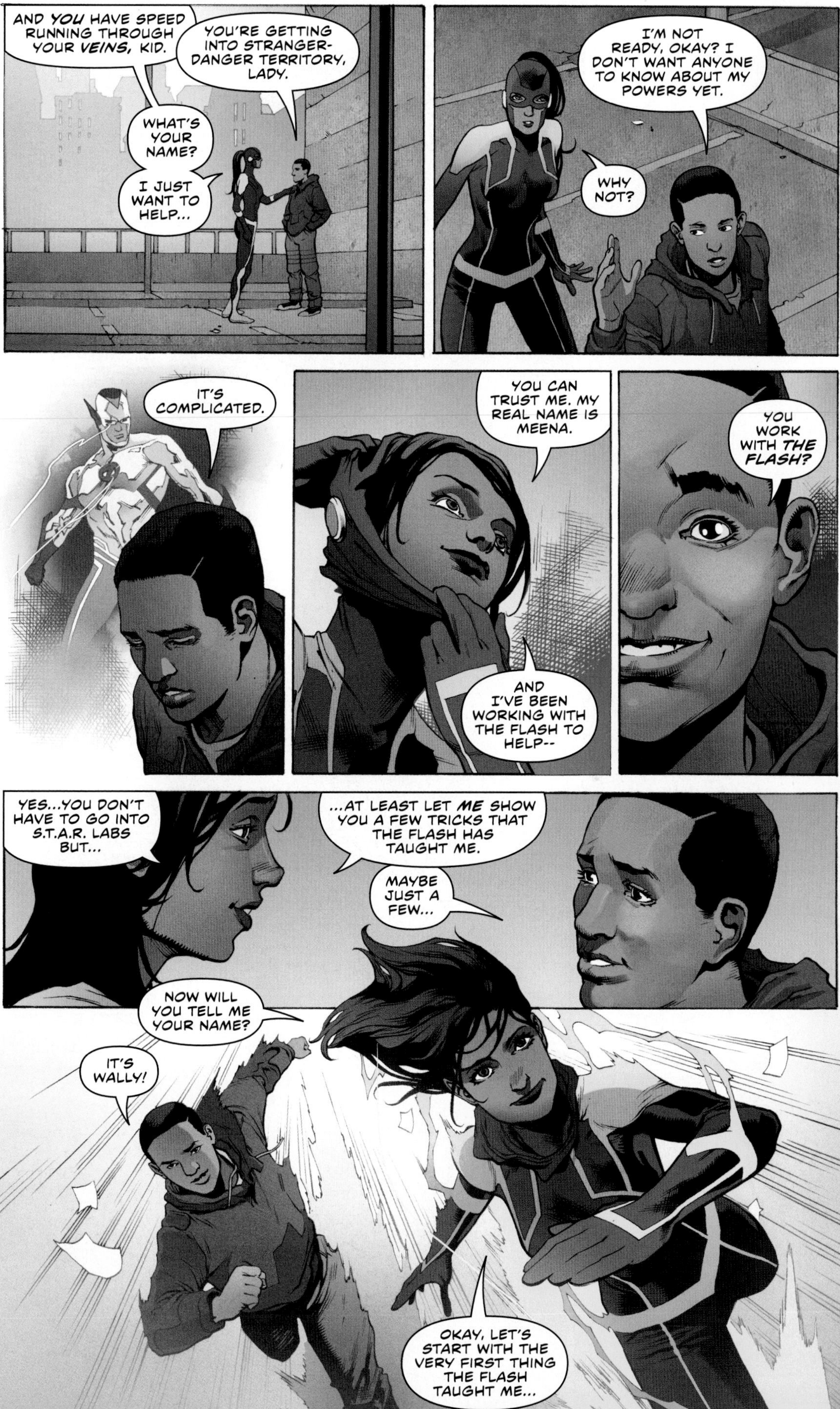
AND YOU HAVE SPEED RUNNING THROUGH YOUR VEINS, KID.
YOU'RE GETTING INTO STRANGER-DANGER TERRITORY, LADY.
WHAT'S YOUR NAME?
I JUST WANT TO HELP...
I'M NOT READY, OKAY? I DON'T WANT ANYONE TO KNOW ABOUT MY POWERS YET.
WHY NOT?
IT'S COMPLICATED.
YOU CAN TRUST ME. MY REAL NAME IS MEENA.
AND I'VE BEEN WORKING WITH THE FLASH TO HELP--
YOU WORK WITH THE FLASH?
YES...YOU DON'T HAVE TO GO INTO S.T.A.R. LABS BUT...
...AT LEAST LET ME SHOW YOU A FEW TRICKS THAT THE FLASH HAS TAUGHT ME.
MAYBE JUST A FEW...
NOW WILL YOU TELL ME YOUR NAME?
IT'S WALLY!
OKAY, LET'S START WITH THE VERY FIRST THING THE FLASH TAUGHT ME...

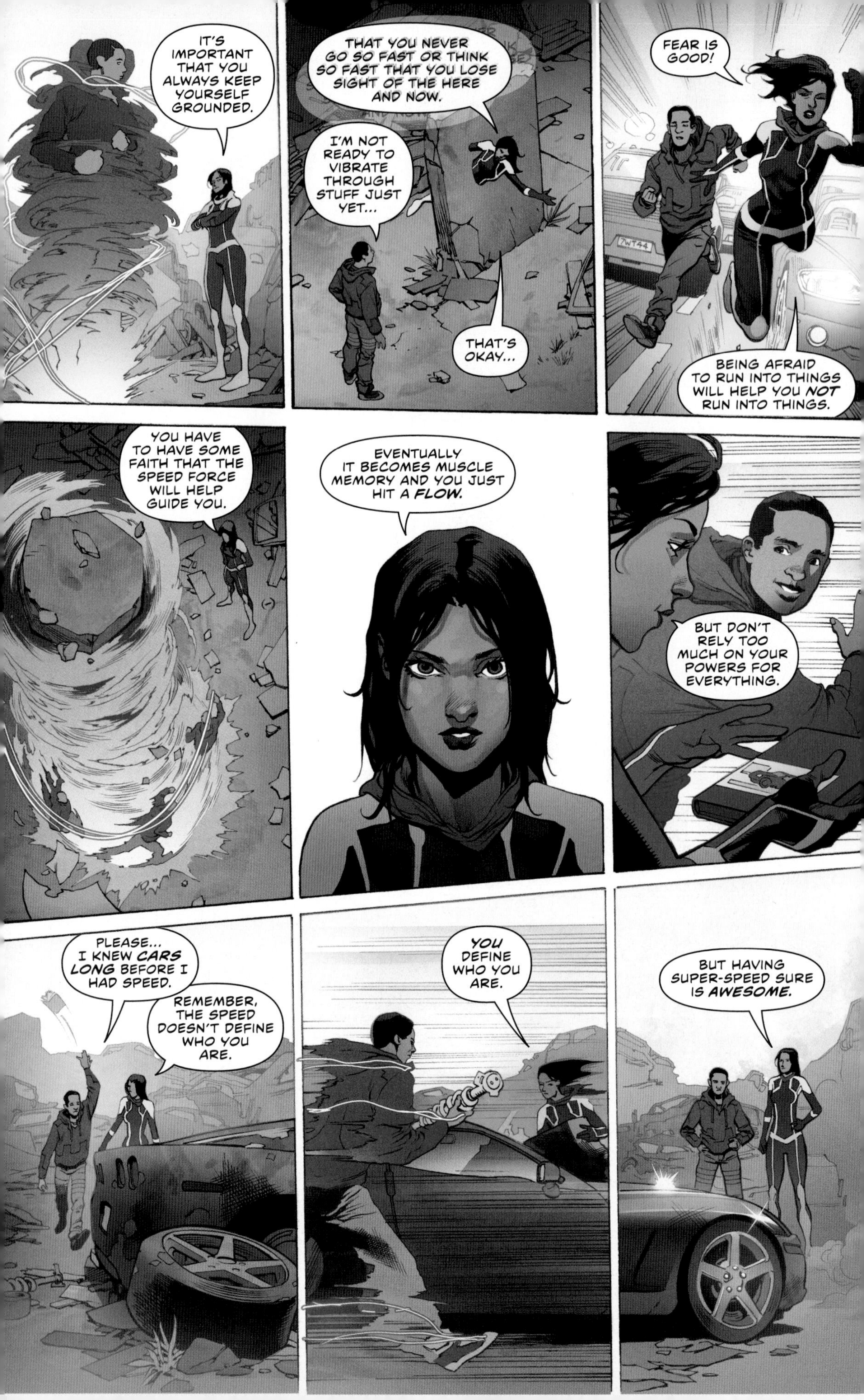
IT'S IMPORTANT THAT YOU ALWAYS KEEP YOURSELF GROUNDED.
THAT YOU NEVER GO SO FAST OR THINK SO FAST THAT YOU LOSE SIGHT OF THE HERE AND NOW.
I'M NOT READY TO VIBRATE THROUGH STUFF JUST YET...
THAT'S OKAY...
FEAR IS GOOD!
BEING AFRAID TO RUN INTO THINGS WILL HELP YOU *NOT* RUN INTO THINGS.
YOU HAVE TO HAVE SOME FAITH THAT THE SPEED FORCE WILL HELP GUIDE YOU.
EVENTUALLY IT BECOMES MUSCLE MEMORY AND YOU JUST HIT A *FLOW.*
BUT DON'T RELY TOO MUCH ON YOUR POWERS FOR EVERYTHING.
PLEASE... I KNEW *CARS LONG* BEFORE I HAD SPEED.
REMEMBER, THE SPEED DOESN'T DEFINE WHO YOU ARE.
YOU DEFINE WHO YOU ARE.
BUT HAVING SUPER-SPEED SURE IS *AWESOME.*

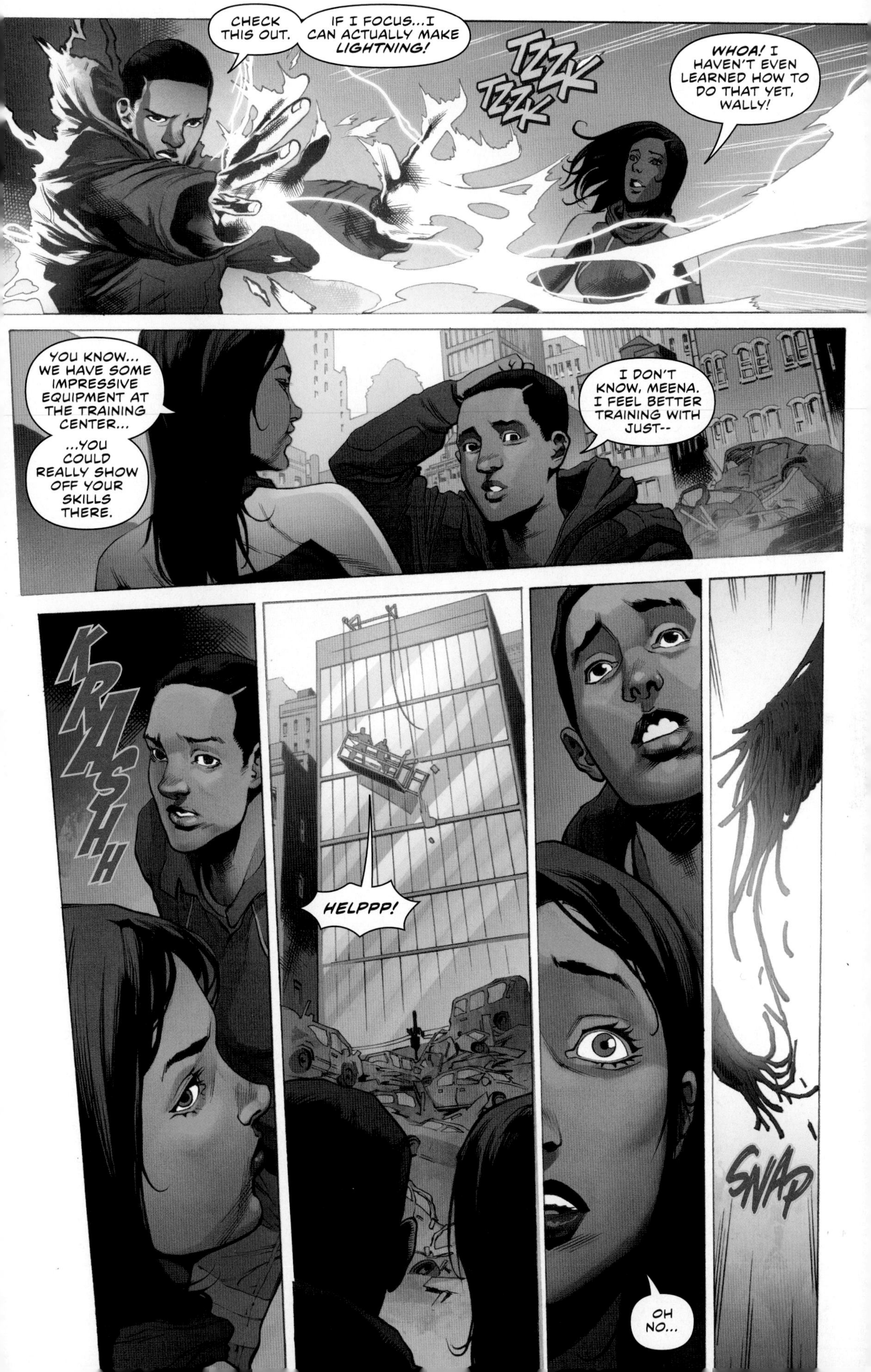
CHECK THIS OUT.
IF I FOCUS...I CAN ACTUALLY MAKE LIGHTNING!
TZZK TZZK
WHOA! I HAVEN'T EVEN LEARNED HOW TO DO THAT YET, WALLY!
YOU KNOW... WE HAVE SOME IMPRESSIVE EQUIPMENT AT THE TRAINING CENTER...
...YOU COULD REALLY SHOW OFF YOUR SKILLS THERE.
I DON'T KNOW, MEENA. I FEEL BETTER TRAINING WITH JUST--
KRASHHH
HELPPP!
OH NO...
SNAP

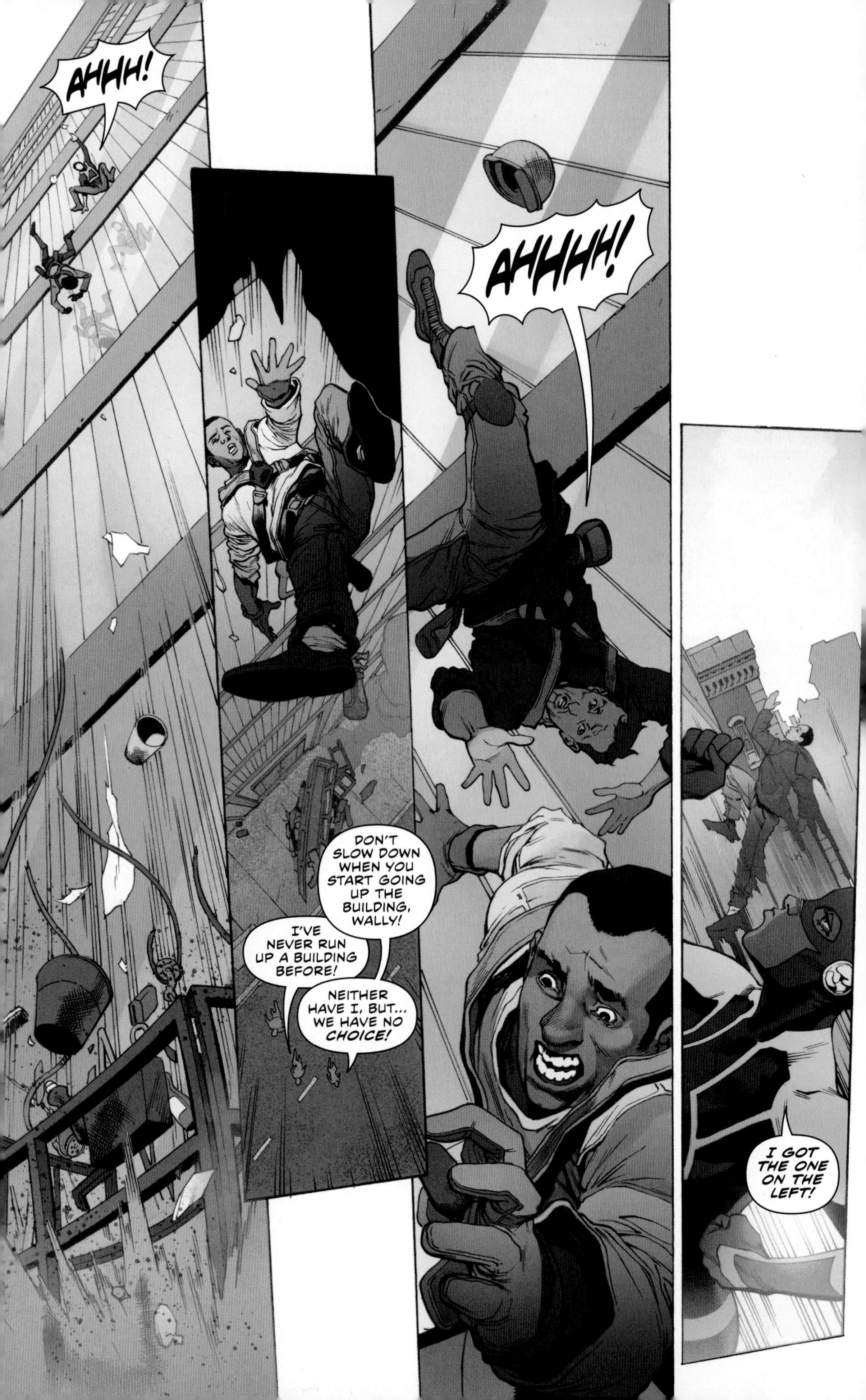
AHHH!
AHHHH!
DON'T SLOW DOWN WHEN YOU START GOING UP THE BUILDING, WALLY!
I'VE NEVER RUN UP A BUILDING BEFORE!
NEITHER HAVE I, BUT... WE HAVE NO CHOICE!
I GOT THE ONE ON THE LEFT!

AND I HAVE THE ONE ON THE RIGHT!

THEY'RE TOO HEAVY!

WHAT NOW?!

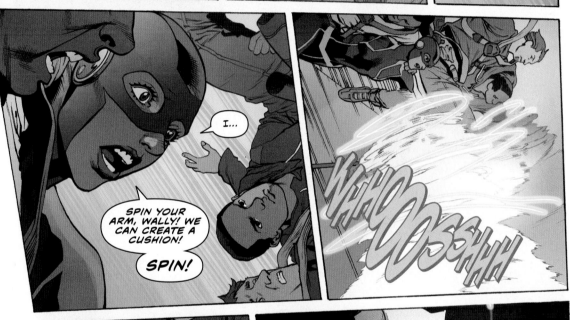

I...

SPIN YOUR ARM, WALLY! WE CAN CREATE A CUSHION!

SPIN!

WHHOOSSHH

WE'RE STILL GOING TOO FAST!

TRUST ME, WALLY!

OOOSSHH

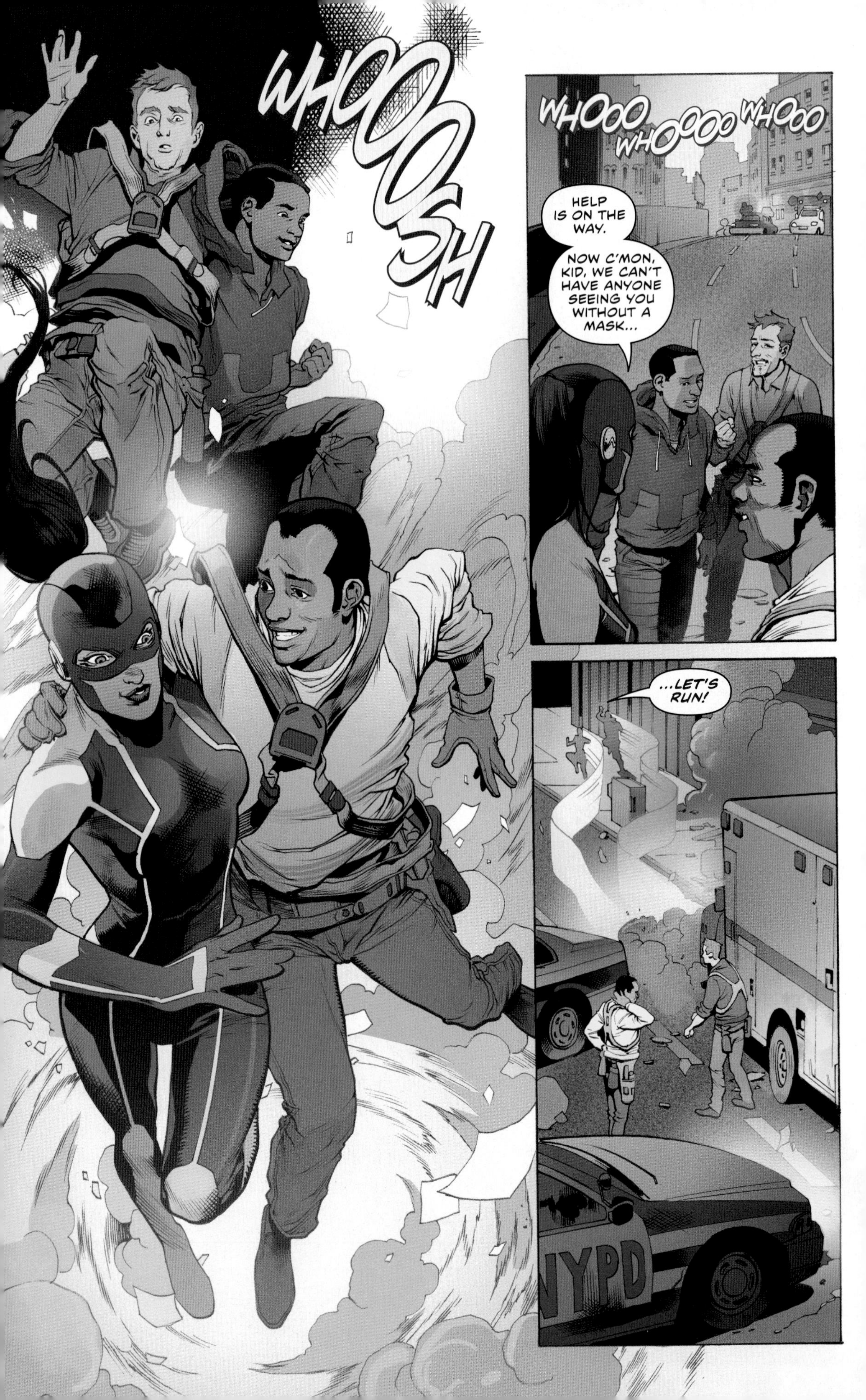
WHOOOOSH
WHOOO
WHOOOOO
WHOOO
HELP IS ON THE WAY.
NOW C'MON, KID, WE CAN'T HAVE ANYONE SEEING YOU WITHOUT A MASK...
...LET'S RUN!
NYPD

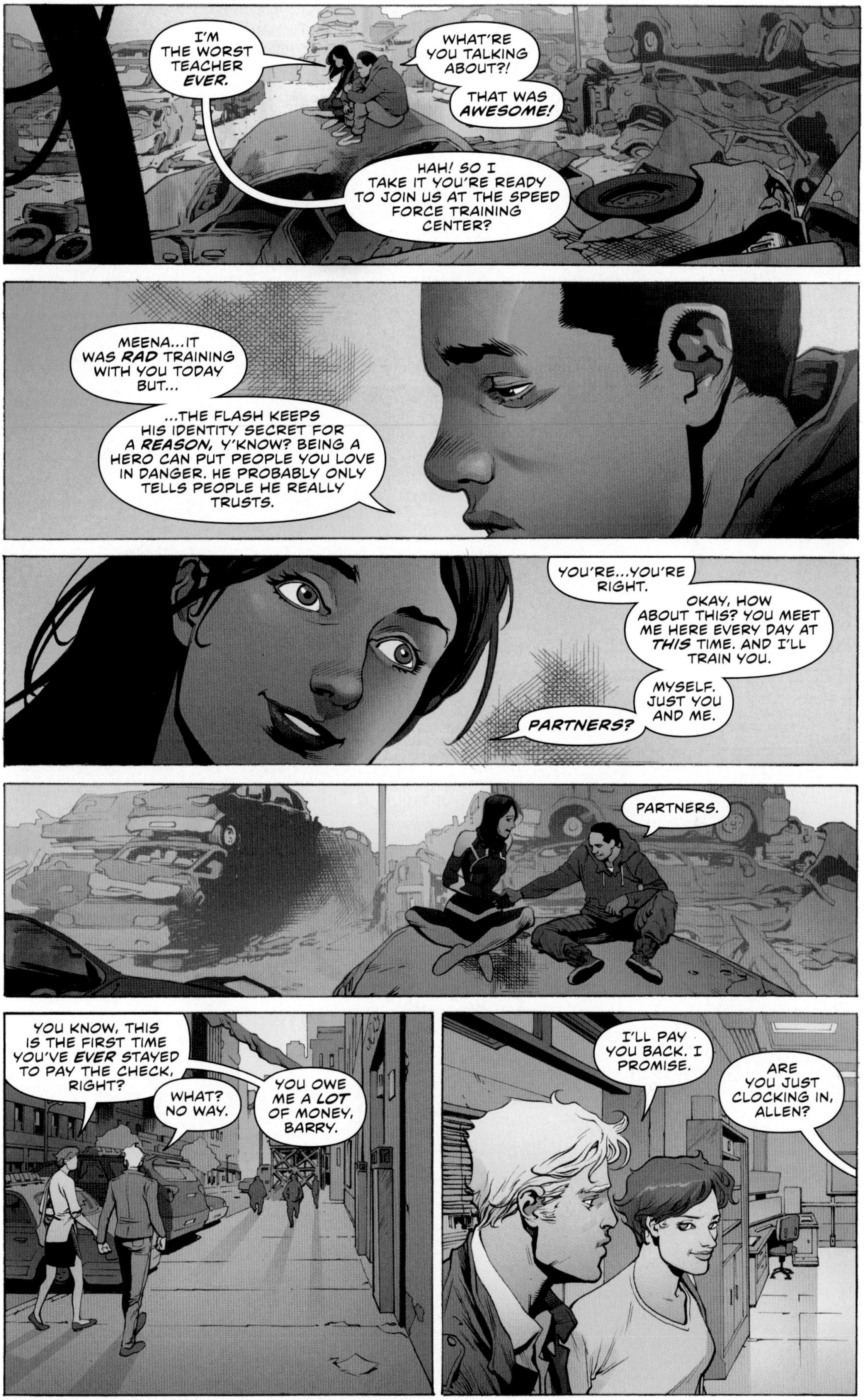
I'M THE WORST TEACHER EVER.
WHAT'RE YOU TALKING ABOUT?!
THAT WAS AWESOME!
HAH! SO I TAKE IT YOU'RE READY TO JOIN US AT THE SPEED FORCE TRAINING CENTER?
MEENA...IT WAS RAD TRAINING WITH YOU TODAY BUT...
...THE FLASH KEEPS HIS IDENTITY SECRET FOR A REASON, Y'KNOW? BEING A HERO CAN PUT PEOPLE YOU LOVE IN DANGER. HE PROBABLY ONLY TELLS PEOPLE HE REALLY TRUSTS.
YOU'RE...YOU'RE RIGHT.
OKAY, HOW ABOUT THIS? YOU MEET ME HERE EVERY DAY AT THIS TIME. AND I'LL TRAIN YOU.
MYSELF. JUST YOU AND ME.
PARTNERS?
PARTNERS.
YOU KNOW, THIS IS THE FIRST TIME YOU'VE EVER STAYED TO PAY THE CHECK, RIGHT?
WHAT? NO WAY.
YOU OWE ME A LOT OF MONEY, BARRY.
I'LL PAY YOU BACK. I PROMISE.
ARE YOU JUST CLOCKING IN, ALLEN?

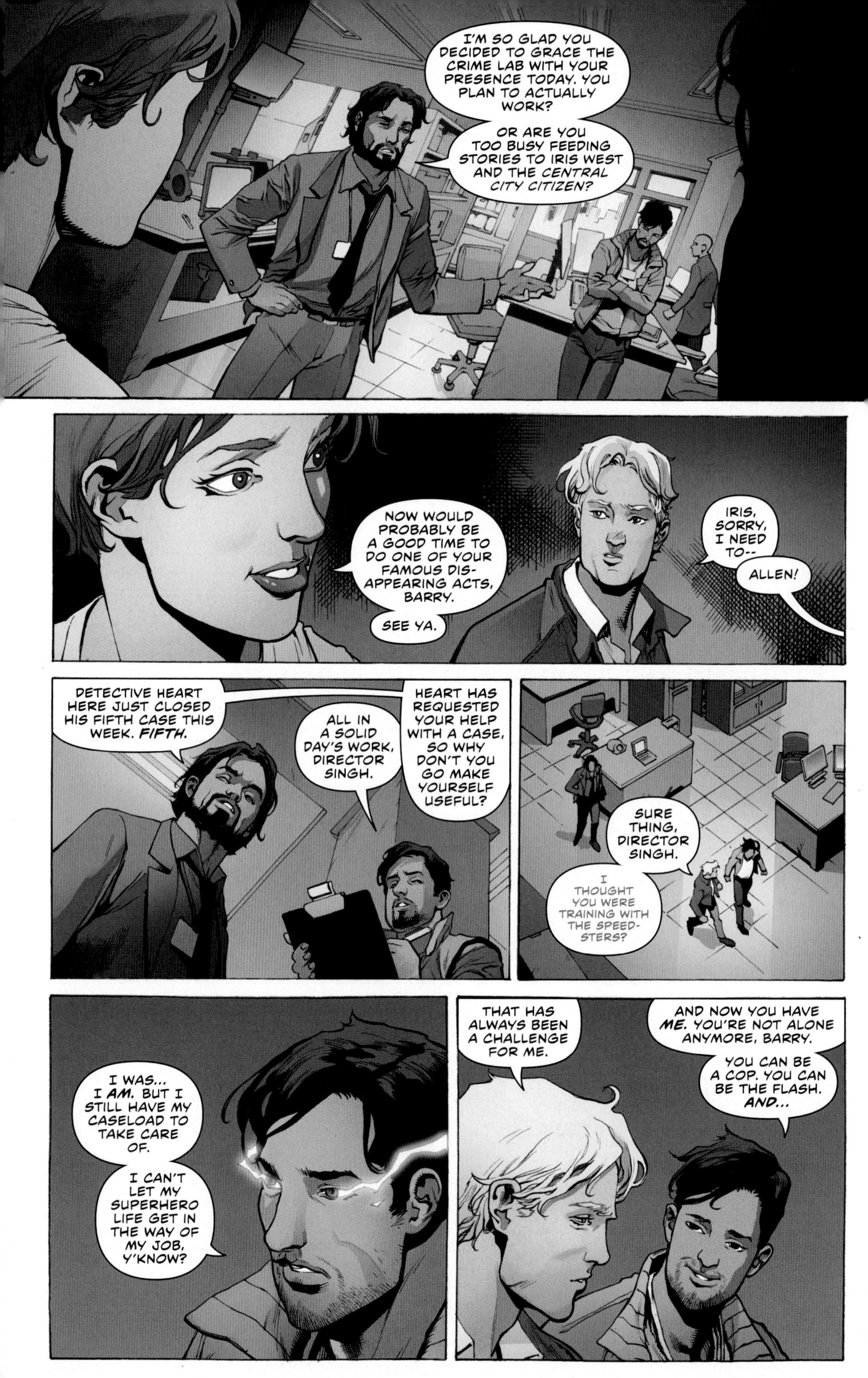
I'M SO GLAD YOU DECIDED TO GRACE THE CRIME LAB WITH YOUR PRESENCE TODAY. YOU PLAN TO ACTUALLY WORK?
OR ARE YOU TOO BUSY FEEDING STORIES TO IRIS WEST AND THE *CENTRAL CITY CITIZEN?*
NOW WOULD PROBABLY BE A GOOD TIME TO DO ONE OF YOUR FAMOUS DIS-APPEARING ACTS, BARRY.
SEE YA.
IRIS, SORRY, I NEED TO--
ALLEN!
DETECTIVE HEART HERE JUST CLOSED HIS FIFTH CASE THIS WEEK. ***FIFTH.***
ALL IN A SOLID DAY'S WORK, DIRECTOR SINGH.
HEART HAS REQUESTED YOUR HELP WITH A CASE, SO WHY DON'T YOU GO MAKE YOURSELF USEFUL?
SURE THING, DIRECTOR SINGH.
I THOUGHT YOU WERE TRAINING WITH THE SPEED-STERS?
I WAS... I ***AM.*** BUT I STILL HAVE MY CASELOAD TO TAKE CARE OF.
I CAN'T LET MY SUPERHERO LIFE GET IN THE WAY OF MY JOB, Y'KNOW?
THAT HAS ALWAYS BEEN A CHALLENGE FOR ME.
AND NOW YOU HAVE ***ME.*** YOU'RE NOT ALONE ANYMORE, BARRY.
YOU CAN BE A COP. YOU CAN BE THE FLASH. ***AND...***

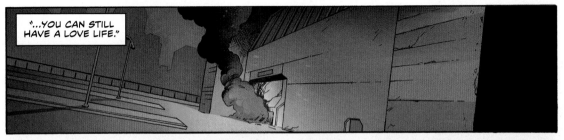

"...YOU CAN STILL HAVE A LOVE LIFE."

WHY ARE THE DOORS SMOKING...?

...OH NO...

...IT'S JUST LIKE GODSPEED'S ATTACK AT IRON HEIGHTS, BUT...CARVER IS STILL IN A COMA...

HELP!

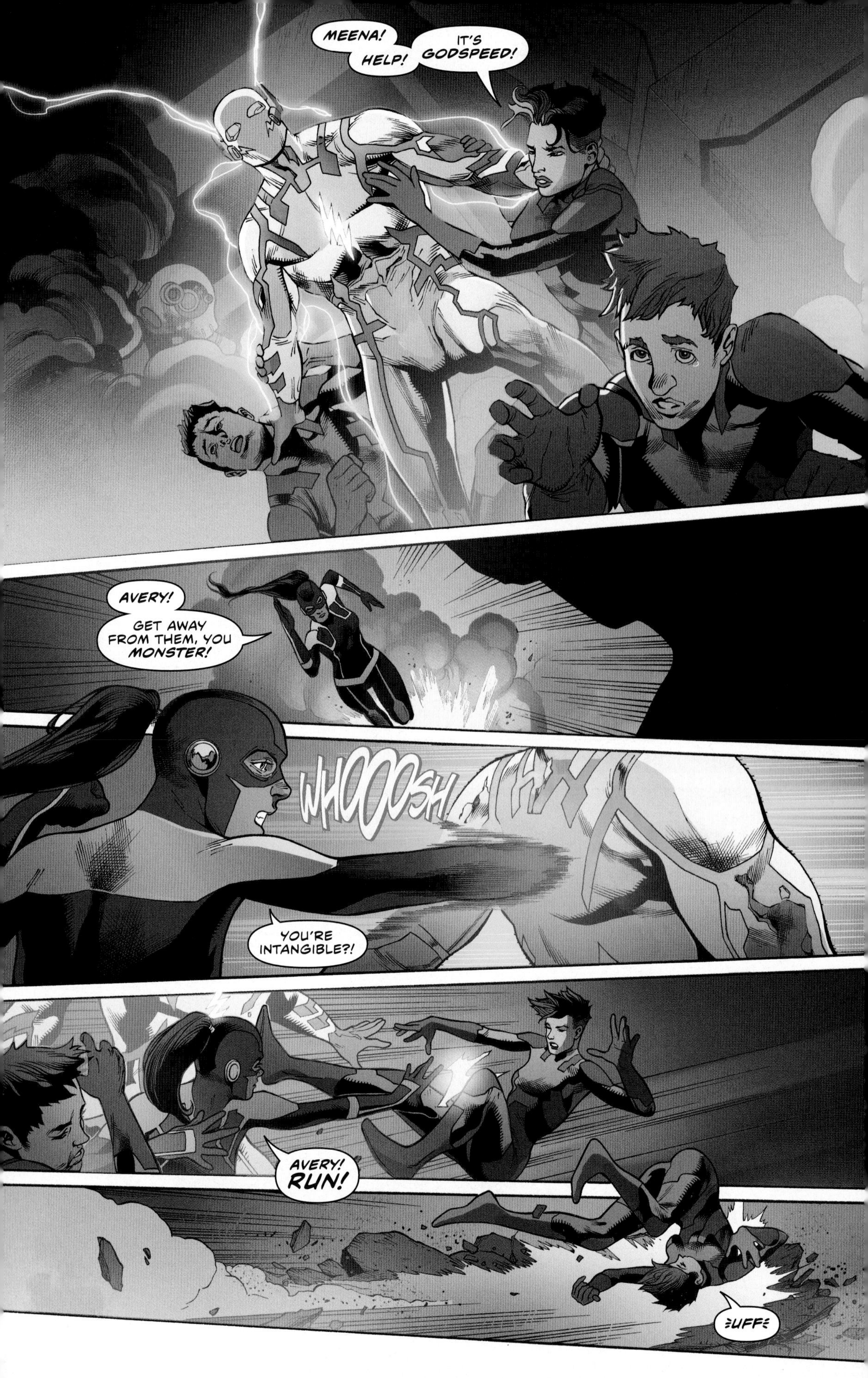

MEENA! HELP!
IT'S GODSPEED!
AVERY! GET AWAY FROM THEM, YOU MONSTER!
WHOOOSH
YOU'RE INTANGIBLE?!
AVERY! RUN!
UFF

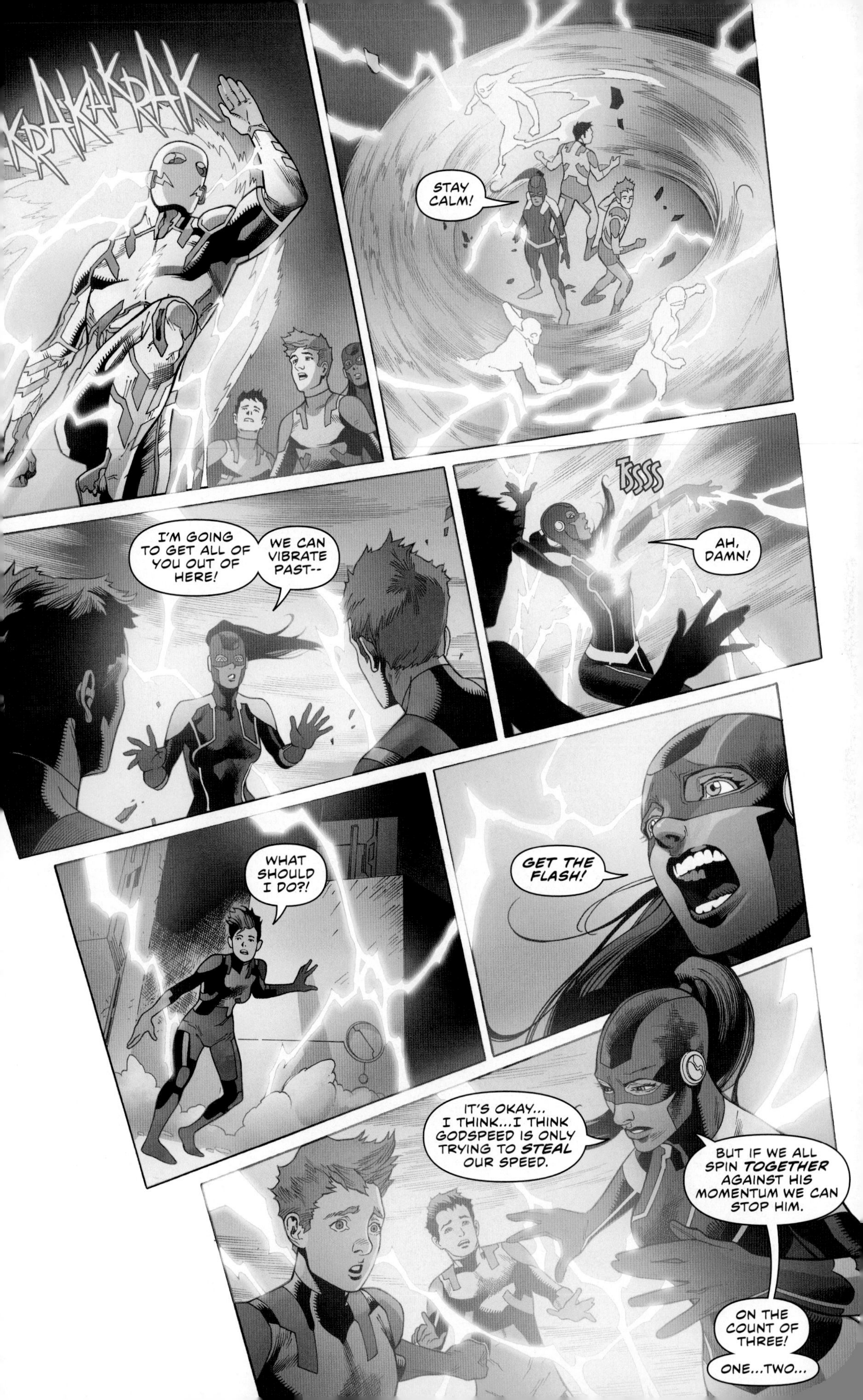
KRAKKAKRAK
STAY CALM!
I'M GOING TO GET ALL OF YOU OUT OF HERE!
WE CAN VIBRATE PAST--
TSSSS
AH, DAMN!
WHAT SHOULD I DO?!
GET THE FLASH!
IT'S OKAY... I THINK...I THINK GODSPEED IS ONLY TRYING TO STEAL OUR SPEED.
BUT IF WE ALL SPIN TOGETHER AGAINST HIS MOMENTUM WE CAN STOP HIM.
ON THE COUNT OF THREE!
ONE...TWO...

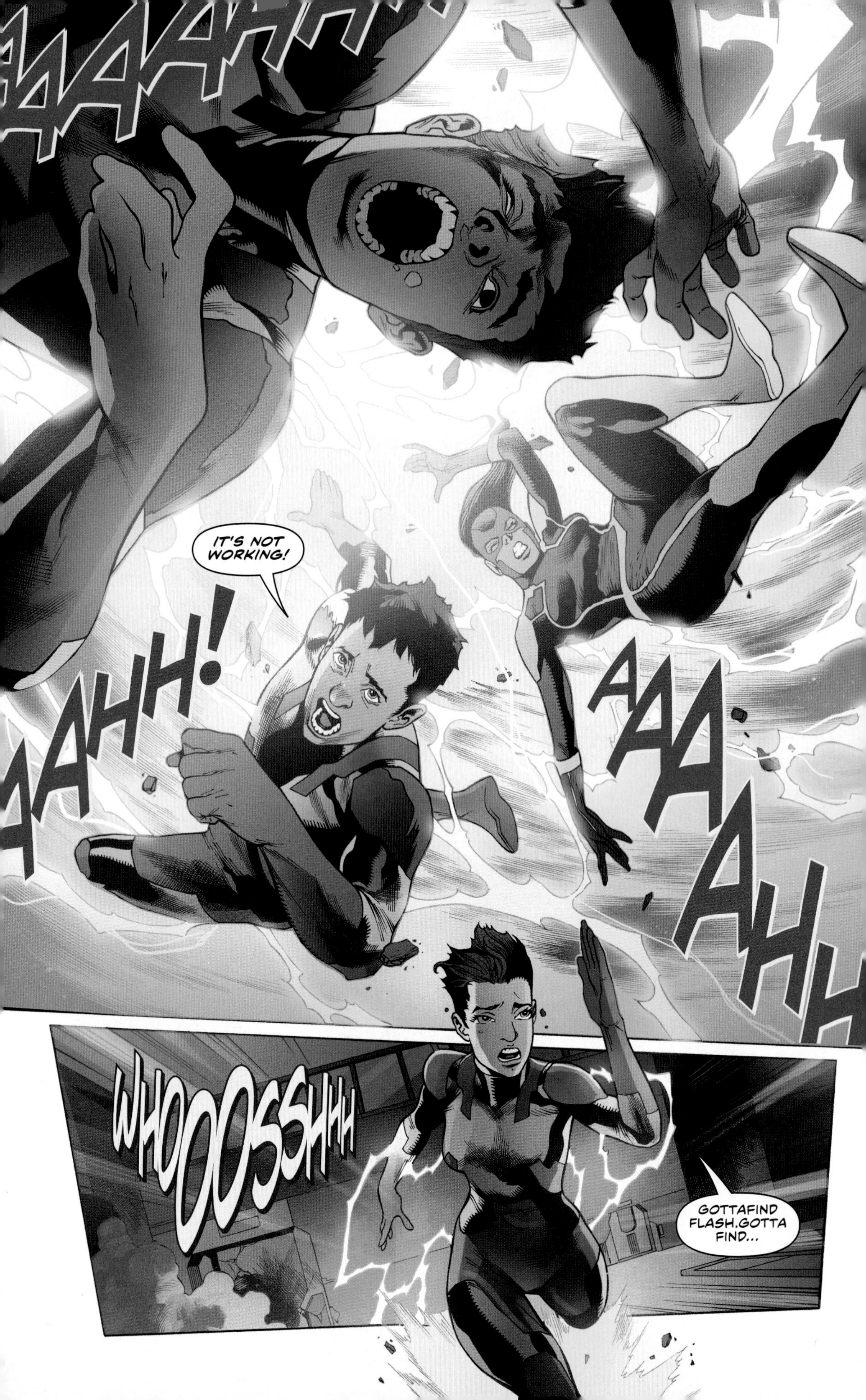
IT'S NOT WORKING!
WHOOOSSHHH
GOTTAFIND FLASH.GOTTA FIND...

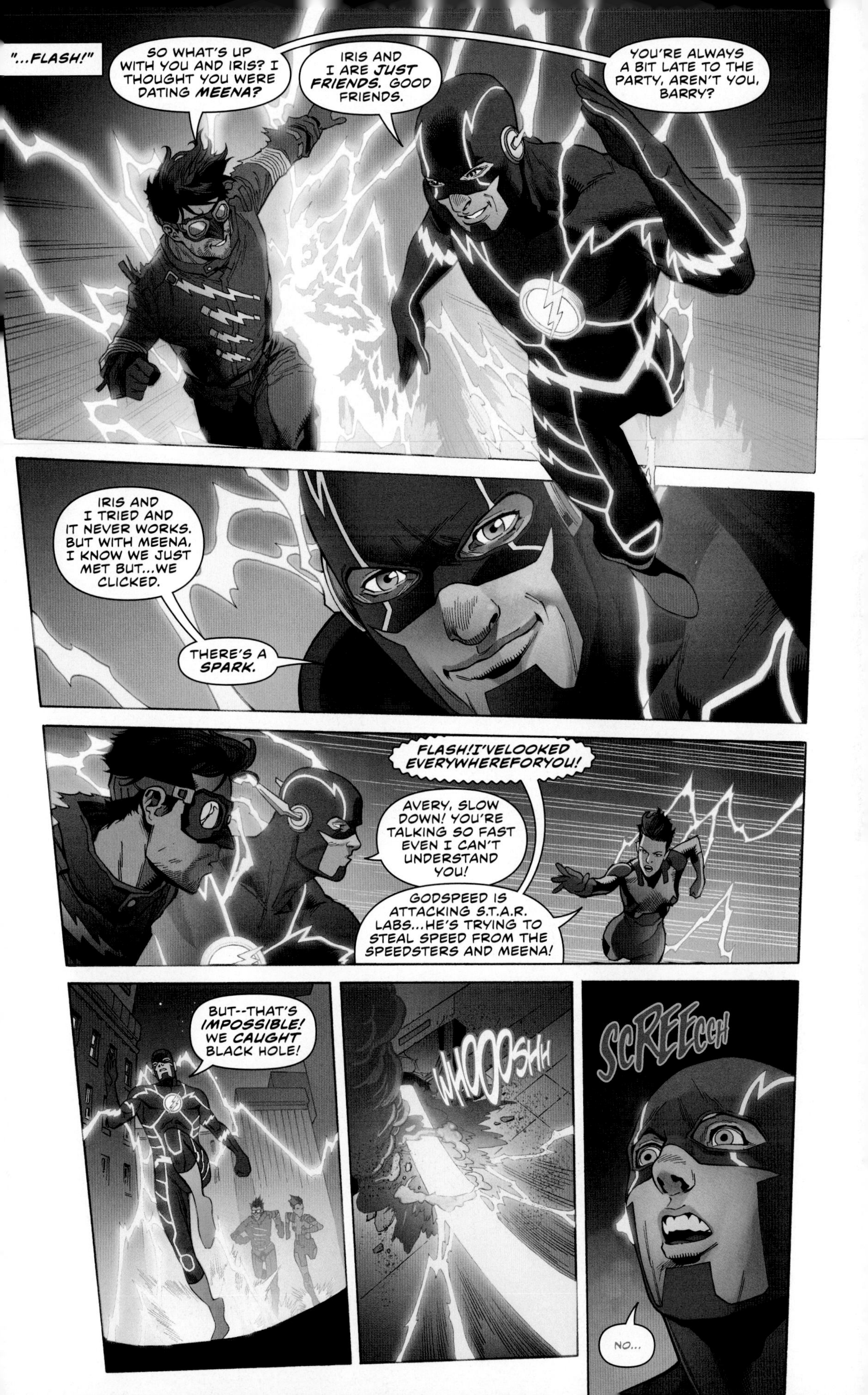
"...FLASH!"
SO WHAT'S UP WITH YOU AND IRIS? I THOUGHT YOU WERE DATING MEENA?
IRIS AND I ARE JUST FRIENDS. GOOD FRIENDS.
YOU'RE ALWAYS A BIT LATE TO THE PARTY, AREN'T YOU, BARRY?
IRIS AND I TRIED AND IT NEVER WORKS. BUT WITH MEENA, I KNOW WE JUST MET BUT...WE CLICKED.
THERE'S A SPARK.
FLASH!I'VELOOKED EVERYWHEREFORYOU!
AVERY, SLOW DOWN! YOU'RE TALKING SO FAST EVEN I CAN'T UNDERSTAND YOU!
GODSPEED IS ATTACKING S.T.A.R. LABS...HE'S TRYING TO STEAL SPEED FROM THE SPEEDSTERS AND MEENA!
BUT--THAT'S IMPOSSIBLE! WE CAUGHT BLACK HOLE!
WHOOOSHH
SCREEccH
NO...

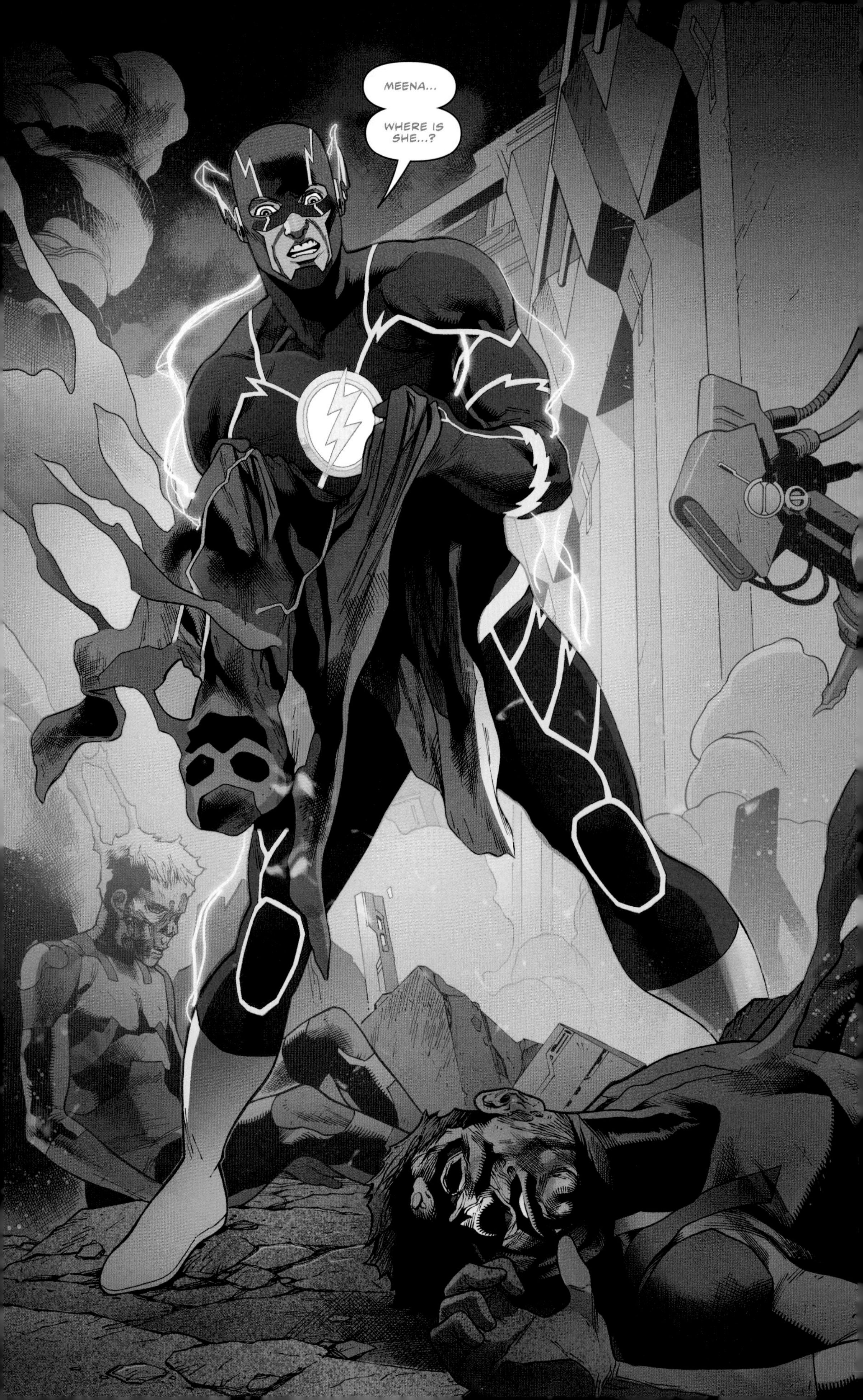
MEENA...
WHERE IS SHE...?

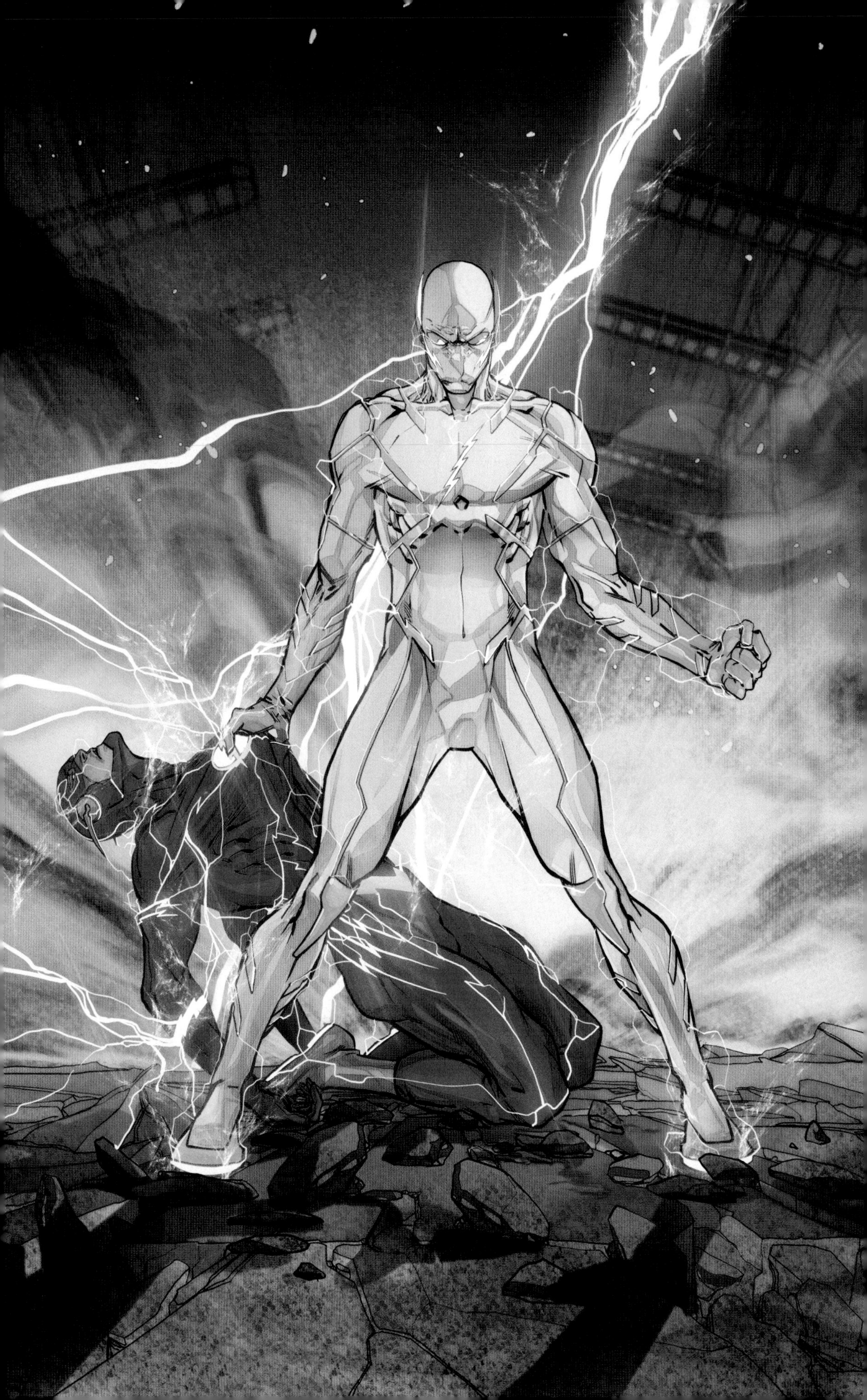

REVENGE

CARMINE DI GIANDOMENICO artist/cover

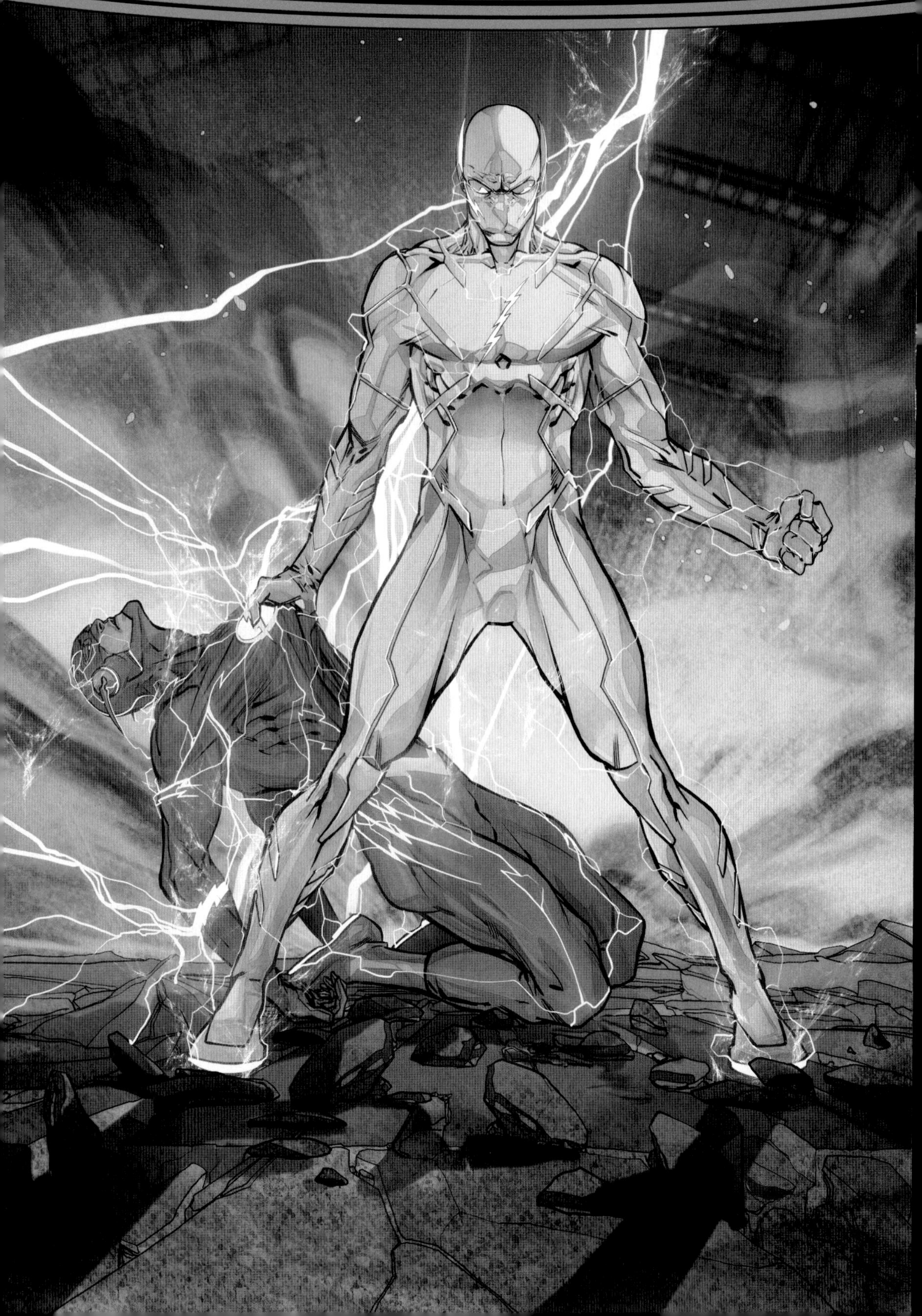

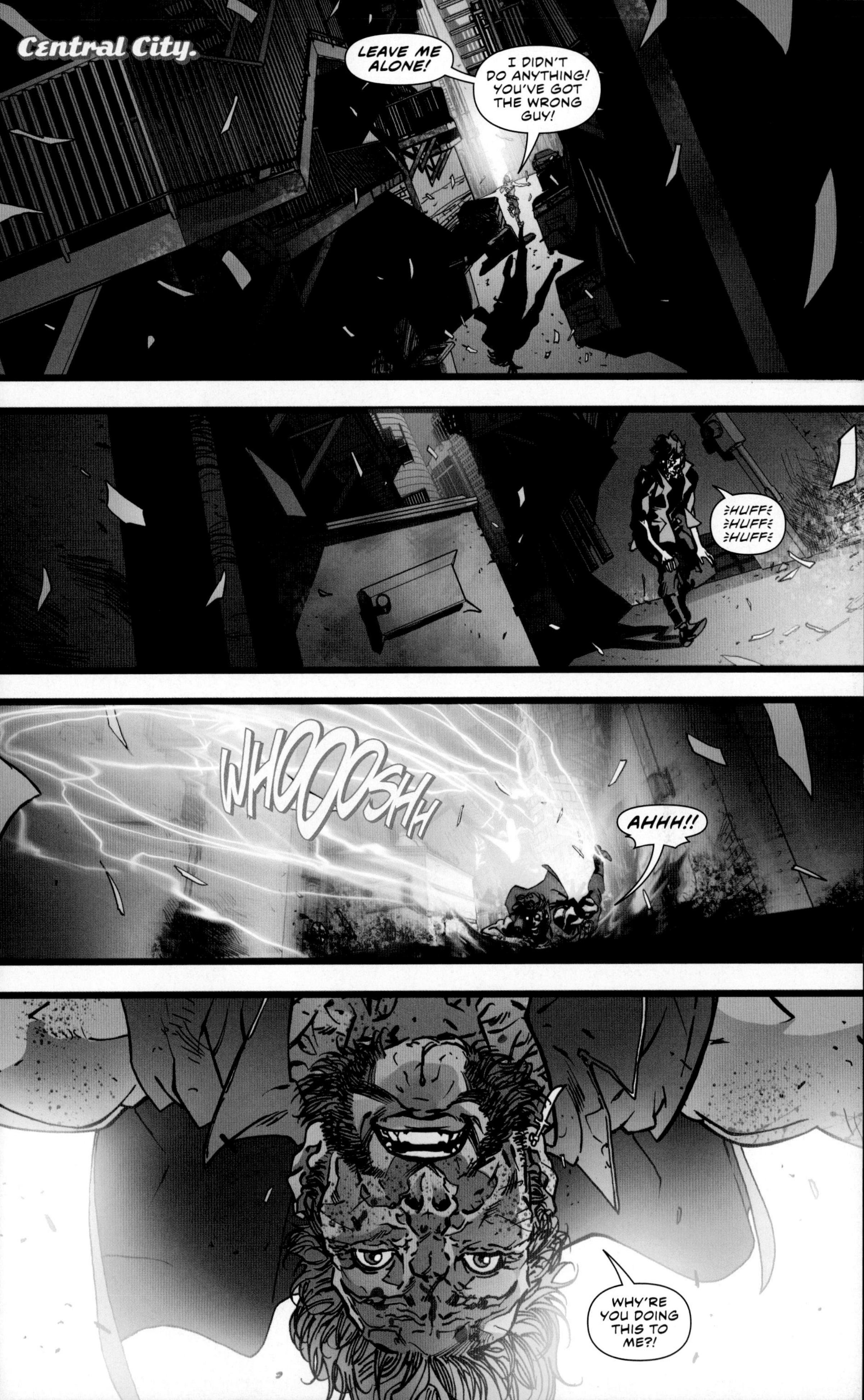
Central City.
LEAVE ME ALONE!
I DIDN'T DO ANYTHING! YOU'VE GOT THE WRONG GUY!
HUFF HUFF HUFF
WHOOOOSHH
AHHH!!
WHY'RE YOU DOING THIS TO ME?!

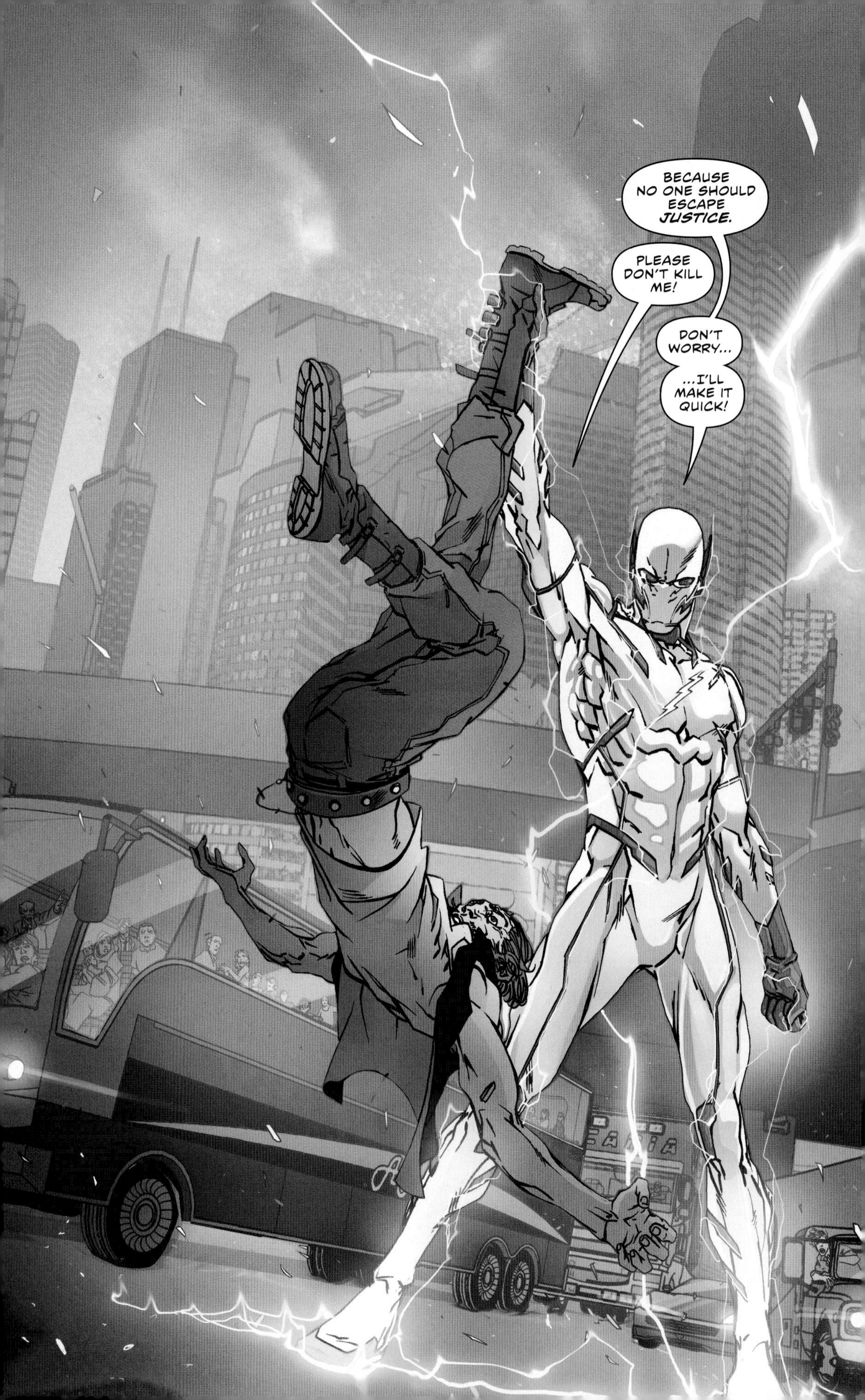
BECAUSE NO ONE SHOULD ESCAPE *JUSTICE*.
PLEASE DON'T KILL ME!
DON'T WORRY...
...I'LL MAKE IT QUICK!

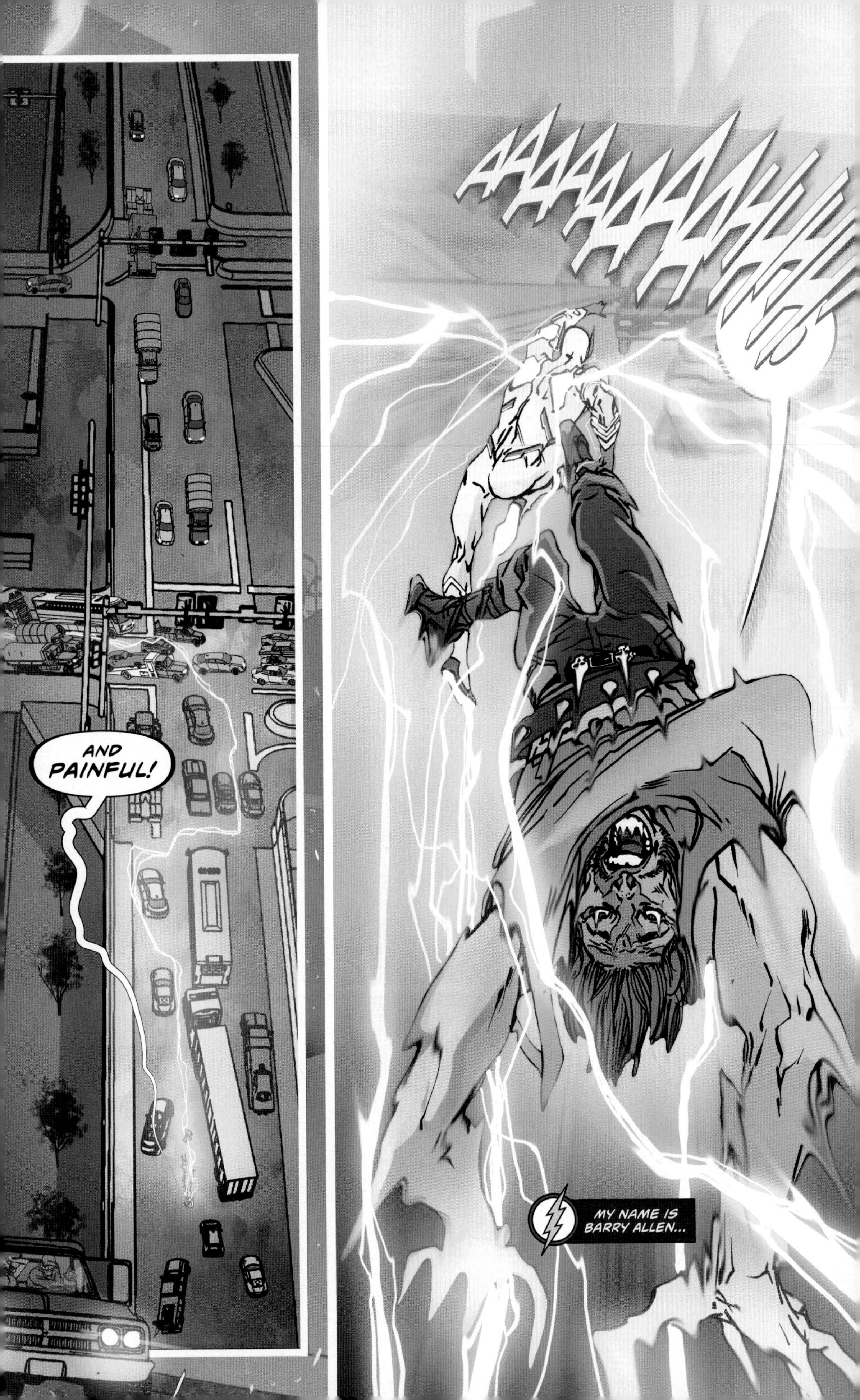
AND PAINFUL!
AAAAAAAAAHHHH
MY NAME IS BARRY ALLEN...

FAILURE.

CENTRAL CITY WAS HIT BY A SPEED STORM THAT GAVE DOZENS OF NORMAL PEOPLE SPEED POWERS JUST LIKE MINE.

ONE STARTED CALLING HIMSELF GODSPEED AND VIOLENTLY STOLE THE SPEED FROM OTHERS, KILLING THEM IN THE PROCESS. I THOUGHT IT WAS DR. CARVER, LEADER OF BLACK HOLE, A FACTION OF ROGUE SCIENTISTS...

S.T.A.R. Labs.

...BUT I WAS WRONG.

I GOT LAZY...AND GODSPEED ATTACKED A GROUP OF SPEEDSTERS, INCLUDING MY GIRLFRIEND, MEENA DHAWAN...

MY FRIEND DETECTIVE AUGUST HEART HAS BEEN TRYING TO HELP ME, BUT I KNOW WHERE HIS PRIORITIES ARE... BLACK HOLE IS THE ONLY CONNECTION HE HAD TO HIS BROTHER'S DEATH.

IRON HEIGHTS IS SAFE AND SECURE, FLASH.

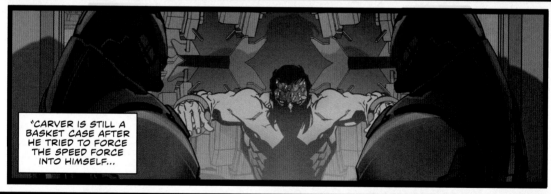

"CARVER IS STILL A BASKET CASE AFTER HE TRIED TO FORCE THE SPEED FORCE INTO HIMSELF...

...AND WITHOUT THEIR LEADER, IT'S LOOKING LIKE THE REMAINING MEMBERS OF BLACK HOLE HAVE GONE INTO HIDING. I'M OUT OF LEADS ON MY BROTHER'S MURDER CASE...

...BILLY PARKS IS STILL OUT THERE...

...BARRY?

BARRY, ARE YOU LISTENING TO ME? MY BROTHER'S CASE HAS GONE COLD AGAIN...?

HM.

HM.

HAVE YOU SLEPT?

WHEN WAS THE LAST TIME YOU LEFT THE LAB?

I SPENT ALL MORNING NOTIFYING THE FAMILIES OF GODSPEED'S VICTIMS, AUGUST.

TELLING THEM THAT THEIR LOVED ONES DIED ON MY WATCH.

YOU SHOULD HAVE LET ME OR ANOTHER DETECTIVE DO THAT.

THE SPEEDSTERS WERE *MY* RESPONSIBILITY.

GODSPEED... BLACK HOLE... I WON'T LET YOUR BROTHER'S CASE BECOME ANOTHER THING THAT I FAILED TO SOLVE.

I NEED TO WORK THE EVIDENCE ON *ALL* THE CASES.

YOU...YOU HAVE DONE *EVERYTHING* FOR THESE *CASES* AS BARRY ALLEN *AND* AS THE FLASH. I KNOW THAT. IT'S PART OF WHO YOU ARE.

IT'S NOT *JUST A CASE* TO ME...IT'S *YOU*... IT'S MEENA.

YOU NEED TO LET YOURSELF GRIEVE, BARRY. MEENA WOULDN'T WANT YOU TO BE PUSHING YOURSELF LIKE THIS.

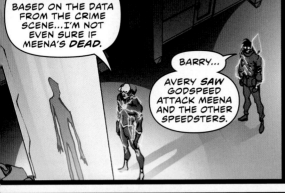

BASED ON THE DATA FROM THE CRIME SCENE...I'M NOT EVEN SURE IF MEENA'S *DEAD.*

BARRY... AVERY *SAW* GODSPEED ATTACK MEENA AND THE OTHER SPEEDSTERS.

MEENA'S SUIT WAS THERE BUT THERE WAS *NO* BODY.

AND WHAT DO WE KNOW ABOUT CRIME SCENES WITH NO BODY?

I THINK...I THINK YOU'RE IN DENIAL.

THE RESULTS FROM MEENA'S SUIT...THEY REMIND ME OF SOMETHING THAT HAPPENED TO *ME* ONCE.

IT WAS...

...A LONG TIME AGO.

BUT THAT'S IMPOSSIBLE.

DON'T START REACHING FOR STRAWS, BARRY... IT'S LIKE YOU ALWAYS SAY...*STAY GROUNDED.* FOLLOW THE EVIDENCE. WE'LL CATCH THIS GUY. *YOU AND ME.*

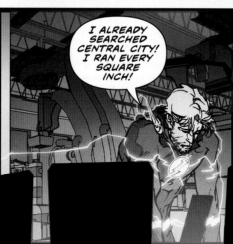

I ALREADY SEARCHED CENTRAL CITY! I RAN EVERY SQUARE INCH!

AND I FOUND *NOTHING.* SO I'M NOT LEAVING THIS LAB AGAIN UNTIL *ALL* THE EVIDENCE HAS BEEN PROCESSED!

BARRY... I KNOW YOU WANT REVENGE BUT--

I WANT *JUSTICE,* AUGUST.

WHEN ARE YOU GOING TO UNDERSTAND THAT?

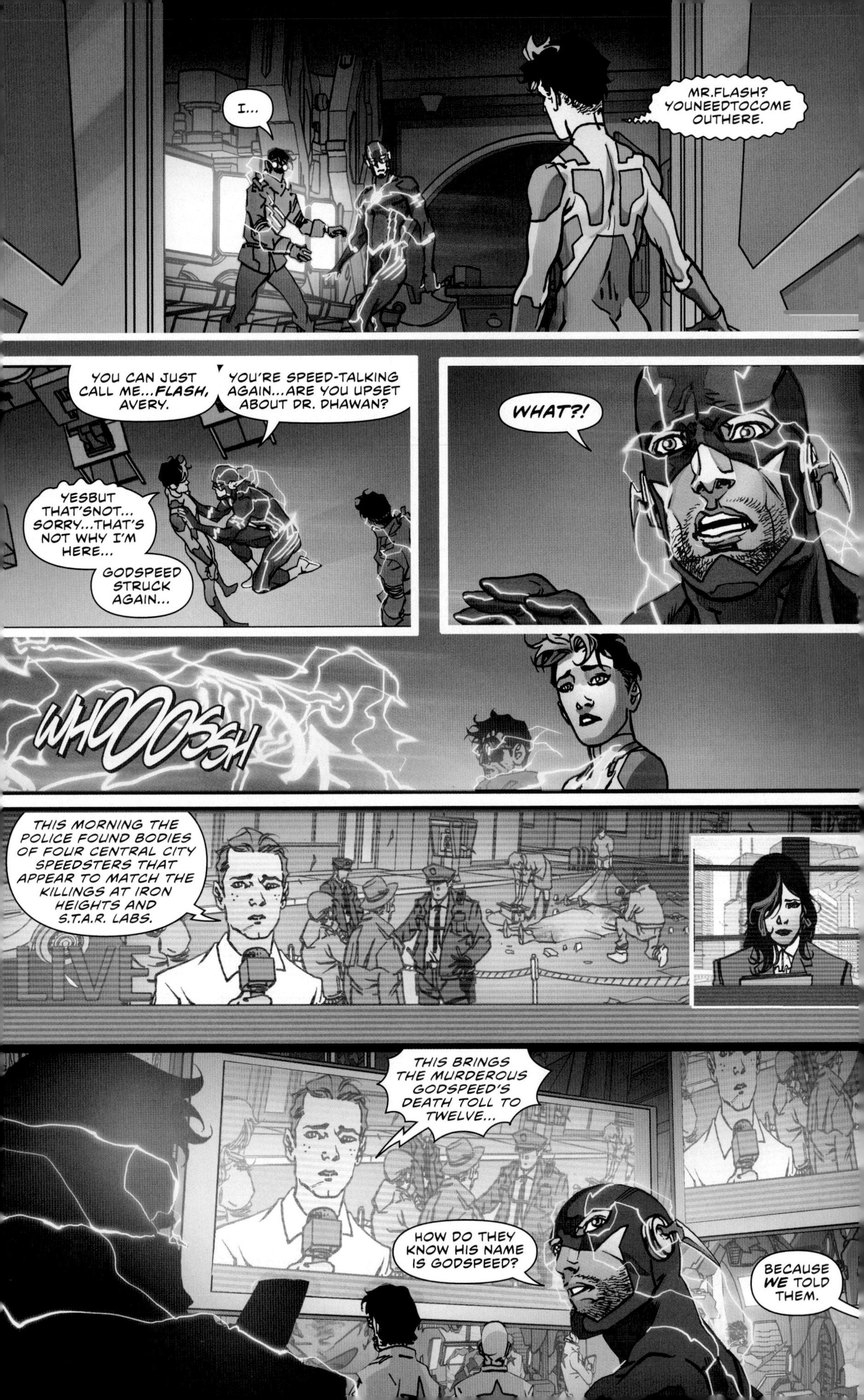
I...
MR.FLASH? YOUNEEDTOCOME OUTHERE.
YOU CAN JUST CALL ME...FLASH, AVERY.
YOU'RE SPEED-TALKING AGAIN...ARE YOU UPSET ABOUT DR. DHAWAN?
YESBUT THAT'SNOT... SORRY...THAT'S NOT WHY I'M HERE...
GODSPEED STRUCK AGAIN...
WHAT?!
WHOOOOSSH
THIS MORNING THE POLICE FOUND BODIES OF FOUR CENTRAL CITY SPEEDSTERS THAT APPEAR TO MATCH THE KILLINGS AT IRON HEIGHTS AND S.T.A.R. LABS.
LIVE
THIS BRINGS THE MURDEROUS GODSPEED'S DEATH TOLL TO TWELVE...
HOW DO THEY KNOW HIS NAME IS GODSPEED?
BECAUSE WE TOLD THEM.

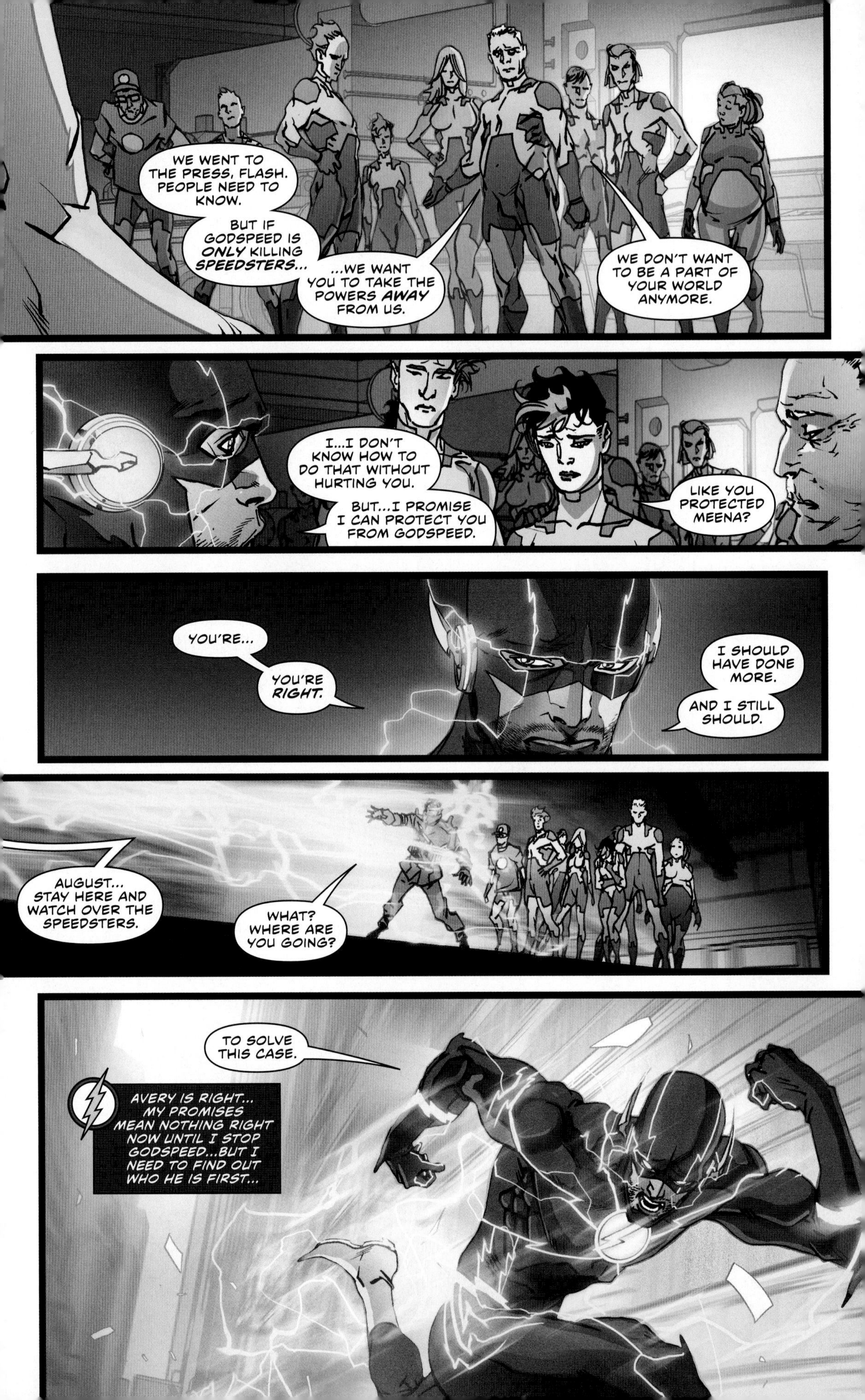
WE WENT TO THE PRESS, FLASH. PEOPLE NEED TO KNOW.
BUT IF GODSPEED IS ONLY KILLING SPEEDSTERS...
...WE WANT YOU TO TAKE THE POWERS AWAY FROM US.
WE DON'T WANT TO BE A PART OF YOUR WORLD ANYMORE.
I...I DON'T KNOW HOW TO DO THAT WITHOUT HURTING YOU.
BUT...I PROMISE I CAN PROTECT YOU FROM GODSPEED.
LIKE YOU PROTECTED MEENA?
YOU'RE...
YOU'RE RIGHT.
I SHOULD HAVE DONE MORE.
AND I STILL SHOULD.
AUGUST... STAY HERE AND WATCH OVER THE SPEEDSTERS.
WHAT? WHERE ARE YOU GOING?
TO SOLVE THIS CASE.
AVERY IS RIGHT... MY PROMISES MEAN NOTHING RIGHT NOW UNTIL I STOP GODSPEED...BUT I NEED TO FIND OUT WHO HE IS FIRST...

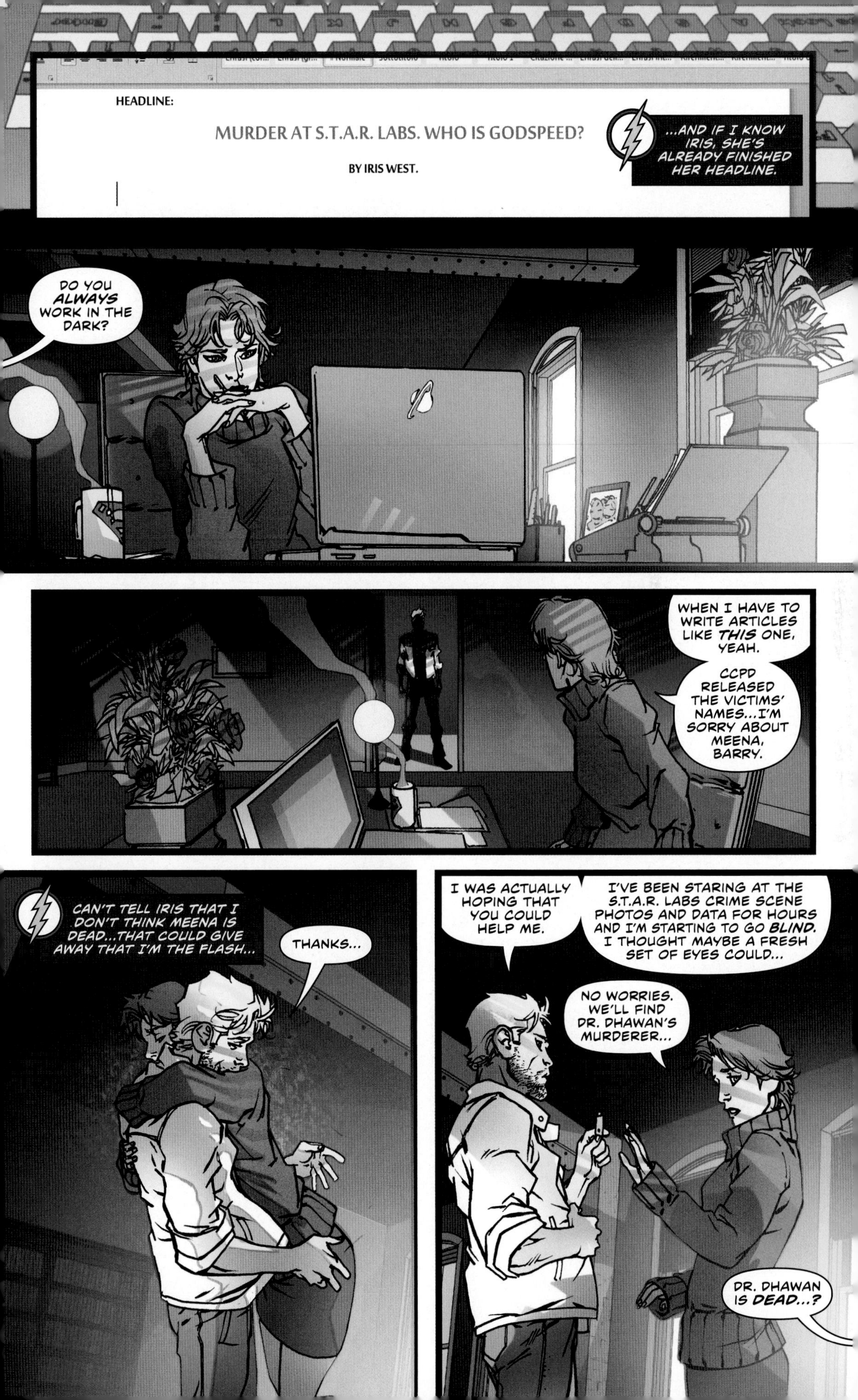

HEADLINE:
MURDER AT S.T.A.R. LABS. WHO IS GODSPEED?
BY IRIS WEST.
...AND IF I KNOW IRIS, SHE'S ALREADY FINISHED HER HEADLINE.
DO YOU ALWAYS WORK IN THE DARK?
WHEN I HAVE TO WRITE ARTICLES LIKE THIS ONE, YEAH.
CCPD RELEASED THE VICTIMS' NAMES...I'M SORRY ABOUT MEENA, BARRY.
CAN'T TELL IRIS THAT I DON'T THINK MEENA IS DEAD...THAT COULD GIVE AWAY THAT I'M THE FLASH...
THANKS...
I WAS ACTUALLY HOPING THAT YOU COULD HELP ME.
I'VE BEEN STARING AT THE S.T.A.R. LABS CRIME SCENE PHOTOS AND DATA FOR HOURS AND I'M STARTING TO GO BLIND. I THOUGHT MAYBE A FRESH SET OF EYES COULD...
NO WORRIES. WE'LL FIND DR. DHAWAN'S MURDERER...
DR. DHAWAN IS DEAD...?

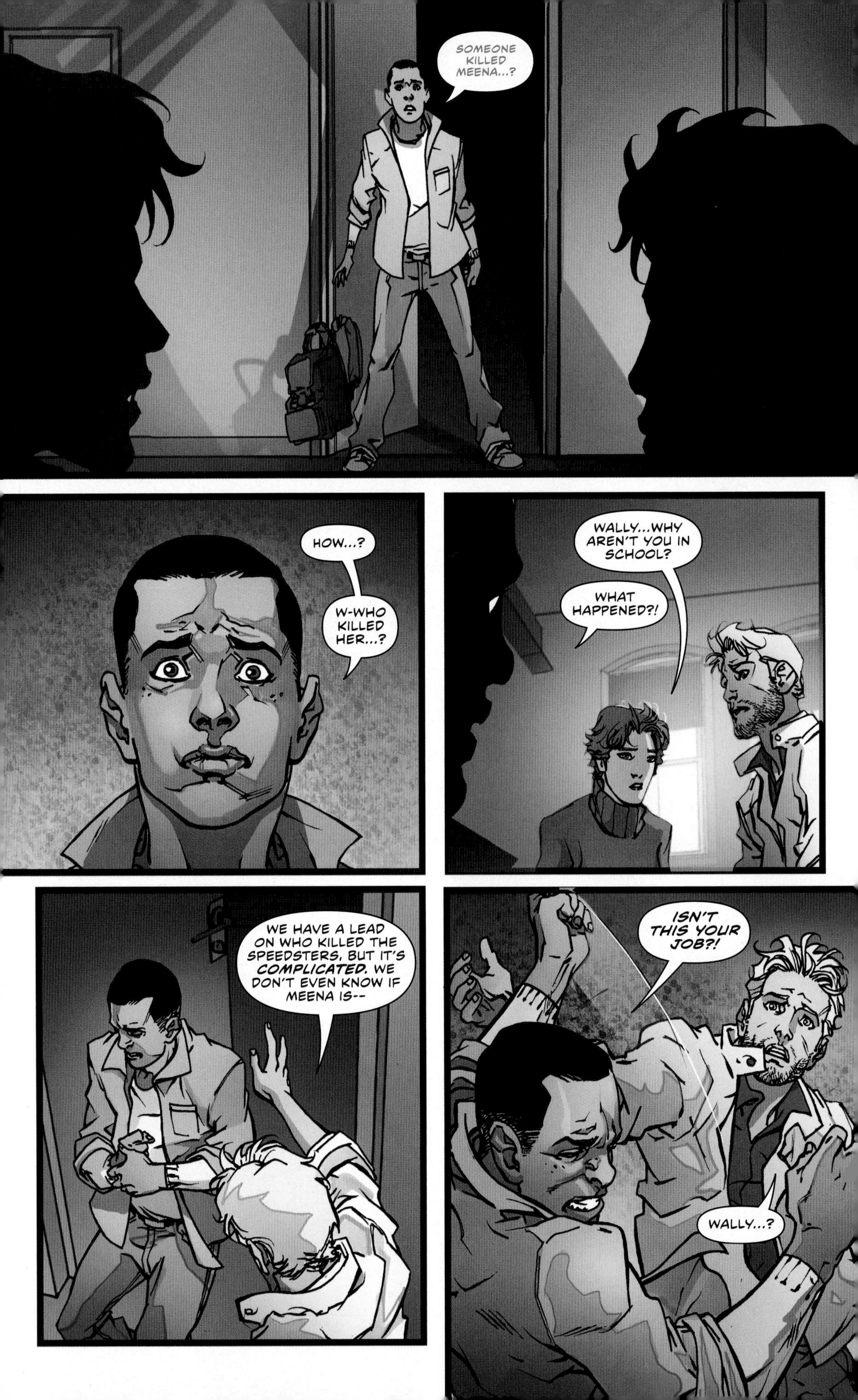
SOMEONE KILLED MEENA...?
HOW...?
W-WHO KILLED HER...?
WALLY...WHY AREN'T YOU IN SCHOOL?
WHAT HAPPENED?!
WE HAVE A LEAD ON WHO KILLED THE SPEEDSTERS, BUT IT'S *COMPLICATED.* WE DON'T EVEN KNOW IF MEENA IS--
ISN'T THIS YOUR JOB?!
WALLY...?

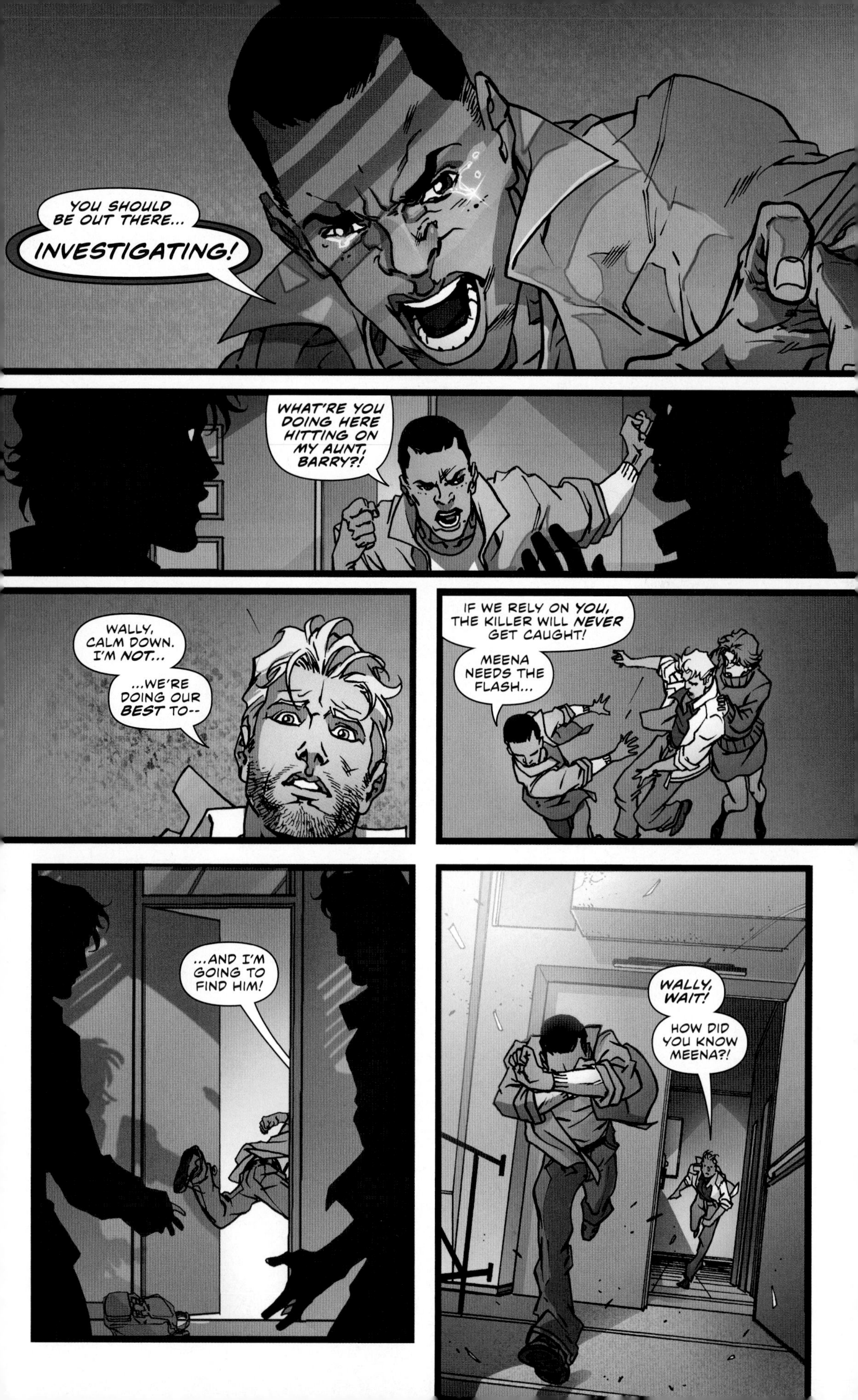
YOU SHOULD BE OUT THERE...
INVESTIGATING!
WHAT'RE YOU DOING HERE HITTING ON MY AUNT, BARRY?!
WALLY, CALM DOWN. I'M NOT...
...WE'RE DOING OUR BEST TO--
IF WE RELY ON YOU, THE KILLER WILL NEVER GET CAUGHT!
MEENA NEEDS THE FLASH...
...AND I'M GOING TO FIND HIM!
WALLY, WAIT!
HOW DID YOU KNOW MEENA?!

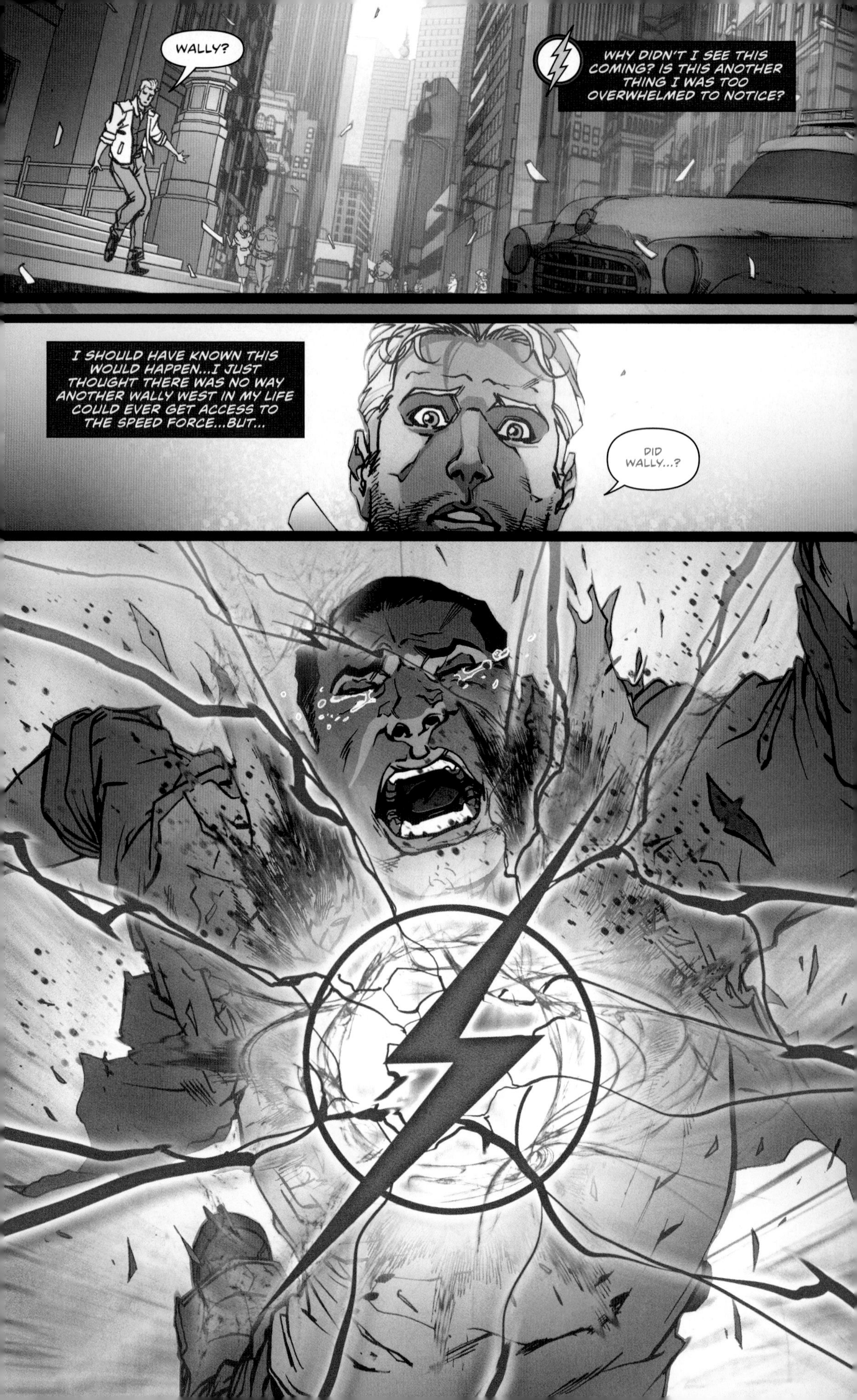
WALLY?
WHY DIDN'T I SEE THIS COMING? IS THIS ANOTHER THING I WAS TOO OVERWHELMED TO NOTICE?
I SHOULD HAVE KNOWN THIS WOULD HAPPEN...I JUST THOUGHT THERE WAS NO WAY ANOTHER WALLY WEST IN MY LIFE COULD EVER GET ACCESS TO THE SPEED FORCE...BUT...
DID WALLY...?

IRIS, WHERE DOES WALLY GO WHEN HE'S UPSET?

LET HIM BE, BARRY--YOU CAN'T MAKE HIM TALK TO US. WALLY WILL COME TO US WHEN HE'S READY.

BUT I THINK I FOUND SOMETHING...

ABOUT GODSPEED?

SORT OF...

THE ONLY CONNECTION BETWEEN ALL THE KILLINGS WAS THAT GODSPEED WAS GOING AFTER CENTRAL CITY CITIZENS WHO WERE STRUCK BY LIGHTNING FROM THE SPEED FORCE STORM, RIGHT?

YES...

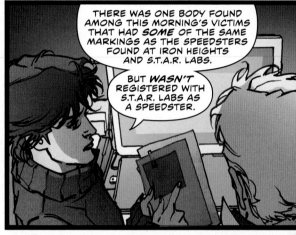

THERE WAS ONE BODY FOUND AMONG THIS MORNING'S VICTIMS THAT HAD *SOME* OF THE SAME MARKINGS AS THE SPEEDSTERS FOUND AT IRON HEIGHTS AND S.T.A.R. LABS.

BUT *WASN'T* REGISTERED WITH S.T.A.R. LABS AS A SPEEDSTER.

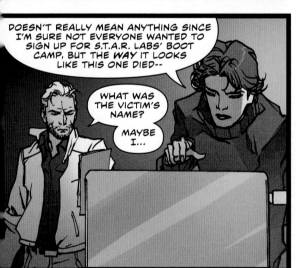

DOESN'T REALLY MEAN ANYTHING SINCE I'M SURE NOT EVERYONE WANTED TO SIGN UP FOR S.T.A.R. LABS' BOOT CAMP, BUT THE *WAY* IT LOOKS LIKE THIS ONE DIED--

WHAT WAS THE VICTIM'S NAME?

MAYBE I...

...OH NO.

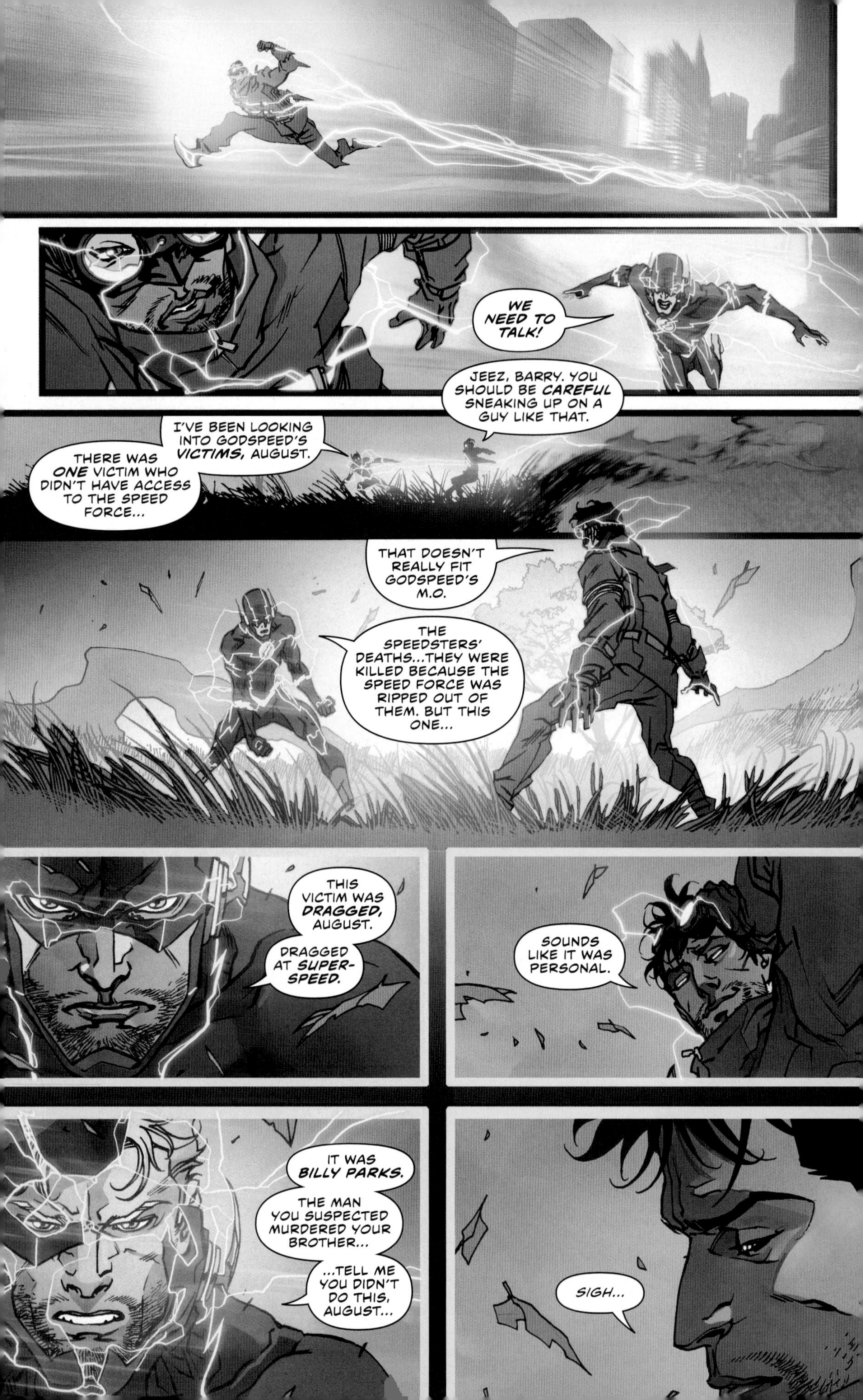

WE NEED TO TALK!
JEEZ, BARRY. YOU SHOULD BE CAREFUL SNEAKING UP ON A GUY LIKE THAT.
I'VE BEEN LOOKING INTO GODSPEED'S VICTIMS, AUGUST.
THERE WAS ONE VICTIM WHO DIDN'T HAVE ACCESS TO THE SPEED FORCE...
THAT DOESN'T REALLY FIT GODSPEED'S M.O.
THE SPEEDSTERS' DEATHS...THEY WERE KILLED BECAUSE THE SPEED FORCE WAS RIPPED OUT OF THEM. BUT THIS ONE...
THIS VICTIM WAS DRAGGED, AUGUST.
DRAGGED AT SUPER-SPEED.
SOUNDS LIKE IT WAS PERSONAL.
IT WAS BILLY PARKS.
THE MAN YOU SUSPECTED MURDERED YOUR BROTHER...
...TELL ME YOU DIDN'T DO THIS, AUGUST...
SIGH...

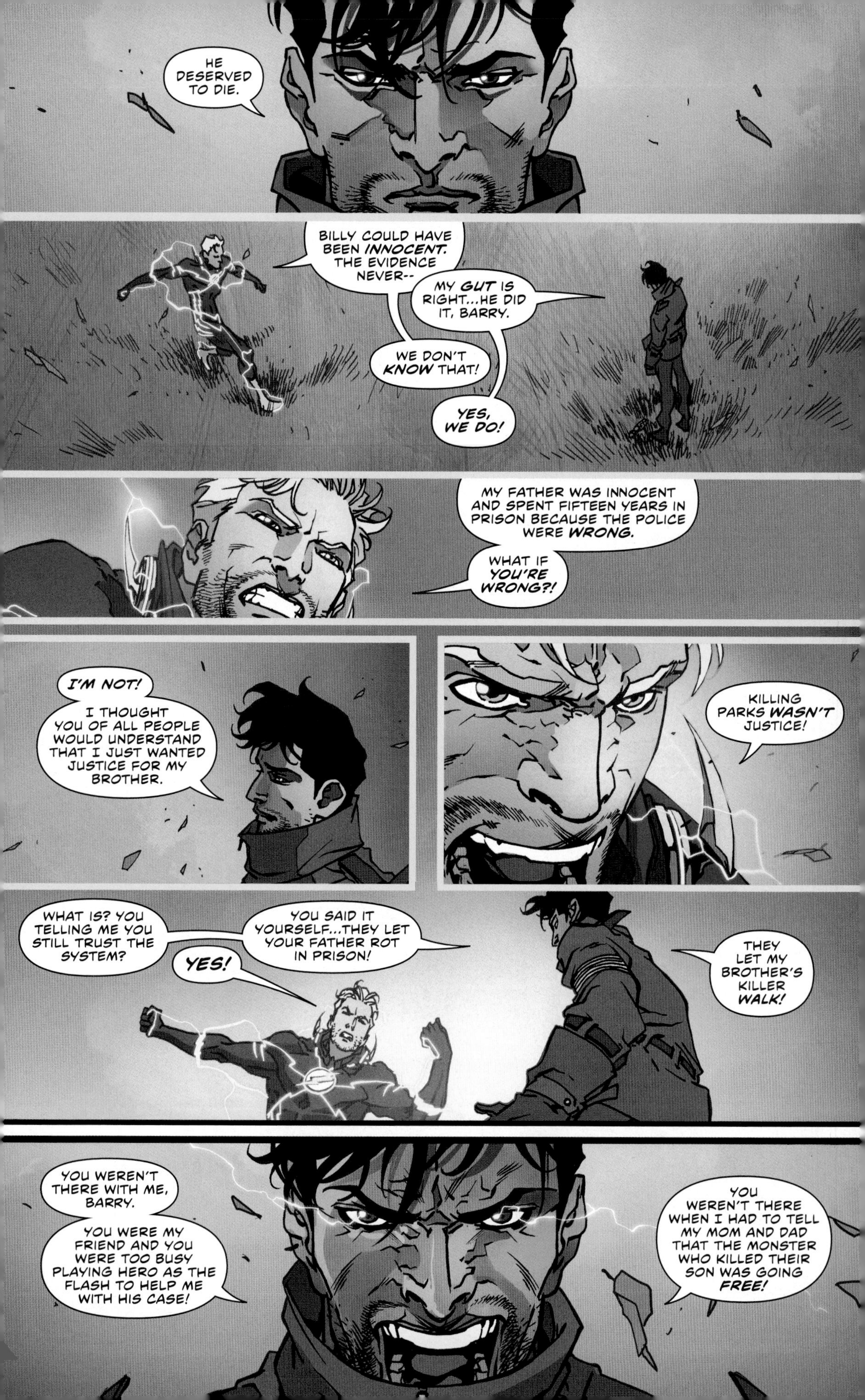
HE DESERVED TO DIE.
BILLY COULD HAVE BEEN INNOCENT. THE EVIDENCE NEVER--
MY GUT IS RIGHT...HE DID IT, BARRY.
WE DON'T KNOW THAT!
YES, WE DO!
MY FATHER WAS INNOCENT AND SPENT FIFTEEN YEARS IN PRISON BECAUSE THE POLICE WERE WRONG.
WHAT IF YOU'RE WRONG?!
I'M NOT!
I THOUGHT YOU OF ALL PEOPLE WOULD UNDERSTAND THAT I JUST WANTED JUSTICE FOR MY BROTHER.
KILLING PARKS WASN'T JUSTICE!
WHAT IS? YOU TELLING ME YOU STILL TRUST THE SYSTEM?
YES!
YOU SAID IT YOURSELF...THEY LET YOUR FATHER ROT IN PRISON!
THEY LET MY BROTHER'S KILLER WALK!
YOU WEREN'T THERE WITH ME, BARRY.
YOU WERE MY FRIEND AND YOU WERE TOO BUSY PLAYING HERO AS THE FLASH TO HELP ME WITH HIS CASE!
YOU WEREN'T THERE WHEN I HAD TO TELL MY MOM AND DAD THAT THE MONSTER WHO KILLED THEIR SON WAS GOING FREE!

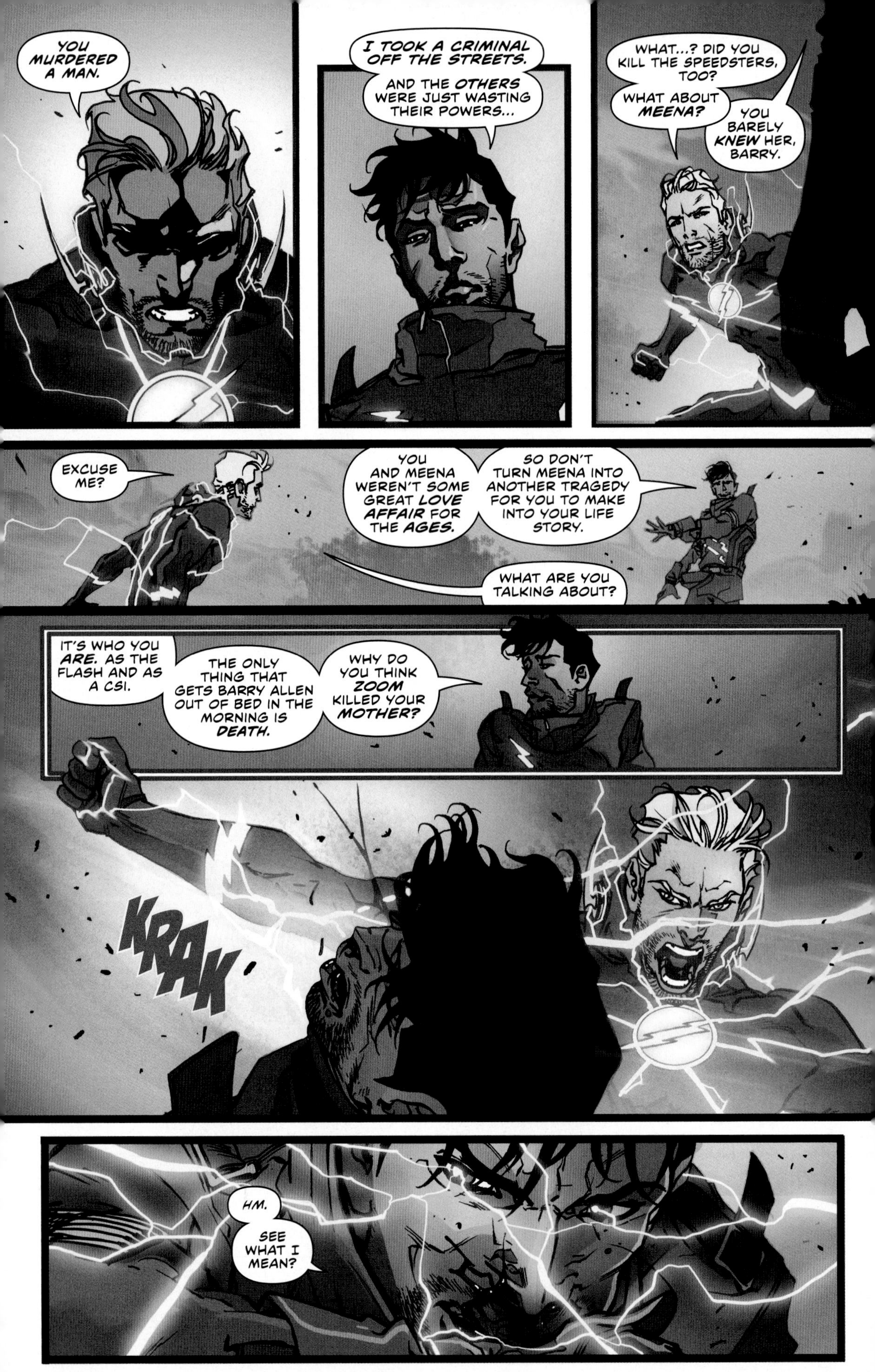
YOU MURDERED A MAN.
I TOOK A CRIMINAL OFF THE STREETS.
AND THE OTHERS WERE JUST WASTING THEIR POWERS...
WHAT...? DID YOU KILL THE SPEEDSTERS, TOO?
WHAT ABOUT MEENA?
YOU BARELY KNEW HER, BARRY.
EXCUSE ME?
YOU AND MEENA WEREN'T SOME GREAT LOVE AFFAIR FOR THE AGES.
SO DON'T TURN MEENA INTO ANOTHER TRAGEDY FOR YOU TO MAKE INTO YOUR LIFE STORY.
WHAT ARE YOU TALKING ABOUT?
IT'S WHO YOU ARE. AS THE FLASH AND AS A CSI.
THE ONLY THING THAT GETS BARRY ALLEN OUT OF BED IN THE MORNING IS DEATH.
WHY DO YOU THINK ZOOM KILLED YOUR MOTHER?
KRAK
HM.
SEE WHAT I MEAN?

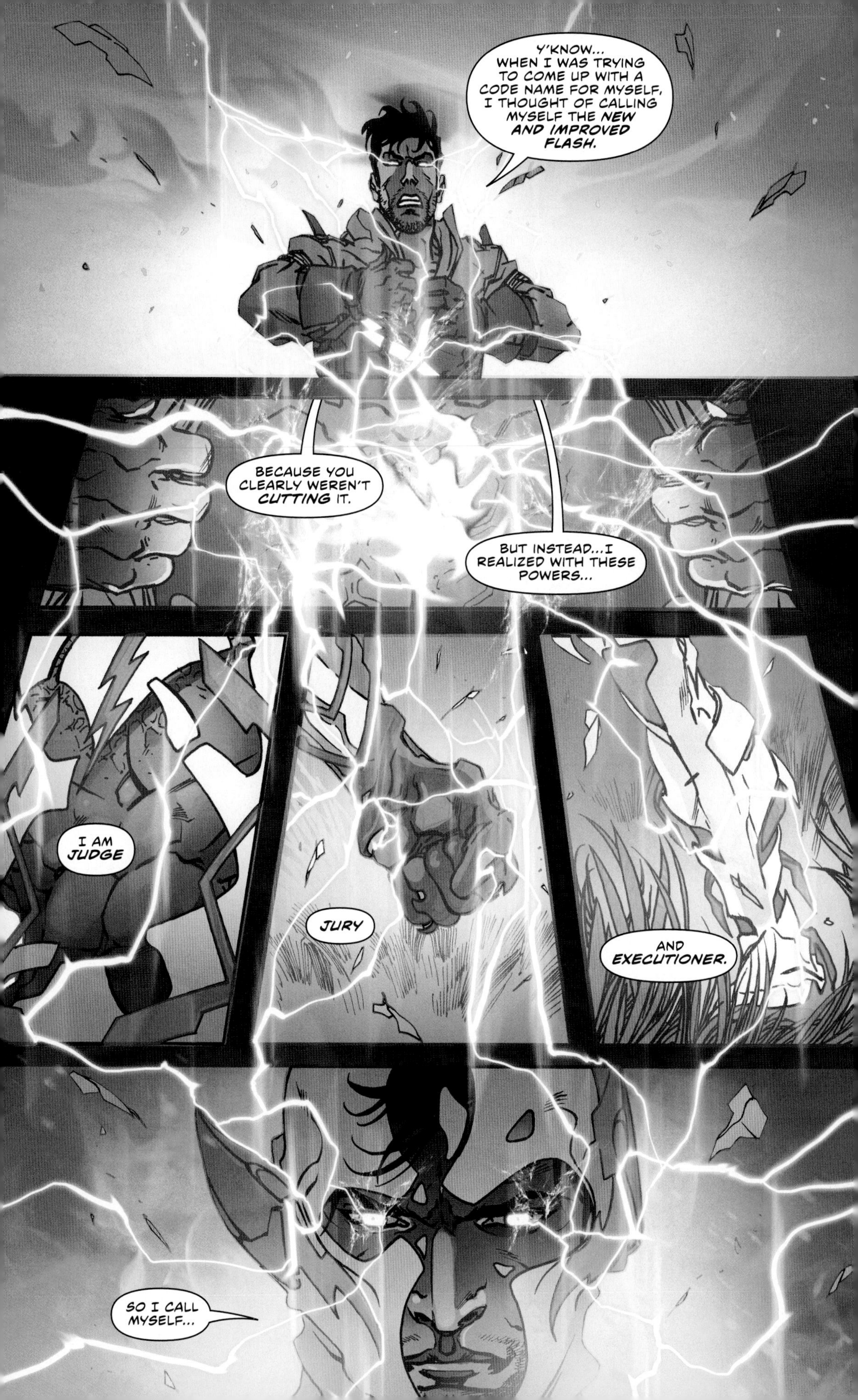
Y'KNOW... WHEN I WAS TRYING TO COME UP WITH A CODE NAME FOR MYSELF, I THOUGHT OF CALLING MYSELF THE *NEW AND IMPROVED FLASH.*
BECAUSE YOU CLEARLY WEREN'T *CUTTING* IT.
BUT INSTEAD...I REALIZED WITH THESE POWERS...
I AM *JUDGE*
JURY
AND *EXECUTIONER.*
SO I CALL MYSELF...

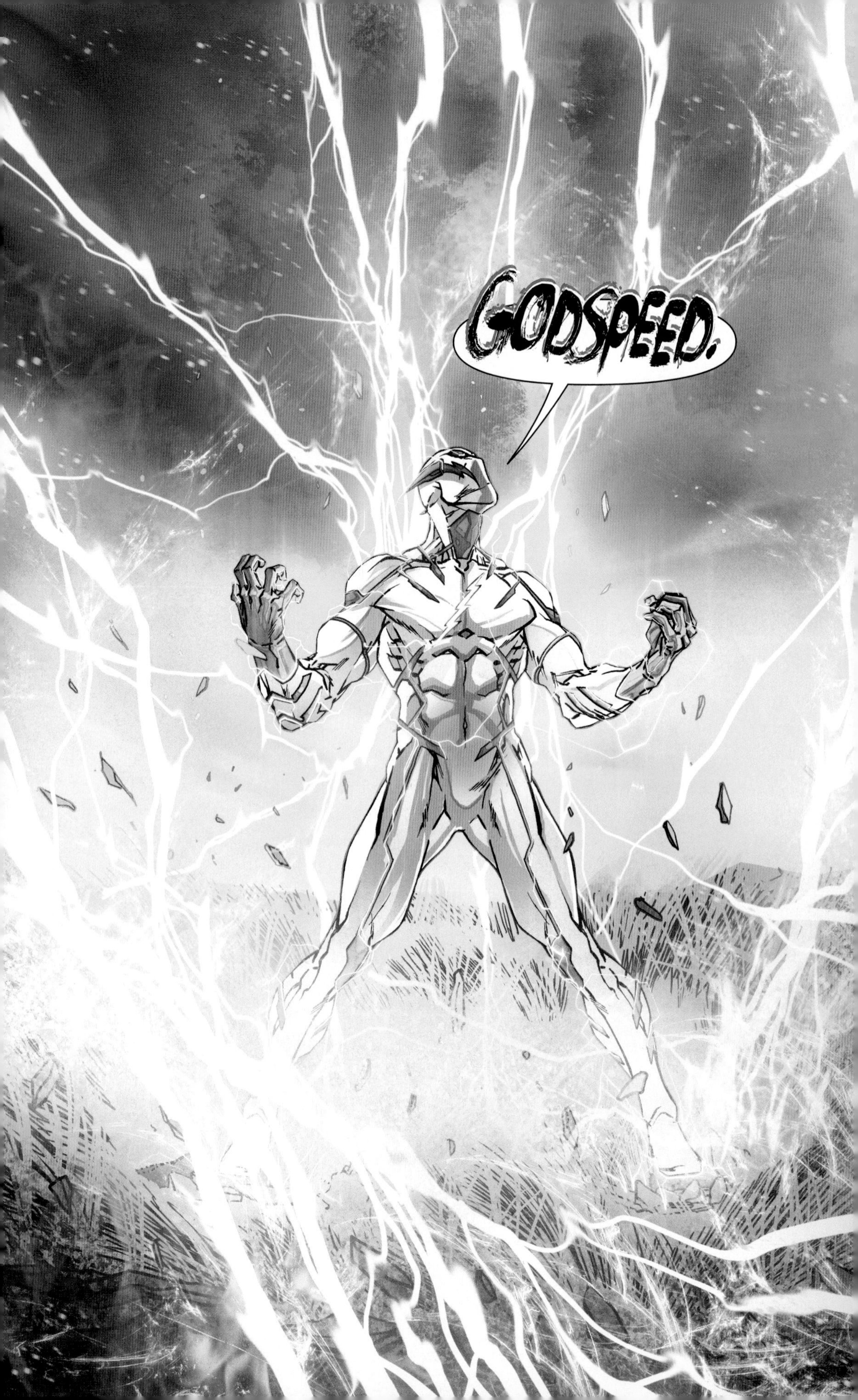
GODSPEED.

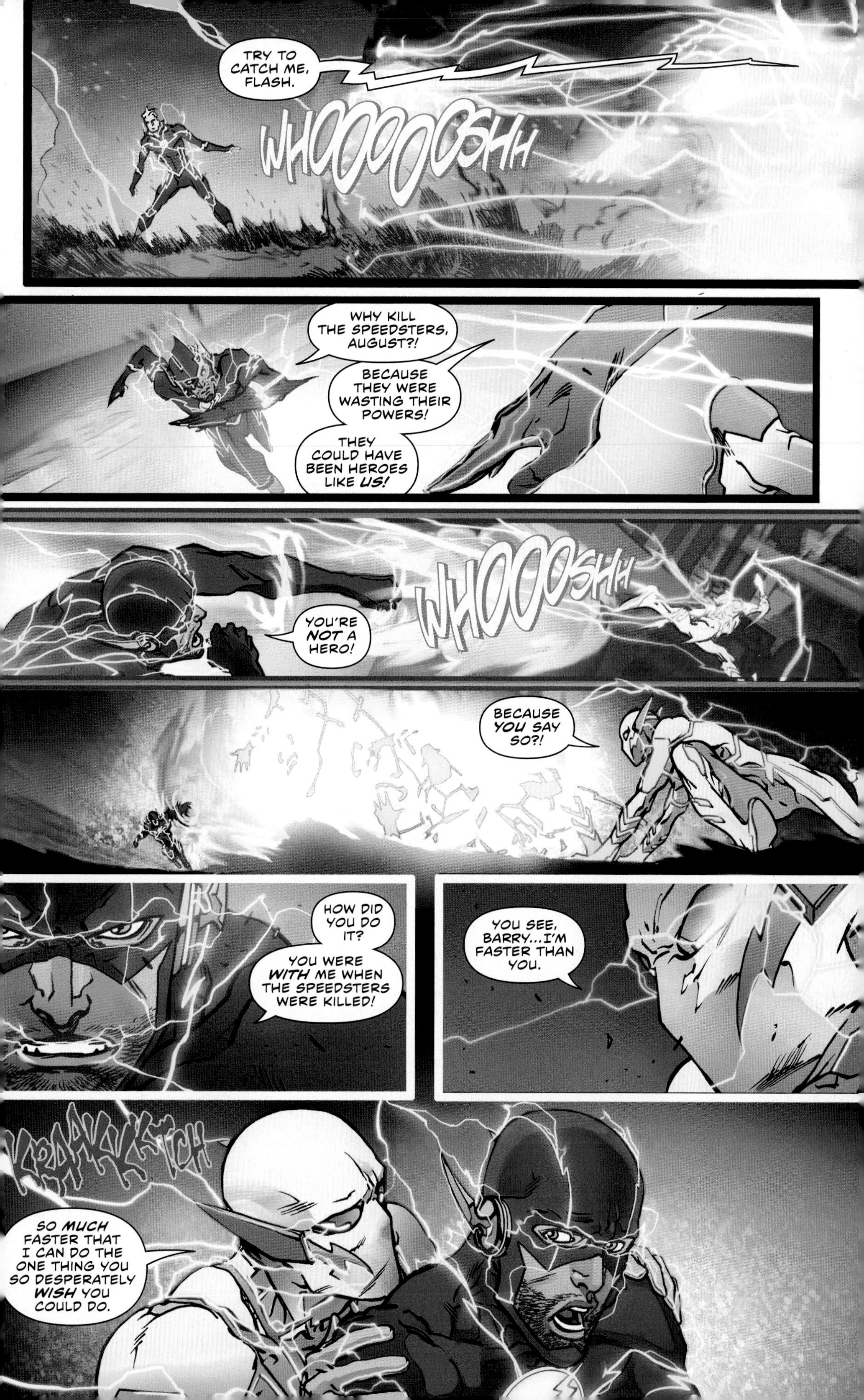
TRY TO CATCH ME, FLASH.
WHOOOOOOOSHH
WHY KILL THE SPEEDSTERS, AUGUST?!
BECAUSE THEY WERE WASTING THEIR POWERS!
THEY COULD HAVE BEEN HEROES LIKE *US!*
YOU'RE *NOT* A HERO!
WHOOOOSHH
BECAUSE *YOU* SAY SO?!
HOW DID YOU DO IT?
YOU WERE *WITH* ME WHEN THE SPEEDSTERS WERE KILLED!
YOU SEE, BARRY...I'M FASTER THAN YOU.
KRAKKKTCH
SO *MUCH* FASTER THAT I CAN DO THE ONE THING YOU SO DESPERATELY *WISH* YOU COULD DO.

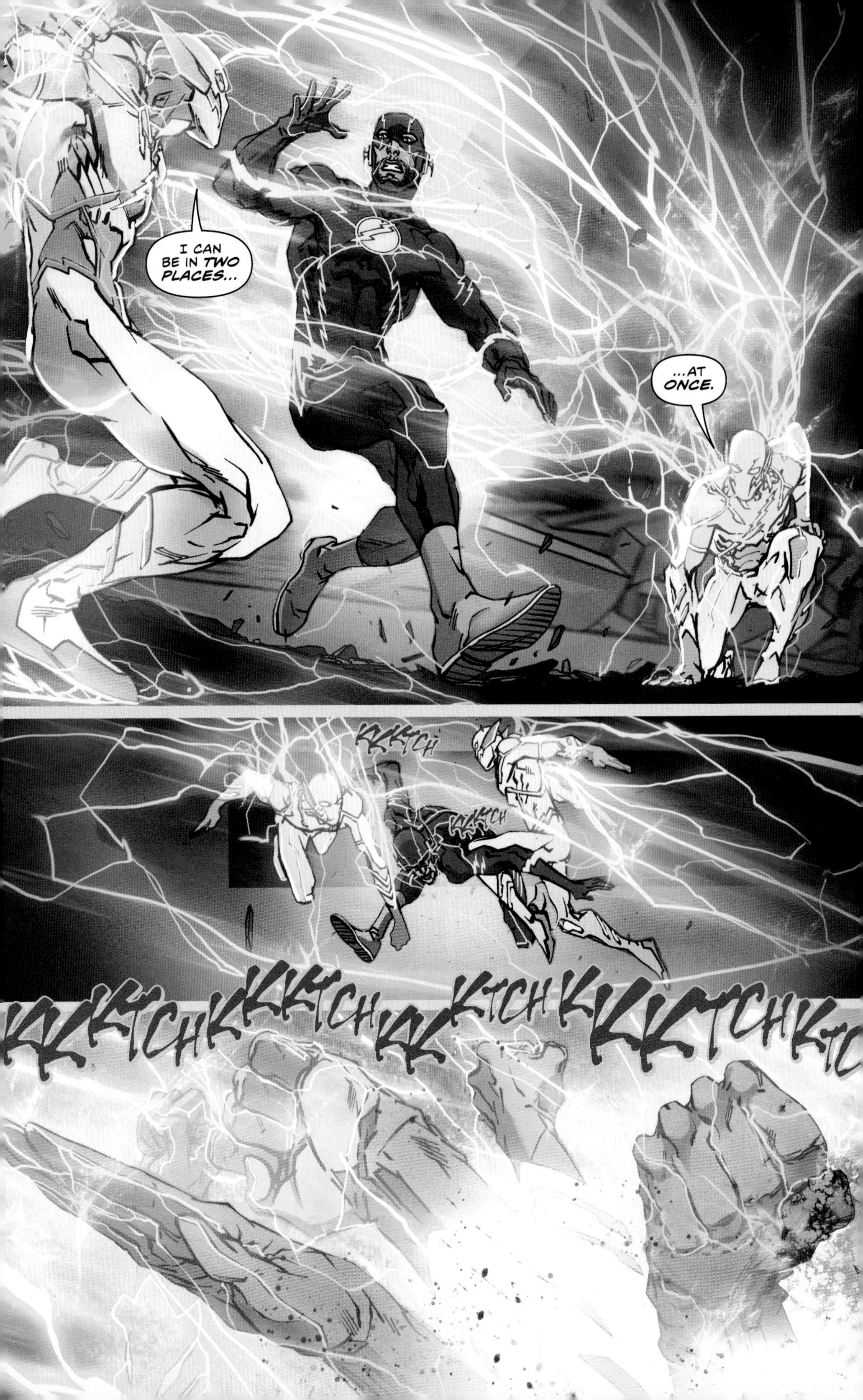
I CAN BE IN *TWO* PLACES...
...AT ONCE.
KKKTCH
KKKTCH

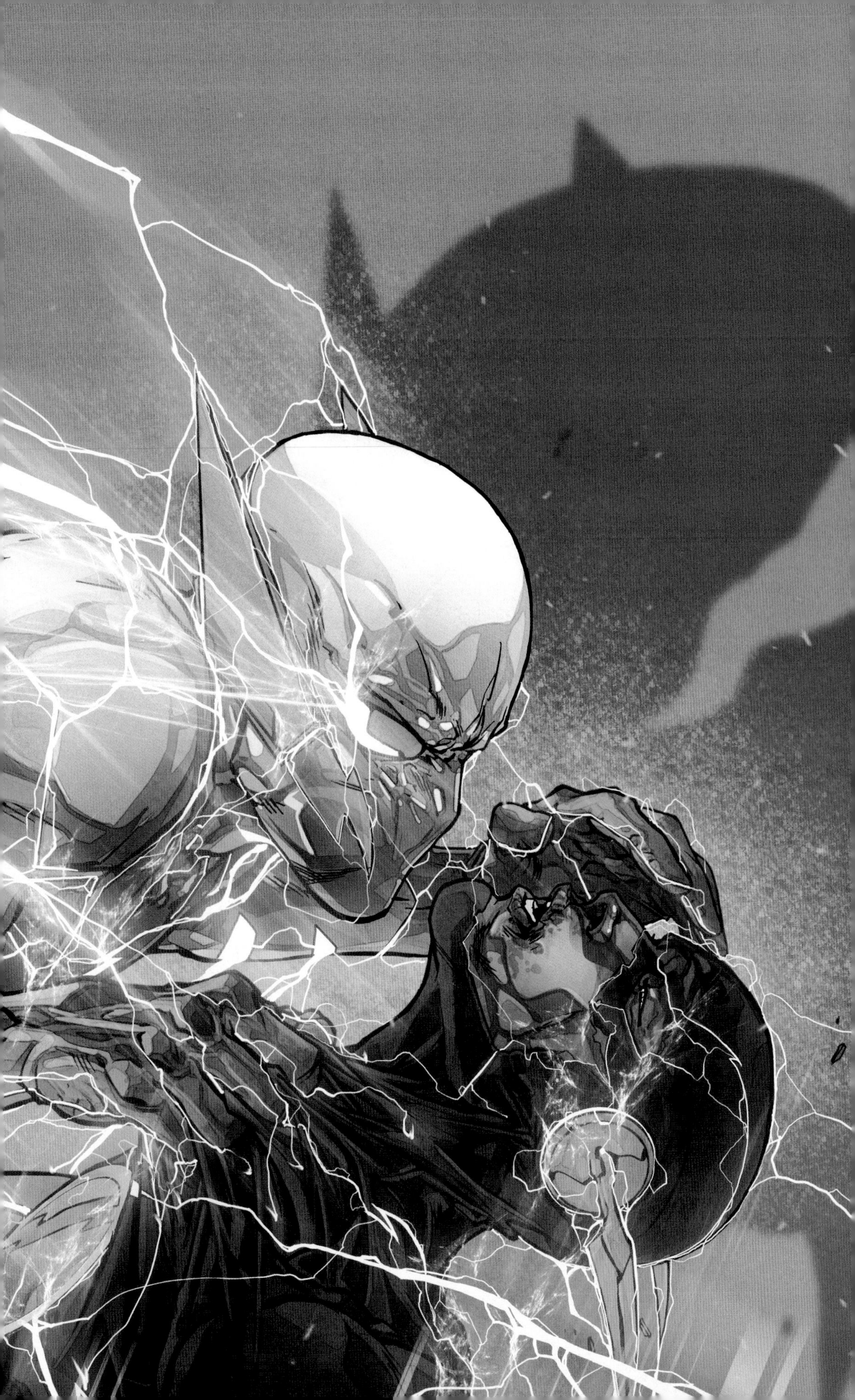

NO MORE SPEEDSTERS

CARMINE DI GIANDOMENICO artist/cover

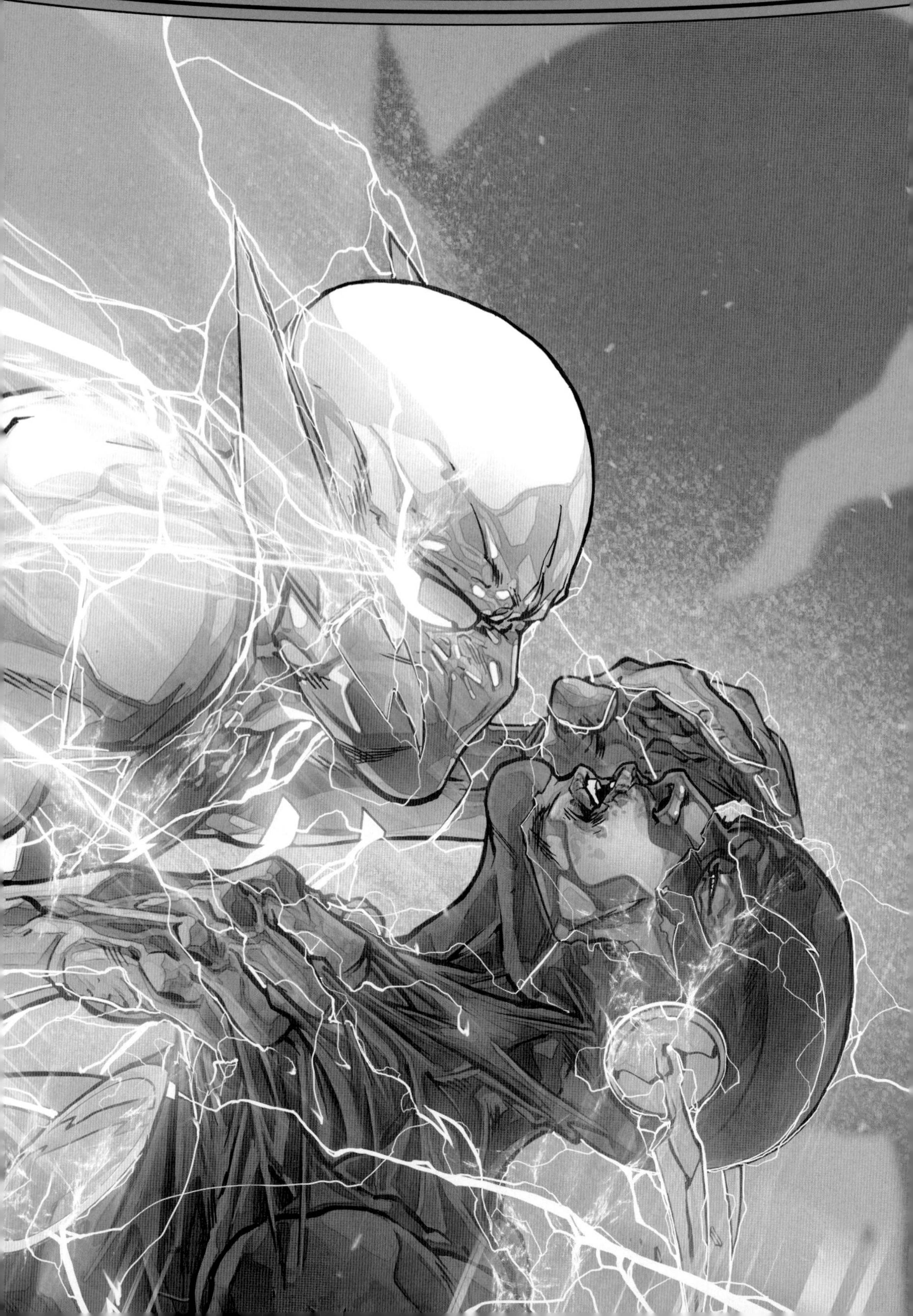

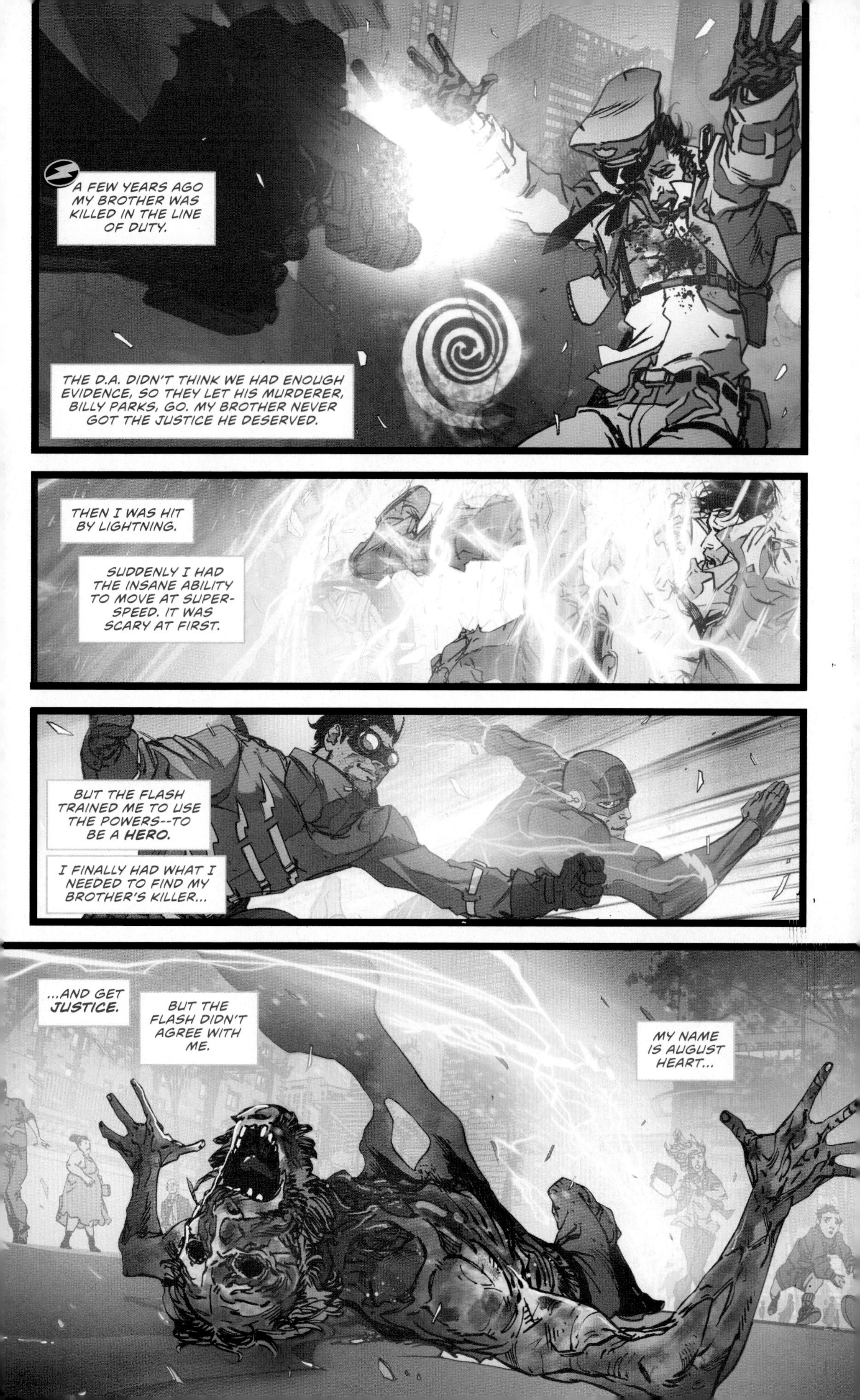
A FEW YEARS AGO MY BROTHER WAS KILLED IN THE LINE OF DUTY.
THE D.A. DIDN'T THINK WE HAD ENOUGH EVIDENCE, SO THEY LET HIS MURDERER, BILLY PARKS, GO. MY BROTHER NEVER GOT THE JUSTICE HE DESERVED.
THEN I WAS HIT BY LIGHTNING.
SUDDENLY I HAD THE INSANE ABILITY TO MOVE AT SUPER-SPEED. IT WAS SCARY AT FIRST.
BUT THE FLASH TRAINED ME TO USE THE POWERS--TO BE A HERO.
I FINALLY HAD WHAT I NEEDED TO FIND MY BROTHER'S KILLER...
...AND GET JUSTICE.
BUT THE FLASH DIDN'T AGREE WITH ME.
MY NAME IS AUGUST HEART...

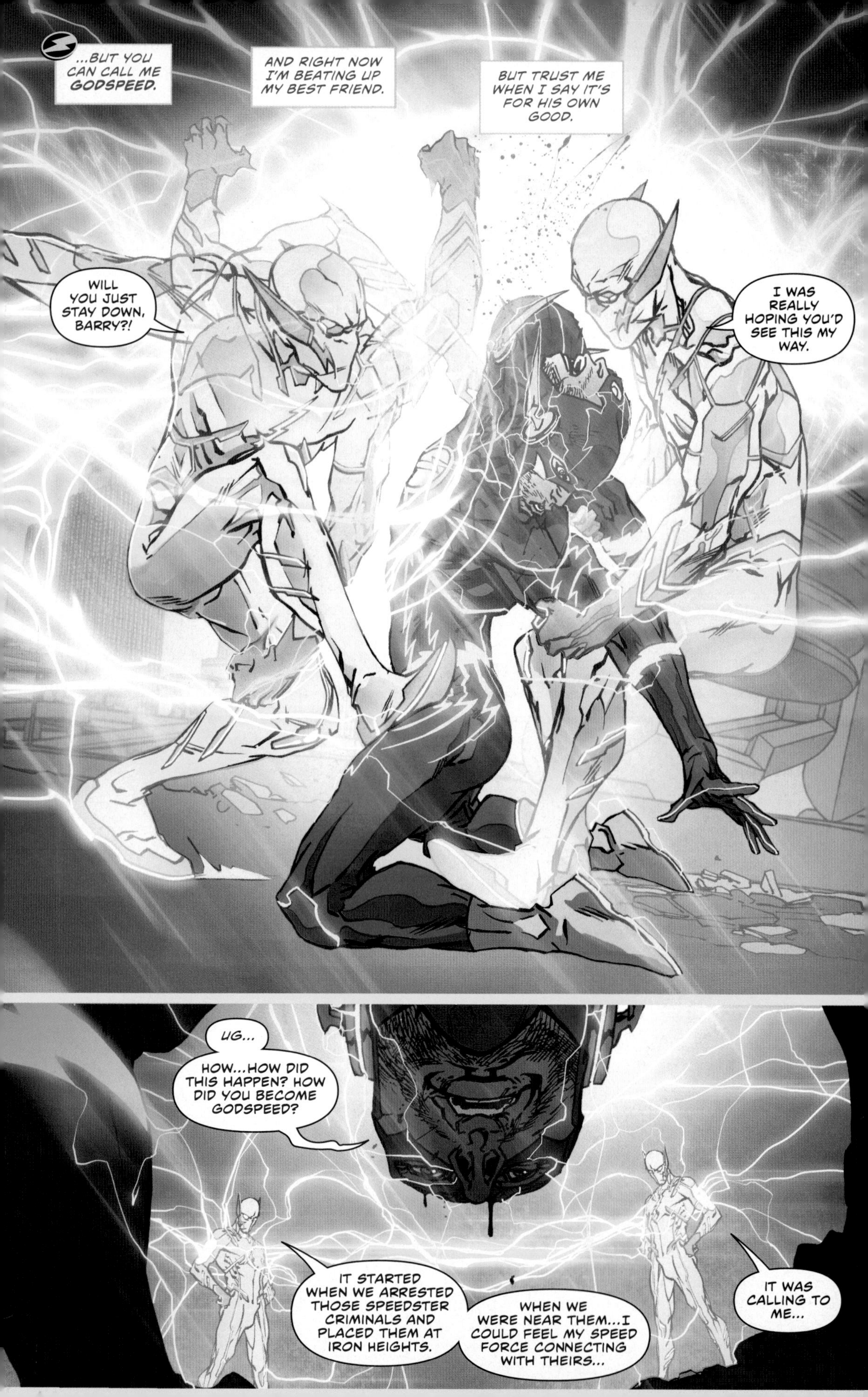
...BUT YOU CAN CALL ME **GODSPEED.**
AND RIGHT NOW I'M BEATING UP MY BEST FRIEND.
BUT TRUST ME WHEN I SAY IT'S FOR HIS OWN GOOD.
WILL YOU JUST STAY DOWN, BARRY?!
I WAS REALLY HOPING YOU'D SEE THIS MY WAY.
UG...
HOW...HOW DID THIS HAPPEN? HOW DID YOU BECOME GODSPEED?
IT STARTED WHEN WE ARRESTED THOSE SPEEDSTER CRIMINALS AND PLACED THEM AT IRON HEIGHTS.
WHEN WE WERE NEAR THEM...I COULD FEEL MY SPEED FORCE CONNECTING WITH THEIRS...
IT WAS CALLING TO ME...

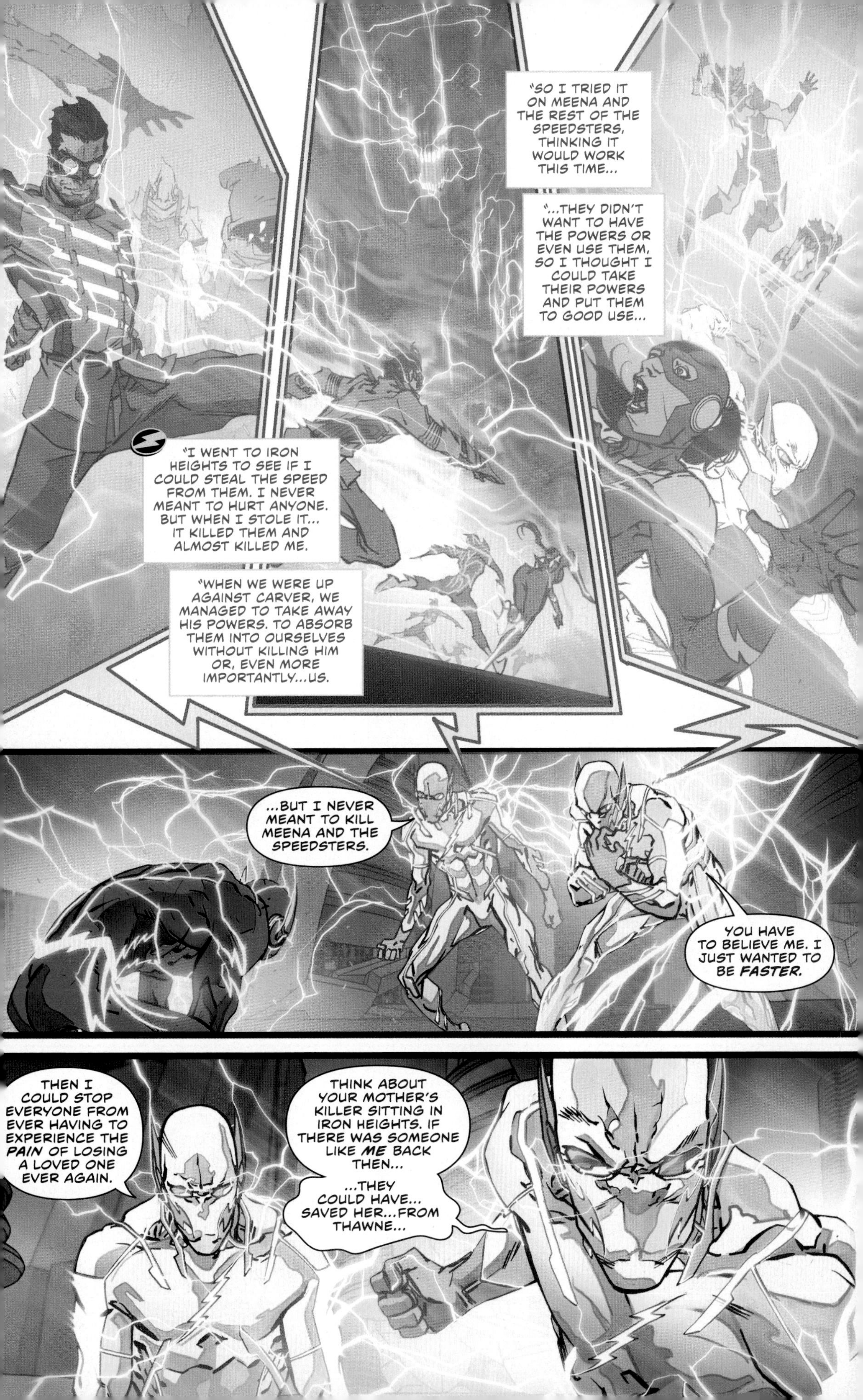
"I WENT TO IRON HEIGHTS TO SEE IF I COULD STEAL THE SPEED FROM THEM. I NEVER MEANT TO HURT ANYONE. BUT WHEN I STOLE IT... IT KILLED THEM AND ALMOST KILLED ME.
"WHEN WE WERE UP AGAINST CARVER, WE MANAGED TO TAKE AWAY HIS POWERS. TO ABSORB THEM INTO OURSELVES WITHOUT KILLING HIM OR, EVEN MORE IMPORTANTLY...US.
"SO I TRIED IT ON MEENA AND THE REST OF THE SPEEDSTERS, THINKING IT WOULD WORK THIS TIME...
"...THEY DIDN'T WANT TO HAVE THE POWERS OR EVEN USE THEM, SO I THOUGHT I COULD TAKE THEIR POWERS AND PUT THEM TO GOOD USE...
...BUT I NEVER MEANT TO KILL MEENA AND THE SPEEDSTERS.
YOU HAVE TO BELIEVE ME. I JUST WANTED TO BE *FASTER.*
THEN I COULD STOP EVERYONE FROM EVER HAVING TO EXPERIENCE THE *PAIN* OF LOSING A LOVED ONE EVER AGAIN.
THINK ABOUT YOUR MOTHER'S KILLER SITTING IN IRON HEIGHTS. IF THERE WAS SOMEONE LIKE *ME* BACK THEN...
...THEY COULD HAVE... SAVED HER...FROM THAWNE...

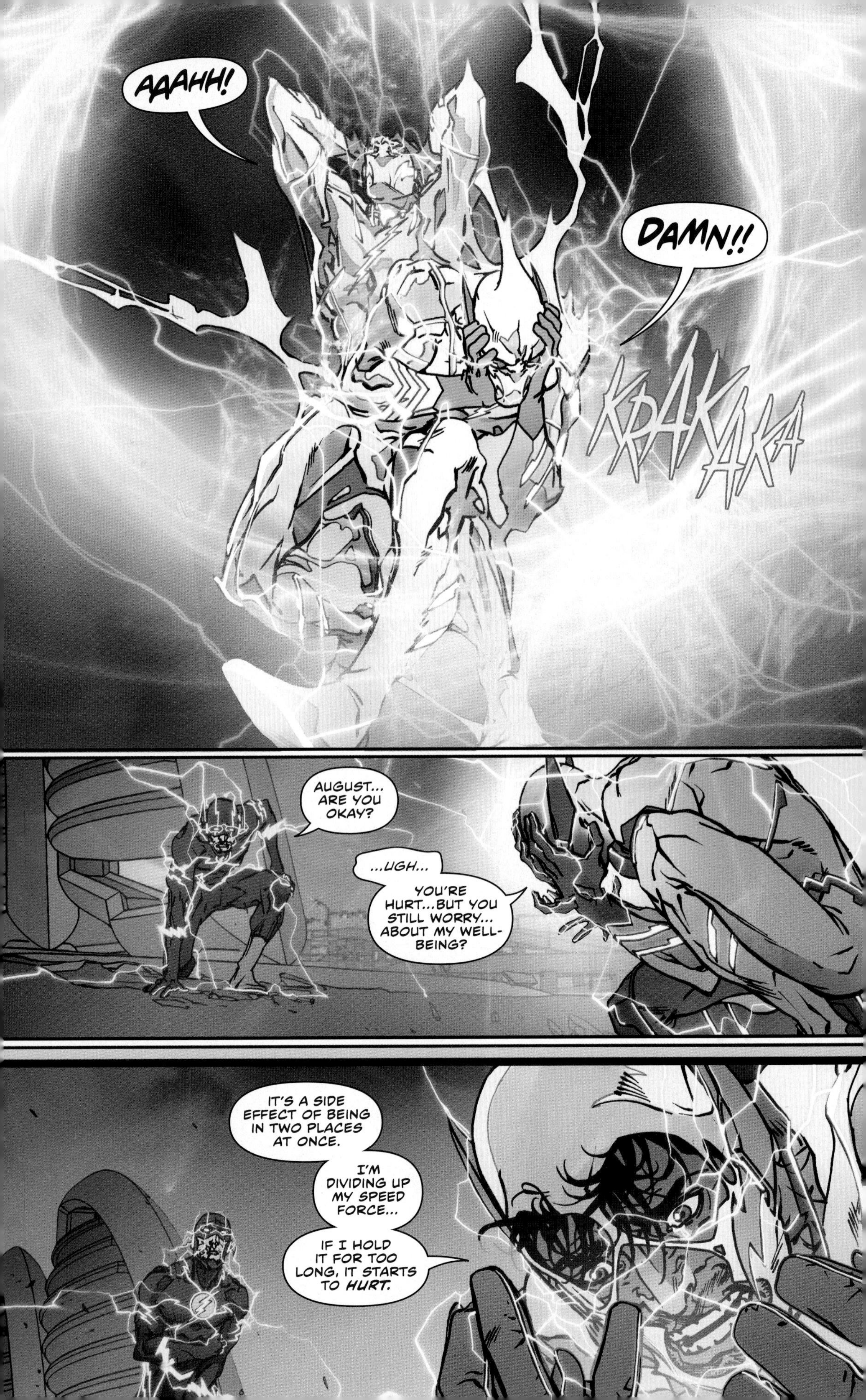
AAAHH!
DAMN!!
KRAKAKAKA
AUGUST... ARE YOU OKAY?
...UGH...
YOU'RE HURT...BUT YOU STILL WORRY... ABOUT MY WELL-BEING?
IT'S A SIDE EFFECT OF BEING IN TWO PLACES AT ONCE.
I'M DIVIDING UP MY SPEED FORCE...
IF I HOLD IT FOR TOO LONG, IT STARTS TO *HURT.*

GOOD.

WHOOOSHH

AH!

NEVER TOOK YOU FOR THE SUCKER PUNCH TYPE, BARRY.

BARRY?

ON THE RUN, HUH?

NO WORRIES. THE CRIMINALS OF CENTRAL CITY WILL GIVE ME PLENTY TO DO...

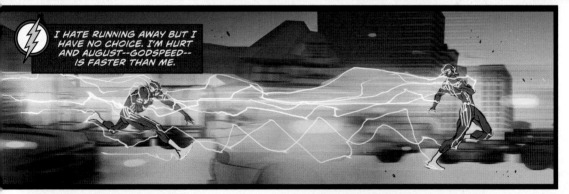

I HATE RUNNING AWAY BUT I HAVE NO CHOICE. I'M HURT AND AUGUST--GODSPEED-- IS FASTER THAN ME.

I NEED...I NEED TIME TO THINK.

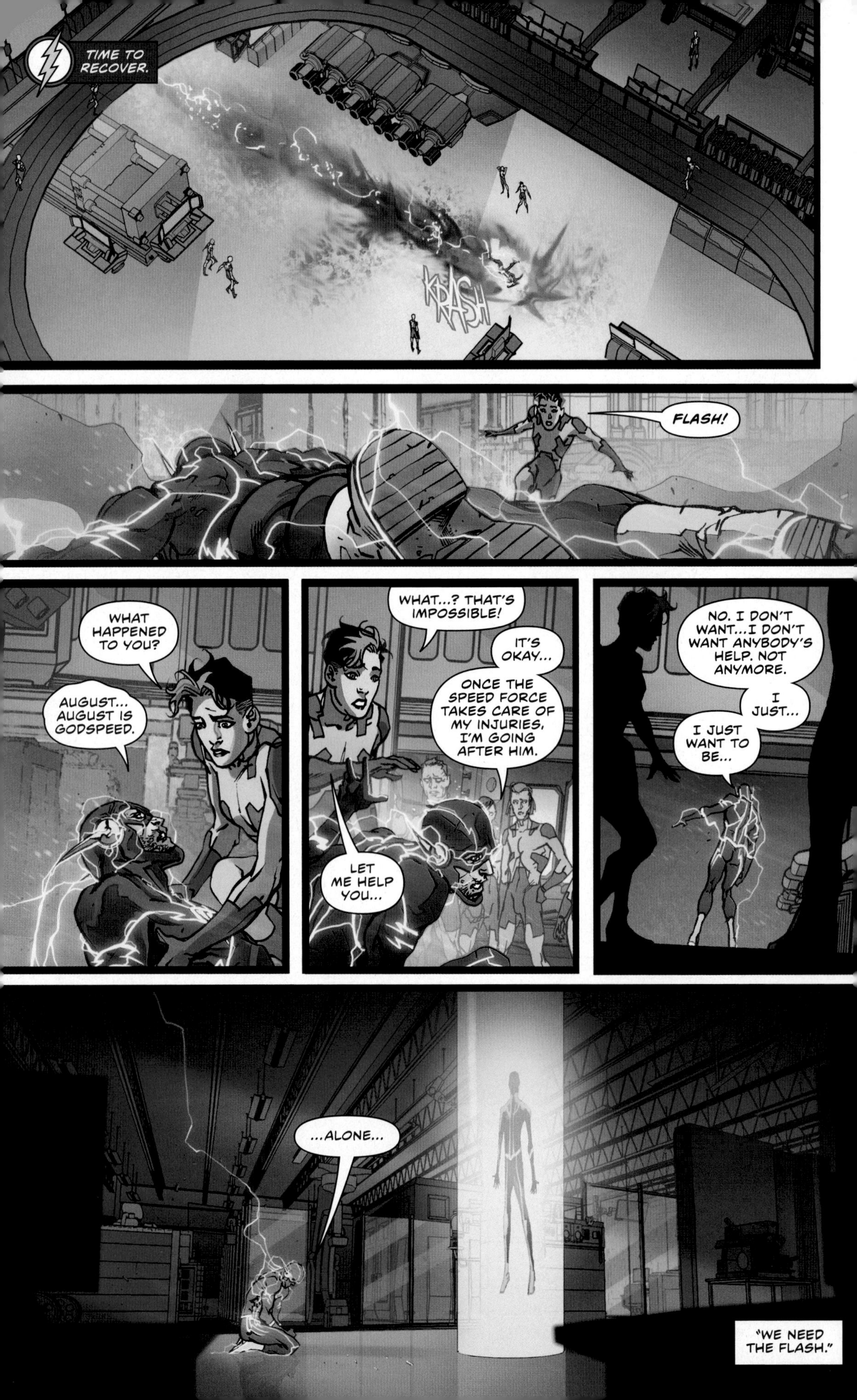
TIME TO RECOVER.
KRASH
FLASH!
WHAT HAPPENED TO YOU?
AUGUST... AUGUST IS GODSPEED.
WHAT...? THAT'S IMPOSSIBLE!
IT'S OKAY...
ONCE THE SPEED FORCE TAKES CARE OF MY INJURIES, I'M GOING AFTER HIM.
LET ME HELP YOU...
NO. I DON'T WANT...I DON'T WANT ANYBODY'S HELP. NOT ANYMORE.
I JUST...
I JUST WANT TO BE...
...ALONE...
"WE NEED THE FLASH."

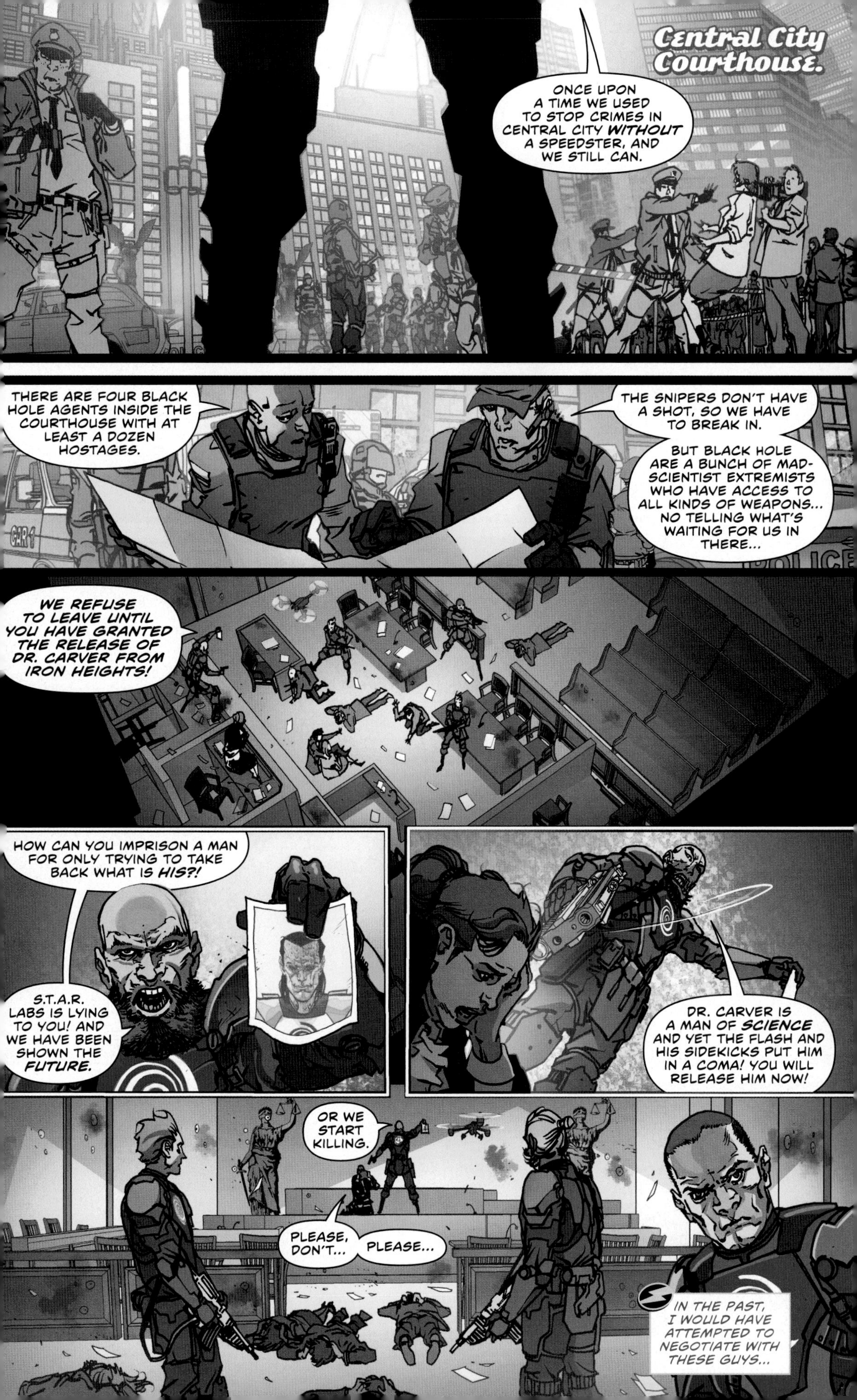
Central City Courthouse.
ONCE UPON A TIME WE USED TO STOP CRIMES IN CENTRAL CITY WITHOUT A SPEEDSTER, AND WE STILL CAN.
THERE ARE FOUR BLACK HOLE AGENTS INSIDE THE COURTHOUSE WITH AT LEAST A DOZEN HOSTAGES.
THE SNIPERS DON'T HAVE A SHOT, SO WE HAVE TO BREAK IN.
BUT BLACK HOLE ARE A BUNCH OF MAD-SCIENTIST EXTREMISTS WHO HAVE ACCESS TO ALL KINDS OF WEAPONS... NO TELLING WHAT'S WAITING FOR US IN THERE...
WE REFUSE TO LEAVE UNTIL YOU HAVE GRANTED THE RELEASE OF DR. CARVER FROM IRON HEIGHTS!
HOW CAN YOU IMPRISON A MAN FOR ONLY TRYING TO TAKE BACK WHAT IS HIS?!
S.T.A.R. LABS IS LYING TO YOU! AND WE HAVE BEEN SHOWN THE FUTURE.
DR. CARVER IS A MAN OF SCIENCE AND YET THE FLASH AND HIS SIDEKICKS PUT HIM IN A COMA! YOU WILL RELEASE HIM NOW!
OR WE START KILLING.
PLEASE, DON'T...
PLEASE...
IN THE PAST, I WOULD HAVE ATTEMPTED TO NEGOTIATE WITH THESE GUYS...

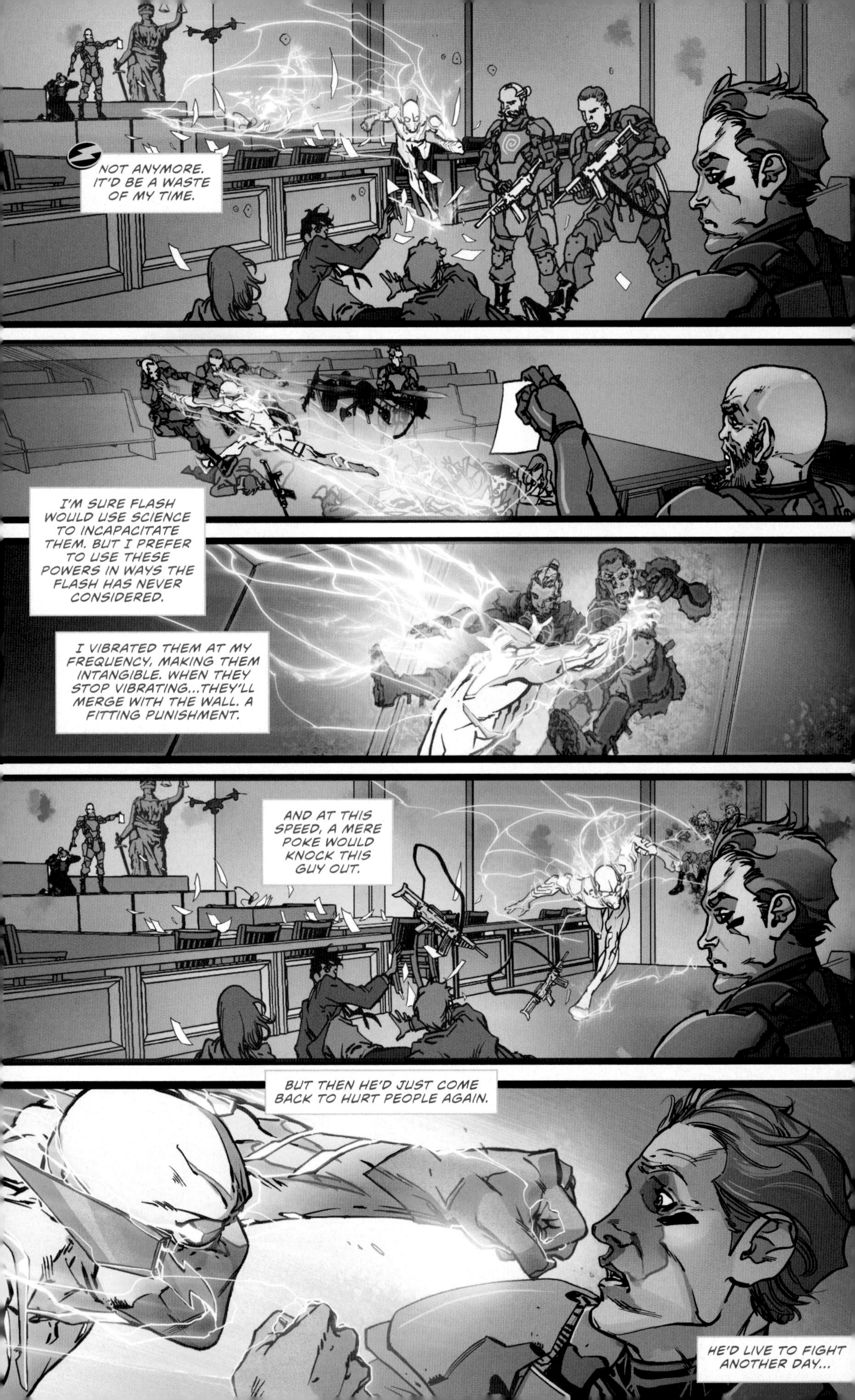
NOT ANYMORE. IT'D BE A WASTE OF MY TIME.
I'M SURE FLASH WOULD USE SCIENCE TO INCAPACITATE THEM. BUT I PREFER TO USE THESE POWERS IN WAYS THE FLASH HAS NEVER CONSIDERED.
I VIBRATED THEM AT MY FREQUENCY, MAKING THEM INTANGIBLE. WHEN THEY STOP VIBRATING...THEY'LL MERGE WITH THE WALL. A FITTING PUNISHMENT.
AND AT THIS SPEED, A MERE POKE WOULD KNOCK THIS GUY OUT.
BUT THEN HE'D JUST COME BACK TO HURT PEOPLE AGAIN.
HE'D LIVE TO FIGHT ANOTHER DAY...

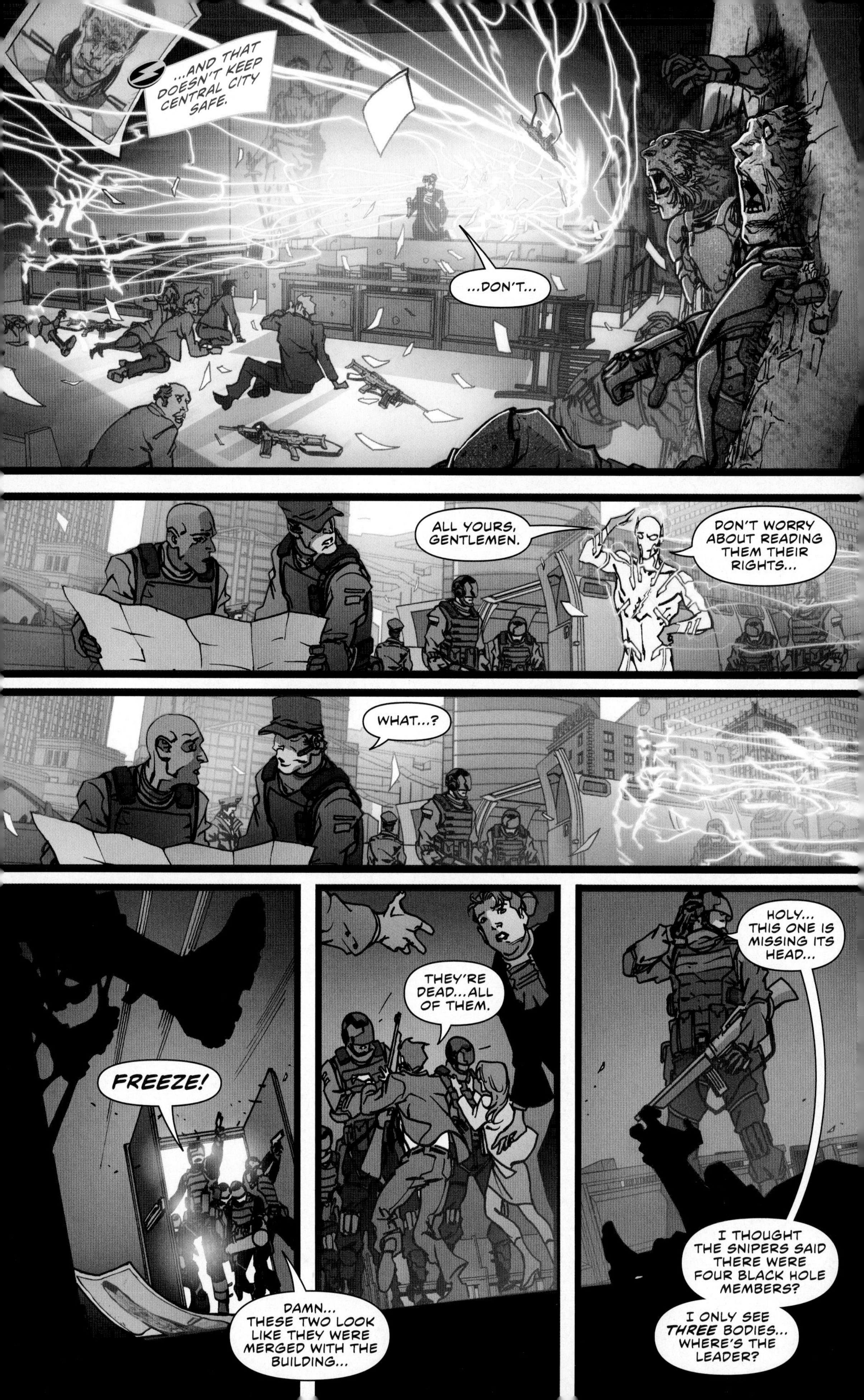
...AND THAT DOESN'T KEEP CENTRAL CITY SAFE.
...DON'T...
ALL YOURS, GENTLEMEN.
DON'T WORRY ABOUT READING THEM THEIR RIGHTS...
WHAT...?
FREEZE!
DAMN... THESE TWO LOOK LIKE THEY WERE MERGED WITH THE BUILDING...
THEY'RE DEAD...ALL OF THEM.
HOLY... THIS ONE IS MISSING ITS HEAD...
I THOUGHT THE SNIPERS SAID THERE WERE FOUR BLACK HOLE MEMBERS?
I ONLY SEE THREE BODIES... WHERE'S THE LEADER?

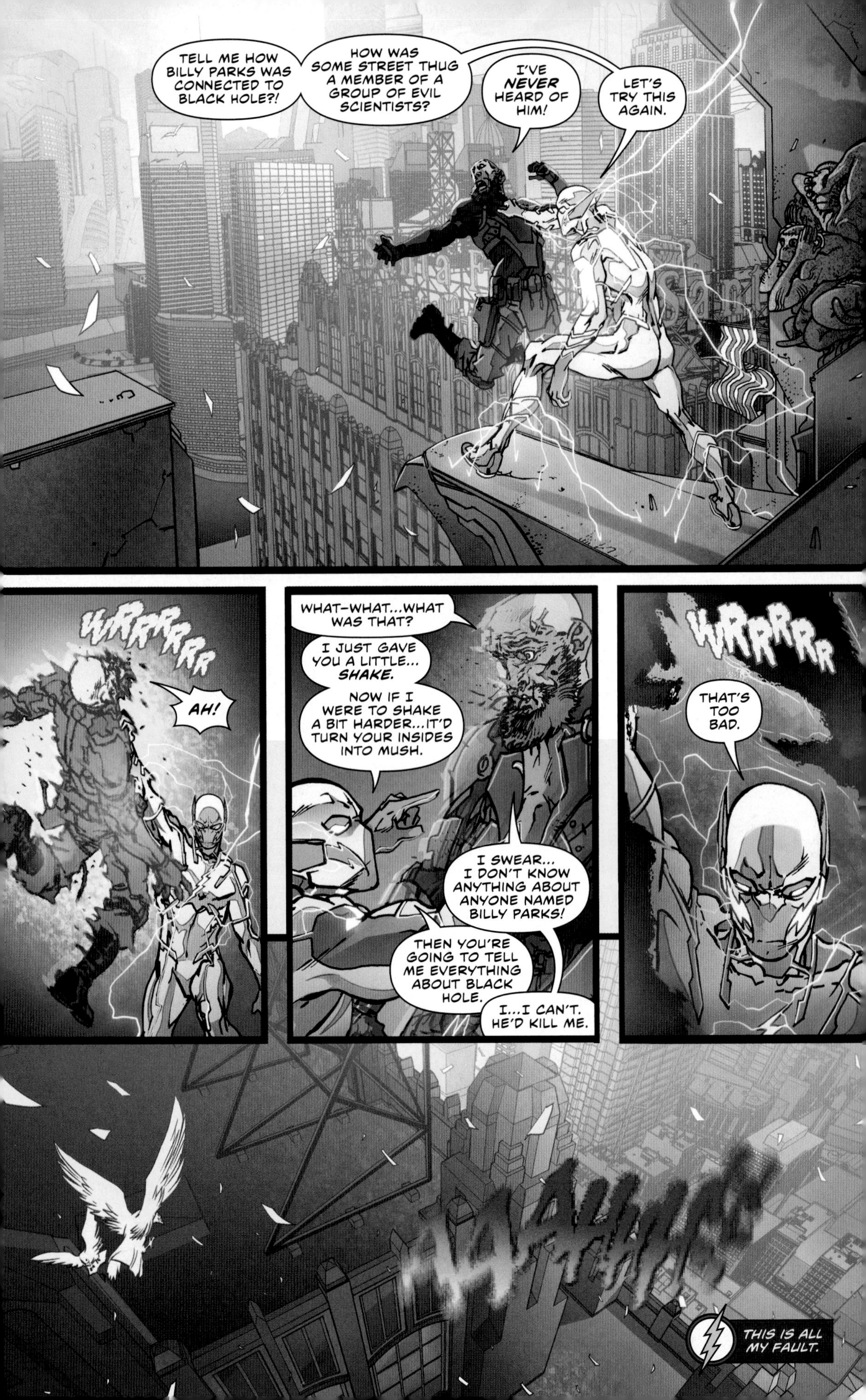
TELL ME HOW BILLY PARKS WAS CONNECTED TO BLACK HOLE?!
HOW WAS SOME STREET THUG A MEMBER OF A GROUP OF EVIL SCIENTISTS?
I'VE *NEVER* HEARD OF HIM!
LET'S TRY THIS AGAIN.
WRRRRRR
AH!
WHAT-WHAT...WHAT WAS THAT?
I JUST GAVE YOU A LITTLE... *SHAKE.*
NOW IF I WERE TO SHAKE A BIT HARDER...IT'D TURN YOUR INSIDES INTO MUSH.
I SWEAR... I DON'T KNOW ANYTHING ABOUT ANYONE NAMED BILLY PARKS!
THEN YOU'RE GOING TO TELL ME EVERYTHING ABOUT BLACK HOLE.
I...I CAN'T. HE'D KILL ME.
WRRRRRR
THAT'S TOO BAD.
THIS IS ALL MY FAULT.

I LET MYSELF GET DISTRACTED WITH THE NEW SPEEDSTERS.

WITH MEENA...

...AND I DIDN'T SEE THAT AUGUST WAS STILL TORTURED ABOUT HIS BROTHER'S DEATH.

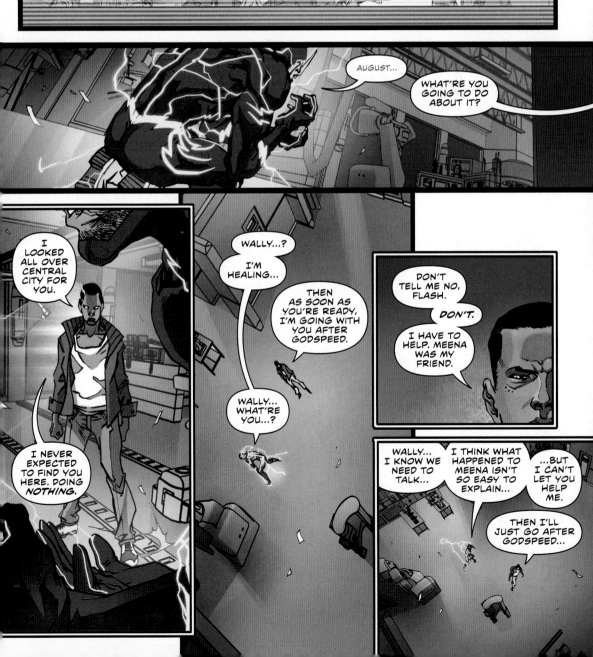

GODSPEED SAVED THE COURTROOM HOSTAGES BUT KILLED THE MEMBERS OF THE SCIENTIST TERROR GROUP KNOWN AS THE BLACK HOLE.

THE CRIME SCENE WAS REPORTED AS..."A HORROR SHOW."

AUGUST...

WHAT'RE YOU GOING TO DO ABOUT IT?

I LOOKED ALL OVER CENTRAL CITY FOR YOU.

I NEVER EXPECTED TO FIND YOU HERE. DOING *NOTHING*.

WALLY...?

I'M HEALING...

THEN AS SOON AS YOU'RE READY, I'M GOING WITH YOU AFTER GODSPEED.

WALLY... WHAT'RE YOU...?

DON'T TELL ME NO, FLASH.

DON'T.

I HAVE TO HELP. MEENA WAS MY FRIEND.

WALLY... I KNOW WE NEED TO TALK...

I THINK WHAT HAPPENED TO MEENA ISN'T SO EASY TO EXPLAIN...

...BUT I CAN'T LET YOU HELP ME.

THEN I'LL JUST GO AFTER GODSPEED...

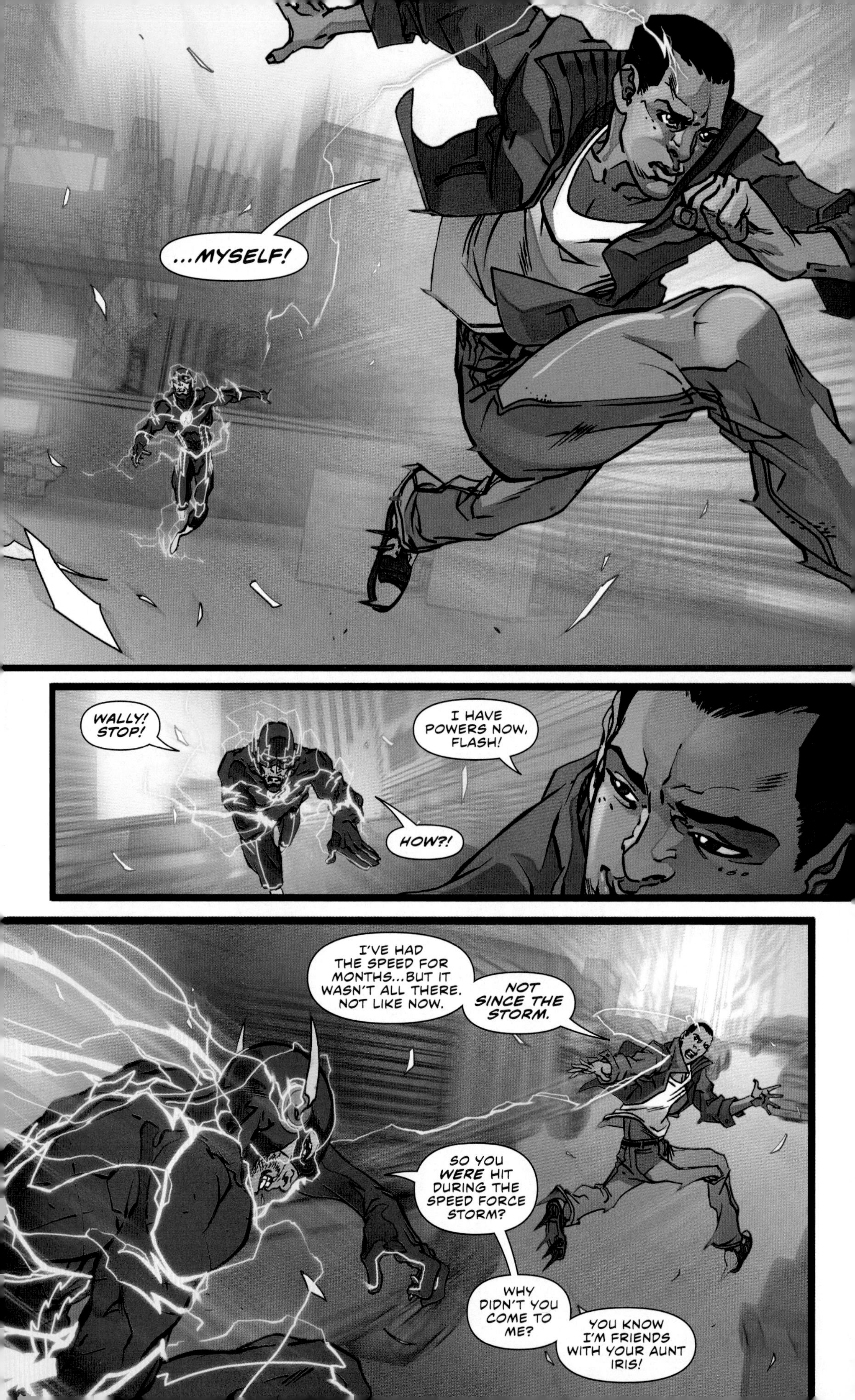
...MYSELF!
WALLY! STOP!
I HAVE POWERS NOW, FLASH!
HOW?!
I'VE HAD THE SPEED FOR MONTHS...BUT IT WASN'T ALL THERE. NOT LIKE NOW.
NOT SINCE THE STORM.
SO YOU WERE HIT DURING THE SPEED FORCE STORM?
WHY DIDN'T YOU COME TO ME?
YOU KNOW I'M FRIENDS WITH YOUR AUNT IRIS!

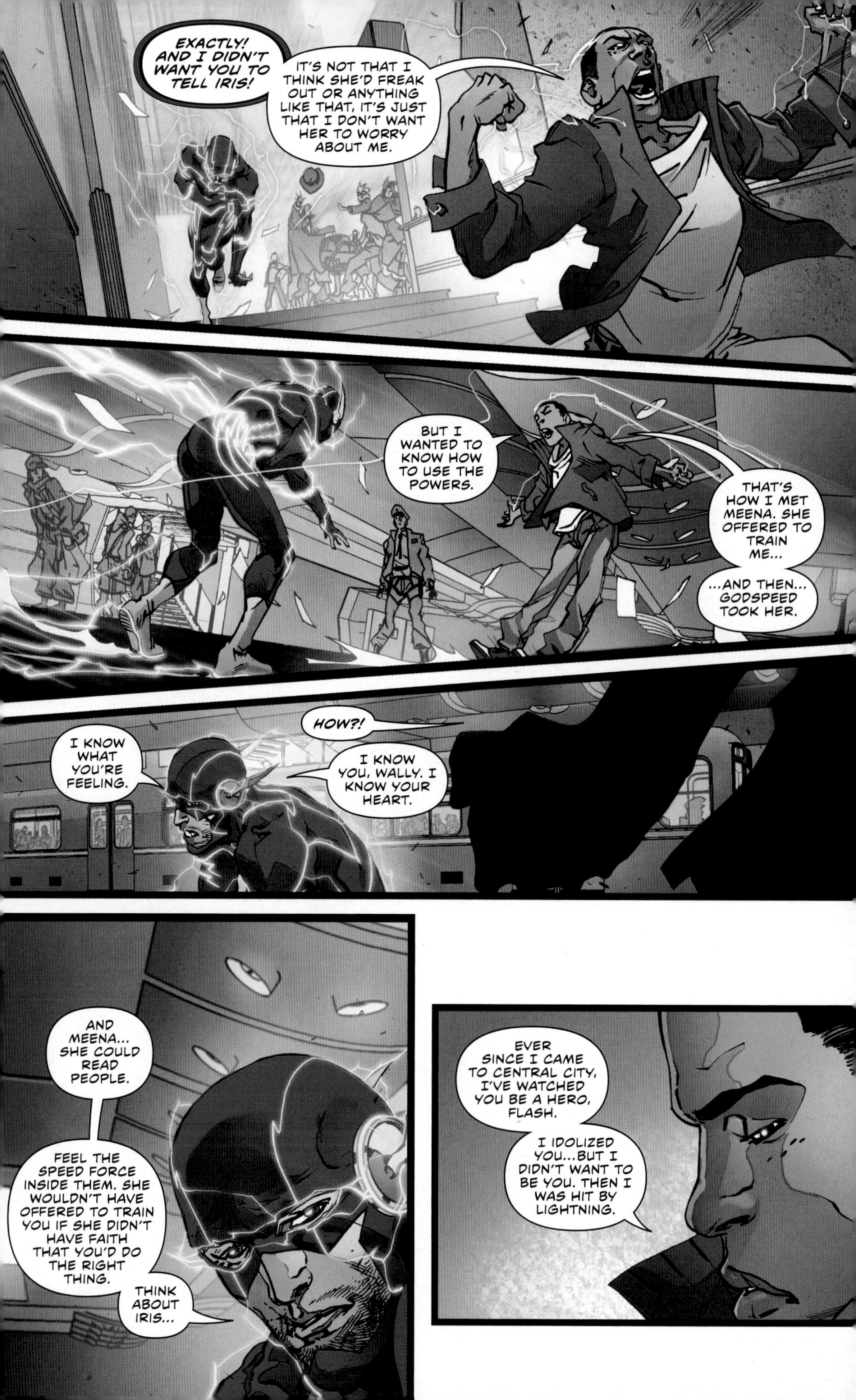
EXACTLY! AND I DIDN'T WANT YOU TO TELL IRIS!
IT'S NOT THAT I THINK SHE'D FREAK OUT OR ANYTHING LIKE THAT, IT'S JUST THAT I DON'T WANT HER TO WORRY ABOUT ME.
BUT I WANTED TO KNOW HOW TO USE THE POWERS.
THAT'S HOW I MET MEENA. SHE OFFERED TO TRAIN ME...
...AND THEN... GODSPEED TOOK HER.
I KNOW WHAT YOU'RE FEELING.
HOW?!
I KNOW YOU, WALLY. I KNOW YOUR HEART.
AND MEENA... SHE COULD READ PEOPLE.
FEEL THE SPEED FORCE INSIDE THEM. SHE WOULDN'T HAVE OFFERED TO TRAIN YOU IF SHE DIDN'T HAVE FAITH THAT YOU'D DO THE RIGHT THING.
THINK ABOUT IRIS...
EVER SINCE I CAME TO CENTRAL CITY, I'VE WATCHED YOU BE A HERO, FLASH.
I IDOLIZED YOU...BUT I DIDN'T WANT TO BE YOU. THEN I WAS HIT BY LIGHTNING.

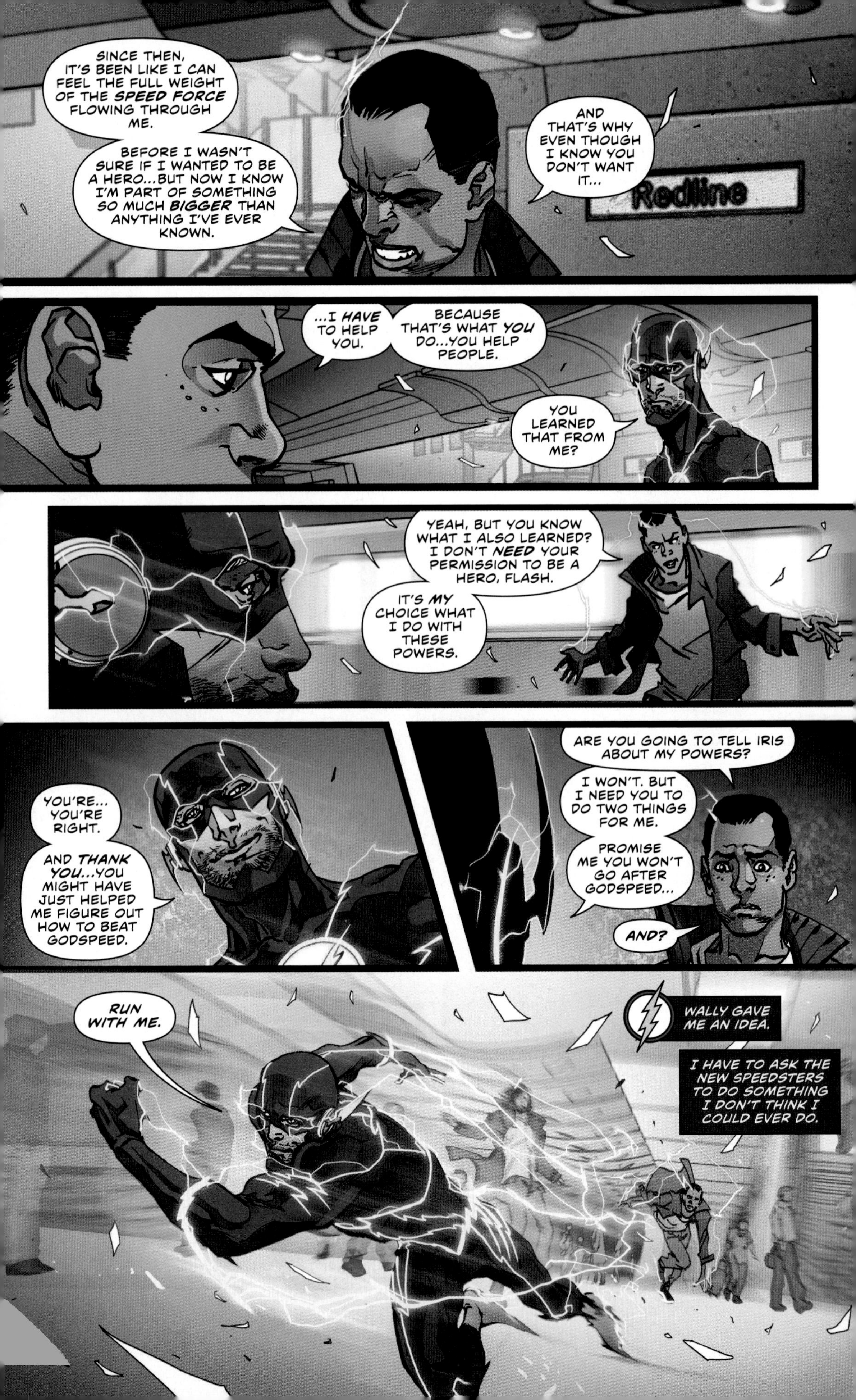
SINCE THEN, IT'S BEEN LIKE I CAN FEEL THE FULL WEIGHT OF THE SPEED FORCE FLOWING THROUGH ME.
BEFORE I WASN'T SURE IF I WANTED TO BE A HERO...BUT NOW I KNOW I'M PART OF SOMETHING SO MUCH BIGGER THAN ANYTHING I'VE EVER KNOWN.
AND THAT'S WHY EVEN THOUGH I KNOW YOU DON'T WANT IT...
Redline
...I HAVE TO HELP YOU.
BECAUSE THAT'S WHAT YOU DO...YOU HELP PEOPLE.
YOU LEARNED THAT FROM ME?
YEAH, BUT YOU KNOW WHAT I ALSO LEARNED? I DON'T NEED YOUR PERMISSION TO BE A HERO, FLASH.
IT'S MY CHOICE WHAT I DO WITH THESE POWERS.
YOU'RE... YOU'RE RIGHT.
AND THANK YOU...YOU MIGHT HAVE JUST HELPED ME FIGURE OUT HOW TO BEAT GODSPEED.
ARE YOU GOING TO TELL IRIS ABOUT MY POWERS?
I WON'T. BUT I NEED YOU TO DO TWO THINGS FOR ME.
PROMISE ME YOU WON'T GO AFTER GODSPEED...
AND?
RUN WITH ME.
WALLY GAVE ME AN IDEA.
I HAVE TO ASK THE NEW SPEEDSTERS TO DO SOMETHING I DON'T THINK I COULD EVER DO.

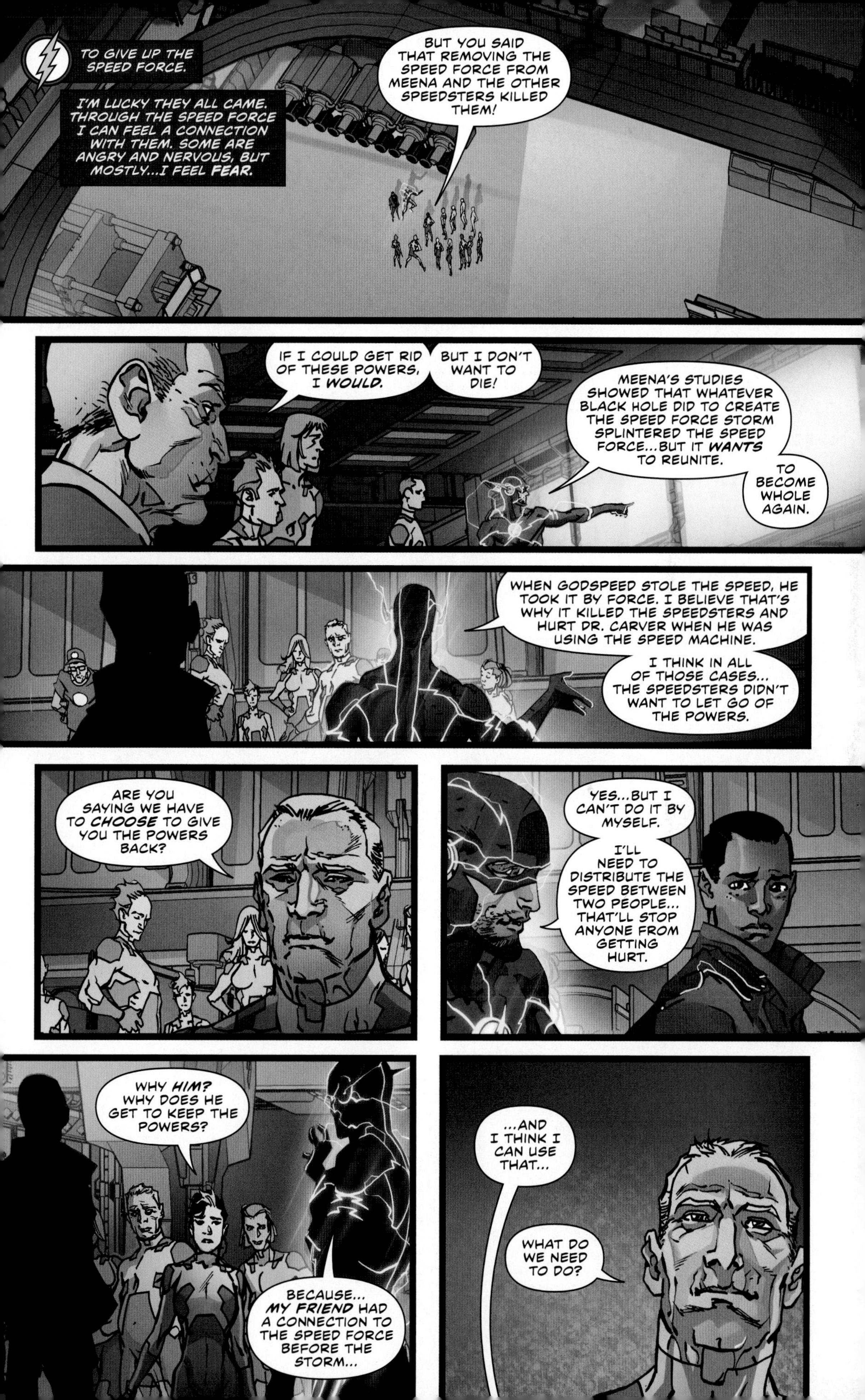
TO GIVE UP THE SPEED FORCE.
I'M LUCKY THEY ALL CAME. THROUGH THE SPEED FORCE I CAN FEEL A CONNECTION WITH THEM. SOME ARE ANGRY AND NERVOUS, BUT MOSTLY...I FEEL FEAR.
BUT YOU SAID THAT REMOVING THE SPEED FORCE FROM MEENA AND THE OTHER SPEEDSTERS KILLED THEM!
IF I COULD GET RID OF THESE POWERS, I WOULD.
BUT I DON'T WANT TO DIE!
MEENA'S STUDIES SHOWED THAT WHATEVER BLACK HOLE DID TO CREATE THE SPEED FORCE STORM SPLINTERED THE SPEED FORCE...BUT IT WANTS TO REUNITE.
TO BECOME WHOLE AGAIN.
WHEN GODSPEED STOLE THE SPEED, HE TOOK IT BY FORCE. I BELIEVE THAT'S WHY IT KILLED THE SPEEDSTERS AND HURT DR. CARVER WHEN HE WAS USING THE SPEED MACHINE.
I THINK IN ALL OF THOSE CASES... THE SPEEDSTERS DIDN'T WANT TO LET GO OF THE POWERS.
ARE YOU SAYING WE HAVE TO CHOOSE TO GIVE YOU THE POWERS BACK?
YES...BUT I CAN'T DO IT BY MYSELF.
I'LL NEED TO DISTRIBUTE THE SPEED BETWEEN TWO PEOPLE... THAT'LL STOP ANYONE FROM GETTING HURT.
WHY HIM? WHY DOES HE GET TO KEEP THE POWERS?
BECAUSE... MY FRIEND HAD A CONNECTION TO THE SPEED FORCE BEFORE THE STORM...
...AND I THINK I CAN USE THAT...
WHAT DO WE NEED TO DO?

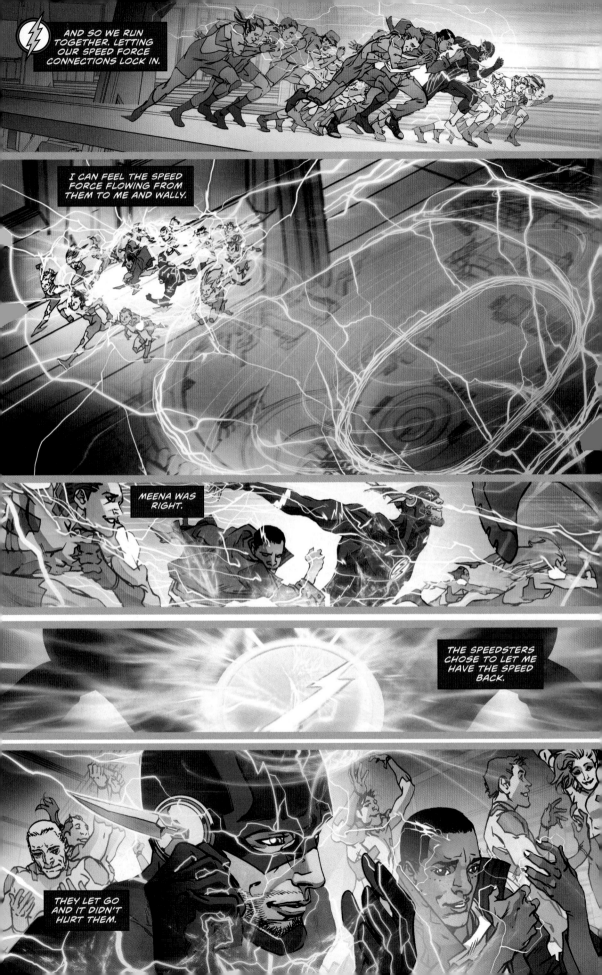

AND SO WE RUN TOGETHER. LETTING OUR SPEED FORCE CONNECTIONS LOCK IN.

I CAN FEEL THE SPEED FORCE FLOWING FROM THEM TO ME AND WALLY.

MEENA WAS RIGHT.

THE SPEEDSTERS CHOSE TO LET ME HAVE THE SPEED BACK.

THEY LET GO AND IT DIDN'T HURT THEM.

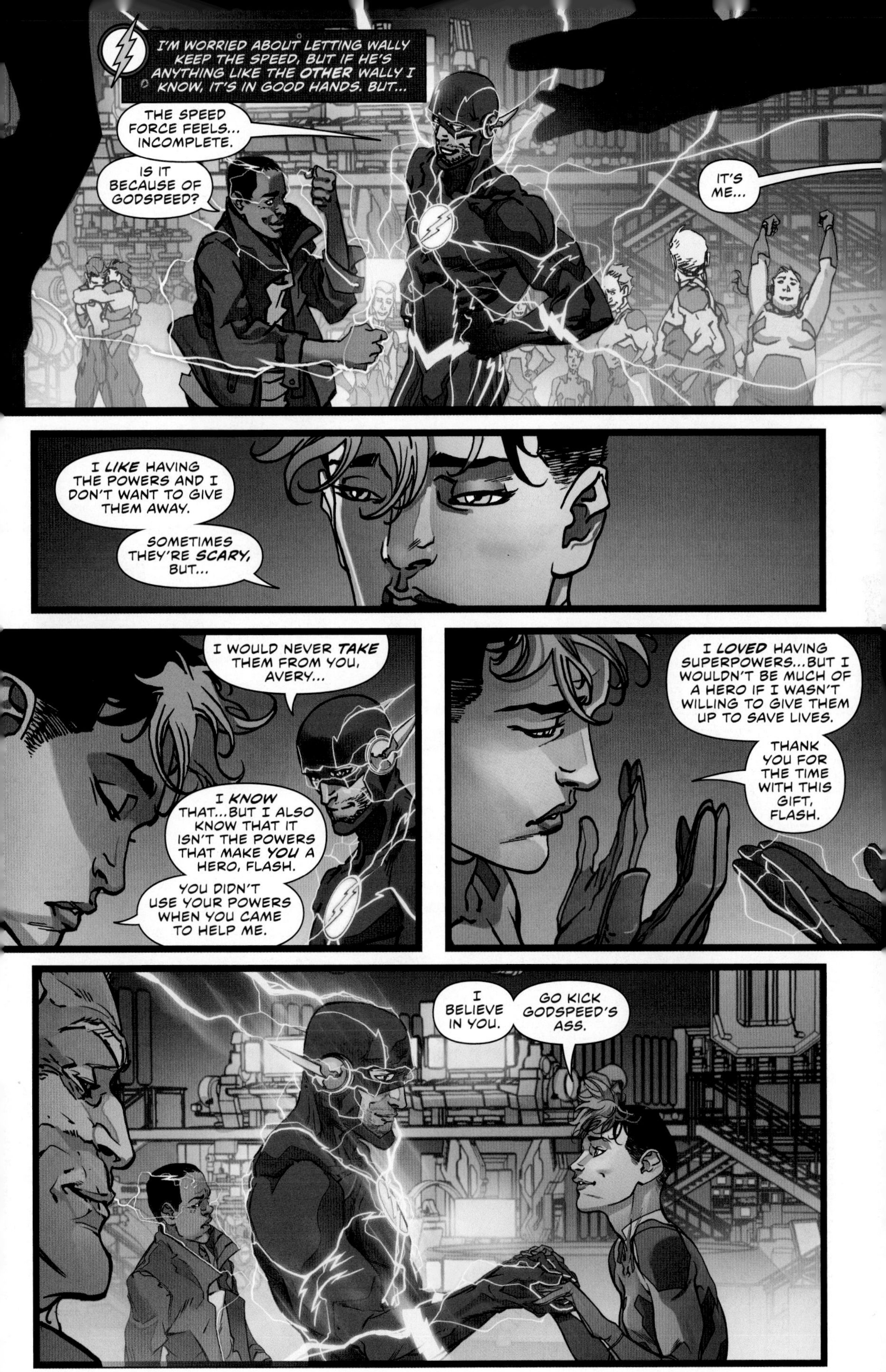
I'M WORRIED ABOUT LETTING WALLY KEEP THE SPEED, BUT IF HE'S ANYTHING LIKE THE OTHER WALLY I KNOW, IT'S IN GOOD HANDS. BUT...
THE SPEED FORCE FEELS... INCOMPLETE.
IS IT BECAUSE OF GODSPEED?
IT'S ME...
I LIKE HAVING THE POWERS AND I DON'T WANT TO GIVE THEM AWAY.
SOMETIMES THEY'RE SCARY, BUT...
I WOULD NEVER TAKE THEM FROM YOU, AVERY...
I KNOW THAT...BUT I ALSO KNOW THAT IT ISN'T THE POWERS THAT MAKE YOU A HERO, FLASH.
YOU DIDN'T USE YOUR POWERS WHEN YOU CAME TO HELP ME.
I LOVED HAVING SUPERPOWERS...BUT I WOULDN'T BE MUCH OF A HERO IF I WASN'T WILLING TO GIVE THEM UP TO SAVE LIVES.
THANK YOU FOR THE TIME WITH THIS GIFT, FLASH.
I BELIEVE IN YOU.
GO KICK GODSPEED'S ASS.

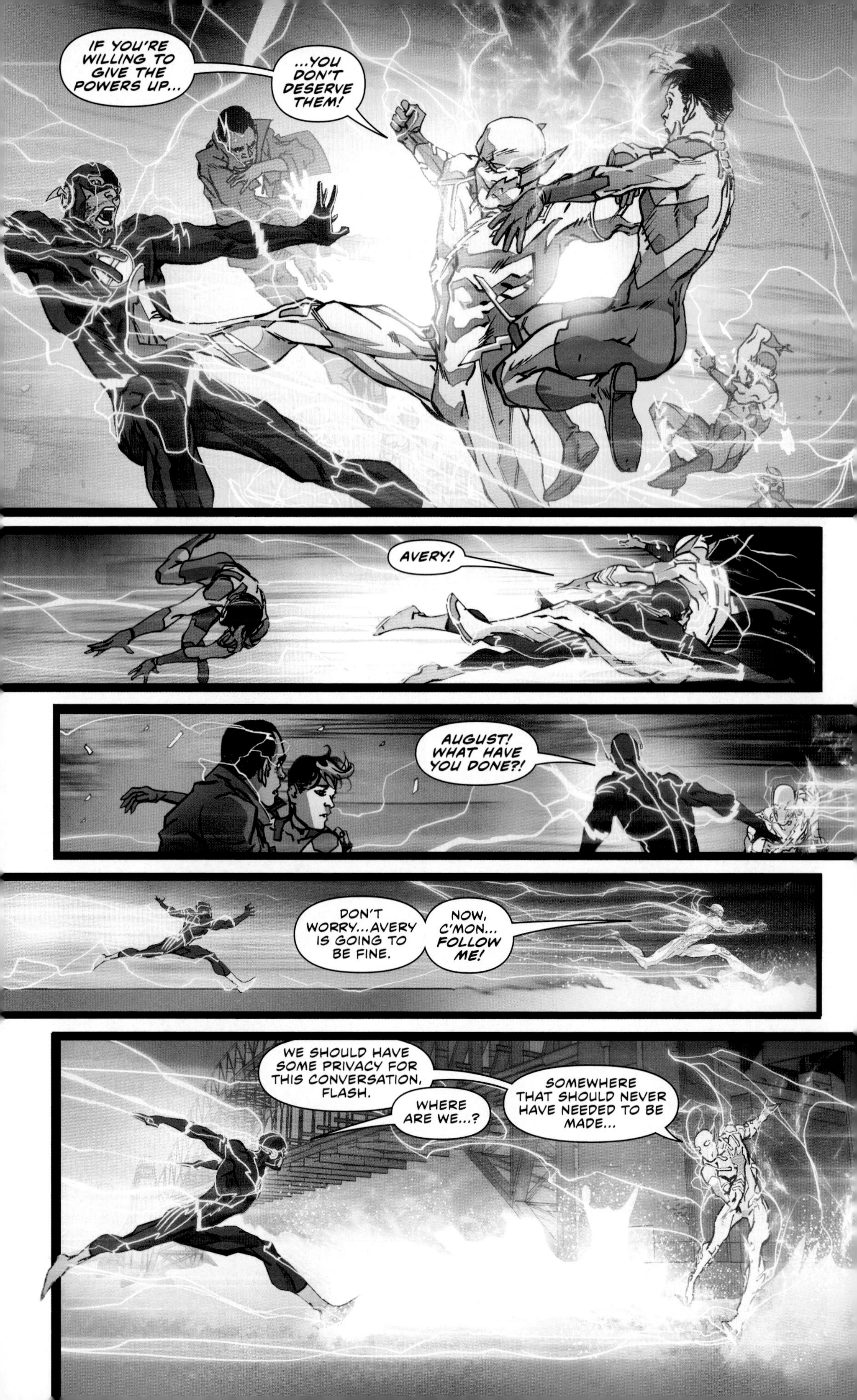
IF YOU'RE WILLING TO GIVE THE POWERS UP...
...YOU DON'T DESERVE THEM!
AVERY!
AUGUST! WHAT HAVE YOU DONE?!
DON'T WORRY...AVERY IS GOING TO BE FINE.
NOW, C'MON... FOLLOW ME!
WE SHOULD HAVE SOME PRIVACY FOR THIS CONVERSATION, FLASH.
WHERE ARE WE...?
SOMEWHERE THAT SHOULD NEVER HAVE NEEDED TO BE MADE...

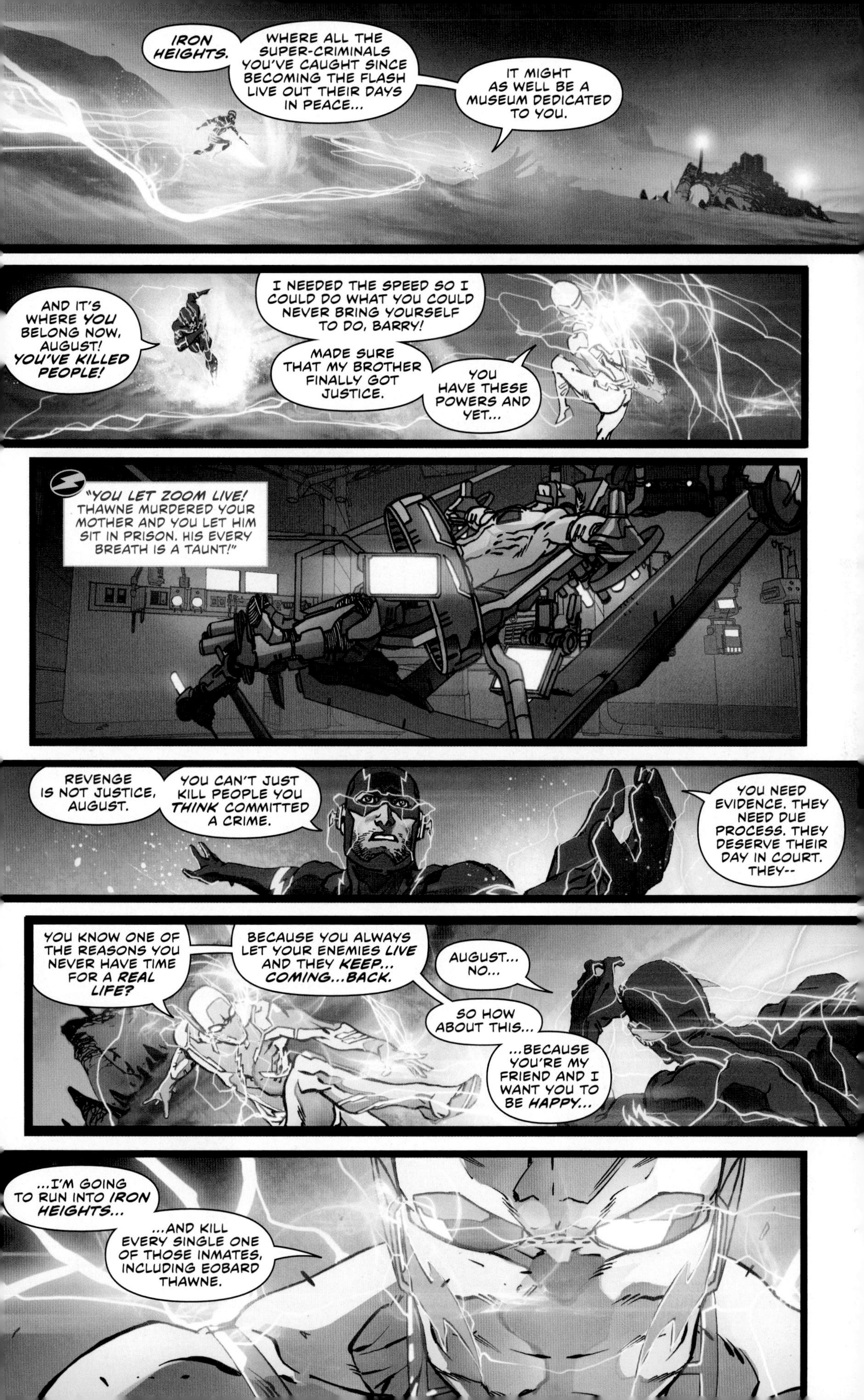
IRON HEIGHTS.
WHERE ALL THE SUPER-CRIMINALS YOU'VE CAUGHT SINCE BECOMING THE FLASH LIVE OUT THEIR DAYS IN PEACE...
IT MIGHT AS WELL BE A MUSEUM DEDICATED TO YOU.
AND IT'S WHERE YOU BELONG NOW, AUGUST! YOU'VE KILLED PEOPLE!
I NEEDED THE SPEED SO I COULD DO WHAT YOU COULD NEVER BRING YOURSELF TO DO, BARRY!
MADE SURE THAT MY BROTHER FINALLY GOT JUSTICE.
YOU HAVE THESE POWERS AND YET...
"YOU LET ZOOM LIVE! THAWNE MURDERED YOUR MOTHER AND YOU LET HIM SIT IN PRISON. HIS EVERY BREATH IS A TAUNT!"
REVENGE IS NOT JUSTICE, AUGUST.
YOU CAN'T JUST KILL PEOPLE YOU THINK COMMITTED A CRIME.
YOU NEED EVIDENCE. THEY NEED DUE PROCESS. THEY DESERVE THEIR DAY IN COURT. THEY--
YOU KNOW ONE OF THE REASONS YOU NEVER HAVE TIME FOR A REAL LIFE?
BECAUSE YOU ALWAYS LET YOUR ENEMIES LIVE AND THEY KEEP... COMING...BACK.
AUGUST... NO...
SO HOW ABOUT THIS...
...BECAUSE YOU'RE MY FRIEND AND I WANT YOU TO BE HAPPY...
...I'M GOING TO RUN INTO IRON HEIGHTS...
...AND KILL EVERY SINGLE ONE OF THOSE INMATES, INCLUDING EOBARD THAWNE.

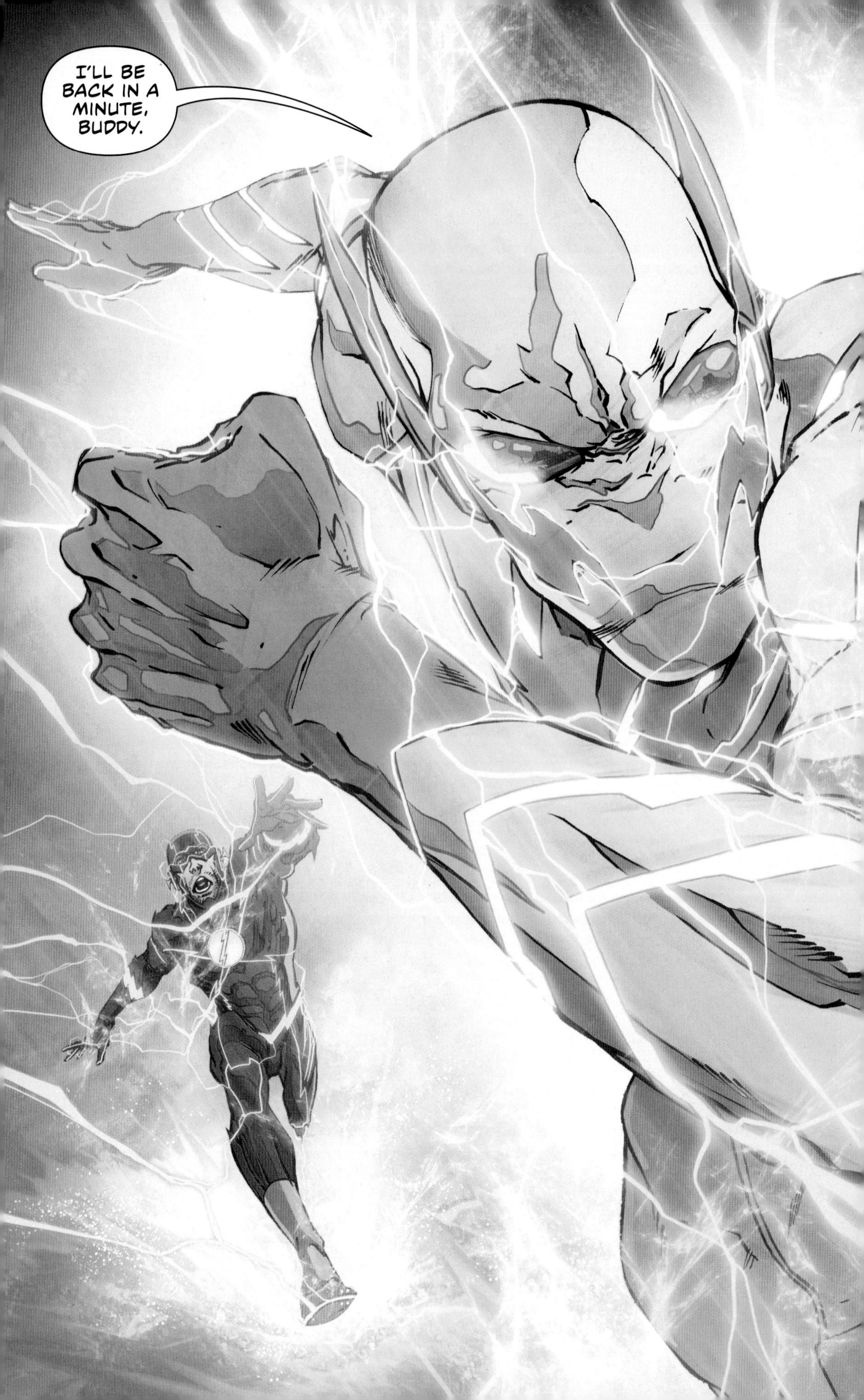
I'LL BE BACK IN A MINUTE, BUDDY.

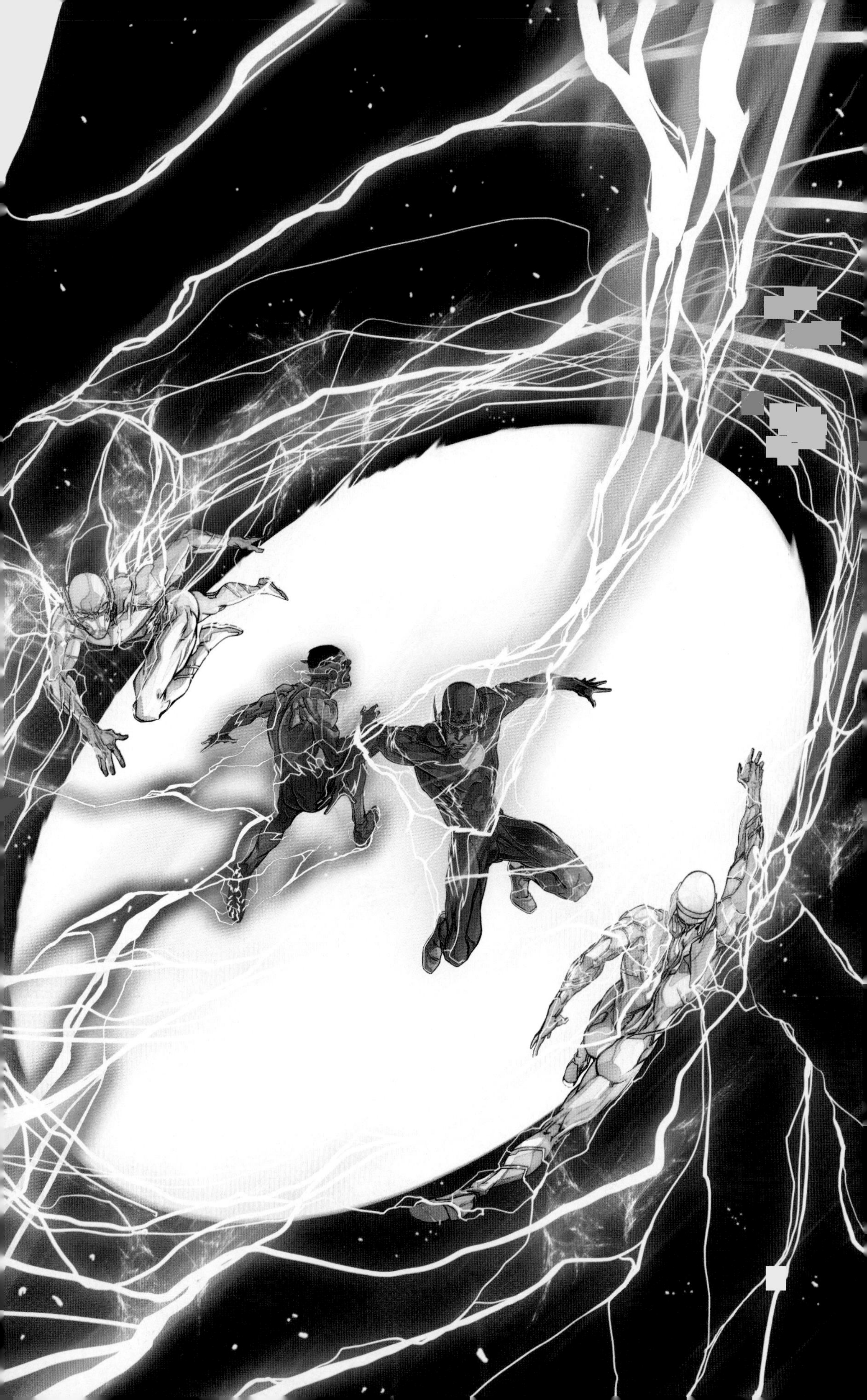

OLD FRIENDS
CARMINE DI GIANDOMENICO artist/cover

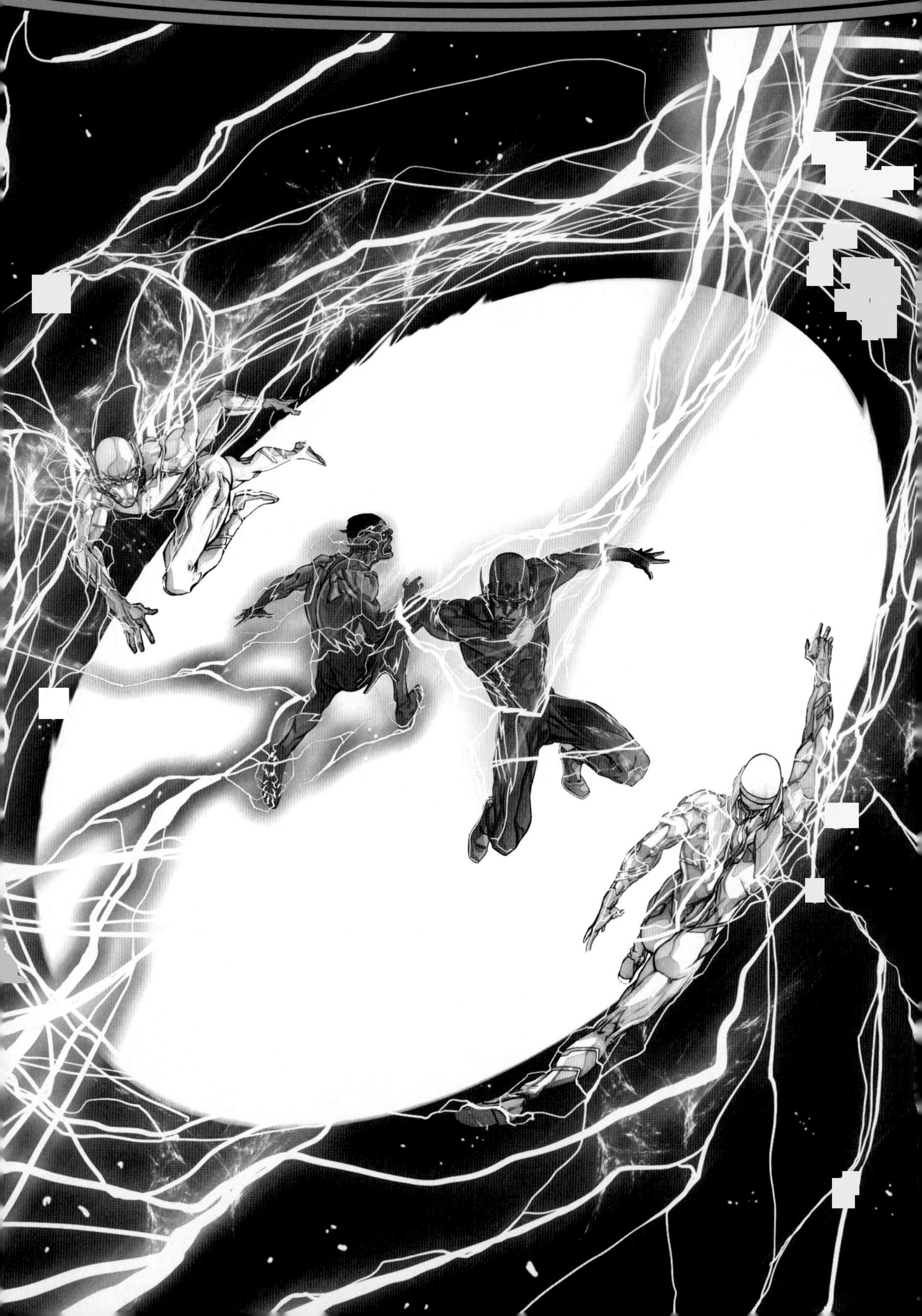

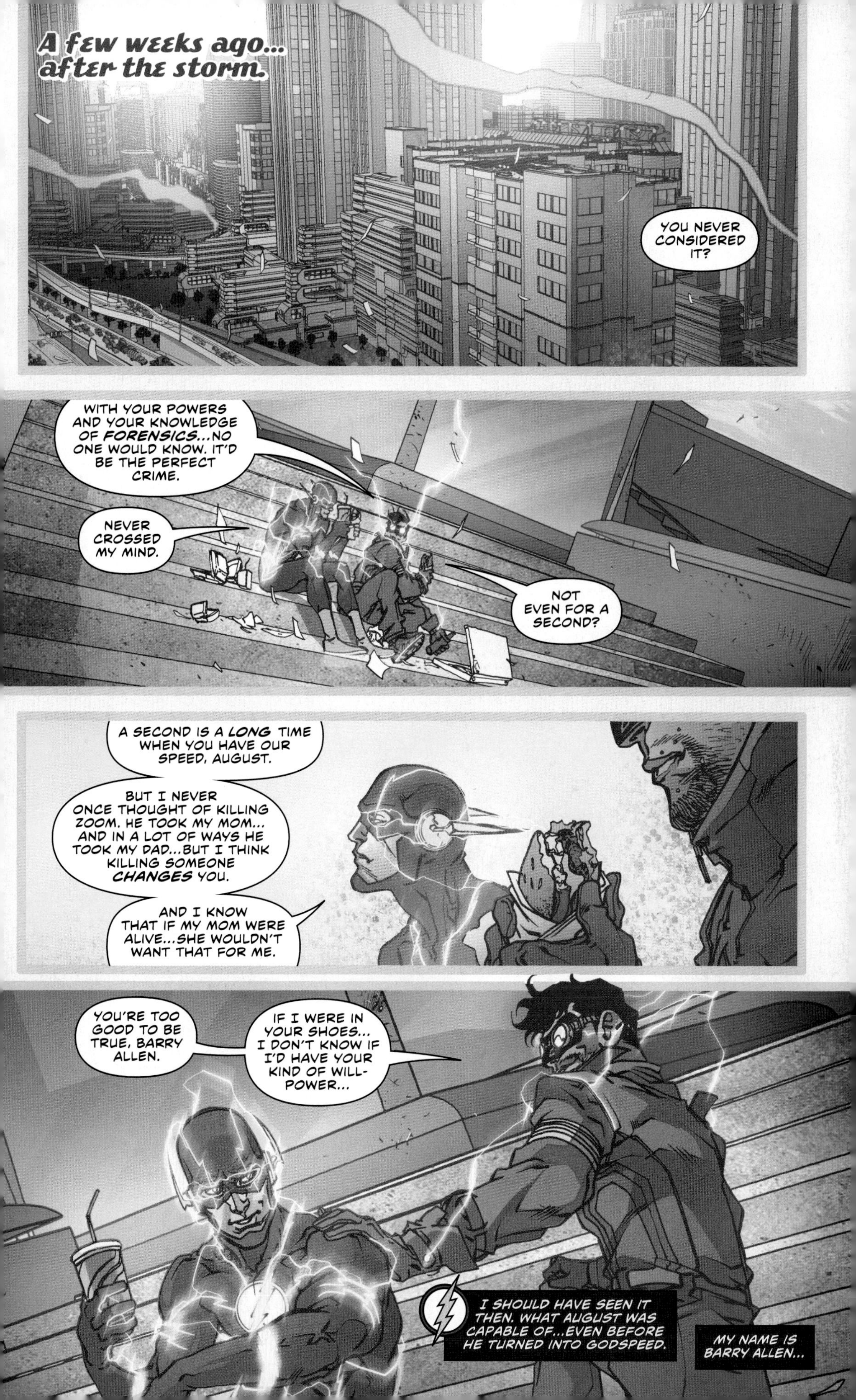
A few weeks ago... after the storm.
YOU NEVER CONSIDERED IT?
WITH YOUR POWERS AND YOUR KNOWLEDGE OF FORENSICS...NO ONE WOULD KNOW. IT'D BE THE PERFECT CRIME.
NEVER CROSSED MY MIND.
NOT EVEN FOR A SECOND?
A SECOND IS A LONG TIME WHEN YOU HAVE OUR SPEED, AUGUST.
BUT I NEVER ONCE THOUGHT OF KILLING ZOOM. HE TOOK MY MOM... AND IN A LOT OF WAYS HE TOOK MY DAD...BUT I THINK KILLING SOMEONE CHANGES YOU.
AND I KNOW THAT IF MY MOM WERE ALIVE...SHE WOULDN'T WANT THAT FOR ME.
YOU'RE TOO GOOD TO BE TRUE, BARRY ALLEN.
IF I WERE IN YOUR SHOES... I DON'T KNOW IF I'D HAVE YOUR KIND OF WILL-POWER...
I SHOULD HAVE SEEN IT THEN. WHAT AUGUST WAS CAPABLE OF...EVEN BEFORE HE TURNED INTO GODSPEED.
MY NAME IS BARRY ALLEN...

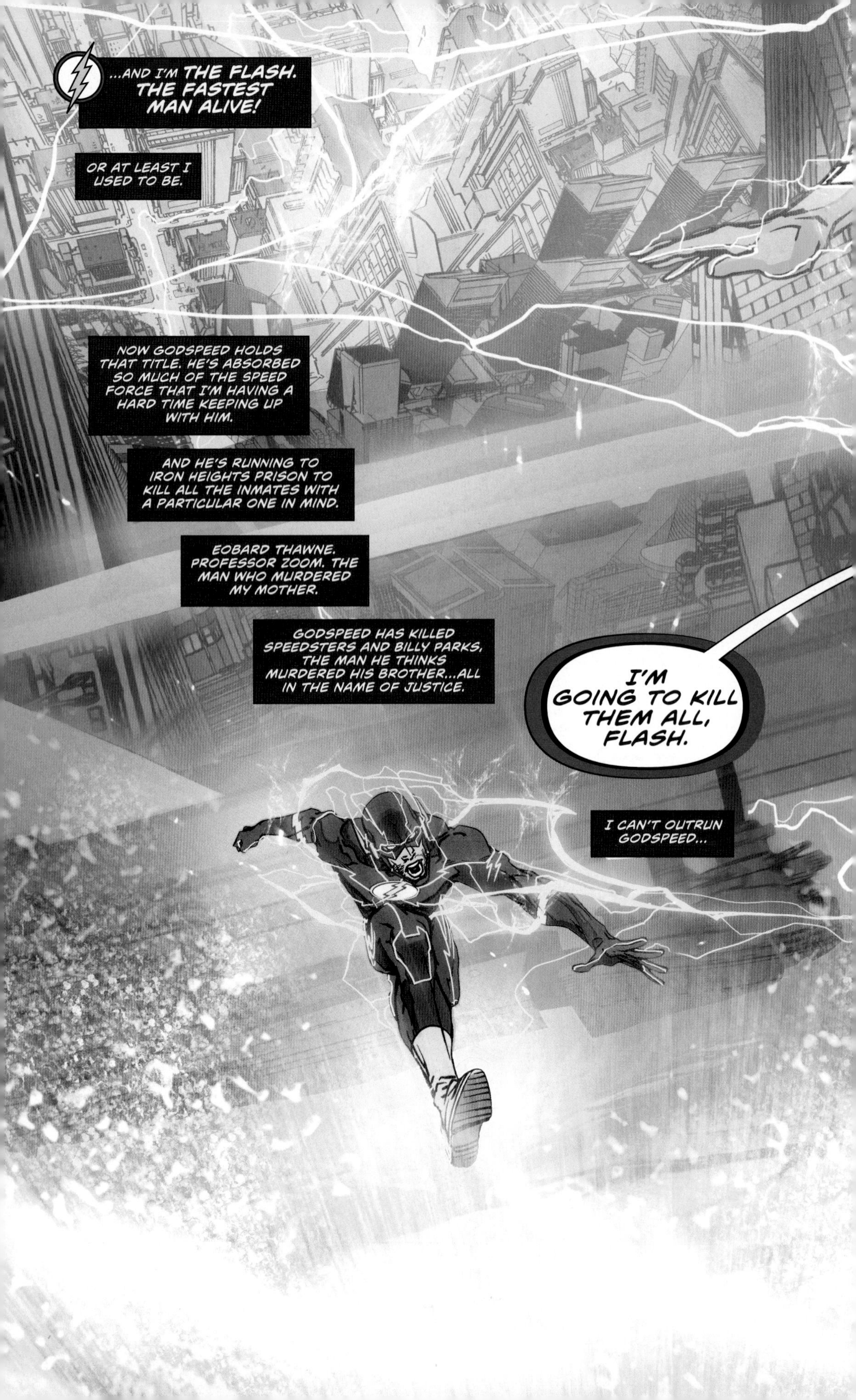
...AND I'M THE FLASH. THE FASTEST MAN ALIVE!
OR AT LEAST I USED TO BE.
NOW GODSPEED HOLDS THAT TITLE. HE'S ABSORBED SO MUCH OF THE SPEED FORCE THAT I'M HAVING A HARD TIME KEEPING UP WITH HIM.
AND HE'S RUNNING TO IRON HEIGHTS PRISON TO KILL ALL THE INMATES WITH A PARTICULAR ONE IN MIND.
EOBARD THAWNE. PROFESSOR ZOOM. THE MAN WHO MURDERED MY MOTHER.
GODSPEED HAS KILLED SPEEDSTERS AND BILLY PARKS, THE MAN HE THINKS MURDERED HIS BROTHER...ALL IN THE NAME OF JUSTICE.
I'M GOING TO KILL THEM ALL, FLASH.
I CAN'T OUTRUN GODSPEED...

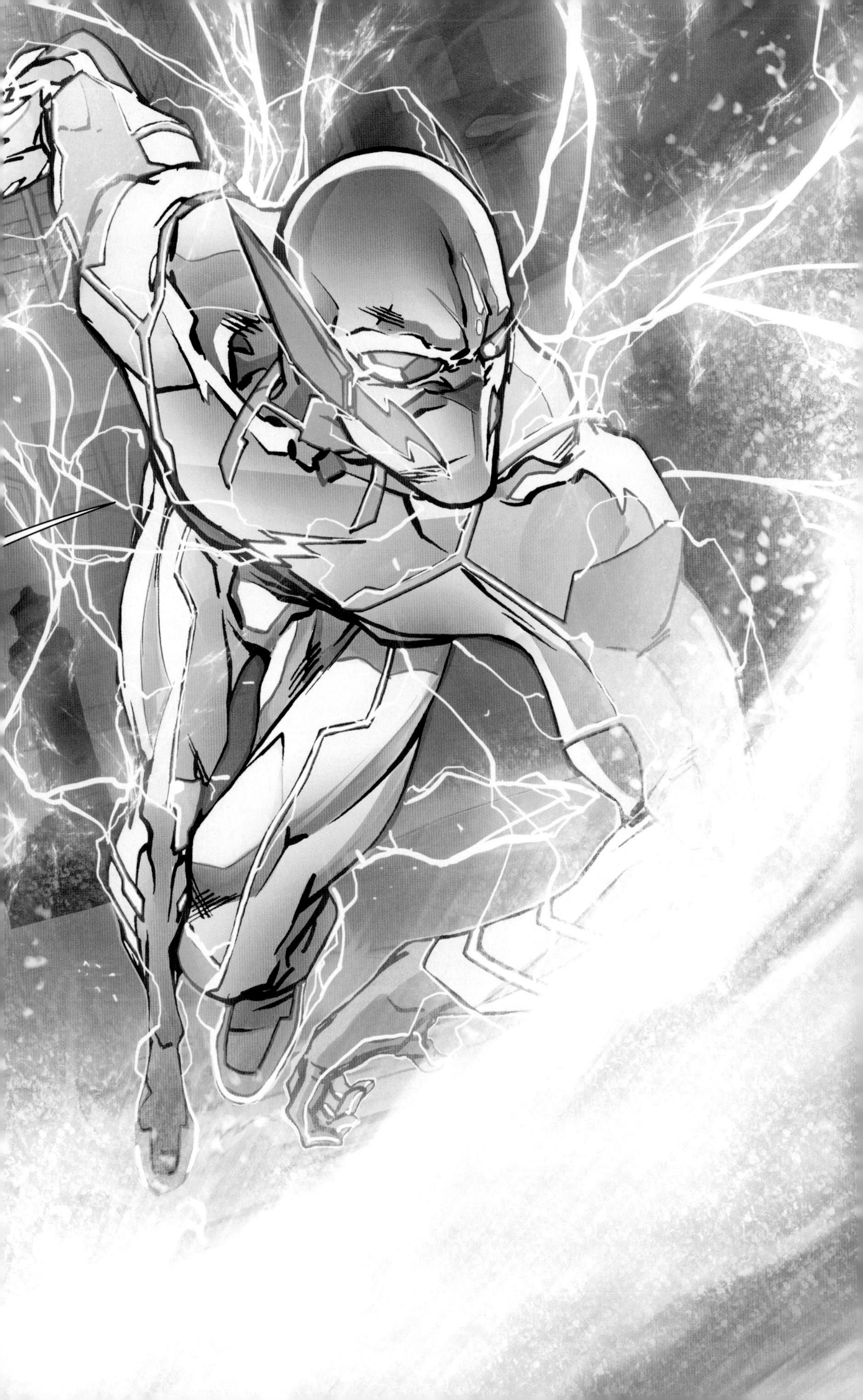

...BUT I CAN OUTSMART HIM.

LIKE TWO RACE CARS, I NEED TO STAY BEHIND GODSPEED, CATCH HIS DRAFT. THAT'S THE ONLY THING LETTING ME STAY CLOSE TO HIM. BUT IT'S NOT WHAT'S GOING TO STOP HIM.

AUGUST NEVER BOTHERED TO LEARN THE **SCIENCE** OF THE SPEED FORCE.

WE'RE BOTH POWER SOURCES CONNECTED TO THE SPEED FORCE BUT WE'RE DIFFERENT **VOLTAGES.**

I CAN FEEL OUR SPEED FORCE ENERGIES LOCKING INTO EACH OTHER...IF I TIE OUR CURRENTS TOGETHER...

...I CAN TEMPORARILY SHORT-CIRCUIT OUR CONNECTION.

WHICH I KNOW IS GOING TO HURT **ME** MORE THAN HIM. IT COULD EVEN TAKE AWAY MY CONNECTION TO THE SPEED FORCE.

BUT IF I DON'T DO THIS, I'LL BE ONE STEP BEHIND HIM AS HE MURDERS THE INMATES RIGHT IN FRONT OF MY EYES.

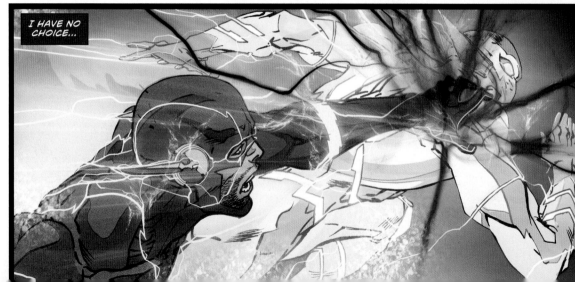

I HAVE NO CHOICE...

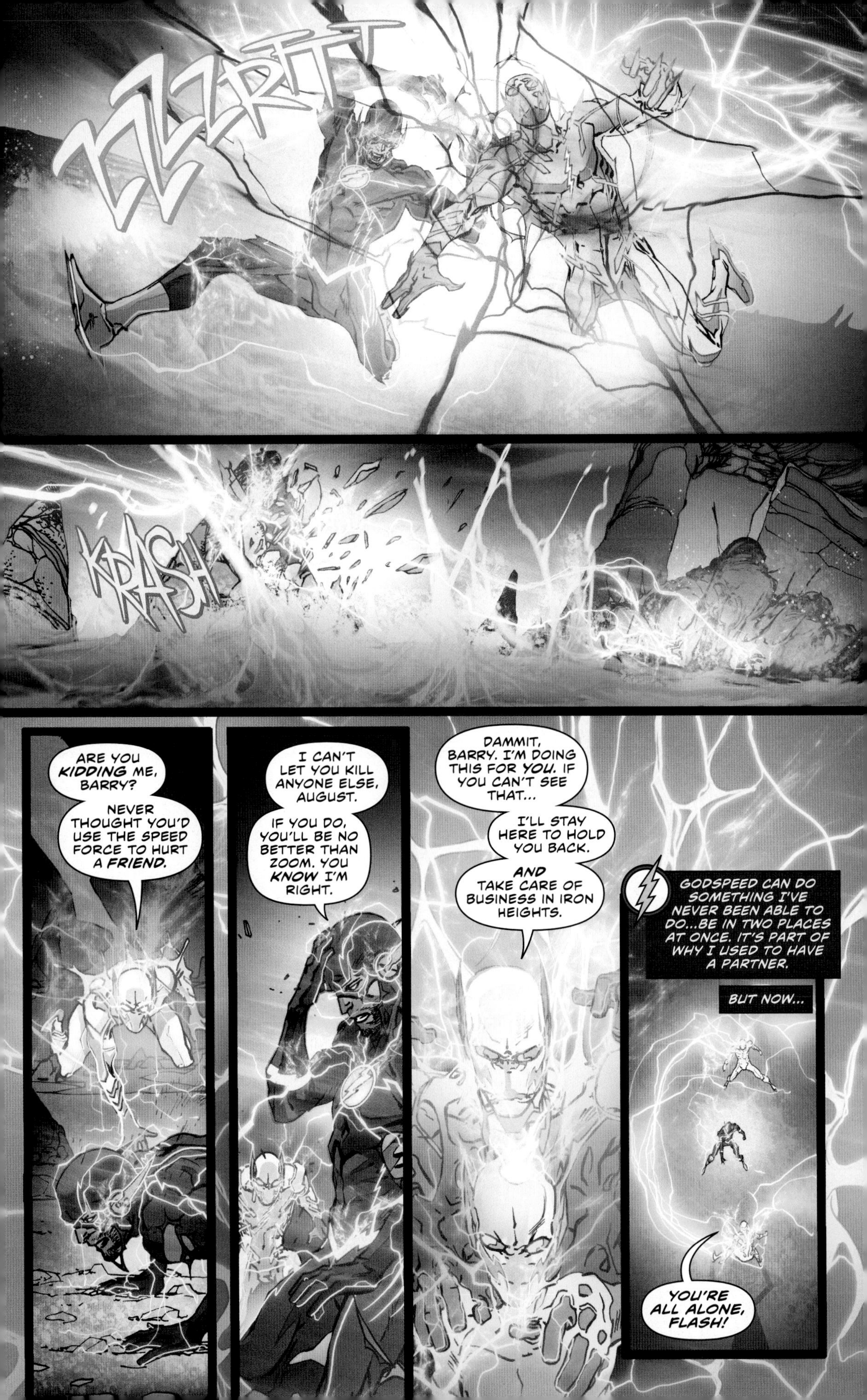
ZZZZRTTT
KRASH
ARE YOU KIDDING ME, BARRY?
NEVER THOUGHT YOU'D USE THE SPEED FORCE TO HURT A FRIEND.
I CAN'T LET YOU KILL ANYONE ELSE, AUGUST.
IF YOU DO, YOU'LL BE NO BETTER THAN ZOOM. YOU KNOW I'M RIGHT.
DAMMIT, BARRY. I'M DOING THIS FOR YOU. IF YOU CAN'T SEE THAT...
I'LL STAY HERE TO HOLD YOU BACK.
AND TAKE CARE OF BUSINESS IN IRON HEIGHTS.
GODSPEED CAN DO SOMETHING I'VE NEVER BEEN ABLE TO DO...BE IN TWO PLACES AT ONCE. IT'S PART OF WHY I USED TO HAVE A PARTNER.
BUT NOW...
YOU'RE ALL ALONE, FLASH!

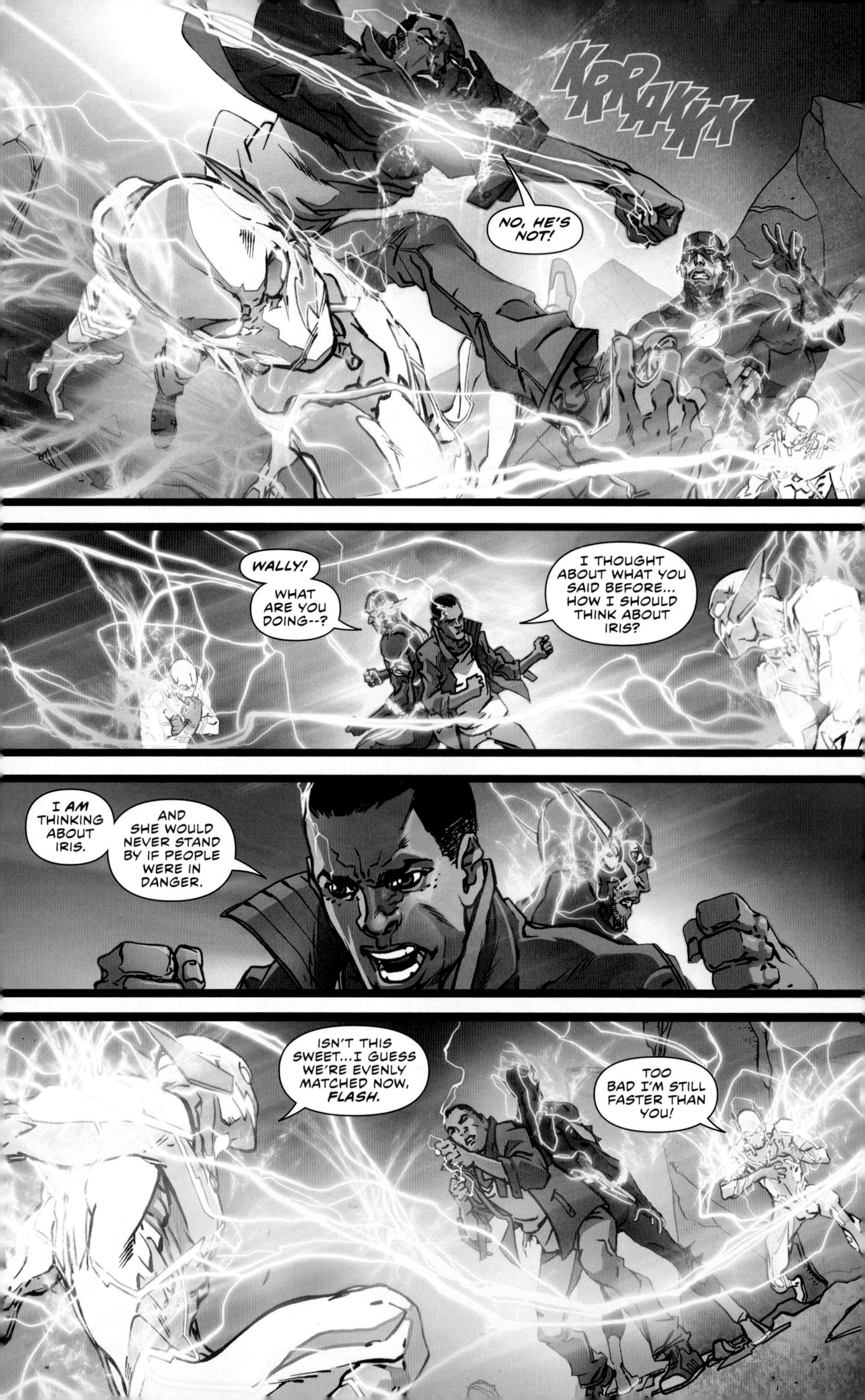
KRRAKKK
NO, HE'S NOT!
WALLY!
WHAT ARE YOU DOING--?
I THOUGHT ABOUT WHAT YOU SAID BEFORE... HOW I SHOULD THINK ABOUT IRIS?
I AM THINKING ABOUT IRIS.
AND SHE WOULD NEVER STAND BY IF PEOPLE WERE IN DANGER.
ISN'T THIS SWEET...I GUESS WE'RE EVENLY MATCHED NOW, FLASH.
TOO BAD I'M STILL FASTER THAN YOU!

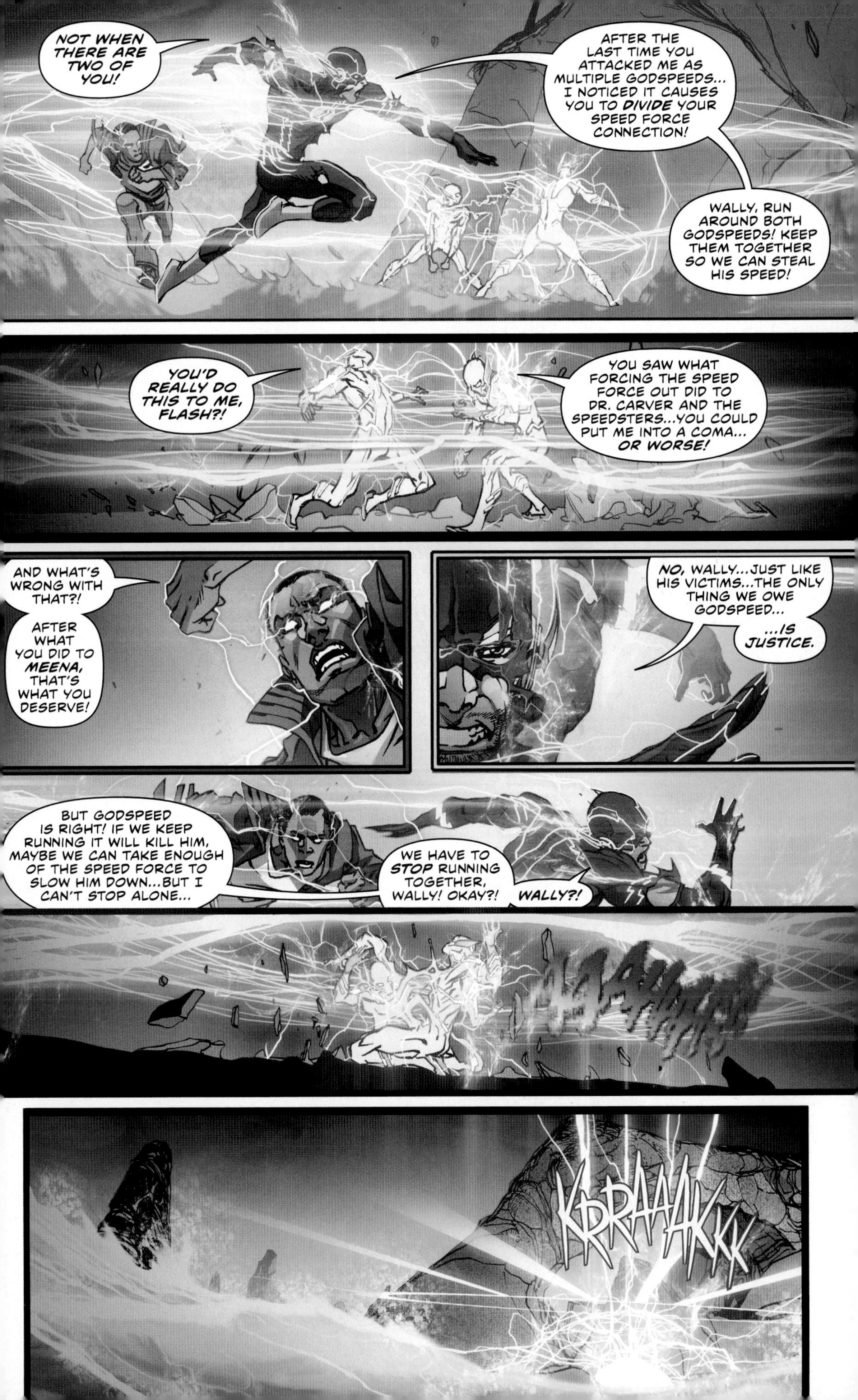
NOT WHEN THERE ARE TWO OF YOU!
AFTER THE LAST TIME YOU ATTACKED ME AS MULTIPLE GODSPEEDS... I NOTICED IT CAUSES YOU TO DIVIDE YOUR SPEED FORCE CONNECTION!
WALLY, RUN AROUND BOTH GODSPEEDS! KEEP THEM TOGETHER SO WE CAN STEAL HIS SPEED!
YOU'D REALLY DO THIS TO ME, FLASH?!
YOU SAW WHAT FORCING THE SPEED FORCE OUT DID TO DR. CARVER AND THE SPEEDSTERS...YOU COULD PUT ME INTO A COMA... OR WORSE!
AND WHAT'S WRONG WITH THAT?!
AFTER WHAT YOU DID TO MEENA, THAT'S WHAT YOU DESERVE!
NO, WALLY...JUST LIKE HIS VICTIMS...THE ONLY THING WE OWE GODSPEED...
...IS JUSTICE.
BUT GODSPEED IS RIGHT! IF WE KEEP RUNNING IT WILL KILL HIM, MAYBE WE CAN TAKE ENOUGH OF THE SPEED FORCE TO SLOW HIM DOWN...BUT I CAN'T STOP ALONE...
WE HAVE TO STOP RUNNING TOGETHER, WALLY! OKAY?!
WALLY?!
KRRAAAKKKK

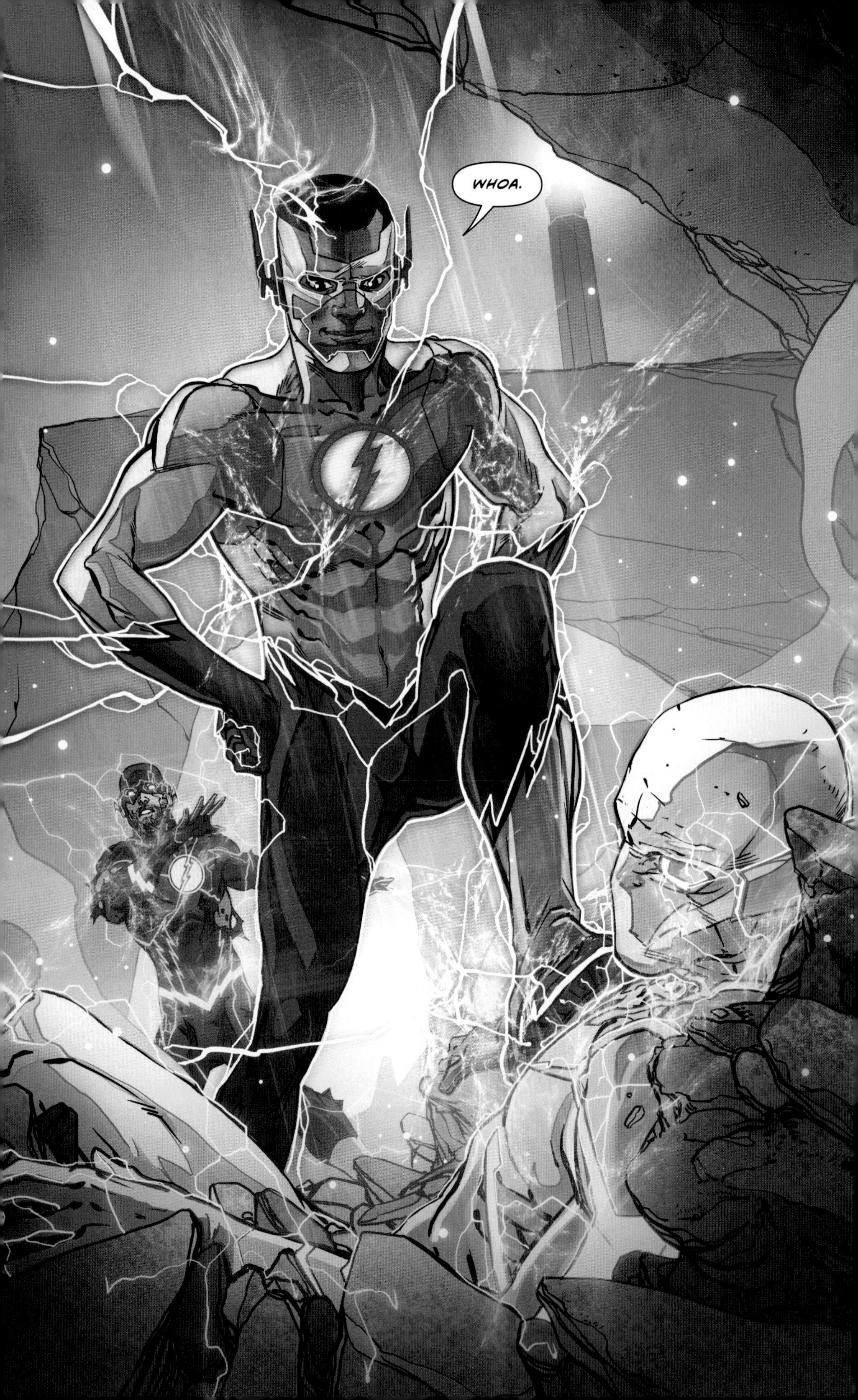
WHOA.

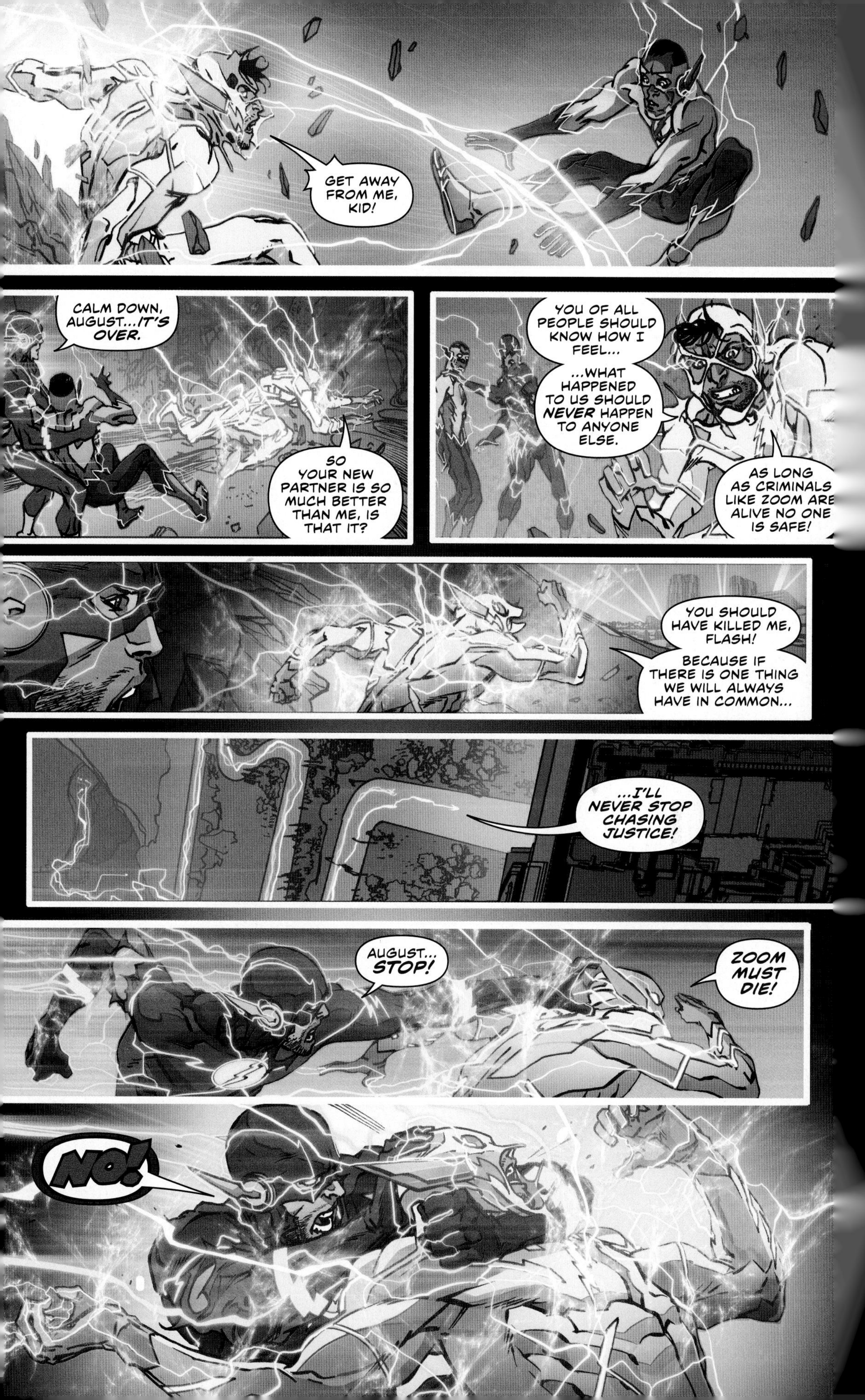
GET AWAY FROM ME, KID!
CALM DOWN, AUGUST...IT'S OVER.
SO YOUR NEW PARTNER IS SO MUCH BETTER THAN ME, IS THAT IT?
YOU OF ALL PEOPLE SHOULD KNOW HOW I FEEL...
...WHAT HAPPENED TO US SHOULD NEVER HAPPEN TO ANYONE ELSE.
AS LONG AS CRIMINALS LIKE ZOOM ARE ALIVE NO ONE IS SAFE!
YOU SHOULD HAVE KILLED ME, FLASH!
BECAUSE IF THERE IS ONE THING WE WILL ALWAYS HAVE IN COMMON...
...I'LL NEVER STOP CHASING JUSTICE!
AUGUST... STOP!
ZOOM MUST DIE!
NO!

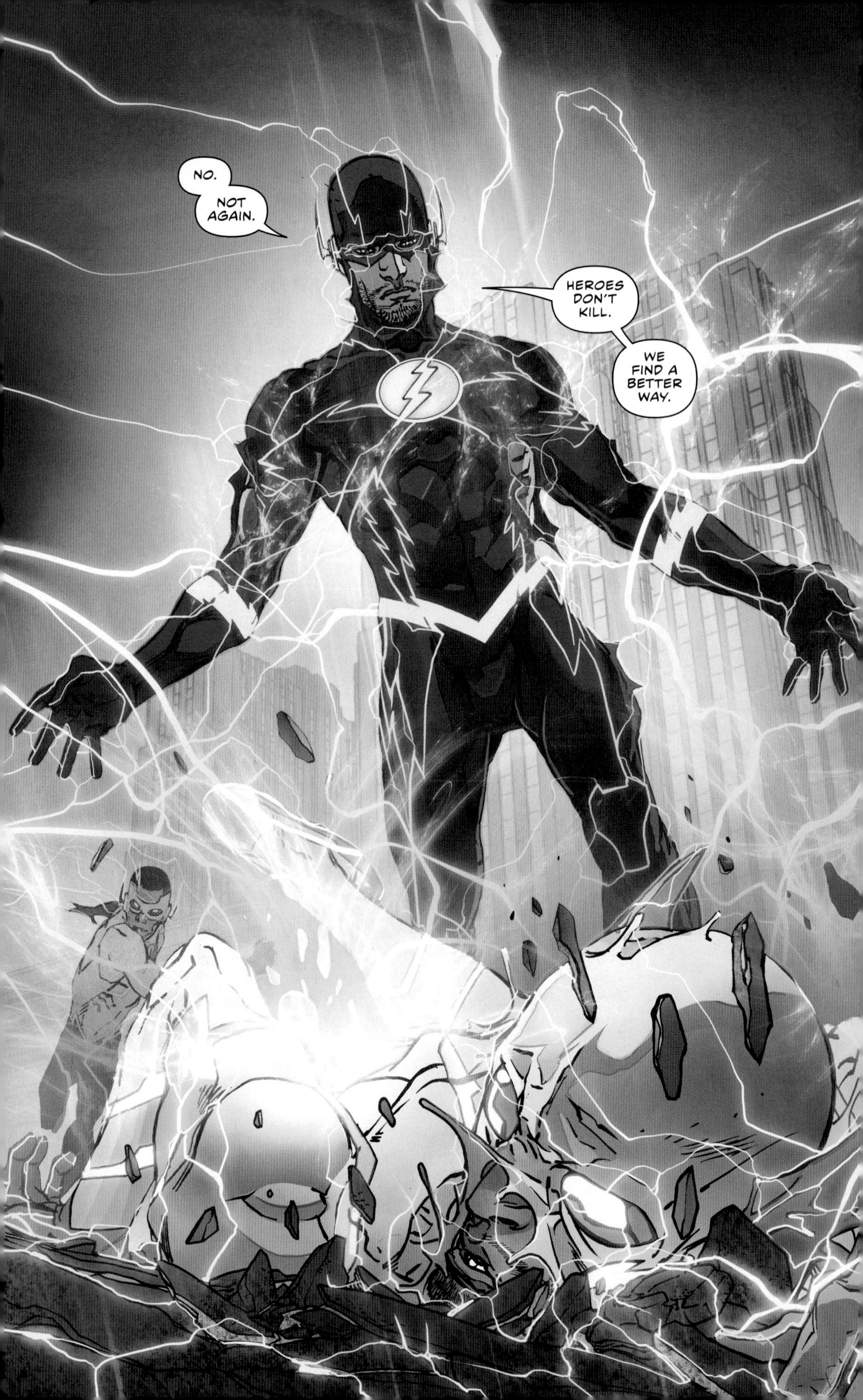
NO.
NOT AGAIN.
HEROES DON'T KILL.
WE FIND A BETTER WAY.

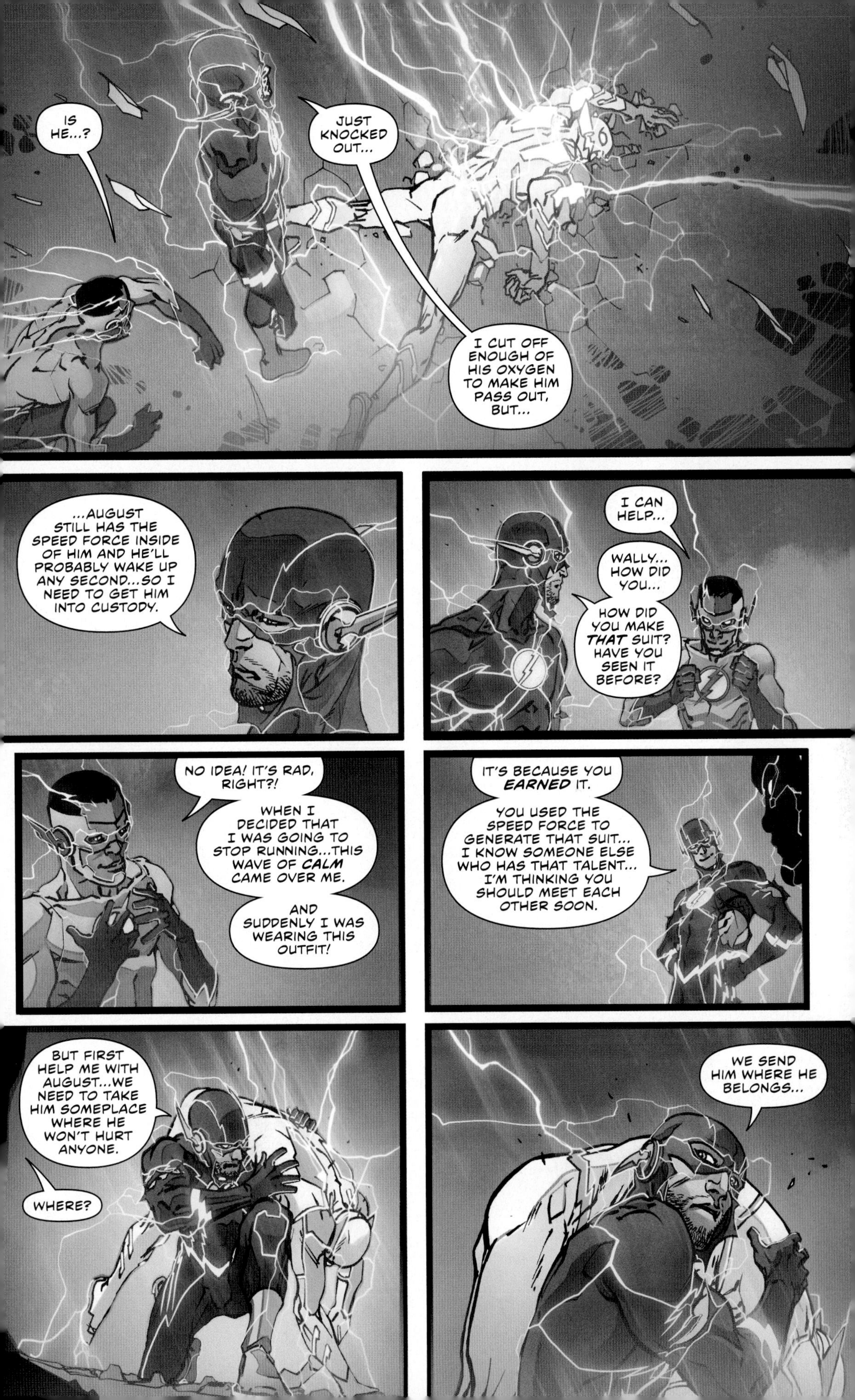
IS HE...?
JUST KNOCKED OUT...
I CUT OFF ENOUGH OF HIS OXYGEN TO MAKE HIM PASS OUT, BUT...
...AUGUST STILL HAS THE SPEED FORCE INSIDE OF HIM AND HE'LL PROBABLY WAKE UP ANY SECOND...SO I NEED TO GET HIM INTO CUSTODY.
I CAN HELP...
WALLY... HOW DID YOU...
HOW DID YOU MAKE *THAT* SUIT? HAVE YOU SEEN IT BEFORE?
NO IDEA! IT'S RAD, RIGHT?!
WHEN I DECIDED THAT I WAS GOING TO STOP RUNNING...THIS WAVE OF *CALM* CAME OVER ME.
AND SUDDENLY I WAS WEARING THIS OUTFIT!
IT'S BECAUSE YOU *EARNED* IT.
YOU USED THE SPEED FORCE TO GENERATE THAT SUIT... I KNOW SOMEONE ELSE WHO HAS THAT TALENT... I'M THINKING YOU SHOULD MEET EACH OTHER SOON.
BUT FIRST HELP ME WITH AUGUST...WE NEED TO TAKE HIM SOMEPLACE WHERE HE WON'T HURT ANYONE.
WHERE?
WE SEND HIM WHERE HE BELONGS...

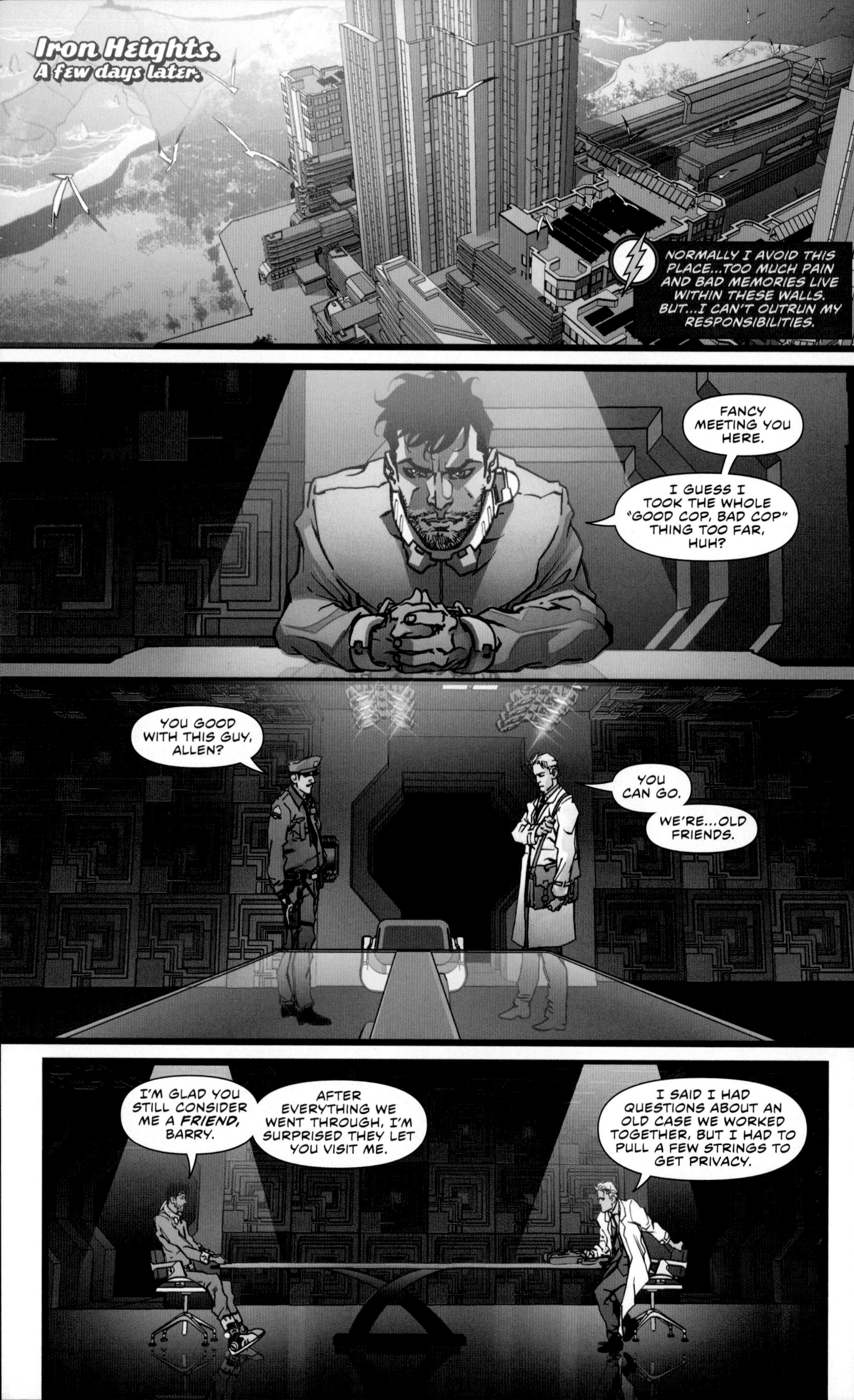
Iron Heights.
A few days later.
NORMALLY I AVOID THIS PLACE...TOO MUCH PAIN AND BAD MEMORIES LIVE WITHIN THESE WALLS. BUT...I CAN'T OUTRUN MY RESPONSIBILITIES.
FANCY MEETING YOU HERE.
I GUESS I TOOK THE WHOLE "GOOD COP, BAD COP" THING TOO FAR, HUH?
YOU GOOD WITH THIS GUY, ALLEN?
YOU CAN GO.
WE'RE...OLD FRIENDS.
I'M GLAD YOU STILL CONSIDER ME A *FRIEND*, BARRY.
AFTER EVERYTHING WE WENT THROUGH, I'M SURPRISED THEY LET YOU VISIT ME.
I SAID I HAD QUESTIONS ABOUT AN OLD CASE WE WORKED TOGETHER, BUT I HAD TO PULL A FEW STRINGS TO GET PRIVACY.

DON'T WORRY. I'M NOT GOING TO TELL ANYONE *OUR* SECRET.

I KEEP TELLING YOU, BARRY. I WAS JUST TRYING TO HELP. I NEVER WANTED ANY INNOCENTS TO GET HURT.

I CAN STILL FEEL A CONNECTION, Y'KNOW...THE SPEED FORCE IS GONE FROM THE OTHER SPEEDSTERS...BUT I CAN SENSE THEM.

"MOST OF THEM ARE *HAPPY* TO BE DONE WITH THE SPEED FORCE. SATISFIED WITH BEING POWERLESS AND LIVING *NORMAL* LIVES AGAIN.

"BUT SOME ARE *UPSET* THAT THEY HAD GREATNESS TAKEN AWAY FROM THEM.

"WISHING THEY HAD ANOTHER CHANCE WITH THE POWERS.

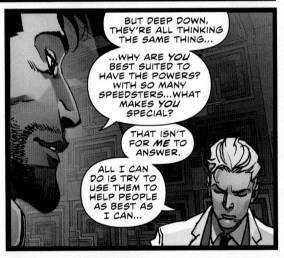

BUT DEEP DOWN, THEY'RE ALL THINKING THE SAME THING...

...WHY ARE *YOU* BEST SUITED TO HAVE THE POWERS? WITH SO MANY SPEEDSTERS...WHAT MAKES *YOU* SPECIAL?

THAT ISN'T FOR *ME* TO ANSWER.

ALL I CAN DO IS TRY TO USE THEM TO HELP PEOPLE AS BEST AS I CAN...

BUT AGAIN...THAT'S WHAT *YOU* THINK IS BEST. PEOPLE LIKE ME...WE THINK YOU CAN DO MORE.

JUST LIKE BILLY PARKS. I *KNOW* HE KILLED MY BROTHER, I COULD TELL JUST BY LOOKING AT HIM, AND SO I USED THOSE POWERS TO GET *JUSTICE*.

ACTUALLY, THAT'S WHY I CAME TODAY.

I STARTED TO LOOK INTO YOUR BROTHER'S CASE AGAIN.

THE FILES WERE DESTROYED THE NIGHT I WAS HIT BY LIGHTNING... BUT I PIECED THEM BACK TOGETHER AND WAS ABLE TO WORK ON THE EVIDENCE.

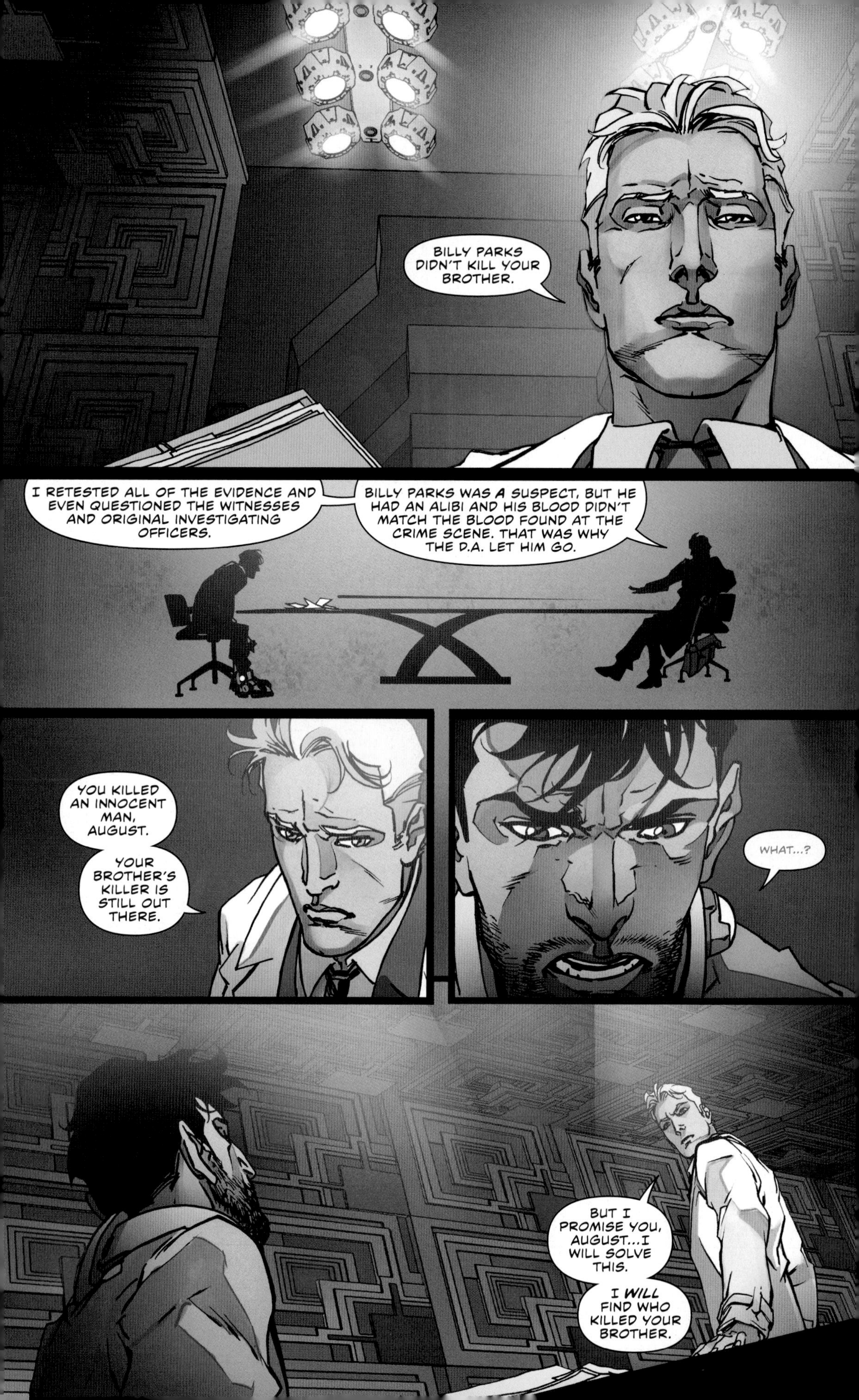
BILLY PARKS DIDN'T KILL YOUR BROTHER.
I RETESTED ALL OF THE EVIDENCE AND EVEN QUESTIONED THE WITNESSES AND ORIGINAL INVESTIGATING OFFICERS.
BILLY PARKS WAS A SUSPECT, BUT HE HAD AN ALIBI AND HIS BLOOD DIDN'T MATCH THE BLOOD FOUND AT THE CRIME SCENE. THAT WAS WHY THE D.A. LET HIM GO.
YOU KILLED AN INNOCENT MAN, AUGUST.
YOUR BROTHER'S KILLER IS STILL OUT THERE.
WHAT...?
BUT I PROMISE YOU, AUGUST...I WILL SOLVE THIS.
I WILL FIND WHO KILLED YOUR BROTHER.

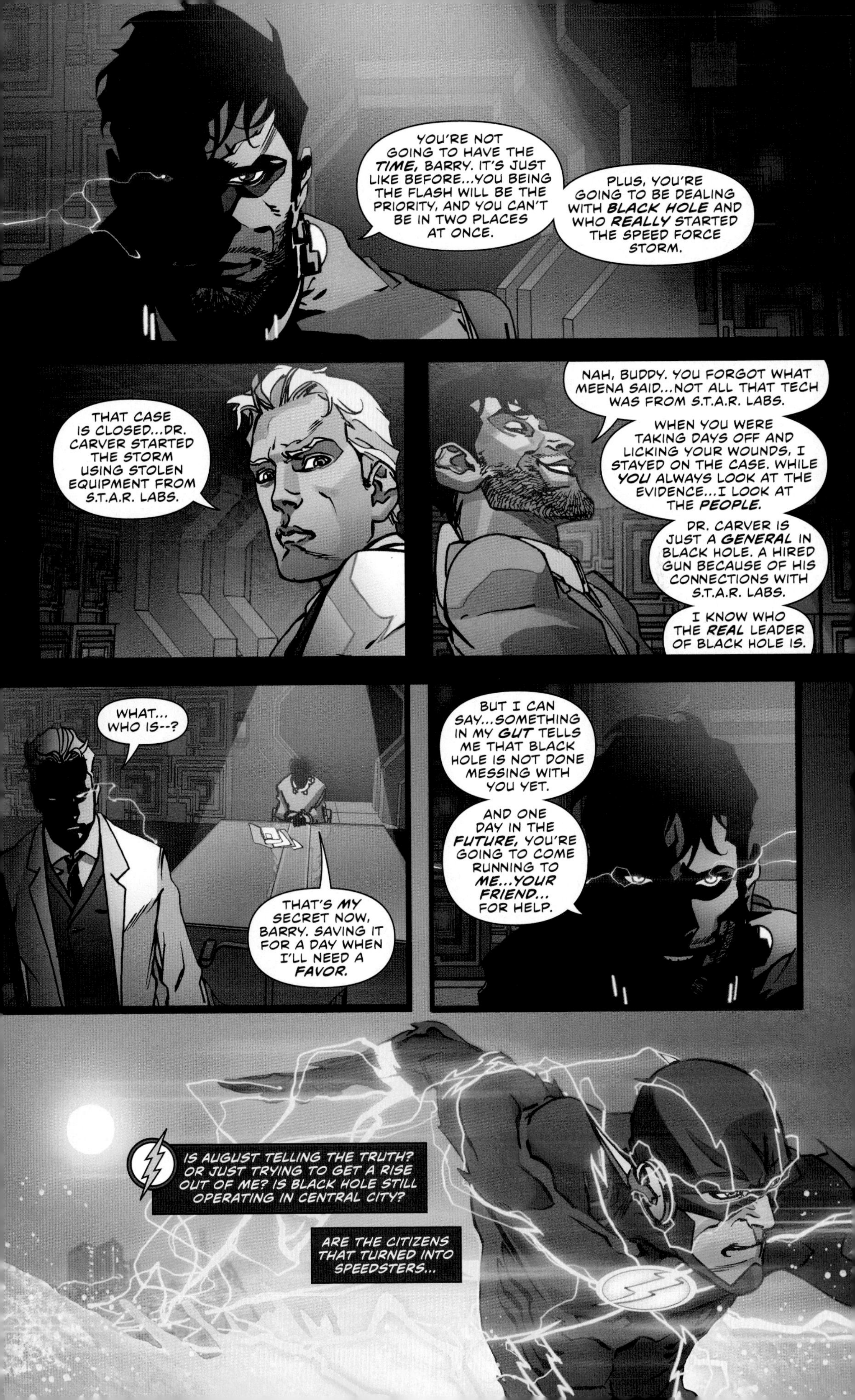
YOU'RE NOT GOING TO HAVE THE TIME, BARRY. IT'S JUST LIKE BEFORE...YOU BEING THE FLASH WILL BE THE PRIORITY, AND YOU CAN'T BE IN TWO PLACES AT ONCE.
PLUS, YOU'RE GOING TO BE DEALING WITH BLACK HOLE AND WHO REALLY STARTED THE SPEED FORCE STORM.
THAT CASE IS CLOSED...DR. CARVER STARTED THE STORM USING STOLEN EQUIPMENT FROM S.T.A.R. LABS.
NAH, BUDDY. YOU FORGOT WHAT MEENA SAID...NOT ALL THAT TECH WAS FROM S.T.A.R. LABS.
WHEN YOU WERE TAKING DAYS OFF AND LICKING YOUR WOUNDS, I STAYED ON THE CASE. WHILE YOU ALWAYS LOOK AT THE EVIDENCE...I LOOK AT THE PEOPLE.
DR. CARVER IS JUST A GENERAL IN BLACK HOLE. A HIRED GUN BECAUSE OF HIS CONNECTIONS WITH S.T.A.R. LABS.
I KNOW WHO THE REAL LEADER OF BLACK HOLE IS.
WHAT... WHO IS--?
THAT'S MY SECRET NOW, BARRY. SAVING IT FOR A DAY WHEN I'LL NEED A FAVOR.
BUT I CAN SAY...SOMETHING IN MY GUT TELLS ME THAT BLACK HOLE IS NOT DONE MESSING WITH YOU YET.
AND ONE DAY IN THE FUTURE, YOU'RE GOING TO COME RUNNING TO ME...YOUR FRIEND... FOR HELP.
IS AUGUST TELLING THE TRUTH? OR JUST TRYING TO GET A RISE OUT OF ME? IS BLACK HOLE STILL OPERATING IN CENTRAL CITY?
ARE THE CITIZENS THAT TURNED INTO SPEEDSTERS...

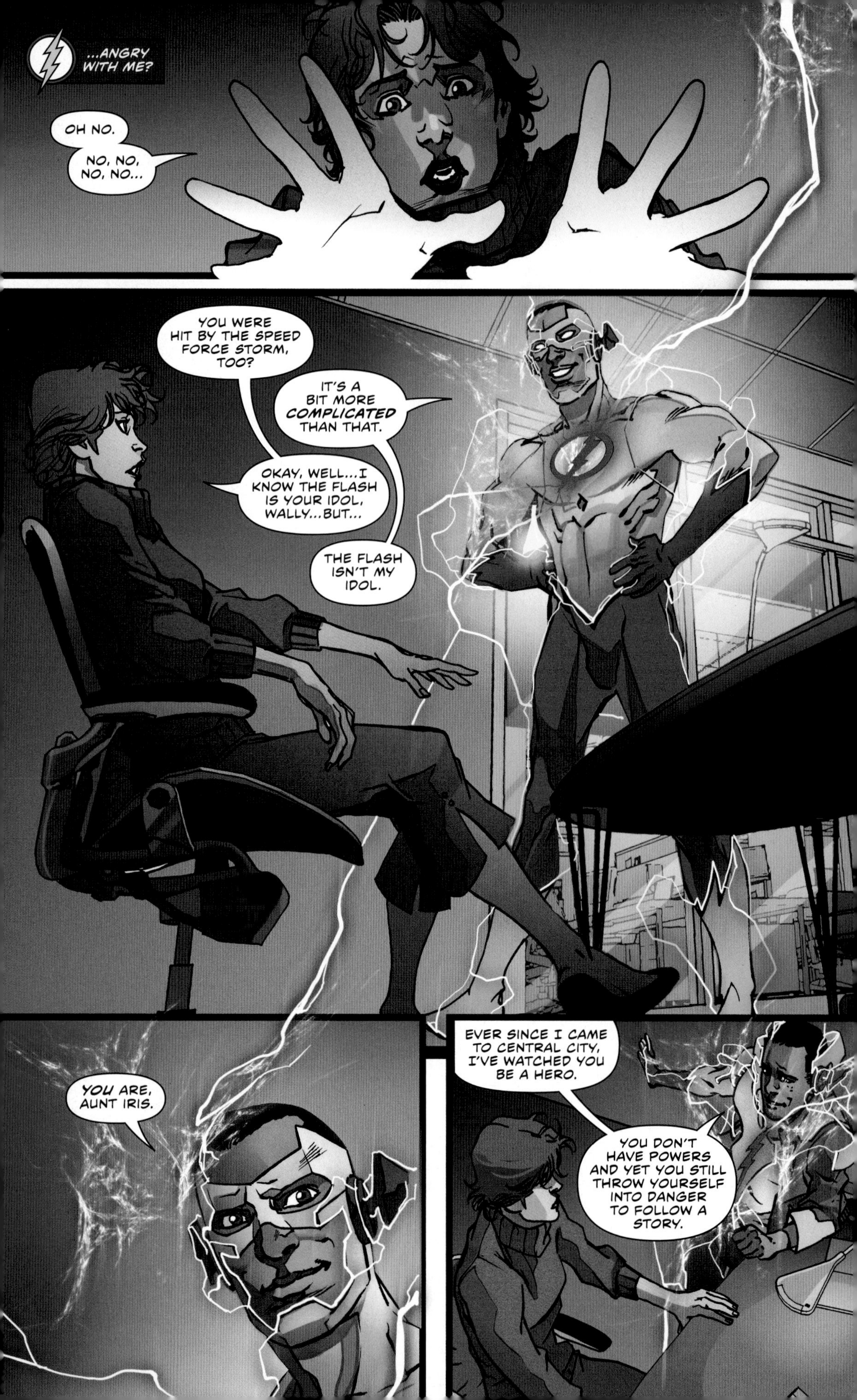
...ANGRY WITH ME?
OH NO.
NO, NO, NO, NO...
YOU WERE HIT BY THE SPEED FORCE STORM, TOO?
IT'S A BIT MORE *COMPLICATED* THAN THAT.
OKAY, WELL...I KNOW THE FLASH IS YOUR IDOL, WALLY...BUT...
THE FLASH ISN'T MY IDOL.
YOU ARE, AUNT IRIS.
EVER SINCE I CAME TO CENTRAL CITY, I'VE WATCHED YOU BE A HERO.
YOU DON'T HAVE POWERS AND YET YOU STILL THROW YOURSELF INTO DANGER TO FOLLOW A STORY.

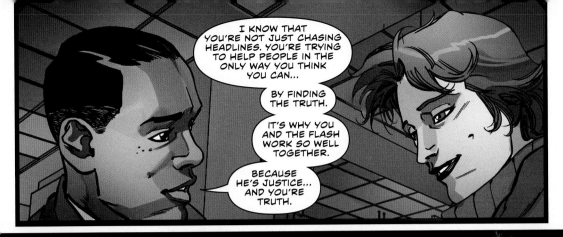

I KNOW THAT YOU'RE NOT JUST CHASING HEADLINES. YOU'RE TRYING TO HELP PEOPLE IN THE ONLY WAY YOU THINK YOU CAN...

BY FINDING THE TRUTH.

IT'S WHY YOU AND THE FLASH WORK SO WELL TOGETHER.

BECAUSE HE'S JUSTICE... AND YOU'RE TRUTH.

WHY...

...WHY DIDN'T YOU TELL ME?

I WAS WORRIED BECAUSE OF WHAT HAPPENED... WITH UNCLE DANIEL...

WHEN HE GOT THE SPEED POWERS...

WALLY... DANIEL IS...

YOU'RE NOT DANIEL.

I KNOW THAT NOW. HELPING THE FLASH SHOWED ME I COULD BE A HERO...JUST LIKE YOU.

YOU KNOW THAT YOU CAN ALWAYS COME TO ME...

BUT I HAVE QUESTIONS.

YOU WOULDN'T BE YOU IF YOU DIDN'T...

I'M STILL A BIT WORRIED THIS COULD BE DANGEROUS...

DON'T WORRY, IRIS...

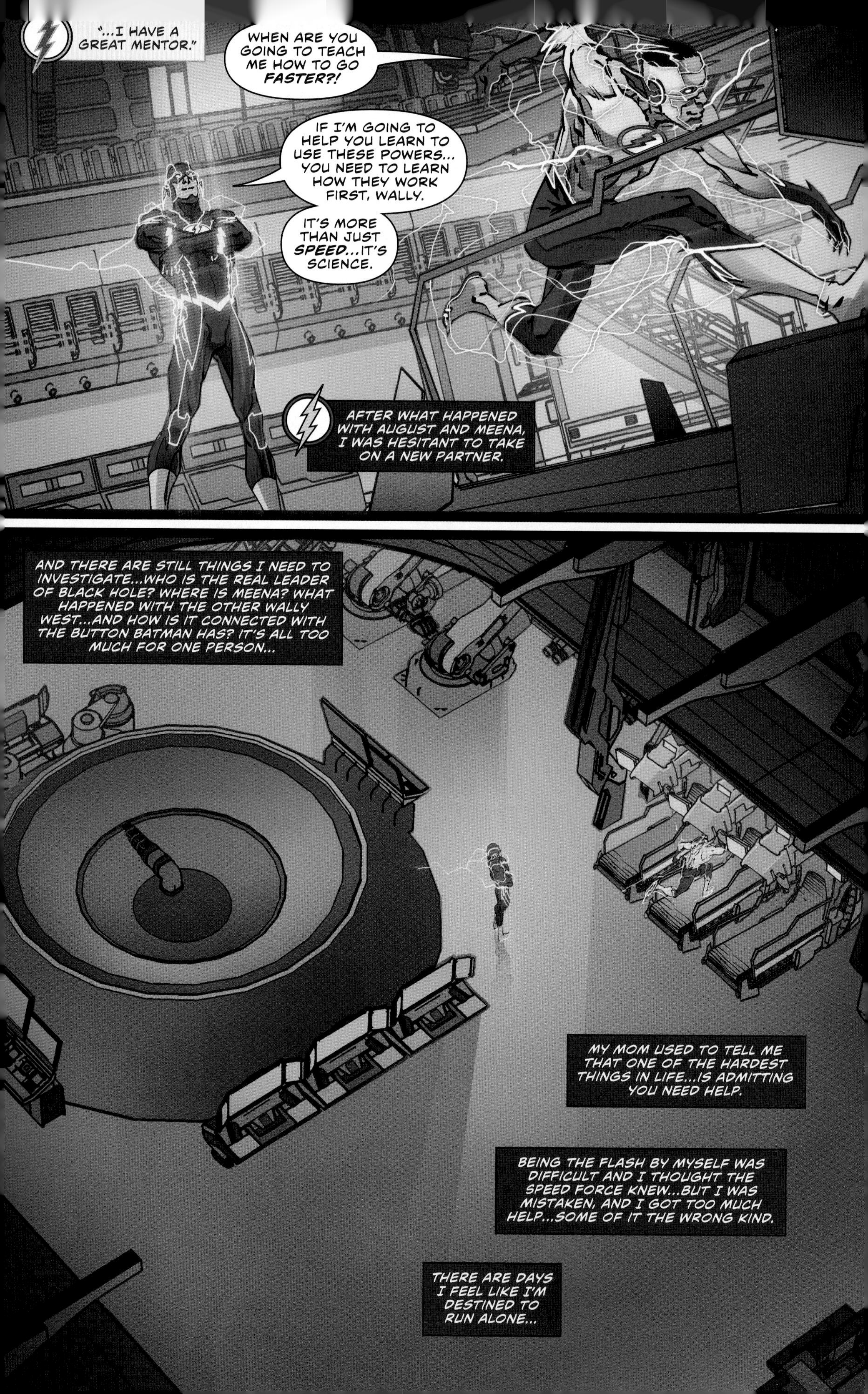
"...I HAVE A GREAT MENTOR."
WHEN ARE YOU GOING TO TEACH ME HOW TO GO FASTER?!
IF I'M GOING TO HELP YOU LEARN TO USE THESE POWERS... YOU NEED TO LEARN HOW THEY WORK FIRST, WALLY.
IT'S MORE THAN JUST SPEED...IT'S SCIENCE.
AFTER WHAT HAPPENED WITH AUGUST AND MEENA, I WAS HESITANT TO TAKE ON A NEW PARTNER.
AND THERE ARE STILL THINGS I NEED TO INVESTIGATE...WHO IS THE REAL LEADER OF BLACK HOLE? WHERE IS MEENA? WHAT HAPPENED WITH THE OTHER WALLY WEST...AND HOW IS IT CONNECTED WITH THE BUTTON BATMAN HAS? IT'S ALL TOO MUCH FOR ONE PERSON...
MY MOM USED TO TELL ME THAT ONE OF THE HARDEST THINGS IN LIFE...IS ADMITTING YOU NEED HELP.
BEING THE FLASH BY MYSELF WAS DIFFICULT AND I THOUGHT THE SPEED FORCE KNEW...BUT I WAS MISTAKEN, AND I GOT TOO MUCH HELP...SOME OF IT THE WRONG KIND.
THERE ARE DAYS I FEEL LIKE I'M DESTINED TO RUN ALONE...

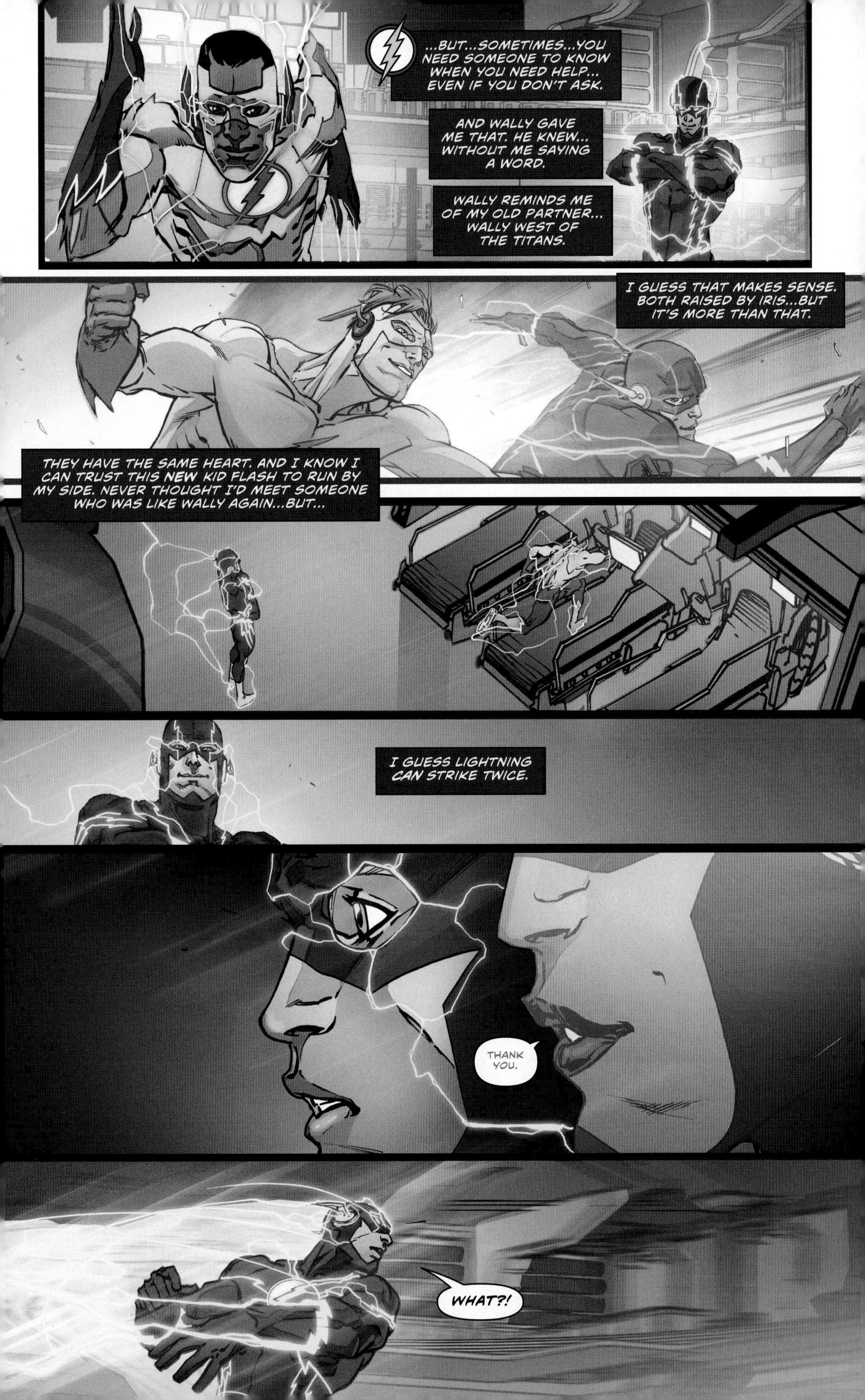
...BUT...SOMETIMES...YOU NEED SOMEONE TO KNOW WHEN YOU NEED HELP... EVEN IF YOU DON'T ASK.
AND WALLY GAVE ME THAT. HE KNEW... WITHOUT ME SAYING A WORD.
WALLY REMINDS ME OF MY OLD PARTNER... WALLY WEST OF THE TITANS.
I GUESS THAT MAKES SENSE. BOTH RAISED BY IRIS...BUT IT'S MORE THAN THAT.
THEY HAVE THE SAME HEART. AND I KNOW I CAN TRUST THIS NEW KID FLASH TO RUN BY MY SIDE. NEVER THOUGHT I'D MEET SOMEONE WHO WAS LIKE WALLY AGAIN...BUT...
I GUESS LIGHTNING CAN STRIKE TWICE.
THANK YOU.
WHAT?!

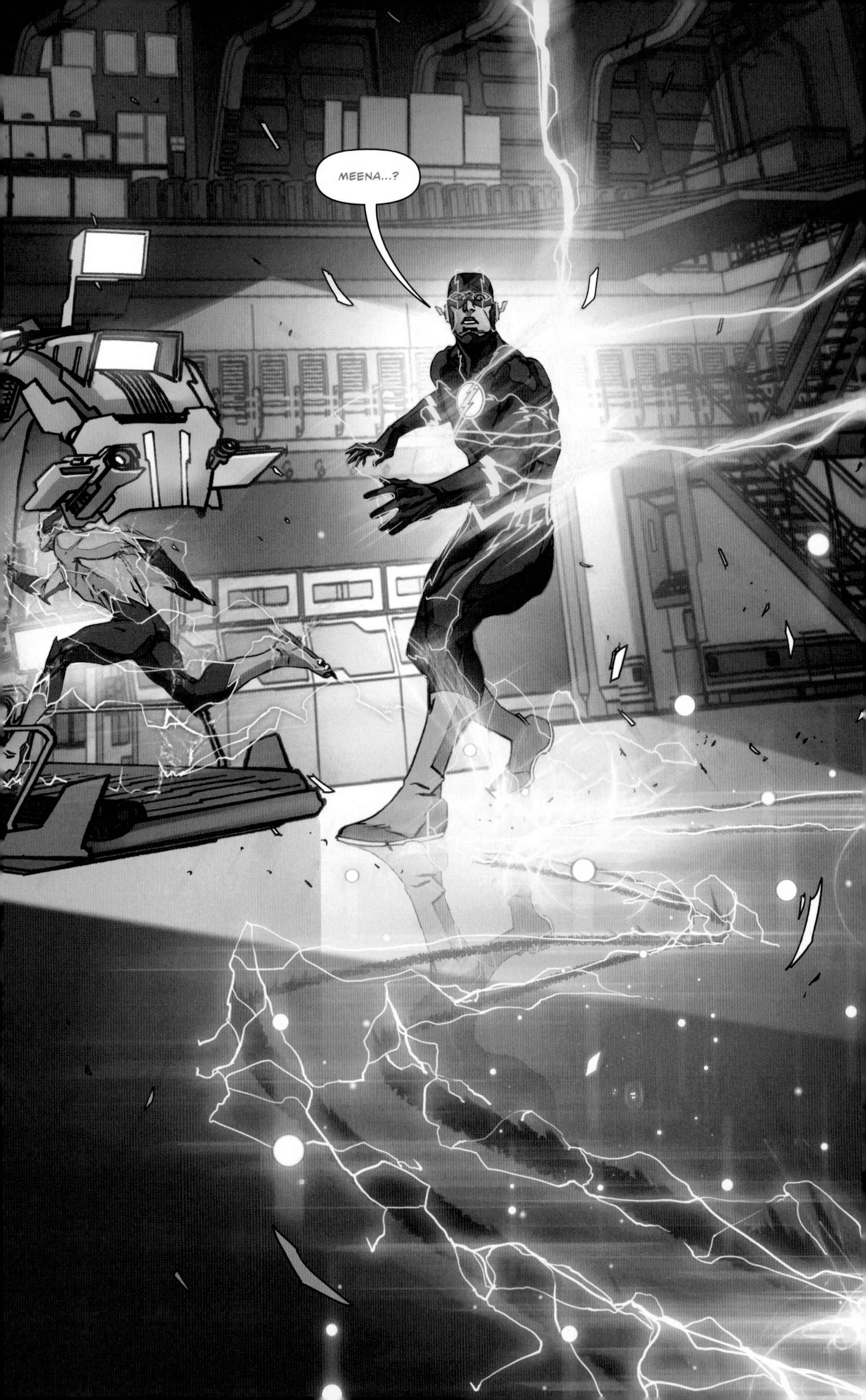
MEENA...?

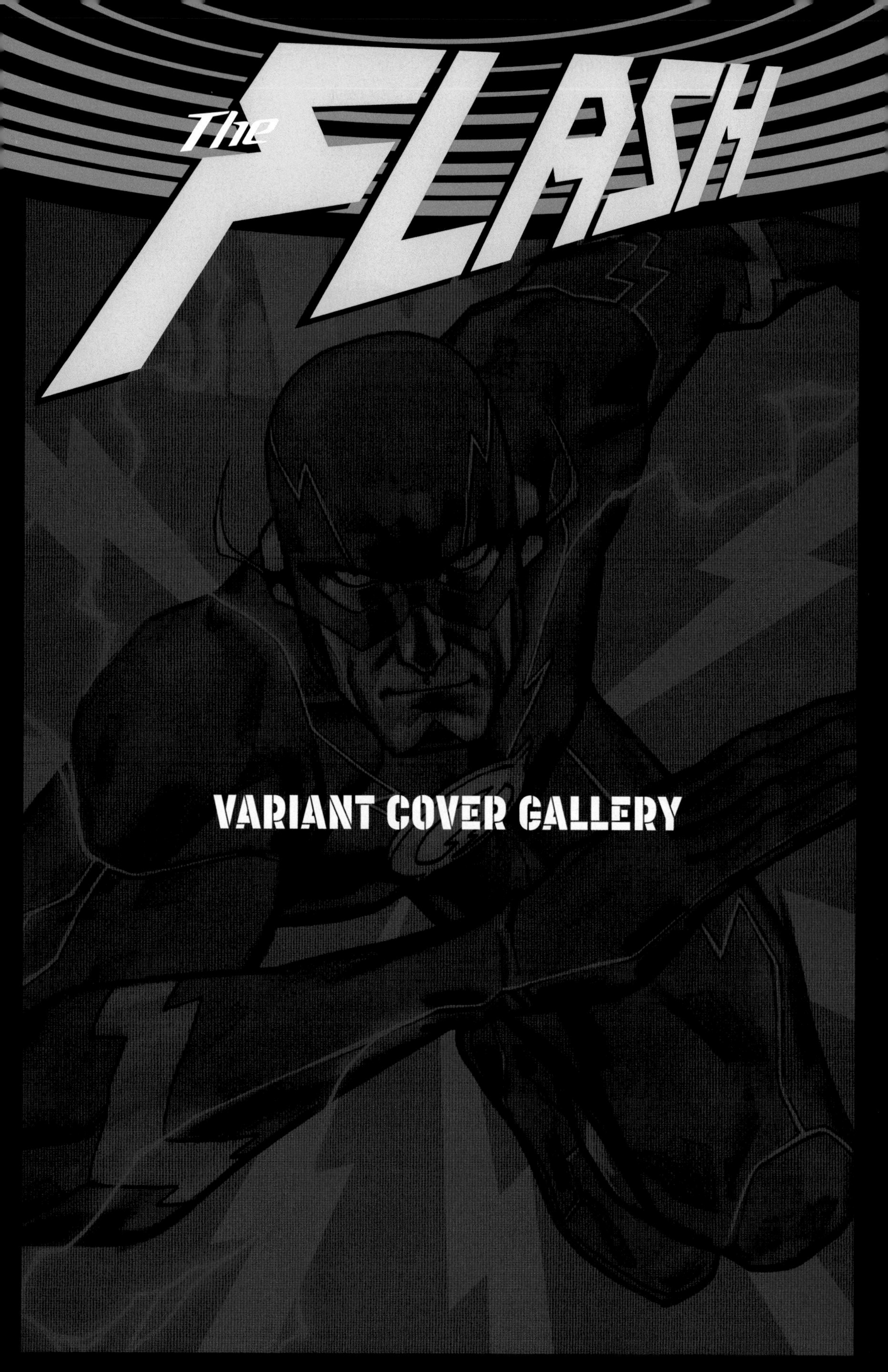
The FLASH

VARIANT COVER GALLERY

THE FLASH: REBIRTH #1 variant by Jason Pearson

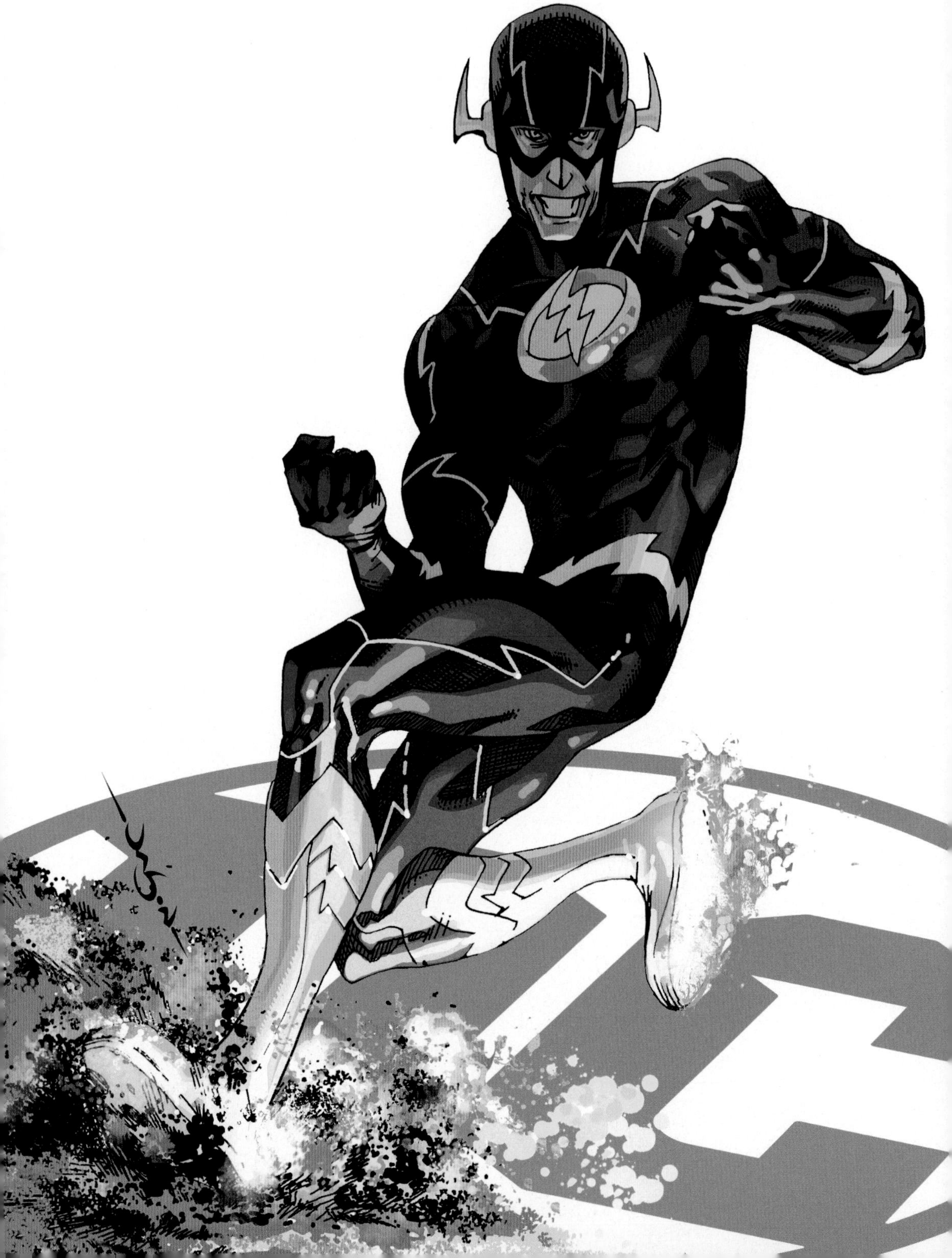

THE FLASH #1 variant by Dave Johnson

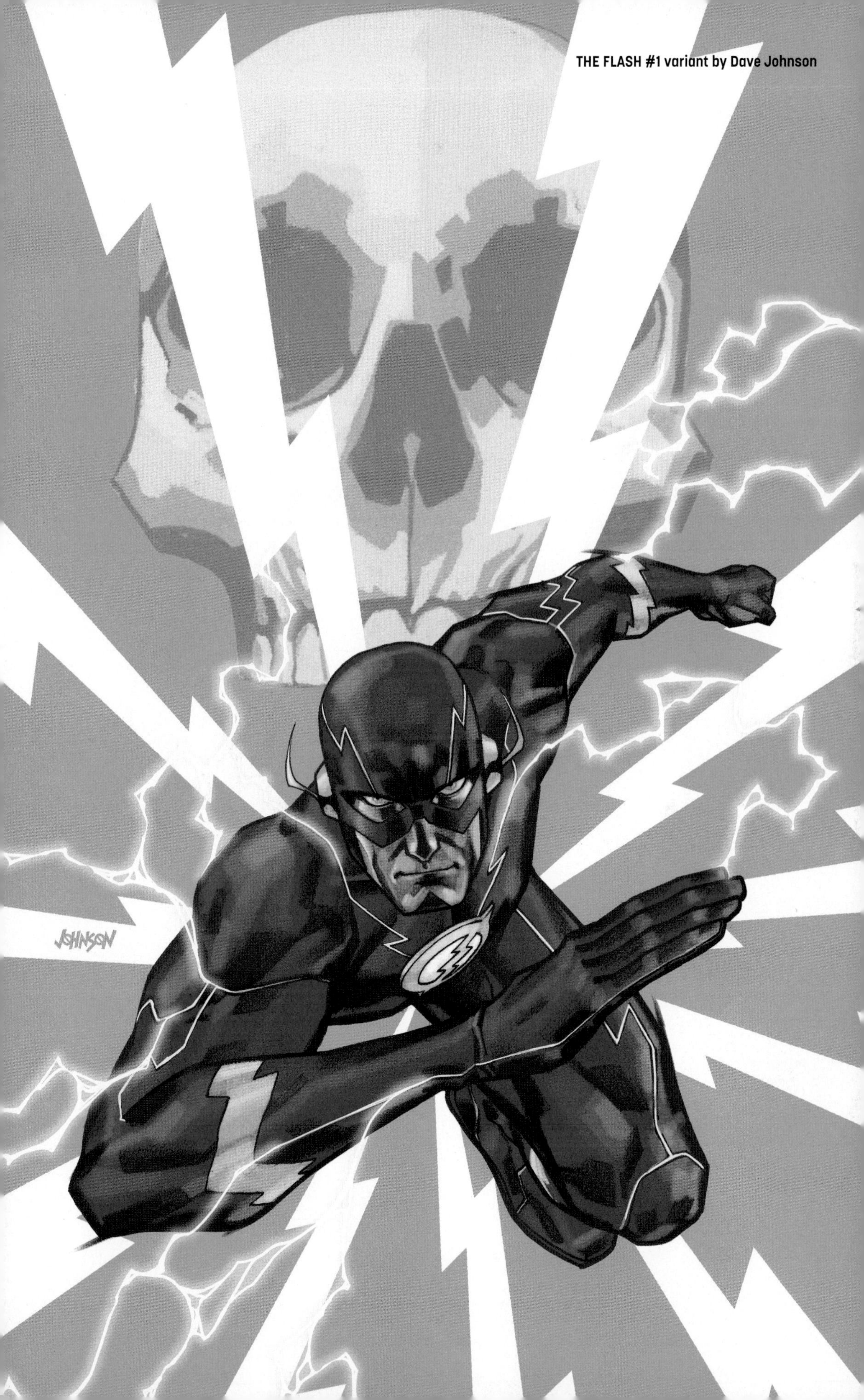
JOHNSON

THE FLASH #2 variant by Dave Johnson

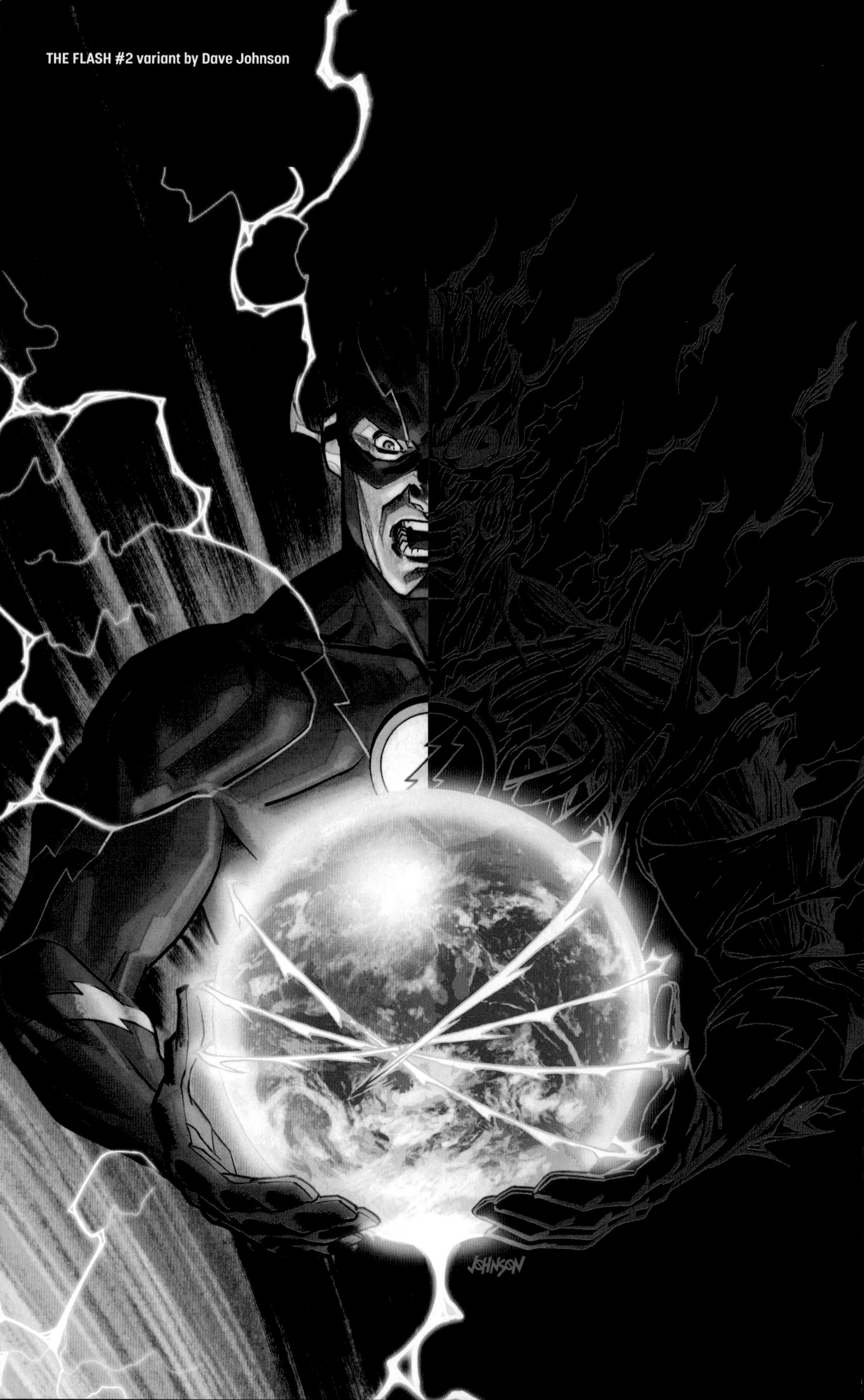
JOHNSON

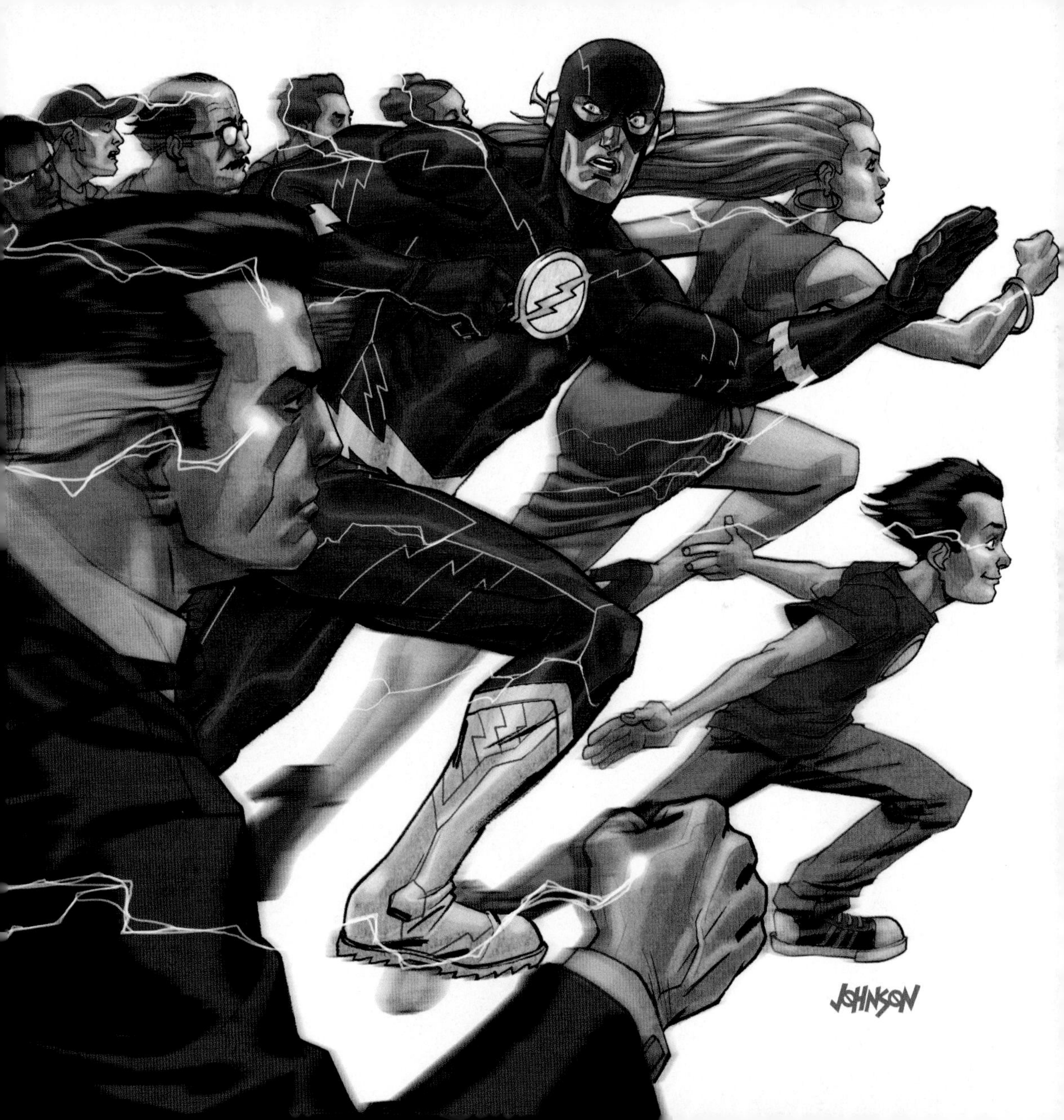
JOHNSON

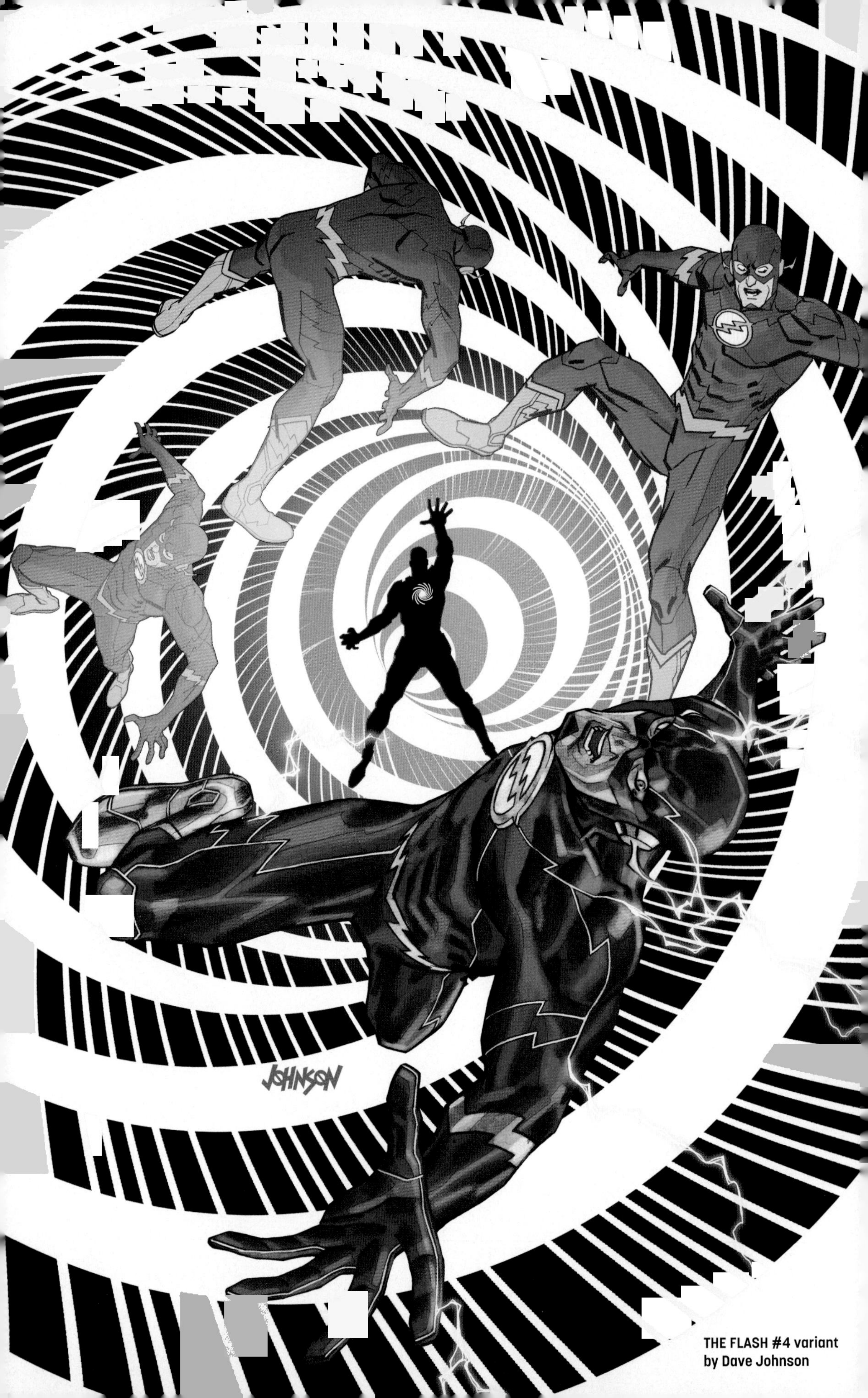
JOHNSON

THE FLASH #4 variant
by Dave Johnson

THE FLASH #3 Variant by Dave Johnson

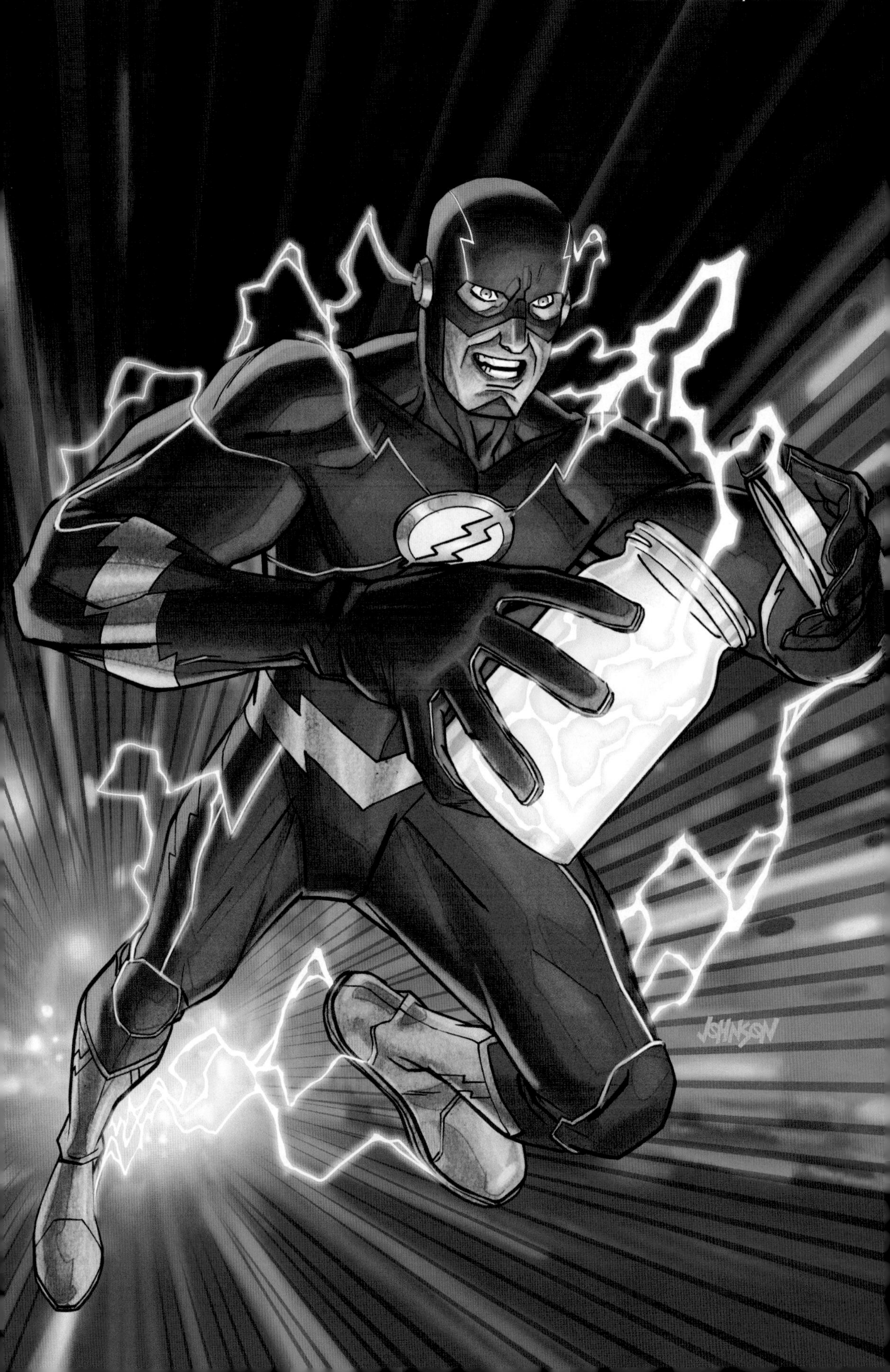
JOHNSON

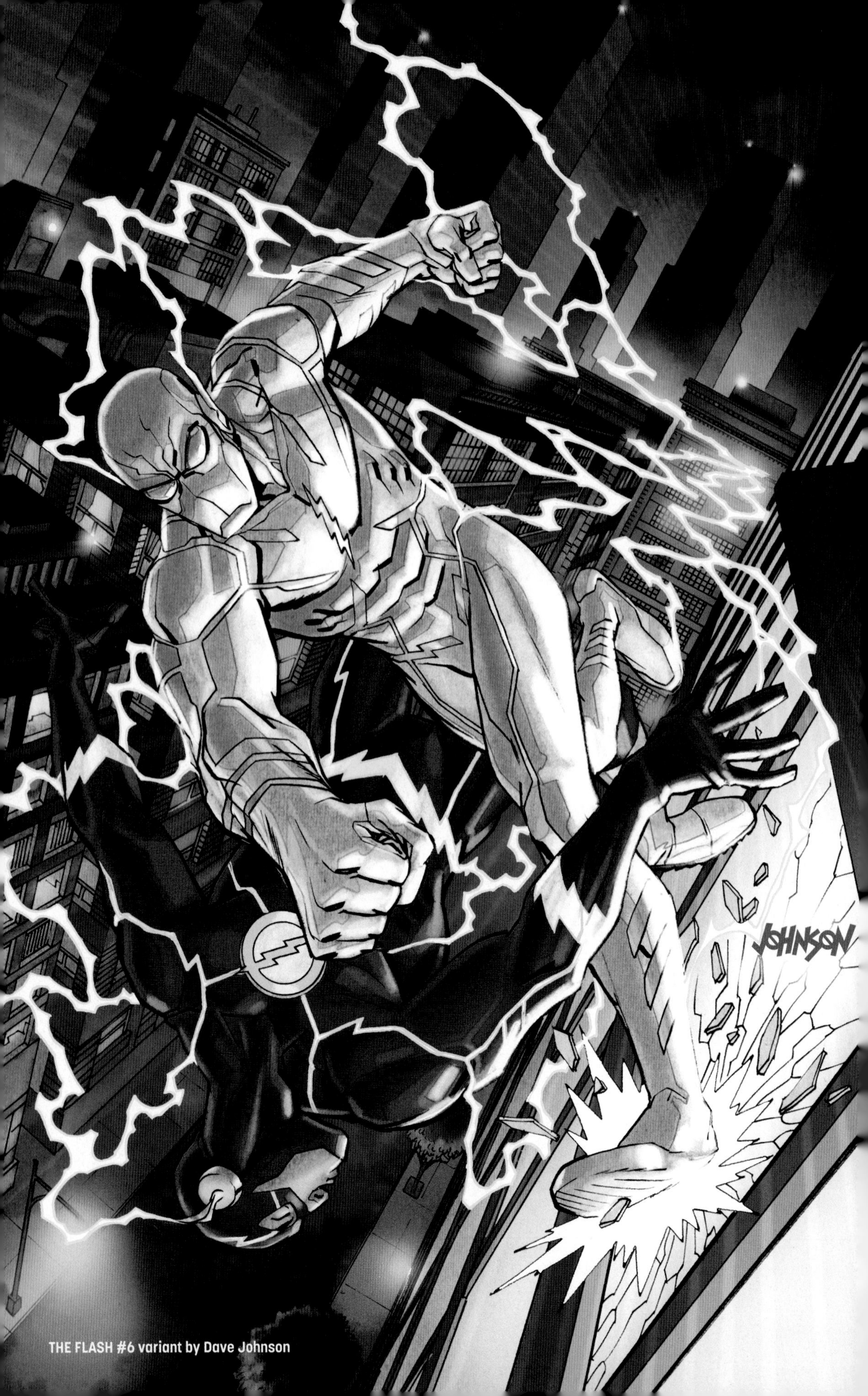
JOHNSON
THE FLASH #6 variant by Dave Johnson

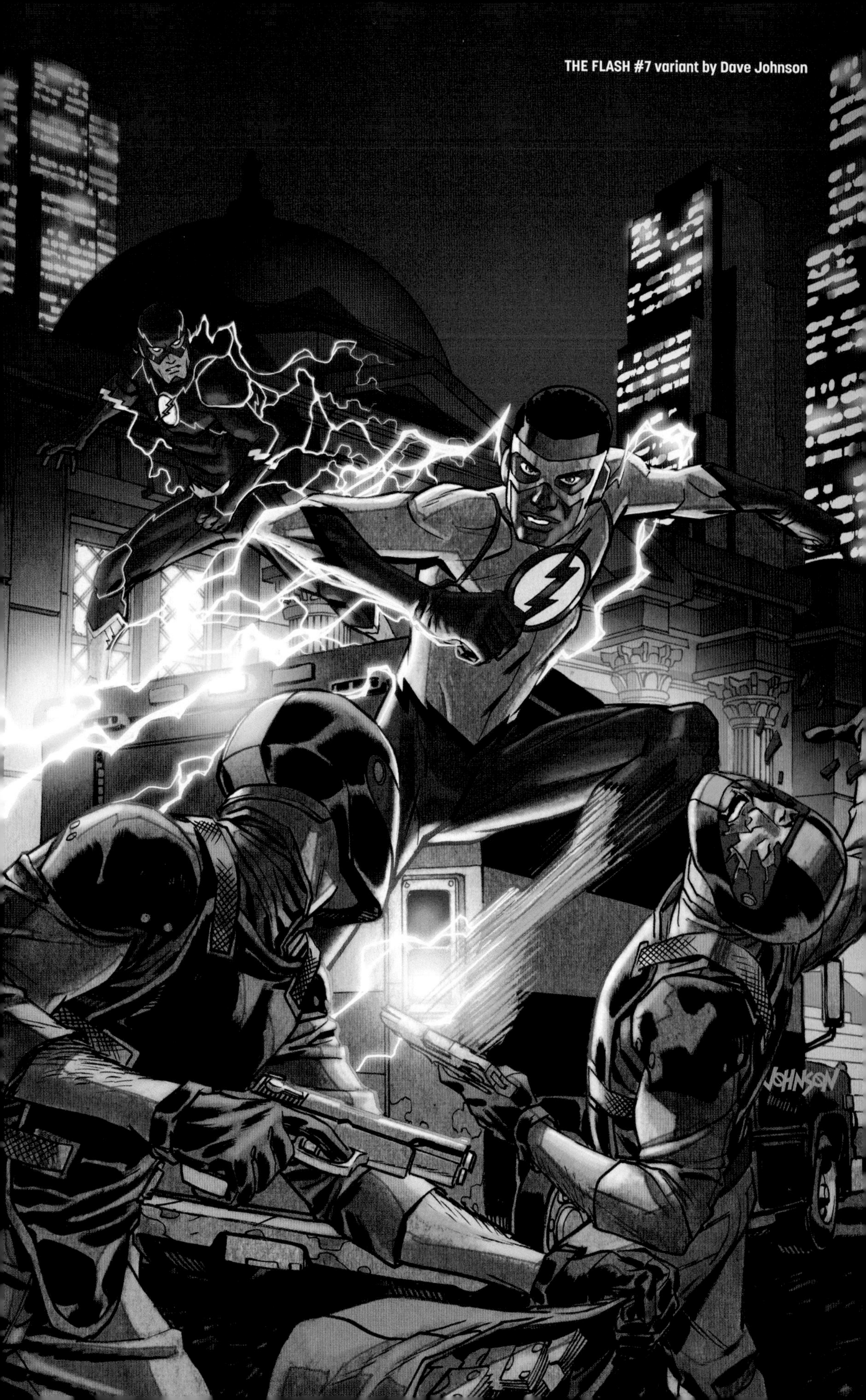
JOHNSON

THE FLASH #7 variant by Dave Johnson

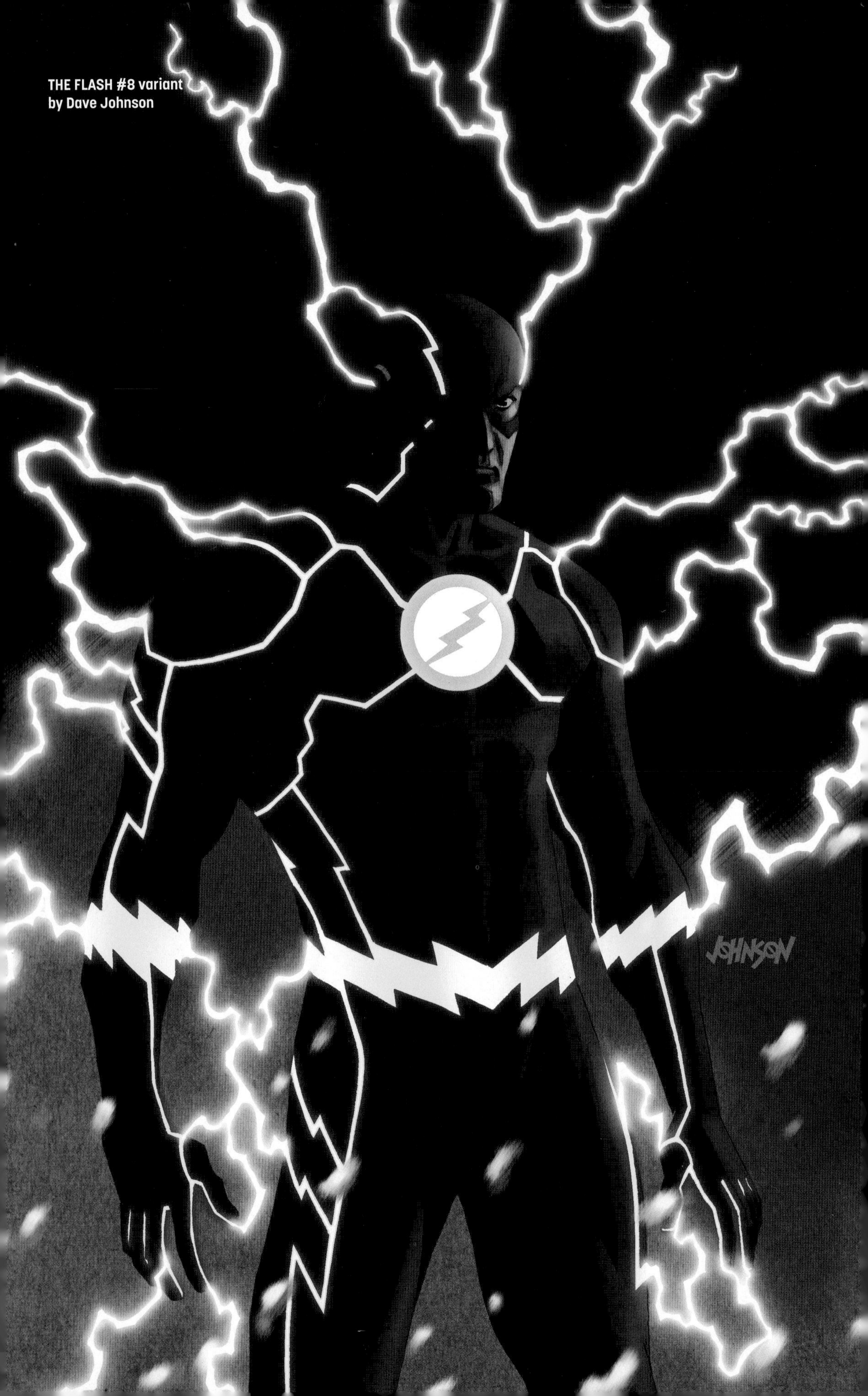
JOHNSON

THE FLASH #8 variant
by Dave Johnson

CHARACTER DESIGNS
by Carmine Di Giandomenico

AUGUST

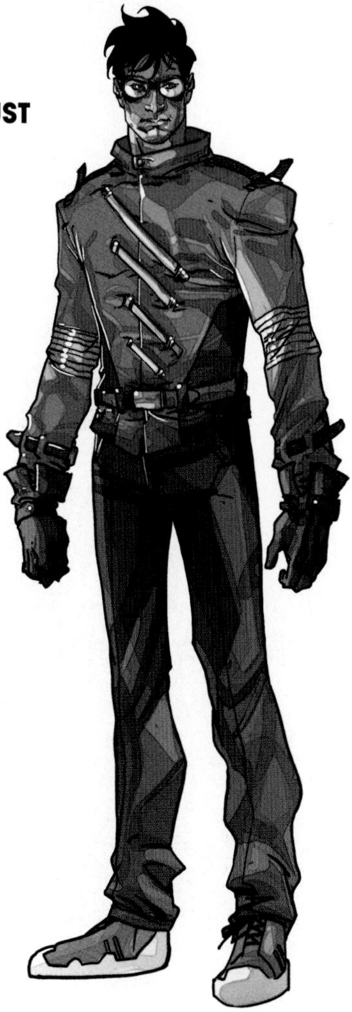

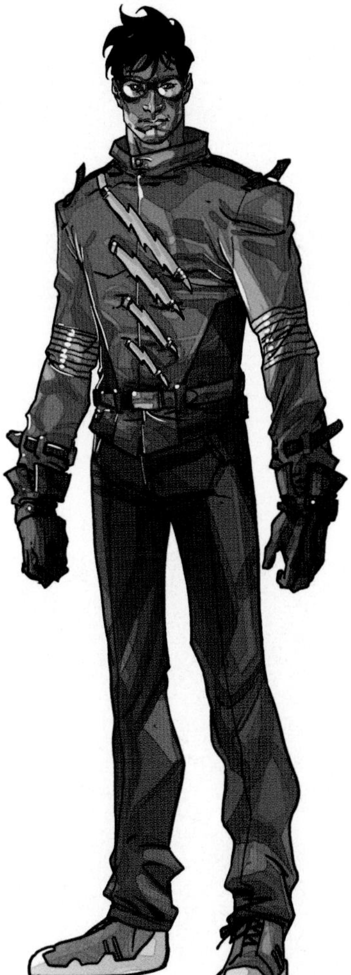

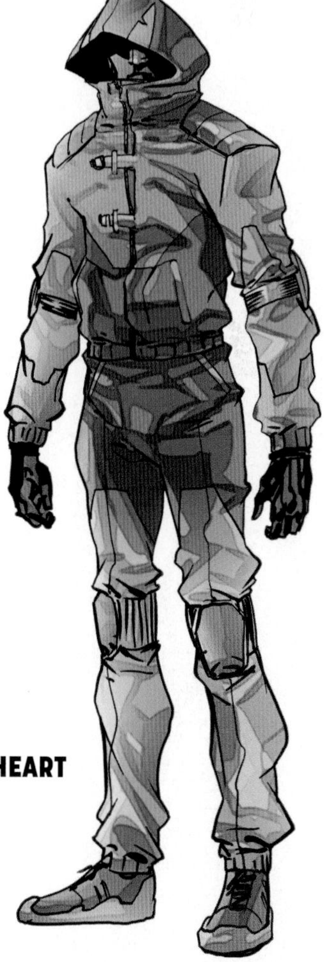

AUGUST HEART

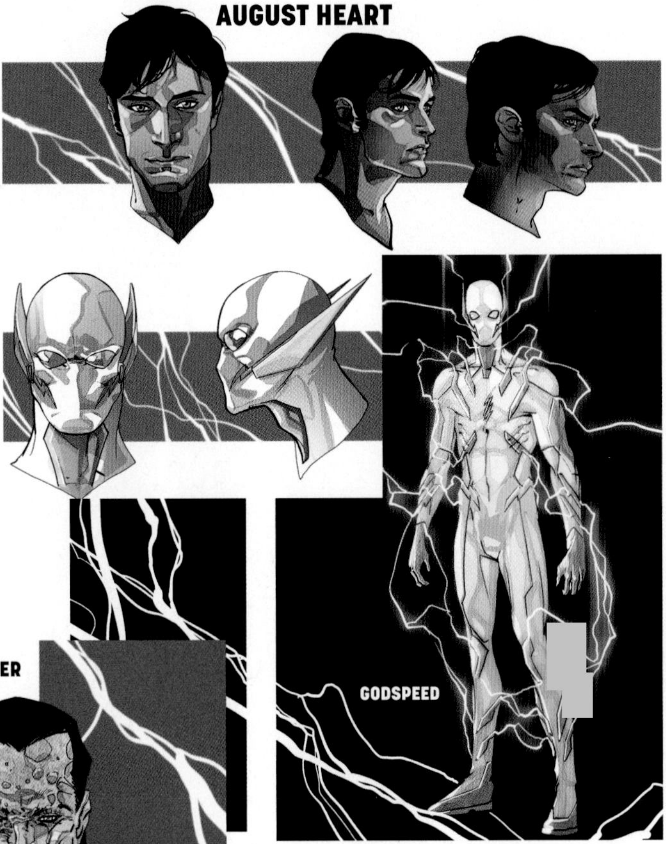
AUGUST HEART
GODSPEED

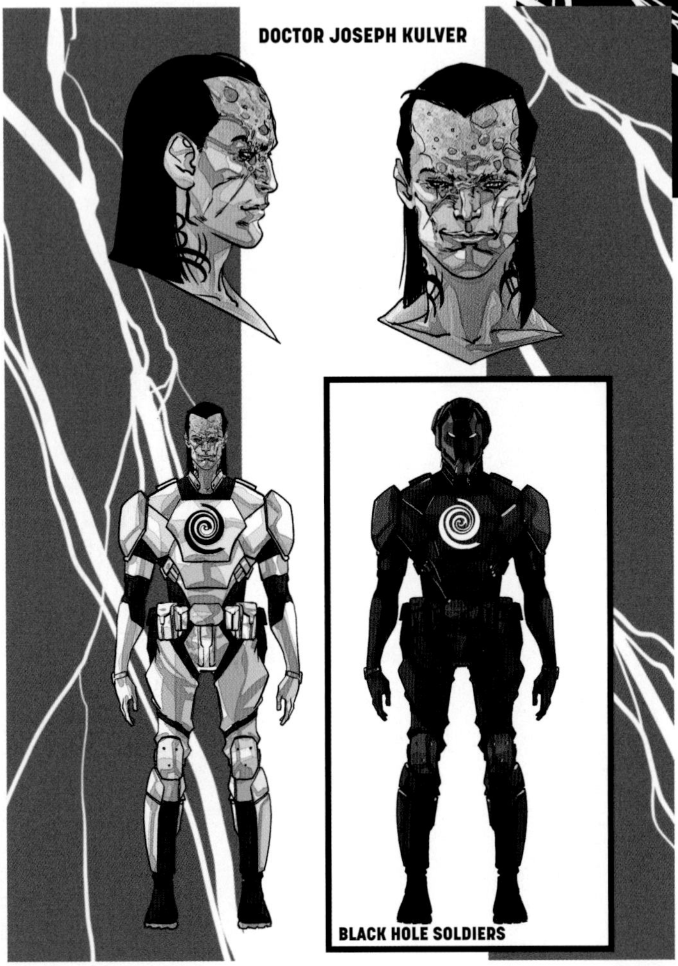
DOCTOR JOSEPH KULVER
BLACK HOLE SOLDIERS

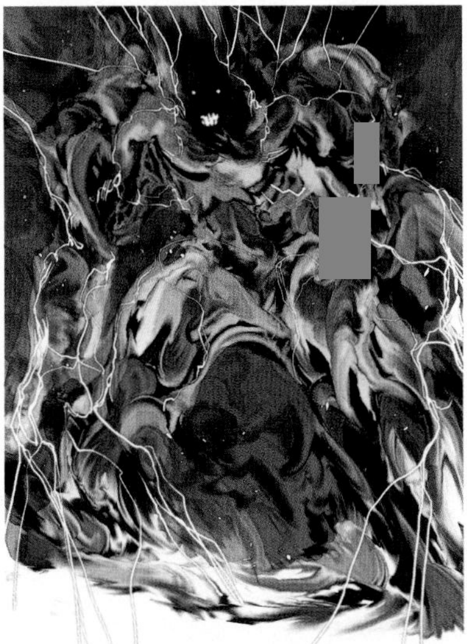

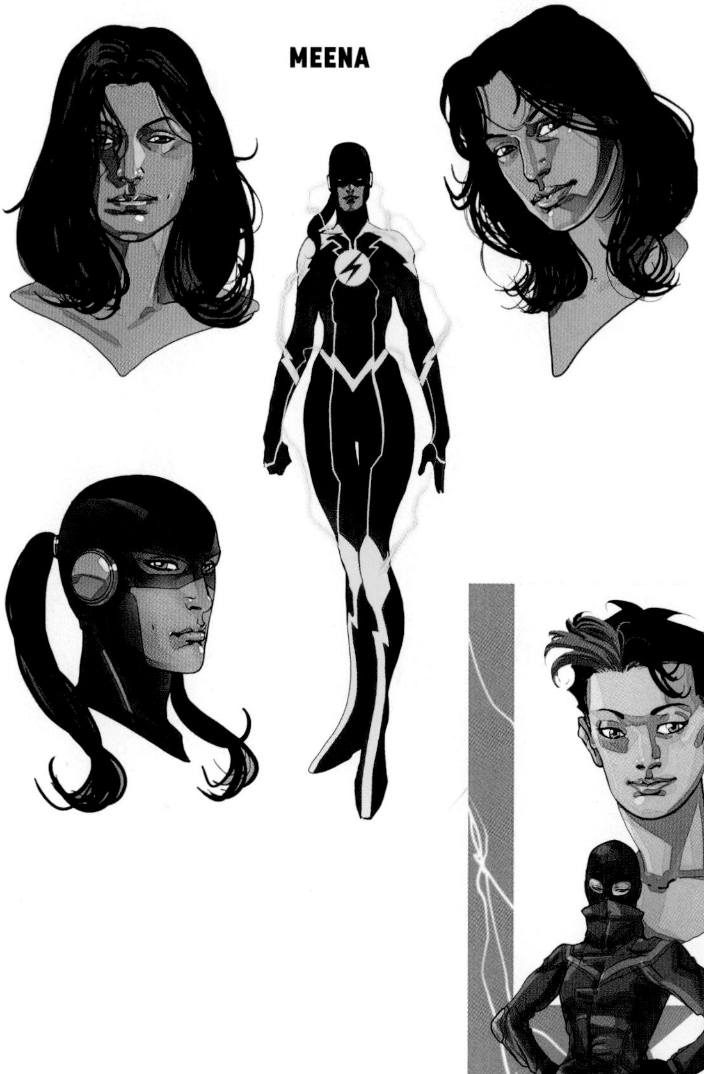
MEENA

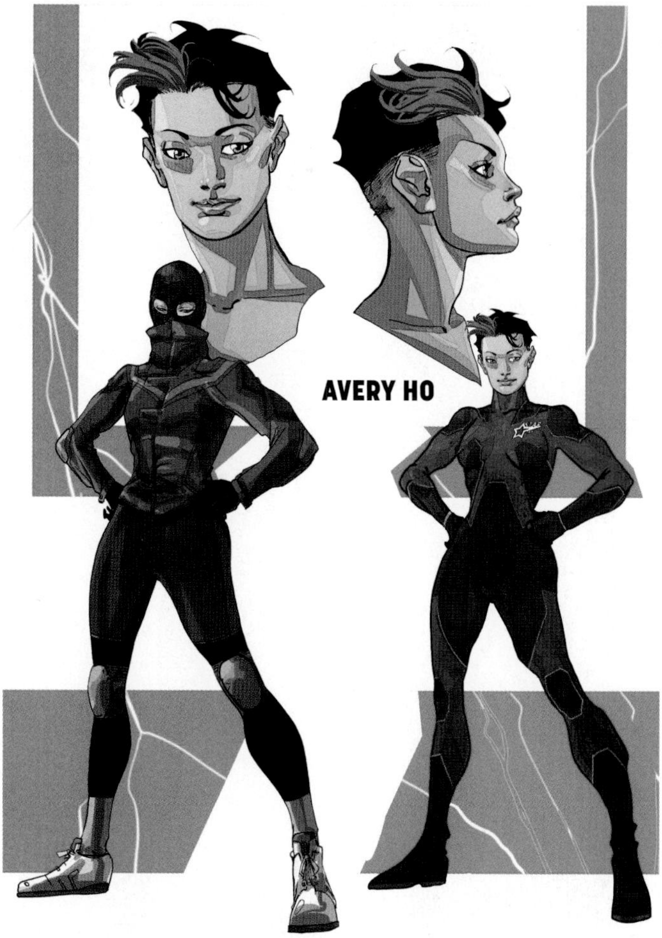
AVERY HO

idea-costume
Speedsters

idea-costume
Speedsters

idea-costume
Speedsters

S.T.A.R.
LABS

idea-costume
Speedsters

S.T.A.R.
LABS

idea-costume
Speedsters

S.T.A.R
LABS

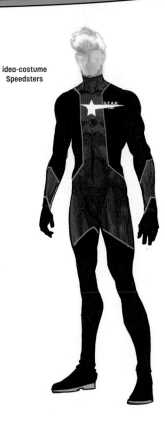